"How do we know a rising power when we see one, what do rising powers want and under what conditions might they be satisfied? Rohan Mukherjee's *Ascending Order* tackles these questions and provides compelling answers that are backed up by solid historical scholarship. The book's distinctive contribution lies in its argument that rising powers seek symbolic equality with the established great powers, and that they look to the institutional openness and procedural fairness of the core institutions of the international system to determine if that equality is achievable. The emphasis on equality, openness, and fairness is truly original and it adds a fascinating normative dimension to the analysis of power transition politics. Mukherjee's arguments warrant the attention of scholars and policymakers grappling with the rise of China and India, and the implications for the established powers such as the United States."

Yuen Foong Khong, Li Ka Shing Professor of Political Science,
Lee Kuan Yew School of Public Policy,
National University of Singapore

"Despite two decades of intensifying struggle – particularly between the United States, Russia, and China – over international order, scholars still know very little about what drives states to contest, reform, or accept the 'rules, norms, and arrangements' of international politics. Based on careful historical research, Rohan Mukherjee argues that key institutions of International order are essentially clubs for great powers. Rising states care about the rules and regulations of those clubs: Can they join? Will they get the same rights as the existing members, or be treated like second-class citizens? The answers to these two questions, Mukherjee shows, have major consequences for the fate of international orders – including the current one. *Ascending Order* is an important and insightful contribution to the academic clubs studying status, power transitions, and international order."

Dan Nexon, Professor of Government and Foreign Service,
Georgetown University, and co-author of *Exit from
Hegemony: The Unraveling of the American Global Order*

"International institutions have been key arenas of contestation and accommodation of the status aspirations of rising powers since the nineteenth century. Here is one of the rare historical treatments of how and when institutions matter for states seeking great power status and the socio-psychological calculations that go behind it. This book is a great addition to the growing literature on international status and power transitions."

T.V. Paul, James McGill Professor of International Relations,
McGill University, Canada, and co-editor of *Status in World Politics*

Ascending Order

Why do rising powers sometimes challenge an international order that enables their growth, and at other times support an order that constrains them? *Ascending Order* offers the first comprehensive study of conflict and cooperation as new powers join the global arena. International institutions shape the choices of rising states as they pursue equal status with established powers. Open membership rules and fair decision-making procedures facilitate equality and cooperation, while exclusion and unfairness frequently produce conflict. Using original and robust archival evidence, the book examines these dynamics in three cases: the United States and the maritime laws of war in the mid-nineteenth century; Japan and naval arms control in the interwar period; and India and nuclear nonproliferation in the Cold War. This study shows that the future of contemporary international order depends on the ability of international institutions to address the status ambitions of rising powers such as China and India.

ROHAN MUKHERJEE is Assistant Professor of International Relations at the London School of Economics and Political Science. He was previously Assistant Professor at Yale-NUS College, Singapore. He holds a PhD in Politics from Princeton University and a BA in Philosophy, Politics, and Economics from the University of Oxford.

Cambridge Studies in International Relations: 160

Ascending Order

Cambridge Studies in International Relations is a joint initiative of Cambridge University Press and the British International Studies Association (BISA). The series aims to publish the best new scholarship in international studies, irrespective of subject matter, methodological approach or theoretical perspective. The series seeks to bring the latest theoretical work in International Relations to bear on the most important problems and issues in global politics.

Ascending Order

Rising Powers and the Politics of Status in International Institutions

ROHAN MUKHERJEE
London School of Economics and Political Science

CAMBRIDGE
UNIVERSITY PRESS

CAMBRIDGE
UNIVERSITY PRESS

University Printing House, Cambridge CB2 8BS, United Kingdom

One Liberty Plaza, 20th Floor, New York, NY 10006, USA

477 Williamstown Road, Port Melbourne, VIC 3207, Australia

314–321, 3rd Floor, Plot 3, Splendor Forum, Jasola District Centre,
New Delhi – 110025, India

103 Penang Road, #05–06/07, Visioncrest Commercial, Singapore 238467

Cambridge University Press is part of the University of Cambridge.

It furthers the University's mission by disseminating knowledge in the pursuit of
education, learning, and research at the highest international levels of excellence.

www.cambridge.org
Information on this title: www.cambridge.org/9781009186810
DOI: 10.1017/9781009186803

First published 2022

A catalogue record for this publication is available from the British Library.

ISBN 978-1-009-18681-0 Hardback

For Shailey

Any claim enforced by equals on equals without recourse to arbitration, no matter whether the issue is of the greatest or the least significance, amounts still to enslavement.

Pericles, in Thucydides, *The Peloponnesian War*, 1.141 (Martin Hammond, trans.)

Contents

Figures

Tables

Acknowledgments

In my journey from doctoral dissertation to first book, I have experienced the tremendous decency, kindness, and generosity of individuals and institutions, many of whom owed me nothing and simply took a chance on a set of ideas shared at a conference or some written words that landed on their desk. The following is my wholly inadequate attempt to acknowledge their contributions.

Aaron Friedberg, John Ikenberry, and Keren Yarhi-Milo helped me light a tiny intellectual flame and keep it alive in the Department of Politics at Princeton University. First drafts took shape during a pre-doctoral fellowship at MIT, where Owen Cote, Brendan Green, Galen Jackson, Vipin Narang, Barry Posen, and Dick Samuels shared their deep knowledge of everything from military technology to archival sources.

The book gained substance during my time as an assistant professor at Yale-NUS College. My colleagues in Global Affairs in particular – Chin-Hao Huang, Steven Oliver, Anju Paul, Navin Rajagobal, Kate Sanger, and Risa Toha – left their imprint on it through innumerable personal and professional kindnesses. Meenakshi Annamalai, Grace Kwan, Vicky Poon, Sarah Ruslan, Jolene Tan, and Kden Tan helped keep the project ticking through grant management, administration, and library resources.

At a workshop on the first draft of the manuscript, Aaron Friedberg, Stacie Goddard, John Ikenberry, Jennifer Lind, Vipin Narang, Jack Snyder, and Keren Yarhi-Milo helped revise and reassemble my arguments and evidence into something worth sharing with the world. I am grateful to Cynthia Ernst for her help in organizing this meeting. Rajesh Basrur, Stephen P. Cohen, Deborah Larson, George Lawson, Manjari Miller, and Jayant Prasad offered vital feedback at other academic gatherings. If there is anything meritorious in this book, it is due to the care and acuity with which all the above scholars treated its evolving contents.

My research benefited immensely from the institutional assistance of librarians and archivists in Princeton, New Jersey; Cambridge, Massachusetts; Singapore; Washington, DC; and New Delhi. Several institutions supported my work, including the Lynde and Harry Bradley Foundation, the Princeton Institute for International and Regional Studies, the Center for International Security Studies, the Mamdouha S. Bobst Center for Peace and Justice, the Niehaus Center for Globalization and Governance, the Stanton Foundation, and Yale-NUS College.

The gargantuan task of research for a book would have been impossible without the help of friends and colleagues who lent a hand at key moments. Nate Hodson and Michelle Mangan put me up in their beautiful home in Washington, DC. Miklos Bankuti made sure I had wheels to get to College Park and back efficiently. As a summer research assistant at Yale-NUS, Ruchika Goel returned to Washington and New Delhi for a second pass at the archives. When the pandemic precluded travel to New Delhi to address a reviewer's queries, Yogesh Joshi most generously shared his own haul of primary documents on India and the International Atomic Energy Agency (IAEA) negotiations.

When it came to the publishing process, Courtney Fung, Evelyn Goh, Devesh Kapur, Raymond Kuo, Darren Lim, Manjari Miller, Nuno Monteiro, Vipin Narang, Dick Samuels, Ben Schupmann, Patrick Thoendel, Srdjan Vucetic, and Keren Yarhi-Milo all took the time to read and critique my book proposal. Alexandre Debs and Rahul Sagar have the dubious distinction of doing the same for the entire manuscript, with Rahul reading multiple drafts of each chapter. Kudrat Virk masterfully copyedited the final version of the manuscript. John Haslam at Cambridge University Press was the perfect editor, not least for picking three anonymous reviewers who read my work sympathetically and offered valuable suggestions that resulted in a much stronger final product than I could have imagined. I am grateful to the editors of Cambridge Studies in International Relations for subsequently adding the book to their series.

I fully expected friends to get tired of hearing about the same project for years on end. On the contrary, they rallied around me, making every little bit of progress worth celebrating. For this, I appreciate Lester Ang, Kokila Annamalai, Kanti Bajpai, Graeme Blair, Nienke Boer, Varanya Chaubey, Courtney Fung, Nirmala George, Kevin

Goldstein, Sinja Graf, Zach Howlett, Caitlin Hutchinson, Ulas Ince, Shalini Jain, Alexander Lanoszka, Nick Lotito, Neena Mahadev, Anit Mukherjee, Karthik Nachiappan, Swapna Kona Nayudu, Elizabeth Nugent, Mridhula Pillay, C. Raja Mohan, Rahul Sagar, Ben Schupmann, Nick Smith, Christina Tarnopolsky, Kriti Vikram, Abhijit Visaria, Christine Walker, and Sara Watson.

Two friends and mentors, Devesh Kapur and David Malone, have profoundly impacted my intellectual and personal development. I continue to learn from and be humbled by the extent to which they have given of themselves to build communities of scholarship that span disciplines, institutions, and continents.

My family is a consistent source of support and encouragement. Utpala Mukherjee, Siddhartha Mukherjee, Navneet and Tekchand Hingorani, and Richa Hingorani are among my greatest cheerleaders. Simita and Tanmoy Brahma were down the road for many years in New Jersey, and have remained so metaphorically, always present when I have needed them.

This book is dedicated to my wife, Shailey Hingorani, who after eleven years still laughs the loudest at my jokes and whom I still find the most interesting person in any room. Her fierce intellect and dedication to leading a life of consequence are the necessary antidote to the moments of self-doubt that accompany academic life. I am excited for the rest of this journey, in our leaky cardboard gondola, toward the salty open sea (with due apologies to Margaret Atwood).

In my better moments, I am also thankful for our cats, Charles and Frida, who engage in constant positional conflict despite living in a world of abundant resources.

Abbreviations

ADB	Asian Development Bank
AEC	Atomic Energy Commission (US)
AIIB	Asian Infrastructure Investment Bank
ASEAN	Association of Southeast Asian Nations
BJP	Bharatiya Janata Party (India)
CCP	Chinese Communist Party
CINC	Composite Index of National Capability
CTBT	Comprehensive Nuclear-Test-Ban Treaty
DAC	Development Assistance Committee (OECD)
DAE	Department of Atomic Energy (India)
DSS	dispute settlement system (WTO)
ENCD	Eighteen-Nation Committee on Disarmament
EU	European Union
G8	Group of Eight
G20	Group of Twenty
GDP	gross domestic product
IAEA	International Atomic Energy Agency
IBSA	India, Brazil, South Africa group
ICBM	intercontinental ballistic missile
IFI	international financial institution
IMF	International Monetary Fund
IST	Institutional Status Theory
LGBTQ+	lesbian, gay, bisexual, transgender, queer/questioning, and others
LIO	liberal international order
MP	Member of Parliament
NAM	Non-Aligned Movement
NDB	New Development Bank
NPT	Treaty on the Non-Proliferation of Nuclear Weapons (Nuclear Non-Proliferation Treaty)

NSG	Nuclear Suppliers Group
OECD	Organisation for Economic Co-operation and Development
P-5	five permanent members (UNSC)
PTBT	Partial Test Ban Treaty
SALT	Strategic Arms Limitation Talks
SCO	Shanghai Cooperation Organization
SDR	Special Drawing Rights (IMF)
UK	United Kingdom
UN	United Nations
UNCHR	United Nations Commission on Human Rights
UNCLOS	United Nations Convention on the Law of the Sea
UNFCCC	United Nations Framework Convention on Climate Change
UNGA	United Nations General Assembly
UNHRC	United Nations Human Rights Council
UNSC	United Nations Security Council
US	United States
WHO	World Health Organization
WTO	World Trade Organization

1 | *Introduction*

In August 1993, as the shadow of the Cold War began its slow retreat, the United Nations (UN) Conference on Disarmament decided the time was ripe to negotiate a treaty banning nuclear tests once and for all. The end of superpower competition had led three of the five official nuclear powers – the United States (US), Russia, and Britain – to announce testing moratoriums, and nonnuclear states were eager for a universal ban.[1] The biggest potential spoiler was China. A "vocal outsider to the global nuclear order"[2] and a "latecomer to the nuclear club,"[3] China had historically viewed test ban efforts as "ploys intended to monopolize nuclear weapons and solidify the larger nuclear powers' advantages."[4]

Beijing had strong security-driven reasons to oppose the Comprehensive Nuclear-Test-Ban Treaty (CTBT) negotiations, as they came to be known. Far from being the geopolitical behemoth it is today, China was a technological laggard compared to other nuclear powers. While the United States was developing advanced first strike and missile defense capabilities that no longer required nuclear testing, China's nuclear forces were still transitioning from liquid-fueled siloed ballistic missiles to solid-fueled mobile missiles, a transition that required smaller and more efficient warhead designs, which required

---

[1] France and China were the other two official nuclear powers.
[2] Nicola Leveringhaus and Kate Sullivan de Estrada, "Between conformity and innovation: China's and India's quest for status as responsible nuclear powers," *Review of International Studies*, 44:3 (2018), 482–503.
[3] Nicola Horsburgh, *China and the Global Nuclear Order: From Estrangement to Active Engagement* (Oxford: Oxford University Press, 2015), 108.
[4] Bates Gill, "Two steps forward, one step back: The dynamics of Chinese nonproliferation and arms control policy-making in an era of reform," in David M. Lampton (ed.), *The Making of Chinese Foreign and Security Policy in the Era of Reform, 1978–2000* (Stanford: Stanford University Press, 2001), 257–288.

further nuclear testing.[5] Zou Yunhua, a senior colonel in the Chinese military and an official delegate at the negotiations, observed, "[T]he CTBT negotiations caught China in the middle of its nuclear weapons program, whereas the United States, Russia, and Britain had completed several development cycles."[6] Put simply, a test ban would make China vulnerable to nuclear coercion (the other nuclear holdout, France, was a US ally and did not face the same predicament).

Unsurprisingly, when negotiations began in Geneva in January 1994, China voiced a number of "treaty-killing positions" that were designed to both reduce the advantages of the established nuclear powers and to leave the door open to certain types of testing for the future reliability and safety of China's limited weapons stockpile.[7] Worse yet, China – and, to a lesser extent, France – kept testing nuclear weapons through the negotiation period, at more than double the rate of its average testing pace.[8] In late 1995, when the United Nations General Assembly (UNGA) set a deadline of September 1996 for a vote on the CTBT, it seemed that China would be the primary cause of deadlock.

Yet, starting in March 1996, China began making a series of concessions that took the world by surprise. Beijing dropped its insistence on maintaining the option of peaceful nuclear explosions, withdrew its proposed inclusion of No First Use and security assurances to non-nuclear states, compromised on the procedure for triggering on-site inspections, and, "in a drastic adjustment of its position," agreed to states using their own technical assets to monitor treaty violations (giving the established powers a major advantage).[9] On July 29, China conducted its last nuclear test and announced a moratorium. On September 24, China signed the CTBT.

What explains this type of cooperation, when a rising power that is clearly at a military and economic disadvantage compared to the great powers, willingly gives up the prospect of substantial relative gains for

[5] Xiangli Sun, "Implications of a comprehensive test ban for China's security policy," Center for International Security and Cooperation, Stanford University (June 1997), 8–9.
[6] Yunhua Zou, "China and the CTBT negotiations," Center for International Security and Cooperation, Stanford University (December 1998), 4.
[7] Alastair Iain Johnston, *Social States: China in International Institutions 1980–2000* (Princeton: Princeton University Press, 2008), 104.
[8] Gill, "Two steps forward," 264.   [9] Zou, "China and the CTBT," 23.

the sake of international agreement? It is possible that India's decision to hold up the treaty gave China cover to make empty promises. However, China made its concessions a number of months before India turned spoiler.[10] China may have also accepted losses in order to restrain Japan's future nuclear development. Japan, however, was one of the biggest votaries of disarmament and a strong treaty, and China's foremost concern was not Japan but US coercion, the potential for which was clearly demonstrated in the Taiwan Strait Crisis of 1995–1996.

The evidence instead overwhelmingly suggests that Chinese leaders were concerned about their country's status as a "responsible major power," a status that was increasingly threatened by a rising chorus of criticism from nuclear and nonnuclear powers alike in the course of the negotiations.[11] France's announcement of a testing moratorium in January 1996 left China particularly isolated among the P-5, the five permanent members of the United Nations Security Council (UNSC) that were also all officially nuclear powers. Against their state's material interests, Chinese leaders weighed their desire for "a legitimate seat at the table" in "a more representative [nuclear] order."[12] Ultimately, it made sense to sacrifice some amount of security in order to "play as an equal among the P-5."[13] Recognition of China's major power identity via membership of the top ranks of the international order was worth preserving at some cost. According to Fan Jishe, a professor at the Central Party School of the Chinese Communist Party (CCP), although China's military-scientific establishment was unhappy, "people who wanted to be part of the international community prevailed."[14]

Although China did not end up ratifying the treaty – nor did the United States – it has consistently supported test ban efforts ever since. This behavior fits with scholarly assessments of Beijing's approach to the global nuclear order as having shifted remarkably since the early

[10] See Rebecca Johnson, "Unfinished business: The negotiation of the CTBT and the end of nuclear testing," United Nations Institute for Disarmament Research, New York (2009), 90–91, 97–102, 126–141.
[11] Johnston, *Social States*, 113.
[12] Horsburgh, *China and the Global Nuclear Order*, 106.
[13] Johnson, "Unfinished business," 122.
[14] Quoted in Richard Salmons, "The role of status in Asia-Pacific international relations," unpublished PhD thesis, Australian National University (June 2018), 194.

1990s toward greater cooperation,[15] including on critical issues such as the North Korean nuclear program.[16] Indeed, since the end of the Cold War, China has cooperated with various parts of the US-led liberal international order (LIO), including the UNSC, the Treaty on the Non-Proliferation of Nuclear Weapons (NPT; also known as the Nuclear Non-Proliferation Treaty), the World Trade Organization (WTO), and the Group of 20 (G20). Cooperation has often been costly for China, for example, in terms of UN interventions disrupting its economic relationships in the Middle East or international nuclear weapons regimes affecting its military posture.

Cooperation was not China's only choice with regard to the CTBT. India provides the counterexample of a rising power that approached the negotiations "confident of ratifying a comprehensive test ban agreement" but ended up bitterly opposed to the final result.[17] Like China, India preferred to link a test ban with disarmament and sought to place the onus on the established nuclear powers to reduce their existing nuclear stockpiles. The negotiations failed to deliver on both counts. The difference was that China was much closer to being treated as an equal member of the great-power club. China was part of the P-5 and an official nuclear weapon state as per the NPT; India was neither. When the dust settled, China's main delegate, Sha Zukang, observed that the treaty was "balanced as a whole."[18] His Indian counterpart, Arundhati Ghose, denounced the CTBT as an "unequal treaty" that would "only succeed in perpetuating a discriminatory status quo."[19] China sought to maintain the status of a responsible major power; India had nothing to lose.

Rising Powers and International Order

As the above example shows, rising powers care about status, or their position in a hierarchy, and are willing to pay significant costs for status relative to the great powers. The international order – the interconnected set of rules and institutions established by great powers

---

[15] Gill, "Two steps forward," 257.
[16] Horsburgh, *China and the Global Nuclear Order*, 120–146.
[17] Karthik Nachiappan, *Does India Negotiate?* (New Delhi: Oxford University Press, 2019), 105.
[18] Quoted in Zou, "China and the CTBT," 25.
[19] Quoted in Nachiappan, *Does India Negotiate?* 127.

for managing conflict and cooperation – is a site of contestation over status, among other things. Rising powers draw inferences about their relative standing from the way they are treated by an international order's core institutions. Some institutional configurations satisfy a rising state's status ambitions and thereby induce cooperative behavior, while other configurations have the opposite effect. This book develops a novel theory, called Institutional Status Theory (IST), to explain the conditions under which rising powers will engage in different strategies to attain or maintain status in the international order.

China's cooperative behavior in the post–Cold War order is puzzling for the bulk of international relations scholarship. Research on power shifts, or "predictable, long-run changes in relative capabilities,"[20] typically views rising powers as prone to dissatisfaction with the international order and likely to challenge it as soon as they are capable. Challenges "almost always" lead to war,[21] because the great powers are unlikely to sit idly by while rising powers go about wrecking global governance. Yet there is no evidence that China and other countries such as India and Brazil are preparing an assault on the international order. If anything, they have signaled a desire to cooperate, conditional on greater *representation* in international institutions, or in Xi Jinping's words, "a more just and equitable international system."[22]

A preoccupation with war in the literature has left much to be learned about how rising powers react to international order. The rise of a new power to prominence in world politics, a process that easily spans decades, is typically telescoped into the moment when it either challenges the established powers or is preempted by them in a military conflict. As a result of this narrow focus, we know a good deal about the regularity with which rising powers and great powers fight, but we know very little about why rising powers might be dissatisfied in the first place. Much of the answer lies in their experiences with international order, or the rules and institutions that they encounter early in their rise.

---

[20] Woosang Kim and James D. Morrow, "When do power shifts lead to war?" *American Journal of Political Science*, 36:4 (1992), 896–922.

[21] Graham Allison, "The Thucydides trap," *Foreign Policy*, 224 (May–June 2017), 80–81.

[22] China Daily, "Full text: President Xi's speech on China-US ties," September 22, 2015.

This book shifts the analytical and empirical lens on power shifts to an earlier stage, well before war is in the picture. It poses two related questions. First, why might a rising power challenge the very international order that has enabled its rise? After all, "by definition, it is doing better than the established powers under *their* rules and institutional arrangements."[23] Second, and conversely, why might a rising power accept a disadvantageous international order when it would be less costly to challenge or disregard it? Over the last decade, a handful of scholars have posed these two questions *separately*.[24] IST offers the most comprehensive and systematic answers to date. Whereas existing works focus mostly on conflict during power shifts, IST offers a single framework that explains a range of rising-power behaviors including conflict and cooperation. It does so by drawing on the growing international relations literature on status in world politics, as well as on insights from club theory in economics and social identity theory in psychology.

IST shows that rising powers will under certain conditions sacrifice their material interests for the sake of membership of the great-power club. Membership entails *symbolic equality* with the great powers, which is a type of status. Two variables influence the strategy a rising power will adopt to achieve its status goals: the *institutional openness* and the *procedural fairness* of an international order's core institutions. A rising power is more likely to support an order whose core institutions are open to new powers joining their leadership ranks, and that treat the rising power in a fair manner. It is more likely to challenge an order that is lacking in these features.

Drawing on archival and other primary sources, I demonstrate the validity of IST in three historical cases: the United States in the British-led Atlantic system of the mid-nineteenth century, Japan in the Washington system of the interwar period, and India in the international order of the Cold War. In each case, status motivations

[23] Randall L. Schweller, "A tale of two realisms: Expanding the institutions debate," *Mershon International Studies Review*, 41 (1997), 1–32.
[24] See Courtney J. Fung, *China and Intervention at the UN Security Council: Reconciling Status* (Oxford: Oxford University Press, 2019); Johnston, *Social States*; Randall L. Schweller and Xiaoyu Pu, "After unipolarity: China's visions of international order in an era of U.S. decline," *International Security*, 36:1 (2011), 41–72; Steven Ward, *Status and the Challenge of Rising Powers* (Cambridge: Cambridge University Press, 2017).

outweigh material factors in shaping the behavior of the rising power with regard to international order. In addition, I demonstrate the plausibility of IST as an explanation for the pattern of China's cooperation and resistance in the contemporary LIO.

Contemporary rising powers, such as China and India, broadly support the LIO because, on balance, it benefits them materially. However, their demands for representation cannot be taken lightly. IST makes this demand intelligible as a claim to symbolic equality with the great powers. Xi Jinping's goal of making "the Chinese nation stand rock-firm in the family of nations" says more about China's status ambitions than it does about China's material calculus.[25] Frustrated by a lack of recognition of their claims, Chinese leaders have in some areas begun to chip away at the legitimacy of the LIO, with potentially deep and damaging long-run consequences.

The rest of this chapter discusses existing approaches to power shifts, which are typically studied through the lens of revisionism. It shows that our knowledge so far of how rising powers navigate the rules and institutions of an international order is incomplete. It introduces IST as a way of addressing important gaps in the literature and discusses the method used to select historical cases for testing the theory. The chapter closes with an outline of the book and a brief discussion of IST's implications.

Existing Approaches to Power Shifts

Rising powers are of great consequence in the international order. As they rise, they obtain the means to challenge the rules and institutions that facilitate their emergence, potentially transforming the foundations of international cooperation and conflict. Understanding why and predicting when rising states will uphold or undermine international order is, therefore, of immense significance.

The existing literature on power shifts and international order frames the problem in terms of revisionism. Revisionist states "seek to change the distribution of goods (territory, status, markets, expansion of ideology, and the creation or change of international law and

---

[25] Xinhua and SCMP Reporters, "Transcript: Xi Jinping's speech at the unveiling of the new Chinese leadership," *South China Morning Post*, November 15, 2012.

institutions)."[26] By contrast, status quo states "prefer to keep things as they are."[27] The literature generally assumes that "all rising powers have some revisionist intentions," and what matters is "whether the challenger harbors limited or revolutionary aims."[28] In fact, almost the entire theoretical canon on power shifts focuses on states whose aims become revolutionary as their power grows to the point of being able to challenge the great powers. Technically, therefore, the study of rising powers thus far has been the study of rising *great* powers, that is, states on the threshold of systemic influence. Given this focus, revisionist behavior is typically defined as expansionism, outright rejection of the international order, or the accumulation of power in a manner that triggers a security dilemma with established powers, often leading to war. By studying power shifts well before radical change is a realistic possibility, IST takes a wider view of rising-power strategies, which may include expansion and conflict but also include reform (a type of revisionism not commonly found in the literature) and cooperation (which is more than just the absence of revisionism).

Theories of revisionism or its absence can be categorized into those that assume material interests, such as wealth and security, on the part of actors and those that assume nonmaterial interests, such as status or recognition. Within each category, theories operate at two different levels of analysis: the state and the international order (individual-level theories of revisionism are less common). Some theories bridge the two levels but still privilege one over the other.

Material Interests

Theories that privilege material interests assume that revisionism is the result either of domestic groups pursuing their respective material interests or of states in the international order doing so. In the former category lie various theories of expansionism arising from domestic politics, going back to Jack Snyder's seminal theory of political

---

[26] Jason W. Davidson, *The Origins of Revisionist and Status-Quo States* (New York: Palgrave Macmillan, 2006), 13.

[27] Jason W. Davidson, "The roots of revisionism: Fascist Italy, 1922–39," *Security Studies*, 11:3 (2002), 125–159.

[28] Stacie E. Goddard, *When Right Makes Might: Rising Powers and World Order* (Ithaca: Cornell University Press, 2018), 4.

logrolling, strategic myths, and over-expansion.[29] For example, Jason Davidson argues that while external threats and opportunities do play a role in driving rising powers to revisionism, they only do so in the presence of powerful nationalist groups within the state that push for aggressive foreign policies.[30] Nationalist groups may also unilaterally instigate revisionism if they are domestically powerful and there are international opportunities available to exploit.[31]

Revisionism's absence can also be due to domestic factors, specifically the absence of powerful nationalist groups. In the US context, Fareed Zakaria argues that for most of the latter half of the nineteenth century, successive administrations that sought to expand abroad failed to raise the necessary economic resources and political support due to the fractious nature of power within the American polity.[32] Jeffrey Meiser offers a similar argument to explain US restraint from the turn of the twentieth century till its entry into World War II.[33] Expansionists in the presidency, in Congress, and in the private sector were continually stymied by the "separation of powers, anti-imperialist norms, and a geographically decentralized electoral system."[34]

Materialist theories of revisionism at the international level are of two types: theories of hegemonic war and of hegemonic peace. The former lie in the domain of power transition theory, which assumes rising powers seek material goals and will axiomatically challenge an international order because it is designed to benefit the great powers.[35] Power transition theory finds that war is most likely when a dissatisfied rising power gets close to overtaking an established great power in terms of economic and military capabilities.[36] A rising power's satisfaction with the international order is tied to the extent to which it benefits materially from the order. Even prestige-related concerns are

---

[29] Jack Snyder, *Myths of Empire: Domestic Politics and International Ambition* (Ithaca: Cornell University Press, 1991).
[30] Davidson, "The roots," 130.   [31] Ibid., 131.
[32] Fareed Zakaria, *From Wealth to Power: The Unusual Origins of America's World Role* (Princeton: Princeton University Press, 1998).
[33] Jeffrey W. Meiser, *Power and Restraint: The Rise of the United States 1898–1941* (Washington, DC: Georgetown University Press, 2015).
[34] Ibid., xvi.
[35] Douglas Lemke and William Reed, "Regime types and status quo evaluations: Power transition theory and the democratic peace," *International Interactions*, 22:2 (1996), 143–164.
[36] Jonathan M. DiCicco, "Power transition theory and the essence of revisionism," *Oxford Research Encyclopedia of Politics* (September 2017).

Table 1.1. *Typology of theories of revisionism among rising powers*

		DOMINANT MOTIVE OF ACTORS	
		Material interests	Status/recognition
	Domestic politics	Expansion/ restraint	Radical revisionism
LEVEL OF ANALYSIS	International order	Hegemonic war/ peace	Identity management

only about "the reputation for power."[37] In other words, prestige is a matter of other states getting out of a rising power's way as it claims a greater share of benefits from the international order.[38]

Theories of hegemonic peace argue that great powers often construct orders that preclude conflict. John Ikenberry argues that such "constitutional orders" are based on a simple bargain: "The leading state agrees to limits on its power – that is, it agrees to operate within an institutionalized political process according to a set of rules and principles – in exchange for the agreement by secondary groups or states to be willing participants in the order."[39] Rising powers are thus assured that their material interests will be protected, and the leading state enjoys prolonged durable power. The typology in Table 1.1 summarizes materialist theories, as well as theories of status or recognition, which are discussed next.

Status/Recognition

Due to their materialist focus, theories of hegemonic war and peace are unable to fully explain why a rising power would challenge an order that benefits it,[40] especially when challenging means risking war with the great powers. In other words, what makes a rising power so

---

[37] Robert Gilpin, *War and Change in World Politics* (Cambridge: Cambridge University Press, 1981), 14.

[38] Daniel Markey, "Prestige and the origins of war: Returning to realism's roots," *Security Studies*, 8:4 (1999), 126–172.

[39] G. John Ikenberry, "Constitutional politics in international relations," *European Journal of International Relations*, 4:2 (1998), 147–177.

[40] DiCicco, "Power transition theory," 25.

dissatisfied that it would seek to upend existing institutional arrangements? Shifting the basis of motivations to nonmaterial factors such as status, Steven Ward argues, "[T]he appearance of permanently obstructed status demands ... push[es] states toward radical revisionist policy combinations."[41] Ward's argument is grounded in domestic politics – status immobility empowers nationalists who use it as a pretext either for replacing moderate leaders or for pushing them to adopt aggressive policies. In the absence of committed nationalists in the domestic political arena, one does not get the all-or-nothing result of radical revisionism.

Finally, status-based theories that locate the sources of revisionism in the international order itself can broadly be termed theories of identity management. Deborah Larson and Alexei Shevchenko's application of social identity theory to international politics has shown, for example, that revisionism is one among a range of strategies that rising powers may adopt in order to maintain their identity or self-concept as major powers.[42] These strategies are not shaped by domestic politics but by the stability and permeability of the social hierarchy of the international order. In a related but distinct vein, Michelle Murray takes up the social process of recognition or misrecognition that constructs a rising power as cooperative or revisionist, respectively, in the eyes of great powers.[43] Misrecognition of a rising power's identity claims can lead to the security dilemma and eventually war between the great powers and the rising power. Recognition offers a pathway to peaceful transition.

IST builds on theories of identity management, which study the impact of international-order-related variables on a state's pursuit of status.

Incompleteness of Existing Approaches

Materialist theories are already poorly equipped to handle the question of revisionism when the latter is defined as a systemic challenge to the

---

[41] Ward, *Status and the Challenge*, 33.
[42] Deborah Welch Larson and Alexei Shevchenko, "Shortcut to greatness: The new thinking and the revolution in Soviet foreign policy," *International Organization*, 57:1 (2003), 77–109; Deborah Welch Larson and Alexei Shevchenko, "Status seekers: Chinese and Russian responses to U.S. primacy," *International Security*, 34:4 (2010), 63–95.
[43] Michelle Murray, *The Struggle for Recognition in International Relations: Status, Revisionism, and Rising Powers* (New York: Oxford University Press, 2019).

international order. However, even when it comes to earlier stages of a power shift, none of the above theories is fully capable of explaining the puzzle at the center of this book, namely, why a rising power might uphold or challenge an international order at great cost to itself.

There are three reasons for the theoretical incompleteness of the literature. First, existing theories take a narrow view of a rising power's strategies. The dominant focus in the literature is on expansion, war, and the radical overturning of norms, rules, and institutions. Very little space is devoted to understanding revisionist behaviors that do not entail military conflict of some sort, let alone straightforward cooperation. Some theories include the absence of conflict as a counterfactual case. For example, Ward and Murray study the United States in the late nineteenth century as an example of status accommodation and recognition, respectively. But the absence of conflict tells us little about the conditions under which a rising power will actively cooperate with the international order, often at significant cost to itself.

Second, existing theories are unable to fully specify the conditions under which rising powers will be (dis)satisfied. In other words, they tell us *why* a rising power may be dissatisfied or *when* it develops revisionist preferences, but not both. For example, theories of power transition and hegemonic war predict when rising powers and great powers will go to war, but they struggle to explain why rising powers are dissatisfied, relying instead on empirical measures – such as alliances, economic benefits, and membership of intergovernmental organizations[44] – that capture the results of dissatisfaction rather than dissatisfaction itself. Ikenberry's theory of hegemonic peace shows why constitutional orders experience less revisionism than other types of order, but it cannot predict when rising powers will be satisfied within constitutional orders. The failure of the interwar order is thus attributed to "idiosyncratic" factors related to US withdrawal rather than factors related to the treatment of Germany and Japan within the order itself.[45] Larson and Shevchenko theorize the conditions under which

---

[44] Steve Chan, "Can't get no satisfaction? The recognition of revisionist states," *International Relations of the Asia-Pacific*, 4 (2004), 207–238; Woosang Kim, "Alliance transitions and great power war," *American Journal of Political Science*, 35:4 (1991), 833–850; Lemke and Reed, "Regime types."

[45] G. John Ikenberry, *After Victory: Institutions, Strategic Restraint, and the Rebuilding of Order after Major Wars* (Princeton: Princeton University Press, 2000), 20.

states will adopt different identity management strategies, but they end up relying on historical disjunctures such as communist revolutions and major wars to model change in the strategies of Russia and China, respectively.[46] At the domestic level, theories of expansionism cannot explain why, despite the constant presence of nationalist groups, expansionism sometimes gains traction in domestic politics and at other times does not. Ward's theory of radical revisionism suggests that nationalists push for aggressive policies when they see their nations hit a status "glass ceiling," but cannot predict when that realization will dawn.[47]

With regard to the present, scholars from diverse theoretical approaches argue that rising powers, such as China and India, are dissatisfied with their lack of representation in the LIO. Left untheorized is the question of why rising powers expect their growing capabilities to translate into a greater voice in international institutions. Scholars of international organization often assume that states value international institutions because they serve a functional purpose.[48] So long as institutions produce functional benefits, states such as China and India should have no reason to demand greater representation or leadership in them; all the more so because leadership, or shouldering greater responsibilities in the international order, is costly.[49] Yet China has not only demanded representation, it has also incurred *greater* uncertainty and *higher* transaction costs by establishing new institutions, such as the Asian Infrastructure Investment Bank (AIIB), that replicate the functions of existing institutions.

Third, and finally, theories of revisionism do not systematically study the content of the international order itself, that is, the rules and institutions designed by great powers. At one end of the spectrum, theories of hegemonic war simply conflate international order and the distribution of power, assigning no causal role to institutions.[50] Thus,

---

[46] Deborah Welch Larson and Alexei Shevchenko, *Quest for Status: Chinese and Russian Foreign Policy* (New Haven: Yale University Press, 2019).

[47] Ward, *Status and the Challenge*, 47, 63.

[48] See Matthew D. Stephen, "Rising regional powers and international institutions: The foreign policy orientations of India, Brazil and South Africa," *Global Society*, 26:3 (2012), 289–309.

[49] Randall Schweller, "Emerging powers in an age of disorder," *Global Governance*, 17:3 (2011), 285–297.

[50] See Woosang Kim and Scott Gates, "Power transition theory and the rise of China," *International Area Studies Review*, 18:3 (2015), 219–226.

as a new power rises, it by definition wants to revise the order to reflect the changing distribution of power. Not only does this approach ignore cooperative and reformist strategies among rising powers, it also "renders any claim about the relationship between interstate power shifts and international order tautological."[51]

At the other end of the spectrum, identity management theories tend to conceive of the international order in overly broad terms, as "the prevailing status hierarchy,"[52] and often conceptually align it with the foreign policies of great powers toward rising powers. States in these models obtain information about their relative standing in the global status hierarchy through their interactions with the great powers.[53] While this assumption is valid, it depends on great-power policies toward rising powers rather than the impact of the international order itself. In the absence of a thicker conception of the institutional "stuff" of the order, we have at best a partial picture of the causal mechanisms by which rising powers might choose to uphold or hold up the international order.

In between these two extremes are theories of expansionism and radical revisionism, which often focus on an order's rules and institutions, but as the *object* of a rising power's revisionism. Rising powers seek to overthrow institutions not because the institutions themselves are flawed – indeed, they provide significant benefits, as discussed earlier – but because they represent a system structured by the great powers that are responsible for denying a rising power's claims to economic resources, security, status, or recognition. This approach too is valid but incomplete, in that it does not examine the role that engagement with the international order itself plays in shaping the strategies of rising powers, to the extent that significant parts of an order may be insulated from turbulence in bilateral relations between a rising power and a great power (as is the case with the present international order and US–China relations).

An exception to theories of revisionism that neglect the institutional aspects of order is Ikenberry's theory of hegemonic peace, which shows that institutions can be designed to reassure rising powers that great

---

[51] Steve Chan, Weixing Hu, and Kai He, "Discerning states' revisionist and status-quo orientations: Comparing China and the US," *European Journal of International Relations*, 25:2 (2019), 613–640.
[52] Larson and Shevchenko, *Quest for Status*, 11.
[53] Murray, *The Struggle for Recognition*, 6–10.

powers will not trample upon their interests. Although the theory itself operates at the aggregate level of international order, Ikenberry characterizes different types of order and their effects on war and peace, with his empirical analysis delving into institutional details to demonstrate the increasingly constitutional nature of the international order since 1815. IST, by contrast, does not assume *longue durée* change in the nature of order and instead explicitly theorizes the institutional features *within* an order that matter for a rising power's status aspirations. IST thus contributes to both theories of hegemonic war and peace and theories of status in world politics.

In all the above conceptions of revisionism, the only dynamic element is the distribution of power. Order itself is commonly viewed in broad and static terms, as "settled arrangements between states" that define their relationships and mutual expectations.[54] Although recent research has sought to analytically separate the distribution of power from the international order,[55] this move perpetuates the notion of an ossified international order juxtaposed against a changing balance of power. As a result, a dissatisfied rising power becomes the proverbial unstoppable force that meets an immovable object, resulting in radical revisionism, hegemonic war, etc. In fact, orders do change for a variety of reasons, and changes in rules and institutions can independently affect rising powers' assessments of the international order, and not always in ways that raise the risk of conflict.

Institutional Status Theory

IST is a theory of identity management that fills important gaps in the study of rising powers and international order. It does so in four ways. First, it focuses on a critical yet ignored period in power transitions – the early stages of a power's rise, when it is relatively weak compared to the great powers but still hungry for recognition. A rising power's approach to the international order is both chronologically and analytically prior to the problem of war in power transitions. Chronologically, although questions of hegemonic war and peace are important, their relevance is restricted to the final stages of a power's

---

[54] Ikenberry, *After Victory*, 23.
[55] Alexander Cooley, Daniel Nexon, and Steven Ward, "Revising order or challenging the balance of military power? An alternative typology of revisionist and status-quo states," *Review of International Studies*, 45:4 (2019), 689–708.

rise. War enters the picture when a rising power amasses sufficient resources to verge on becoming a great power and either mounts an outright challenge against existing great powers or is itself subject to preventive attack. Most scholars ignore the considerable political engagement and contentiousness that precede this stage – often for decades – as great powers seek to preserve their privileges within an international order and rising powers seek a greater role. This state of contentiousness also describes the international order today.

Analytically, the manner in which prior conflicts are resolved within the international order shapes the course of events as a rising power grows increasingly powerful. As the shift from British to US hegemony in the early twentieth century demonstrates, war is not inevitable during a power shift. Sometimes, great powers can accommodate the concerns of a rising power, turning it into a votary of the international order. At other times, as in the case of Germany during the same time period, a rising power's concerns remain unmet, and this dissatisfaction contributes to an eventual military confrontation. The politics of power shifts within the international order may contribute to the eventual occurrence or absence of major war.

Second, IST sheds light on a range of rising-power strategies and behaviors that most existing theories overlook. As Randall Schweller notes, "not all rising powers are dangerous revisionists" and "not every revisionist seeks to overthrow the existing order."[56] By defining status as symbolic equality with the great powers, IST introduces a further innovation to the status literature, which typically focuses on "valued attributes" or status markers that rising powers pursue to substantiate their status.[57] Not only do these attributes change over time but most of the items included in these attribute categories – such as wealth, military capabilities, and war-fighting ability – tend to load the dice in favor of predicting conflict. A rising power that pursues material goals as a status marker is likely to come up against the material interests of great powers soon enough.

---

[56] Randall Schweller, "Rising powers and revisionism in emerging international orders," *Valdai Papers*, 16 (May 2015), 1–15.

[57] Deborah Welch Larson, T. V. Paul, and William C. Wohlforth, "Status and world order," in T. V. Paul, Deborah Welch Larson, and William C. Wohlforth (eds.), *Status in World Politics* (Cambridge: Cambridge University Press, 2014), 3–29.

By focusing on status as symbolic equality with the great powers in institutional settings, IST not only opens up space for alternative approaches to acquiring status but also frees status markers from their historical specificity and enables theorizing about rising-power behaviors across different historical orders within a single framework. Importantly, IST does not exclude competition or conflict as a possible outcome but instead *subsumes* it in a broader theory of rising-power strategies. Some challenges to the international order, such as Japan's challenge to the Washington system in the early 1930s, set off a chain of events that end in war. Other challenges, such as India's challenge to the nuclear nonproliferation regime in the early 1970s, weaken an order's legitimacy over time and threaten its existence at a more gradual pace.

Challenging an international order is costly, and institutions may not always be inimical to a rising power's material interests or status concerns. There are good reasons, therefore, for states to follow rules or seek to change them if they fail to meet expectations. The question is: When will states choose cooperation, reform, or revision? IST's third advantage is the ability to answer this question by setting out the conditions under which rising powers will enact different types of strategies. In doing so, it operationalizes two variables underlying social identity theory – the permeability and legitimacy of the social hierarchy – that have not yet been systematically tested against empirical evidence. Larson and Shevchenko, in producing the only book-length work that engages with the impact of these variables on a state's choice of identity management strategies, conduct a plausibility probe on Russian and Chinese foreign policies to show that further research in this area is warranted.[58] This book fulfills that task.

Fourth, and finally, IST focuses squarely on rules and institutions. Doing so amplifies the theory's other strengths. Institutions are the concrete manifestations of international order that rising powers encounter early in their rise. As social environments thick with rule-based interstate interactions, they offer a venue in which one can observe behaviors other than radical revisionism and expansionism. They also allow for more precise definition and measurement of variables such as permeability (through membership and access rules) and legitimacy (through formal and informal procedures). As a theory that

---

[58] Larson and Shevchenko, *Quest for Status*, 234.

locates the sources of revisionism (and other strategies) at the international level, IST offers a meso-level analysis of rising powers in international order compared to the macro-level approaches of theories of hegemonic war and peace, and identity management.

Theory and Hypotheses

In keeping with much of the literature on status, IST assumes that in addition to material ends, rising powers value symbolic ends. Chief among these is membership of the great-power club, or symbolic equality with the great powers. This equality is a type of status, or position in a hierarchy. As they rise, states develop major-power identity – they see themselves as important actors in the international order and seek recognition of this identity in the design and functioning of the order itself. In doing so, they do not necessarily want to become great powers overnight. Conscious of their material inadequacy and the costs of leadership, they seek symbolic equality in anticipation of becoming great powers in the future. Drawing on club theory in economics, I argue that great-power status is an association good, one whose value depends on *who else* owns it. Rising powers value association with the great powers through membership of the great-power club. Further, drawing on social identity theory, I show that power shifts are not only about status denial and ensuing conflict. Rather, under certain conditions, rising powers will cooperate in order to earn or maintain status.

Social identity theory shows that lower-status groups engage in a range of strategies to close the status gap with higher-status groups. These strategies include (1) cooperation to climb the status hierarchy, (2) competition to undermine the status hierarchy, and (3) efforts to alter the criteria by which status is measured. In applying this paradigm to international relations, scholars have not systematically explained the conditions under which states might choose one strategy over another. This is where social identity theory itself can help. It suggests two variables that influence a lower-status group's choice of strategy: the permeability of social groups and the legitimacy of the social hierarchy.

IST focuses on the core institutions of the international order, an inherently social hierarchy where states meet at the negotiating table instead of the battlefield. I develop two new variables that are

Table 1.2. *Strategies of rising powers toward the international order*

		INSTITUTONAL OPENNESS	
		High	Low
PROCEDURAL FAIRNESS	High	Cooperate	Expand
	Low	Reframe	Challenge

analogous to group permeability and system legitimacy: *institutional openness* and *procedural fairness*, respectively. An open institution has few barriers to new powers joining its leadership ranks – the Council of the European Union's (EU) rotating presidency, for example, allows each member a turn at the helm. A procedurally fair institution treats higher-ranked and lower-ranked states on equal terms – the UNGA, for example, gives each country one vote. As shown in Table 1.2, the conjunction of these two variables produces four hypotheses regarding the strategies rising powers will pursue to earn or maintain status in an institutional setting.

IST predicts that a rising power faced with an institution that is relatively open and procedurally fair will be more likely to *cooperate* with its rules in order to earn status, or symbolic equality with the great powers. Conversely, a relatively closed and procedurally unfair institution will cause the rising power to *challenge* the institution as a way of asserting its claim to status. In between are two other scenarios. If an institution is relatively closed but procedurally fair, a rising power will seek to *expand* the set of criteria for institutional leadership. Alternatively, if an institution is relatively open but procedurally biased toward the great powers, a rising power will seek to *reframe* the rules in order to put itself on a more equal footing with them.

Case Selection

A sound method for testing the above hypotheses requires cases that are similar in all attributes except institutional openness and procedural fairness. This criterion makes it difficult to meaningfully compare international institutions dealing with very different types of issues. The many dissimilarities between security institutions and economic institutions, for example, prevent us from drawing reasonable inferences about the behavior of rising powers across these domains. A similar problem arises when trying to compare rising powers with different histories, cultures, and leaders. To avoid these pitfalls, I examine the rise of a single power over time within one type of institution: security institutions. Further, this method addresses the challenge posed by the historical evolution of international order from being primarily security-focused prior to World War II to being focused on many different issues from 1945 onward. Focusing on security institutions makes historical comparison and generalization more viable.

This book adds significant new empirical material to the study of rising powers, status, and international order. It is the first to develop detailed case studies, based on extensive primary evidence, of the status politics of power shifts in successive international orders since 1815. Specifically, I test IST in three distinct historical cases of a rising power and its approach to a core security institution of an international order. The first case looks at the United States and the 1856 Declaration of Paris on the maritime laws of war, the first near-universal instrument of codified international law, in the British-led Atlantic system of the mid-nineteenth century. The second case focuses on Japan and the 1922 Washington Naval Treaty, the centerpiece of the so-called Washington system of the interwar years. The third case examines India and the 1970 Nuclear Non-Proliferation Treaty, one of the few areas of superpower agreement during the Cold War. The unit of analysis in each case is the political and military leadership of the rising power. Complete details of the case selection process are available in the Appendix.

Each of these institutions – the Declaration of Paris, the Washington Naval Treaty, and the Nuclear Non-Proliferation Treaty – was at the core of an international order fashioned by the great powers in the aftermath of a major war. In each case, the rising power was faced with an order that it could support, challenge, or try to amend. In keeping with IST, I find that the rising powers drew inferences about their status from the design and functioning of these institutions. In moments of significant change in institutional openness and/or procedural fairness, they adjusted their status-seeking strategies accordingly. Overall, IST finds greater support in the empirical record than explanations based on material interests at the state and domestic levels.

Material factors naturally played a role in a rising power's decision-making. However, in moments when states faced major opportunities to earn status or faced a significant threat to their potential status, leaders were willing to let material interests take a back seat.

The findings of each case study also contribute substantially to the study of these historical episodes themselves, shedding new light on pivotal events such as the United States' initial enthusiasm for protecting neutral rights in maritime law and subsequent rejection of the Declaration of Paris which did exactly that; Japan's overly cooperative approach to the Washington Conference of 1921–1922 and subsequent rejection of the entire system a decade later; and India's initial support for multilateral efforts at nonproliferation, despite a growing nuclear threat from China, and its subsequent decision to test a nuclear device after the NPT came into effect. IST challenges existing explanations for these events and offers a new framework in which to make better sense of them.

A fourth case, that of China in the contemporary LIO, serves as a plausibility probe for IST's validity across issue areas and institutions. The findings broadly support IST's predictions, showing that China has been more cooperative in parts of the international order that are relatively open and procedurally fair (to China), including the UNSC, WTO, the nuclear order, and the G20. In other parts that are either closed or unfair – such as the International Monetary Fund (IMF), World Bank, and the UN Framework Convention on Climate Change (UNFCCC) – China has pursued reform strategies aimed at greater inclusion or fairness for itself. When these have failed, China has indirectly challenged the order by establishing new institutions, especially in global economic governance. Finally, in parts of the order that are closed and unfair from China's perspective – the UN system of human rights in particular – Beijing has challenged the order by seeking to delegitimize it.

The empirical research for the historical cases is based on four sets of sources. First, original archival documents collected from the National Archives at College Park, Maryland; the Library of Congress in Washington, DC; the National Archives of India in New Delhi; and the Nehru Memorial Museum and Library in New Delhi. The Japan case, in particular, contains evidence from previously unseen secret cables exchanged between senior Japanese officials in Tokyo, Washington, London, and a handful of European capitals. Originally

in coded Japanese, these cables were intercepted by the US government, deciphered, and translated during the Washington Conference of
1921–1922.

The second set of sources is composed of published documentary
collections such as the American State Papers, Foreign Relations of the
United States, The Diplomacy of Japan, proceedings of the Washington
Naval Conference, transcripts of the meetings of the UN's Eighteen-
Nation Committee on Disarmament (ENCD) during the Cold War, and
various official publications of the Government of India. The third set
includes memoirs, books, and articles written by political leaders, military officials, and official negotiators. Finally, I rely on secondary
sources in all four empirical chapters, and especially in the case of
China in the LIO, due to the contemporary nature of the case and the
difficulty of obtaining primary evidence for it.

Plan of the Book

Chapter 2 lays down the conceptual foundations of Institutional Status
Theory. It situates IST in the literature on status in world politics, and
on social identity in particular. It elaborates on the concept of status as
an intrinsic value and as a role that entails symbolic equality with
higher-status actors, as distinct from status as a set of valued attributes.
It discusses the psychological and social foundations of IST, in particular its relationship to and difference from constructivist theory. Finally,
the chapter theorizes the great-power club and international institutions as sites of status struggles.

Chapter 3 discusses IST itself as well as the research design of the
book. It provides a detailed exposition of the key variables of the theory:
the status-seeking strategies of rising powers, institutional openness, and
procedural fairness. It discusses the causal mechanism that explains the
impact of openness and fairness on a rising power's status and corresponding choice of strategy. It generates four possible strategies a state
may follow: cooperate, challenge, expand, and reframe. On research
design, the chapter describes the scope conditions of the theory, definitions of key concepts, case selection, research methodology and sources,
and the observable implications of the theory and how they differ from
the observable implications of alternative (materialist) explanations.

Chapter 4 focuses on the United States in the Atlantic system of the
nineteenth century. It traces the United States' status concerns from the

early nineteenth century leading up to the 1856 Declaration of Paris. It examines the US approach to the maritime laws of war during this period and derives expectations for how the United States would react to an international agreement such as the Declaration of Paris from two competing perspectives: material interests and IST. It tests these hypotheses through a detailed account of the US approach to the international maritime order from the 1820s, when the United States began rising, to 1856, when the Declaration of Paris became the first universal instrument of international law; as well as in the opening stages of the Civil War when the Union government strongly considered signing the Declaration. It finds that contrary to the commercial interests and status aspirations that influenced initial US support for the maritime laws of war, the country's leaders rejected the Declaration of Paris and sought to undermine it through an alternative (failed) treaty, because the United States was excluded from the deliberations leading to the Declaration and US leaders viewed the Declaration as relegating America to the status of a second-rate power.

Chapter 5 focuses on Japan and the Washington system in the interwar period. It traces Japan's status concerns from the late nineteenth century leading up to the 1922 Washington Naval Treaty. It examines Japan's approach to naval power after World War I and derives expectations for how Japan would react to an international agreement such as the Washington Naval Treaty from two competing perspectives: material interests and IST. It tests these hypotheses through a detailed account of Japan's approach to and positions in the Washington Conference of 1921–1922. It finds that although Japan faced a growing threat to its interests from the United States in the Western Pacific, Japan accepted greater restraints on warship construction in order to maintain its access to the great-power club, alongside Britain and the United States, as part of the "Big Three" at the conference. Subsequently, the US Immigration Act of 1924, which unprecedentedly banned Japanese immigration to America, served as a major betrayal of Japan's sacrifices for the sake of the international order, thus altering Japanese assessments of the openness and fairness of the Washington system. It convinced many moderates that the West would never consider Japan its equal, and it empowered anti-treaty factions in the navy to begin the costly process of abrogating Japan's commitment to the Washington system.

Chapter 6 focuses on India and the international order of the Cold War. It traces India's status concerns from independence in 1947 leading up to the advent of the NPT in the late 1960s. It examines India's approach to nuclear weapons during this period and derives expectations for how India would react to an international treaty such as the NPT from two competing perspectives: material interests and IST. It tests these hypotheses through a detailed account, based on primary sources, of India's approach to nuclear proliferation and positions taken in the International Atomic Energy Agency (IAEA) negotiations of 1954–1956 and in the Eighteen-Nation Committee on Disarmament from 1962 to 1969. It finds that although India faced a major nuclear threat from China, India supported nonproliferation and universal nuclear disarmament, so long as the international nuclear negotiations allowed symbolic equality with the great powers and the door to joining the nuclear club remained open. When the superpowers drafted an NPT that effectively froze the number of recognized nuclear powers for the next twenty-five years, Indian assessments of the openness and fairness of the international order changed, leading India to reject the NPT and undertake the very costly and risky step of testing a nuclear weapon.

Chapter 7 offers a plausibility probe of IST in the case of China and the contemporary liberal international order. The LIO – a multifaceted set of institutions covering a range of security and non-security issues – has contributed immensely to China's economic growth, diplomatic influence, and national security. China, nonetheless, opposes some and embraces other parts of the international order. The chapter shows that existing theories of revisionism struggle to explain this pattern of cooperation and discord in China's approach. It then traces China's status aspirations in the post–Cold War period and applies IST's predictions to China's stances in various prominent international institutions. The chapter concludes that IST can broadly apply in this case across institutions and issue areas, though further research is required to decisively demonstrate this claim.

Chapter 8 recapitulates IST's central assumptions and predictions, as well as the findings from the case studies. It identifies a number of empirical patterns emerging from the cases, which suggest areas for future research. The chapter also identifies alternative methodologies for testing IST and concludes with a discussion of IST's implications for theories of power shifts and international order. Finally, it discusses the policy implications of IST for the future of the liberal international order.

Implications of the Book

Rising powers through the ages have been sensitive to their status relative to the great powers. Even if lacking in relative military power, they value symbolic equality with the great powers. Openness and fair play in the international order are important indicators of this equality. Exclusion and bias are powerful drivers of conflict.

The Peloponnesian War in ancient Greece is a classic of the international relations canon, often studied as a paradigmatic case of power transition. In Thucydides' account of the war, he claimed that the real reason that "forced the war" was "the growth of Athenian power and Spartan fear of it."[59] This telling gives short shrift to "the grievances of either side,"[60] which clearly played a role in the buildup to war. Prestige, by the admission of the Athenians, was a key element – in addition to fear and interest – in their decision to build an empire after defeating the Persian armies of Xerxes.[61] Athens was particularly resentful of being criticized by Sparta and its allies for expanding its empire. This was, after all, what all great powers did. The Spartan position smacked of a double standard. According to the Athenians, "None of our critics enquires why this charge is not laid against other imperial powers elsewhere whose treatment of their subjects is less moderate than ours."[62] Upon receiving an ultimatum from Sparta to end sanctions against the city-state of Megara or face war, the Athenian general Pericles exhorted his countrymen, "stand firm on this, and you will make it clear to them that they would do better to treat you as equals."[63] The rise of Athenian power may indeed have provoked fear in Sparta, but the Athenian unwillingness to back down was driven by concerns of prestige and unfair treatment by Sparta.

IST shows us that the desire for symbolic equality permeates international politics, even outside power transitions. In a more historicized vein, Isaiah Berlin treated nationalism as an expression of "the inflamed desire of the insufficiently regarded to count for something

---

[59] Thucydides, *The Peloponnesian War*, trans. Martin Hammond (Oxford: Oxford University Press, 2009), 13.
[60] Ibid.
[61] Ibid., 37–38. See also Gregory Crane, "Power, prestige, and the Corcyrean affair in Thucydides," *Classical Antiquity*, 11:1 (1992), 1–27.
[62] Ibid., 38–39.   [63] Ibid., 69.

among the cultures of the world."[64] Germany, according to him, was destined to challenge the international order of the early twentieth century precisely because it had "remained on the edges of the great renaissance of Western Europe."[65] E. H. Carr observed that prior to World War I, Italian writers described their country as a "proletarian nation, using the term in the sense of 'under-privileged'."[66] Over time, "the struggle for equality became, in accordance with the ordinary laws of political power, indistinguishable from the struggle for pre-dominance."[67] Amassing power and declaring war on the international order increasingly became a viable mode of earning status.

Even when hegemonic war is unlikely, as in the contemporary international order, we find status concerns prominent in the minds of statesmen. In June 2020, at a meeting of the foreign ministers of Russia, India, and China to commemorate the seventy-fifth anniversary of the end of World War II, India's foreign minister S. Jaishankar reminded his counterparts that the postwar global order "did not give India due recognition" for its contribution to the Allied victory.[68] It was time, therefore, to not only "rectify the past" but also to push for "reformed multilateralism" that could reflect the reality of a contemporary order of 193 countries compared to the 50 countries that founded the United Nations.[69] Institutional reform would give India its rightful place relative to the great powers in the international order.

The attention rising powers, in particular, give to their status within the international order shows that even seemingly innocuous institutional arrangements can have significant consequences for the order and for international security writ large. Neglecting the status concerns of rising powers can lead international institutions to inadvertently undermine their own objectives, sometimes with disastrous consequences. An arms control treaty may produce an arms race, and a nuclear nonproliferation treaty may create a new nuclear power. At a

---

[64] Isaiah Berlin, "The bent twig: A note on nationalism," *Foreign Affairs*, 51:1 (1972), 11–30.

[65] Ibid., 17.

[66] E. H. Carr, *The Twenty Years' Crisis, 1919–1939* (1939; repr. London: Palgrave Macmillan, [2016]), 209.

[67] Ibid.

[68] S. Jaishankar, "EAM's opening remarks at the RIC trilateral foreign ministers' video conference," Ministry of External Affairs, Government of India (June 23, 2020).

[69] Ibid.

more macro level, in the interwar period, for example, the Soviet Union's exclusion from the international order contributed to its sense of isolation and eventual antagonism toward core diplomatic institutions such as the League of Nations by the late 1930s.[70] The opposite phenomenon is just as consequential. An international order that accommodates the status concerns of a rising power may be more successful in co-opting it, as was the case for India in the mid-2000s when the United States officially recognized it as a de facto nuclear power.

These findings have obvious contemporary significance: they shed light on the behavior we see (and can expect to see) from rising powers, such as China and India, within the US-led international order. Given that large-scale military conflict between major powers is unlikely in the nuclear age, the core institutions of the international order become even more salient as venues for contests of influence between rising and great powers. Status within the social hierarchies of these institutions is both a source and measure of a state's influence. This book offers a timely account of the politics of status within international orders from the perspective of rising powers.

* * *

[70] Deborah Welch Larson, "New perspectives on rising powers and global governance: Status and clubs," *International Studies Review*, 20 (2018), 247–254.

2 | *Conceptual Foundations*

According to the dominant view of rising powers in international relations, these states inevitably challenge the international order in which they are rising. Charles Kindleberger, a well-known proponent of the idea that international stability requires an active leading power, nonetheless argued that this system becomes "unstable over time in much the same way that a Pax Britannica, Pax Americana, balance-of-power system, or oligopoly is unstable."[1] There is always a rising challenger, either from outside the system or from within it. Rising powers allegedly turn into challengers because the international order is rigged in favor of the great powers. Robert Gilpin, in his widely read book on international political change and hegemonic war, argued that the "social arrangements" of the international system "tend to reflect the relative powers of the actors involved."[2] As the balance of power changes, rising powers – that seek to continue growing richer and more secure – find the rigged international order blocking their path. When they can, they attempt to change it. Eventually, these efforts create a substantial conflict of interest with the great powers, leading to major war and the creation of a new order.

Revisiting Standard Assumptions

A number of assumptions are built into this theoretical picture. First, great powers are self-centered: They want to, and do, benefit disproportionately from the international order that they build and manage. Second, a rising power is dissatisfied: It wants to maximize wealth and security to an extent deemed impossible under the existing international order. Third, a rising power is an insatiable revisionist:

[1] Charles P. Kindleberger, "Dominance and leadership in the international economy: Exploitation, public goods, and free rides," *International Studies Quarterly*, 25:2 (1981), 242–254.
[2] Gilpin, *War and Change*, 9.

28

Nothing short of fundamental change in the international order will suit its interests. It seeks not merely to replace the great powers at the head of a well-oiled benefits machine but to replace the machine entirely.

These assumptions are plausible at first glance. Great powers are often the architects of international order, especially in the aftermath of major wars.[3] Great powers also stick together as comanagers of the international order, ensuring that its various institutions perform their intended functions. Management typically entails the making, revision, interpretation, justification, and enforcement of rules, as well as the overall protection of the order.[4] Again, great powers have significant room to rig this activity for their own benefit. Rising powers, which surely care about wealth and security, may well feel that the order does not serve their interests. They may seek to fundamentally overhaul it.

Each of the above three assumptions can be challenged, however, with good reason. Scholars have demonstrated, for example, that great powers do not (and often simply cannot) create international orders to exclusively serve themselves and their allies.[5] Instead, to make their power more durable, they often build an order that provides public goods.[6] Rising powers by definition have grown and prospered within the existing international order, hence it seems odd that they would be dissatisfied with it. Randall Schweller and Xiaoyu Pu pose the puzzle: "Why would an increasingly powerful state that is growing faster than its established competitors want to overthrow the very system under which it is benefiting (given its unmatched growth rate) more than any other state?"[7] The answer can only be that a rising power expects to do

[3] Kalevi J. Holsti, *Peace and War: Armed Conflicts and International Order 1648–1989* (Cambridge: Cambridge University Press, 1991).
[4] Hedley Bull, *The Anarchical Society: A Study of Order in World Politics* (1977; 3rd ed. London: Palgrave, 2002), 68–71.
[5] Margit Bussmann and John R. Oneal, "Do hegemons distribute private goods? A test of power-transition theory," *Journal of Conflict Resolution*, 51:1 (2007), 88–111.
[6] G. John Ikenberry, *Liberal Leviathan: The Origins, Crisis, and Transformation of the American World Order* (Princeton: Princeton University Press, 2011); Charles P. Kindleberger, *The World in Depression, 1929–1939* (Berkeley: University of California Press, 1973); Stephen D. Krasner, "State power and the structure of international trade," *World Politics*, 28:3 (1976), 317–347.
[7] Schweller and Pu, "After unipolarity," 51.

even better under an alternative framework.[8] This contention is object-
ively impossible to verify, since there is no counterfactual scenario of a
different international order.[9] If it is a subjective belief, then it raises
the question of what might cause a rising power to believe that the
international order is rigged or unacceptable. In thinking about the
answer, as this chapter will show, we have to venture outside the realm
of purely material motivations, such as wealth and security, and into
the realm of symbolic motivations, such as status.

The link between dissatisfaction and revisionism is also unclear.
Some dissatisfied rising powers seek to challenge an international order
that has benefited them, while others do not. The comparison between
the United States and Germany, both rising in a British-dominated
international order in the late nineteenth century, is commonplace in
the literature. As Susan Sample observes, both Germany and the
United States were reaping "enormous benefits through Pax
Britannica," and both had ongoing disputes with Britain at the time.[10]
Why, then, did Germany challenge the international order while the
United States did not? A similar observation could be made about
countries such as China and India today, which benefit immensely
from the US-led international order and yet are also challenging some
aspects of it and not others.

In addition to the literature discussed in the previous chapter,
scholars often frame the issue of revisionism in terms of time. The
puzzle here is why a dissatisfied rising power would undertake the
costly act of challenging the international order when it can simply
wait until it is powerful enough to become top dog.[11] The literature
offers two types of answers. First, it is not the rising power that
necessarily initiates the challenge but an established great power that
preemptively picks a fight out of insecurity.[12] Second, there is

---

[8] Douglas Lemke and William Reed, "Power is not satisfaction: A comment on de
Soysa, Oneal, and Park," *Journal of Conflict Resolution*, 42:4 (1998), 511–516.
[9] John R. Oneal, Indra de Soysa, and Yong-Hee Park, "But power and wealth are
satisfying: A reply to Lemke and Reed," *Journal of Conflict Resolution*, 42:4
(1998), 517–520.
[10] Susan G. Sample, "Power, wealth, and satisfaction: When do power transitions
lead to conflict?" *Journal of Conflict Resolution*, 62:9 (2018), 1905–1931.
[11] A. F. K. Organski, *World Politics* (1958; repr. New York: Random House,
[1968]), 333.
[12] Daniel S. Geller, "Power transition and conflict initiation," *Conflict
Management and Peace Science*, 12:1 (1992), 1–16.

something intrinsic to certain rising powers that makes them predisposed to revisionism or risky behavior generally.[13] Both explanations hinge on how we define and measure concepts such as dispute initiation and risk tolerance. Both also beg the question in different ways. A great power's optimal policy should be to try to integrate a rising power into the prevailing order, instead of initiating disputes that might lead to war.[14] If disputes are the result of a rising power's truculence, then we still need to know what it is that makes a rising power more prone to revisionist or risky behavior.

Institutional Status Theory (IST), developed in this chapter and the next, approaches the question of revisionism by examining how the design and functioning of core institutions in the international order impact a rising power's aspirations. These aspirations are related to not just security and economics but also a rising power's desired *status* as a major power. Status can be conferred or denied, producing incentives for cooperative or conflictual behavior, respectively, among its aspirants. A rising power encounters the international order early in its rise, well before the possibility of war with any great powers enters the picture. Without an understanding of the institutional politics of this stage, our overall account of international political change remains incomplete. A theory of the respective conditions under which a rising power will uphold or challenge the core institutions of an international order can illuminate why some rising powers become or remain dissatisfied as they grow. It can also suggest ways in which great powers might ameliorate the grievances of a rising power early in its trajectory, thereby reducing the likelihood of a military challenge later.

The rest of this chapter discusses how IST relates to existing work on status and power shifts, and lays out the conceptual foundations of the theory.

Status Research and Power Shifts

A growing body of research on nonmaterial state motivations, specifically focused on status, has studied behaviors that seem counterintuitive from a strictly materialist standpoint. Status is commonly defined

---

[13] Kim and Morrow, "When do power shifts."
[14] Richard Ned Lebow and Benjamin Valentino, "Lost in transition: A critical analysis of power transition theory," *International Relations*, 23:3 (2009), 389–410.

as "collective beliefs about a given state's ranking on valued attributes."[15] Valued attributes may be entirely independent of material factors. Nordic countries, for example, have the status of international peacemakers that uphold the central norms of the contemporary international order.[16] South Korea, Singapore, Finland, and Canada enjoy the status of having the best-performing education systems in the world.[17]

Status theories predict that a state may be willing to pay significant costs to earn or maintain status. Lilach Gilady shows that states often spend extensively on projects of dubious economic or military value for reasons of prestige.[18] Michelle Murray argues that rising powers, in order to secure their identities as major powers, acquire advanced military capabilities that are "understood to be emblematic of major power status."[19] Often, status-seeking goes well beyond conspicuous consumption and status symbols. Jonathan Renshon shows that individuals – including statesmen – frequently choose to engage in military conflict when their group or country's status is threatened.[20] Steven Ward traces the emergence of radical revisionism among rising powers to "the appearance of permanently obstructed status demands."[21]

These theories help us better understand dissatisfaction and why a rising power may challenge an international order that provides significant economic and security benefits. This is, of course, only part of the picture. As noted in Chapter 1, research on status and power shifts overwhelmingly focuses on major war or radical revisionism as the outcome to be explained.[22] Given that rising powers experience decades of growth before they reach a point where military conflict

---

[15] Larson et al., "Status and world order," 7.
[16] See Peter Viggo Jakobsen, Jens Ringsmose, and Hakon Lunde Saxi, "Prestige-seeking small states: Danish and Norwegian military contributions to US-led operations," *European Journal of International Security*, 3:2 (2018), 256–277.
[17] Richard Little, "Foreword," in Benjamin de Carvalho and Iver B. Neumann (eds.), *Small States and Status Seeking: Norway's Quest for International Standing* (New York: Routledge, 2015), xiii–xv.
[18] Lilach Gilady, *The Price of Prestige: Conspicuous Consumption in International Relations* (Chicago: University of Chicago Press, 2018).
[19] Murray, *The Struggle for Recognition*, 7.
[20] Jonathan Renshon, *Fighting for Status: Hierarchy and Conflict in World Politics* (Princeton: Princeton University Press, 2017).
[21] Ward, *Status and the Challenge*, 33.
[22] On the conflict orientation of status theories more generally, see Renshon, *Fighting for Status*, 10–14.

over the fate of the international order is a possibility, understanding what makes them satisfied or dissatisfied *as they rise* can provide a more comprehensive understanding of the entire process of power transition, not just its denouement. Redirecting analytical attention in this way has two productive effects. First, it brings the international order – the set of rules, norms, and institutions designed by the great powers to manage cooperation and conflict among states – into clearer focus. New powers must negotiate the institutions of the international order from the very beginning of their rise, yet we know very little about how they do so. Second, it reveals a range of state strategies with regard to the international order that includes conflict but also reformism and cooperation.

The status paradigm is well equipped to take on these new research problems. Although not directly concerned with power shifts, scholars who have applied social identity theory in international relations have studied the types of behavior motivated by the desire for standing in a hierarchy. They show that the desire to possess or retain a certain high-status identity can cause states to continually find ways to "manage" their identities through the vagaries of international and domestic politics. Deborah Larson and Alexei Shevchenko show, in the case of Russia and China, that the choice of a particular identity management strategy depends on features of the international status hierarchy.[23] Anne Clunan's work on Russia looks within the state at historical memory and elite contestation as key ingredients in the management of national identity.[24] James Lee argues that China's post–Cold War grand strategy reflects a desire to maintain a distinct identity and is fundamentally not hostile to the international order.[25]

This literature is, nonetheless, incomplete in three important respects. First, it does not systematically focus on rising powers. While there are numerous works on individual countries such as Russia, China, Japan, and India – not all of which are studied as rising powers – a testable and generalizable theory of status-seeking strategies among rising powers has not yet been developed. Second, the literature takes a macro-level view of the international order, often

[23] Larson and Shevchenko, *Quest for Status.*
[24] Anne L. Clunan, *The Social Construction of Russia's Resurgence* (Baltimore: Johns Hopkins University Press, 2009).
[25] James Jungbok Lee, "Will China's rise be peaceful? A social psychological perspective," *Asian Security*, 12:1 (2016), 29–52.

describing it in terms of deep norms such as sovereignty or simply aligning it with the policies of great powers toward rising powers. While these factors are not unimportant, the literature has tended to overlook the role of institutions themselves as independent variables. In China's case, for example, the continued emphasis on a distinctive identity in the post–Cold War order is only made possible due to the myriad institutional avenues through which China can develop a public image consonant with its desired identity. It is no surprise, therefore, that a number of contemporarily focused works have focused on specific institutions as sites of China's quest for status.[26]

Third, and finally, social identity theories have not properly outlined the conditions under which a state might pick one status-seeking strategy over another. In part, this is because most studies have focused on a single country within a short time frame, typically in the post–Cold War era. Larson and Shevchenko have recently made an important break with this pattern by developing a theory of Russian and Chinese foreign policy in which the permeability and stability of the international status hierarchy are key variables.[27] However, their work self-consciously does not systematically operationalize or test these variables. Although change in their analysis happens unpredictably based on major wars or revolutions, their *longue durée* analysis of Russia and China is a valuable first step toward a more comprehensive theory of status-seeking in international orders.

The Concept of Status

IST offers the first systematic account of rising-power strategies within the core institutions of an international order. In IST, states are the primary actors in world politics, and they are unitary. Although this is not empirically accurate, it is a simplifying assumption that allows us to more clearly predict state behavior. If a theory assumes that a state values its security, then the underlying assumption is that – even though a state cannot "feel" insecure – dangers to the state appear

---

[26] For example, Fung, *China and Intervention*; Oliver Stuenkel, "Emerging powers and status: The case of the first BRICs summit," *Asian Perspective*, 38:1 (2014), 89–109; Shogo Suzuki, "Seeking 'legitimate' great power status in post-Cold War international society: China's and Japan's participation in UNPKO," *International Relations*, 22:1 (2008), 45–63.

[27] Larson and Shevchenko, *Quest for Status*.

threatening, at the very least, to those in charge of making and execut-
ing policy, if not to all groups and individuals within the state.[28]
Similarly, Renshon observes that "threats to group status are likely
to be felt by individuals just as strongly as if it was a threat to their
personal status position."[29]

Status as an Intrinsic Value

States are rational. They pursue courses of action that will most likely
help attain their desired goals. Scholars of major-power politics often
assume that states value only one goal: power, which comes from
economic and military capabilities. This assumption leads to the claim
that "in international politics prestige [or status] is at most the pleasant
by-product of policies whose ultimate objectives are not the reputation
for power but the substance of power."[30] Status, in this account, is a
means of conserving and thereby enhancing a state's power by not
having to use it. This claim is not theoretically useful. It is a simplifying
assumption that does not help explain the behavior of rising powers in
an international order. If, as Gilpin argues, a rising power's dissatisfaction is due to its reputation for power lagging behind its actual
power, simply providing other states with more information or more
accurate information could solve this problem.[31] The definition of
status as the reputation for power cannot explain why rising powers
do not simply remain content with an international order that facilitates their rise.

The opposite approach assumes that power itself is a means to other,
nonmaterial ends.[32] Henry Kissinger, writing about the Concert of
Europe, rejected the idea that it represented a balance of power.
"While states may appear to the outsider as factors in a security

[28] See Jonathan Mercer, "Feeling like a state: Social emotion and identity,"
International Theory, 6:3 (2014), 515–535.

[29] Renshon, *Fighting for Status*, 44.

[30] Hans J. Morgenthau, *Politics among Nations: The Struggle for Power and Peace*
(New York: Alfred A. Knopf, 1948), 55–56. See also Kenneth N. Waltz, "The
emerging structure of international politics," *International Security*, 18:2
(1993), 44–79.

[31] Marina G. Duque, "Recognizing international status: A relational approach,"
International Studies Quarterly, 62 (2018), 577–592.

[32] Martha Finnemore, "Legitimacy, hypocrisy, and the social structure of
unipolarity," *World Politics*, 61:1 (2009), 58–85.

arrangement," he argued, "they consider themselves as expressions of historical forces. It is not the equilibrium as an end that concerns them ... but as a means towards realizing their historical aspirations in relative safety."[33] Accordingly, it might be said that power is a means to status, with the latter constituting a state's historical aspirations. For example, Ann Hironaka challenges the traditional view of "military competition as a sensible endeavor that is necessary to ensure power and security."[34] Instead, she argues, "the Great Powers wage war to maintain their identity and status as Great Powers."[35] However, if military power is what confers status, then we cannot explain why rising powers sometimes accept constraints on their military power, for example by signing arms control agreements that benefit the great powers more.

To avoid the pitfalls of defining interests exclusively in terms of either power or status, IST assumes that states value both these goals. The case for power as a state goal has been made extensively in international relations. High status, in this account, can at best add to a state's power; it cannot ensure survival. Yet states appear to be "obsessed" with their status.[36] If status is only somewhat valuable as a means, it follows that states must be obsessed with status because they value it *as an end*.[37] This view is increasingly commonplace. Scholars have described prestige or status as "one of the three essential causes of human quarrel,"[38] as something sought for the "psychological satisfaction" of "superiority by comparison to fellow actors,"[39] as central to the identity of rising powers,[40] and as "an effective claim to social esteem in terms of privileges" that are analytically distinct from

---

[33] Henry Kissinger, *A World Restored: Metternich, Castlereagh and the Problems of Peace, 1812–22* (Boston: Houghton Mifflin, 1957), 171.

[34] Ann Hironaka, *Tokens of Power: Rethinking War* (New York: Cambridge University Press, 2017), 18.

[35] Ibid., 17.

[36] Allan Dafoe, Jonathan Renshon, and Paul Huth, "Reputation and status as motives for war," *Annual Review of Political Science*, 17 (2014), 371–393.

[37] Glenn H. Snyder, "Process variables in neorealist theory," *Security Studies*, 5:3 (1996), 167–192.

[38] Markey, "Prestige and the origins of war," 136, drawing on Hobbes.

[39] Tudor A. Onea, "Between dominance and decline: Status anxiety and great power rivalry," *Review of International Studies*, 40 (2014), 125–152.

[40] Murray, *The Struggle for Recognition*, 6–7.

material resources.[41] The psychological evidence supports these assumptions, showing that, irrespective of sex, race, culture, age, or personality type, the desire for status is a fundamental human motive, one that is distinct from power, wealth, or social belonging.[42]

Renshon argues that status and power have "common ancestors," that is, wealth or military capabilities.[43] IST is compatible with this assumption, though it should be recognized that capabilities are not the only source of status. In the case of rising powers, symbolic equality with the great powers is an independent source of status. Situations may arise where the twin goals of power and status come into conflict with each other. IST's premise is not that states *only* value status, but that, under certain conditions, states will give up some amount of security or economic gain to earn or maintain status. Symbolic goals in this theory are pursued rationally.[44]

Status as Symbolic Equality

Status is typically defined as a state's position in a deference hierarchy that is based on some valued attributes or markers – what Reinhard Wolf terms trait-status.[45] Scholars variously list these attributes as "wealth, coercive capabilities, culture, demographic position,

---

[41] Duque, "Recognizing international status," 578. See also Richard Ned Lebow, *A Cultural Theory of International Relations* (Cambridge: Cambridge University Press, 2008), 541; William C. Wohlforth, "Unipolarity, status competition, and great power war," *World Politics*, 61:1 (2009), 28–57.

[42] Cameron Anderson, John Angus D. Hildreth, and Laura Howland, "Is the desire for status a fundamental human motive? A review of the empirical literature," *Psychological Bulletin*, 141:3 (2015), 574–601.

[43] Renshon, *Fighting for Status*, 42.

[44] Ibid., 51–52. For the opposite view that status denial produces negative emotions, such as anger and shame, that shape state behavior, see Deborah Welch Larson and Alexei Shevchenko, "Russia says no: Power, status, and emotions in foreign policy," *Communist and Post-Communist Studies*, 47 (2014), 269–279. These two positions are in fact compatible, since emotions are the foundation of rational action. See Jonathan Mercer, "Rationality and psychology in international politics," *International Organization*, 59:1 (2005), 77–106. Thus, to say status (or security) is pursued rationally is to say that actors value status (or security) because it carries positive emotion.

[45] Reinhard Wolf, "Taking interaction seriously: Asymmetrical roles and the behavioral foundations of status," *European Journal of International Relations*, 25:4 (2019), 1186–1211.

sociopolitical organization, and diplomatic clout,"[46] or "advanced technology, military victories, and institutional reforms,"[47] or "battleships, aircraft carriers, and nuclear weapons."[48] This approach creates some difficulties for the study of status during power shifts. First, the attributes most commonly listed in the literature are material, that is, components of a state's economic and military power. It is difficult, therefore, to distinguish state behavior motivated by power – in terms of both external goals and narrow bureaucratic interests – from behavior motivated by status, and consequently to decisively make the case for either motivation when theory meets the empirical record.

Second, and relatedly, the choice of material attributes fits well with the goal of most status theories, which is to predict conflict, but it is unsuitable for the purposes of IST, which is to predict rising-power strategies toward international order. If status markers prominently include military technology and war-fighting, then the pursuit of status will likely lead to strategic competition between rising powers and great powers. However, defining the basis of hierarchy in material terms loads the dice in favor of competition and underplays the significance of noncompetitive approaches to international order.

Third, and finally, as Wolf points out, theories that rely on trait-status assume a state monitors public beliefs about its acquisition of socially valuable traits. The empirical record shows instead that "status-conscious governments overwhelmingly care about the way in which *significant others treat them* and frequently protest against behavior they consider as disrespectful."[49] Traits may add to the prestige of a state but do not automatically translate into deference without a measure of the behavior of significant Others. Rising powers, thus, care less about how the world perceives them than about how the great powers treat them. Within the international order, by extension, rising powers care about how rules and institutions created by the great powers treat them.

IST draws on an alternative conception of status as "an *identity* or membership in a group,"[50] or what Wolf calls role status.[51] This

---

[46] Larson et al., "Status and world order," 7.
[47] Ward, *Status and the Challenge*, 3.
[48] Murray, *The Struggle for Recognition*, 6.
[49] Wolf, "Taking interaction seriously," 1188, emphasis added.
[50] Renshon, *Fighting for Status*, 4, emphasis in original.
[51] Wolf, "Taking interaction seriously," 1193.

approach is more suitable to the study of power shifts, where "major power status is an identity in international society and as such its formation depends on recognition from the established powers."[52] States may pursue material goods as status markers, but in the context of international order the most important source of status for a rising power is *symbolic equality* with the great powers, which is instantiated by the manner in which rules and institutions treat a state relative to the great powers. Two actors are symbolically equal if prevailing social norms, rules, and institutions recognize them as having equal rights and claims to a certain identity. Symbolic equality does not entail material equality. Rising powers, especially in the earlier stages of their rise, are significantly weaker than great powers. Yet, by virtue of their increasing capabilities and trait-status, they seek role status at par with the great powers. In particular, they seek membership of the great-power club as major powers, or states that have a vital role to play in the management of international order.

In domestic society, the desire for symbolic equality is most commonly studied with regard to groups with unequal capabilities and trait-status. In the context of race and gender – where symbolic equality can be understood as "legal standards of equal citizenship" – some scholars have associated symbolic equality with tokenism, a hollow formal equality that masks significant material inequalities.[53] A much larger literature, however, views symbolic equality as a powerful motivator of group behavior. In the 2000s, for example, although civil unions would have materially guaranteed equality for same-sex couples in the United States, LGBTQ+ activists widely emphasized marriage equality, keeping in mind "the potentially transformative effect of reconfiguring ideas of legitimate family arrangements to include same-sex couples."[54]

---

[52] Murray, *The Struggle for Recognition*, 56.

[53] Robert Frederick Burk, "Symbolic equality: The Eisenhower administration and Black civil rights, 1953–1961," unpublished PhD thesis, University of Wisconsin-Madison (1982), 3. See also Barbara Cameron, "From equal opportunity to symbolic equity: Three decades of federal training policy for women," in Isabella Bakker (ed.), *Changing Spaces: Gender and State Responses to Economic Restructuring in Canada* (Toronto: University of Toronto Press, 1996), 55–81.

[54] Kenneth Sherrill and Alan Yang, "From outlaws to in-laws," *Public Perspective* (January/February 2000), 20–23. See also Nancy K. Kubasek, Alex Frondorf, and Kevin J. Minnick, "Civil union statutes: A shortcut to legal equality for

Demands for social reform are often concurrent demands for resource redistribution and symbolic equality. Lower-caste groups in India mobilize not just for access to resources but also over the naming of airports, the erection of statues, and other symbols of equality with upper-caste groups.[55] Women in the United States continue to mobilize in favor of the Equal Rights Amendment, not because it materially affects their life chances, but because it serves as "a critical symbol of equality in everyday life."[56] States that initially ratified the amendment in the 1970s signaled to women that they had a claim to "the highest goals in not only their family and work-related lives, but ... in their political lives as well."[57]

In some contexts, the attainment of symbolic equality can induce cooperation between different social groups. Proponents of common schooling argue that common schools "symbolise society's recognition of children's common humanity, and of children's equal right to respect and recognition," which may in turn counterbalance some of the negative lived experiences of minority communities.[58] In other contexts, contests over symbolic equality can lead to conflict. National controversy over demands for Albanian to be counted as an official language was an important cause of Macedonia's ethnic insurgency in 2001, as well as a major stumbling block in ensuing peace talks. The "bitter core of the dispute" was "symbolic and psychological," which outweighed any considerations of the cost of including a second language in all government business.[59] Similar political clashes over the inclusion of certain languages in official currency notes have troubled other multilingual societies.[60]

same-sex partners in a landscape littered with Defense of Marriage Acts," *University of Florida Journal of Law and Public Policy*, 15:2 (2004), 229–259.

[55] Muthukaruppan Parthasarathi, "Paramakudi violence: Against dalits, against politics," *Economic and Political Weekly*, 46:44/45 (2011), 14–17.

[56] Jocelyn Elise Crowley, "Moving beyond tokenism: Ratification of the Equal Rights Amendment and the election of women to state legislatures," *Social Science Quarterly*, 87:3 (2006), 519–539.

[57] Ibid., 524.

[58] J. Mark Halstead, "In place of a conclusion: The common school and the melting pot," *Journal of Philosophy of Education*, 41:4 (2007), 829–842.

[59] Risto Karajkov, "Macedonia's 2001 ethnic war: Offsetting conflict: What could have been done but was not?" *Conflict, Security & Development*, 8:4 (2008), 451–490.

[60] Marcela Veselkovaa and Julius Horvath, "National identity and money: Czech and Slovak lands 1918–2008," *Nationalities Papers*, 39:2 (2011), 237–255.

Often, symbolic equality is valuable *because* it masks material inequality, thus allowing unequal groups to get along. The EU's neighbors, such as Ukraine and Egypt, are more willing to cooperate with the EU when they are described as partners, giving them "symbolic recognition as potential members of the club," rather than as Wider Europe or Europe's neighborhood, which relegates them to "a grey zone on its edges."[61] Harald Müller and Carsten Rauch similarly argue that the Concert of Europe was stable because its members "were treated as equals, asymmetries in real power notwithstanding," and this norm "eliminated the risk of growing status dissatisfaction," which could have otherwise destabilized the concert.[62]

Taken together, the above examples show that lower-ranked social groups – including states – seek symbolic equality with higher-ranked groups as an instantiation of status, or a desirable position in a deference hierarchy. In the domain of power shifts, IST presumes that institutional features, such as openness and procedural fairness, contribute to the "symbolic neutralization of power differences" that is necessary for stability in an international order.[63] By the same token, the denial of symbolic equality can cause instability.

The Psychological and Social Foundations of IST

The foundations of IST lie in what Jacques Hymans has called psychological constructivism, a type of theorizing that connects "individuals' cognitive and emotional tendencies and their deeper collective identities."[64] IST probes the effects of social interaction between states on a rising power's pursuit of fundamental human motives such as status, belonging, and fairness. It has much in common with constructivist theories of international relations, yet differs substantially from them by virtue of being grounded in psychology. The theory presumes

---

[61] Dimitar Bechev and Kalypso Nicolaidis, "From policy to polity: Can the EU's special relations with its 'neighbourhood' be decentred?" *Journal of Common Market Studies*, 48:3 (2010), 475–500.

[62] Harald Müller and Carsten Rauch, "Conclusion: Managing power transitions with a concert of powers," in Harald Müller and Carsten Rauch (eds.), *Great Power Multilateralism and the Prevention of War: Debating a 21st Century Concert of Powers* (Abingdon: Routledge, 2018), 244–256.

[63] Ibid., 248.

[64] Jacques E. C. Hymans, "The arrival of psychological constructivism," *International Theory*, 2:3 (2010), 461–467.

that "the structures of human association are determined primarily by shared ideas rather than material forces" and that these shared ideas construct identities and interests.[65] The pursuit of status as a desirable social identity is only possible in the context of preexisting social categories that intersubjectively assign meaning to ideas such as great power, rising power, democracy, autocracy, and so on in world politics.[66] Social categories precede individuals, and state leaders are "born" into international society in the way that individuals are born into an already structured society.[67] IST is thus a theory of "actor behavior in existing hierarchies."[68] Certain leadership roles such as that of a great power are desirable because they are tied to social status and social authority by virtue of the various social expectations built into them.[69]

However, IST stops short of arguing that status-seeking is *constituted* by "the basic fact of sociality."[70] Rather, there is something fundamentally psychological about the self-esteem that status provides to individuals that explains the motive for status-seeking, while sociality explains the substance. For biological and/or evolutionary reasons, humans seek positive distinctiveness for their groups relative to others. This "biological *push*" is accompanied by a "social world *pull*" that explains the substance of desirable identities in different cultures and eras.[71] Put differently, psychology shows us that states universally desire status, while sociology – the basis of constructivism – answers the question of "status *as what*,"[72] which depends on the intersubjective meanings of various identities in the international order.

---

[65] Alexander Wendt, *Social Theory of International Politics* (Cambridge: Cambridge University Press, 1999), 1.

[66] Ibid., 224.

[67] Jan E. Stets and Peter J. Burke, "Identity theory and social identity theory," *Social Psychology Quarterly*, 63:3 (2000), 224–237.

[68] Ayşe Zarakol, "Theorising hierarchies: An introduction," in Ayşe Zarakol (ed.), *Hierarchies in World Politics* (Cambridge: Cambridge University Press, 2017), 1–14.

[69] Sebastian Harnisch, "Role theory and the study of Chinese foreign policy," in Sebastian Harnisch, Sebastian Bersick, and Jörn-Carsten Gottwald (eds.), *China's International Roles* (New York: Routledge, 2016), 3–21.

[70] Vincent Pouliot, "Setting status in stone: The negotiation of international institutional privileges," in Paul et al. (eds.), *Status in World Politics*, 192–215.

[71] Dan Allman, "The sociology of social inclusion," *SAGE Open* (January–March 2013), 1–16, emphases in original.

[72] Renshon, *Fighting for Status*, 35, emphasis in original.

IST both overlaps with and differs from constructivism in another important respect, with regard to the agency of the Self. It assumes, with constructivism, that "actions continually produce and reproduce conceptions of Self and Other, and as such identities and interests are always in process," even if they can be modeled as given in particular scenarios.[73] The status of being a member of the great-power club is a role identity: It entails the existence of Others with relevant counter-identities and shared expectations of the role.[74] Great powers cannot act like great powers if other states do not accord them the recognition of the identity they claim. Similarly, rising powers may pursue the traits of great power but cannot claim equal membership of the club if significant Others, the great powers themselves, do not accord them that recognition. Since "identity is a dynamic process from which action flows and in turn sustains identity," a disjuncture between externally recognized roles and internally held role identities can cause ontological insecurity – instability in one's sense of self over time – among states,[75] a possibility that is exacerbated during times of uncertainty, such as power shifts.[76]

The constructivist assumption at this point is that, given a conflict between internally held and socially recognized identities, the latter wins.[77] Empirical work in this vein emphasizes the process of socialization or internalization by which states take on new identities or groups of states subscribe to new norms.[78] IST, drawing on theories of social identity, takes a different approach. In contrast to the view of the state as a "receptacle for others' expectations,"[79] IST sees the Self as reflexive in that "it can take itself as an object and can categorize,

---

[73] Wendt, *Social Theory*, 36.   [74] Ibid., 227.
[75] Jennifer Mitzen, "Ontological security in world politics: State identity and the security dilemma," *European Journal of International Relations*, 12:3 (2006), 341–370.
[76] Priya Chacko, "A new 'special relationship'? Power transitions, ontological security, and India-US relations," *International Studies Perspectives*, 15 (2014), 329–346.
[77] Mitzen, "Ontological security," 359.
[78] Martha Finnemore and Kathryn Sikkink, "International norm dynamics and political change," *International Organization*, 52:4 (1998), 887–917; Johnston, *Social States*.
[79] Deborah Welch Larson, "How identities form and change: Supplementing constructivism with social psychology," in Vaughn P. Shannon and Paul A. Kowert (eds.), *Psychology and Constructivism in International Relations* (Ann Arbor: University of Michigan Press, 2011), 57–75.

classify, or name itself in particular ways in relation to other social categories or classifications."[80] States are not modeled as individuals in this account, but rather as groups represented in interstate interactions by a coterie of national leaders. These leaders both embody the group's social identity and have the domestic political authority to shape it. As Larson and Shevchenko note, "given effective leadership, groups can decide to whom they should be compared and over what dimensions."[81] Indeed, leaders under various experimental conditions have been found to have the authority to alter group norms, an ability that is stronger at times of identity-related uncertainty (an endemic condition of power shifts).[82] The implication being that if an externally recognized role and internally held identity conflict, a state can reject the role or try to alter it in ways that align with its identity. Interaction is vital for sustaining identity, but identity formation is more a function of individual or group agency than interaction itself.[83]

International Order, the Great-Power Club, and Institutions

Theorists of power transition such as A. F. K. Organski define international order as a system of relations with lesser states established by a powerful state, in which certain rules of deference become standardized over time.[84] In this view, the distribution of power produces

[80] Stets and Burke, "Identity theory," 224.
[81] Larson and Shevchenko, *Quest for Status*, 19.
[82] Dominic Abrams, Georgina Randsley de Moura, José M. Marques, and Paul Hutchison, "Innovation credit: When can leaders oppose their group's norms?" *Journal of Personality and Social Psychology*, 95:3 (2008), 662–678; Michael J. Barone and Robert D. Jewell, "The innovator's license: A latitude to deviate from category norms," *Journal of Marketing*, 77:1 (2013), 120–134; Nir Halevy, Yair Berson, and Adam D. Galinsky, "The mainstream is not electable: When vision triumphs over representativeness in leader emergence and effectiveness," *Personality and Social Psychology Bulletin*, 37:7 (2011), 893–904; David E. Rast, Amber M. Gaffney, Michael A. Hogg, and Richard J. Crisp, "Leadership under uncertainty: When leaders who are non-prototypical group members can gain support," *Journal of Experimental Social Psychology*, 48:3 (2012), 646–653.
[83] Larson, "How identities form," 61. By contrast, the symbolic interactionism underlying constructivism also assumes a reflexive Self but privileges interaction as constitutive of state behavior. See Rebecca Adler-Nissen, "The social Self in international relations: Identity, power and the symbolic interactionist roots of constructivism," *European Review of International Studies*, 3:3 (2016), 27–39.
[84] Organski, *World Politics*, 353.

order, implying that power shifts will automatically revise order as rising powers seek to impose their own rules. This mechanistic approach does not capture the societal nature of international politics, where material power is not the only dimension on which states seek recognition.[85] IST relies instead on Hedley Bull's canonical definition of international order as "a pattern of activity that sustains the elementary or primary goals of the society of states."[86] International society exists when a group of states recognize their common interests and common values, and develop rules and institutions to govern their relations with each other.[87] The primary goals (or values) of international society include preserving itself, maintaining the independence of individual member states, maintaining international peace, and ensuring that social life within states is stable.[88]

Societal theories of international order do not deny the existence of an international hierarchy of power. Rather, they argue that this hierarchy is embedded in a social hierarchy. Material power is a source of trait-status, but it does not guarantee recognition as a great power, for example, which involves legitimation of a state's authority to play a determinative role in establishing, maintaining, and enforcing rules that govern international life.[89] States perform these functions through "basic institutions," such as the balance of power, international law, diplomacy, great power management, and war.[90] These basic institutions operate through international organizations and instruments of international law, both of which are the central focus of IST under the rubric of "international institutions" (for analytical convenience). While it may be difficult to know what states think (if at all) of basic institutions such as the balance of power or diplomacy, the reaction of states to the manifestations of these basic institutions in the "settled rules and arrangements between states that define and guide their interaction" is more evident.[91]

---

[85] Cameron G. Thies and Mark David Nieman, *Rising Powers and Foreign Policy Revisionism: Understanding BRICS Identity and Behavior Through Time* (Ann Arbor: University of Michigan Press, 2017), 2.

[86] Bull, *The Anarchical Society*, 8.   [87] Ibid., 13.   [88] Ibid., 16–18.

[89] Ibid., 64–71.

[90] Ibid., xxxv. See also the role of "fundamental institutions," such as contractual international law and multilateral diplomacy, in Christian Reus-Smit, *The Moral Purpose of the State: Culture, Social Identity, and Institutional Rationality in International Relations* (Princeton: Princeton University Press, 1999).

[91] Ikenberry, *Liberal Leviathan*, 12.

Great powers are central to any conception of international order. They manage the international order through rules and institutions, or "legalised hegemony."[92] To endure, an order and its leaders must be acceptable to its members. While leadership can be attained and maintained for a while through "arm-twisting and bribery,"[93] coercion and inducements are costly.[94] To be truly enduring, an order and its leadership must be based not only on power but also on authority, or rightful rule.[95] International orders can be thought of as "configurations of political authority," or "normatively sanctioned ways of distributing legitimate political power."[96] International authority rests on sovereign states legitimizing some amount of sovereign inequality by accepting the privileged role of great powers in the international order.[97]

At the same time, there is an element of indirect bribery, in that great powers do not rig the international order purely or even disproportionately for their own benefit. If they did, we would not observe new powers rising. As many scholars have argued, the international order does in fact provide public goods and benefits to other states as well.[98] IST thus assumes that great powers manage the international order through a mix of coercion, inducements, and legitimacy. Coercion and inducements influence the material goals of rising powers, whereas legitimacy influences their symbolic goals. Just as a rising power's

---

[92] Gerry Simpson, *Great Powers and Outlaw States: Unequal Sovereigns in the International Legal Order* (Cambridge: Cambridge University Press, 2004), x.

[93] Kindleberger, "Dominance and leadership," 243.

[94] Christian Reus-Smit, "Power, legitimacy, and order," *The Chinese Journal of International Politics*, 7:3 (2014), 341–359.

[95] David A. Lake, *Hierarchy in International Relations* (Ithaca: Cornell University Press, 2011), 8.

[96] Reus-Smit, "Power, legitimacy, and order," 348.

[97] Shunji Cui and Barry Buzan, "Great power management in international society," *The Chinese Journal of International Politics*, 9:2 (2016), 181–210. For the contrary view that hierarchy is ubiquitous in social life, leaving subordinate states with little choice in taking on their respective roles, see Vincent Pouliot, "Against authority: The heavy weight of international hierarchy," in Zarakol (ed.), *Hierarchies in World Politics*, 113–133.

[98] Bussmann and Oneal, "Do hegemons distribute private goods?"; Indra de Soysa, John R. Oneal, and Yong-Hee Park, "Testing power-transition theory using alternative measures of national capabilities," *Journal of Conflict Resolution*, 41:4 (1997), 509–528; Lebow and Valentino, "Lost in transition," 395; Ronald L. Tammen, "The Organski legacy: A fifty-year research program," *International Interactions*, 34:4 (2008), 314–332.

support may be bought through preferential trade policies, so may it be earned through legitimate rules and institutions.

The Great-Power Club

The great powers form an exclusive club of the highest material capabilities and status. They are not only "in the front rank in terms of military strength," but also "recognized by others to have ... certain special rights and duties."[99] Great-power privileges are essentially rule-making privileges – they have "the authority to structure the norms and rules that guide the international order."[100] The club-like nature of great powers, although frequently referred to in the status literature, has not been theorized in any depth.[101] Doing so can illuminate relations between states inside and outside the club. Economic theory tells us that for great-power status to be a traditional club good, it must be non-rivalrous (up to a point) and excludable. Non-rivalry means admitting a new member to the club is costless (up to a point), and excludability means great powers can prevent countries from joining the club.

Club goods are different from private and public goods because the membership size of the group and the provision of the good are interdependent allocation decisions.[102] The non-rivalrous property of club goods declines as more members join the club. Beyond a point, the costs of congestion overwhelm the benefits of adding new members. A common example: For the same level of facilities, each new dues-paying member of a golf club reduces the cost of membership for any single member (assuming equal cost sharing). However, as more new members are added without any change in the size of the club's facilities, the benefit to each individual member of the club declines due to crowding.[103]

---

[99] Bull, *The Anarchical Society*, 194–196.
[100] Murray, *The Struggle for Recognition*, 15.
[101] An exception is Lora Anne Viola, *The Closure of the International System: How Institutions Create Political Equalities and Hierarchies* (Cambridge: Cambridge University Press, 2020), 60–70. In their account, however, states only value club membership for material reasons.
[102] Todd Sandler and John Tschirhart, "Club theory: Thirty years later," *Public Choice*, 93 (1997), 335–355.
[103] Ibid., 337–338.

Club theory assumes a world of material costs and benefits.[104] In such a world, the membership dues of the great-power club would be the cost of managing the international order. The membership benefit would be pecuniary only: say, protection money paid to the great powers by other states in the form of preferential trade, access to resources, etc. In this world, the optimal size of the great-power club – the size at which crowding begins to set in – would be larger than what we actually observe, since the pot of benefits for members would be limited only by the total financial capacity of states outside the club.

Status, however, is a positional good – its supply is socially scarce.[105] The great powers are privileged not just because they are better able to provide order than other states, but because the great-power club is not just any club: It "stands as the preeminent social fact of the state system."[106] Demand for great-power status rests on the fact that only a few states can have it. The principal benefit of great-power club membership is not material – each great power could achieve material ends, such as survival and security, independently – but rather the "substantial prestige and deference from all members of the state system."[107] Due to the social scarcity of great-power status, the great powers have an incentive to keep their club small. The optimal size of the great-power club is, therefore, much smaller than it would be if the benefits of membership were purely material.

The concept of association goods combines the positionality of status and the club-like nature of great powers.[108] The value of association goods depends neither on their market price nor strictly on the number of consumers, but rather on who the other consumers are: "By acquiring such a commodity a person tries to gain association, in the eyes of fellow human beings, with its other recipients."[109] Membership of a club that restricts membership to social elites would qualify as an

---

[104] Economists have acknowledged that certain clubs become unattractive for members as more members join because of prestige reasons (see Yew-Kwang Ng, "The economic theory of clubs: Optimal tax/subsidy," *Economica*, 41:163 (1974), 308–321), but the dominant assumption behind crowding is material scarcity.

[105] Fred Hirsch, *Social Limits to Growth* (1977; repr. London: Taylor & Francis, [2005]), 27; Renshon, *Fighting for Status*, 33–35.

[106] Hironaka, *Tokens of Power*, 3–4.   [107] Ibid., 15.

[108] Kaushik Basu, "A theory of association: Social status, prices and markets," *Oxford Economic Papers*, 41:4 (1989), 653–671.

[109] Ibid., 653.

association good, as do prestigious prizes such as the Nobel Prize and the Booker Prize. Members of these clubs value their membership because of the rules by which it is allocated – to the most socially, intellectually, or artistically talented individuals, for example – rather than the market value of their medal or prize money.[110] The great-power club, like the Nobel Prize, is at the very top of the general hierarchy in its status community. It holds a monopoly on the conferral of great-power status upon states. Although states can pursue power through other means such as building up their own economies and militaries, or allying with powerful states, they cannot attain great-power status without associating with other great powers. The club is, therefore, not only small but also tight-knit, because members have no alternative sources for what they principally get from it. In the language of institutional economics, the exit cost for each member – "the difference between the value received from membership in the group and the value that is gained from the member's best alternative" – is prohibitively high.[111]

Great-power status entitles certain states to managerial privileges in the international order. It is also an identity with which rising powers want to associate themselves, as major powers. Rising powers cannot simply increase their material capabilities to the point of parity with the great powers in order to gain the status benefits of association. They need to be admitted into the great-power club precisely because "there is status associated with being admitted."[112] Club membership implies symbolic equality between members, which does not entail material equality. Recipients of the Nobel Prize need not have published as much as past prizewinners, and members of an elite country club need not have identical financial endowments. In every club, there may be members who are less "capable" than other members. However, the very fact of their membership in the club gives them the same role status as other members *relative to non-members*, thus compensating for disparities in capabilities or trait-status. IST is thus a theory about what rising powers do to gain recognition as symbolic equals of the great powers (and not a theory about the status hierarchy of the great-power club itself).

[110] Ibid.
[111] Michael Hechter, *Principles of Group Solidarity* (Berkeley and Los Angeles: University of California Press, 1987), 46.
[112] Basu, "A theory of association," 654.

The great-power club relies on shared understandings and norms between states, as well as on institutions, as a means of coordinating who counts as a member and what privileges are accorded to them. Institutions may exclude – and historically have excluded – states for all manner of reason, including on grounds of political ideology, race, and "civilization."[113] At minimum, the price of membership is the ability and willingness to manage the international order, which would in effect reduce the cost of management for those already in the club. Rising powers, as aspiring members, seek recognition of their suitability for this role,[114] which may entail undertaking costly actions to support the status quo.

International Institutions and Status Struggles

The hierarchical nature of the international order and the privileged position of the great power club are manifested in international institutions, or formal and informal sets of rules and procedures designed by states to achieve common objectives.[115] Institutions – especially those that are central to the existence and functioning of an international order – perform recognition functions that make them vital to the ambitions of rising powers. Caroline Fehl and Katja Freistein show how institutions, being embedded in the already stratified social environment of the international order, reproduce inequalities through processes of *categorization* and *distribution*.[116] In other words, institutions assign states to different social categories and distribute material and nonmaterial resources across these categories. These functions are vital for recognition, because states' claims to specific role identities

---

[113] Gerrit W. Gong, *The Standard of 'Civilization' in International Society* (Oxford: Oxford University Press, 1984); Steven Ward, "Race, status, and Japanese revisionism in the early 1930s," *Security Studies*, 22:4 (2013), 607–639.

[114] Murray, *The Struggle for Recognition*, 15; Duque, "Recognizing international status," 578.

[115] This definition draws on Douglass C. North's definition of "organizations." In contrast, "institutions," for him, are the deep rules of the game (akin to Bull's "fundamental institutions"). See Douglass C. North, *Institutions, Institutional Change and Economic Performance* (Cambridge: Cambridge University Press, 1990), 3–5.

[116] Caroline Fehl and Katja Freistein, "Organising global stratification: How international organisations (re)produce inequalities in international society," *Global Society*, 34:3 (2020), 285–303.

are unintelligible without an institutional architecture that defines roles and their attendant privileges. Thomas Müller shows, for example, that institutional reform in the League of Nations in the mid-1920s led to the sanctification of the great powers – a reflection of the broader social hierarchy – as permanent members of the League's Executive Council.[117] In this manner, the institutionalization of roles facilitates shared expectations of what it means to be a great power, a major power, and so on.[118]

The existence of multiple types of status in the international order (traits and roles) may potentially confuse statesmen about their country's relative standing. However, when it comes to the great-power club, the asymmetrical nature of roles ensures that participants are "fully aware of their relative rank."[119] This is particularly true of the international orders the world has seen since the early nineteenth century (the focus of this book), which have institutionalized the notion of great power management. There is no ambiguity in the mind of an Indian or Brazilian diplomat of the difference in rank at the United Nations Security Council between their country and the five permanent members. Indeed the clear demarcation of club membership in this manner makes institutions particularly attractive venues for rising powers to definitively attain symbolic equality with the great powers. It is telling, for example, that India and Brazil have even proposed permanent UNSC membership for themselves *without* veto power, thus accepting less power over decision-making in exchange for a seat at the highest table.[120]

The multilateral and public nature of institutions makes them particularly suitable for status-seeking. An international institution offers rising powers a single venue in which to make their status claims to a collective audience of great powers. More importantly, it provides a single set of formal and informal rules and procedures designed and

---

[117] Thomas Müller, "Institutional reforms and the politics of inequality reproduction: The case of the League of Nations' Council Crisis in 1926," *Global Society*, 34:3 (2020), 304–317.

[118] Wendt, *Social Theory*, 227.

[119] Wolf, "Taking interaction seriously," 1194. See also T. V. Paul and Mahesh Shankar, "Status accommodation through institutional means: India's rise and the global order," in Paul et al. (eds.), *Status in World Politics*, 165–191.

[120] Oliver Stuenkel, "Leading the disenfranchised or joining the establishment? India, Brazil, and the UN Security Council," *Carta Internacional*, 5:1 (March 2010), 53–63.

maintained by the great powers against which a rising power can judge the degree of symbolic equality accorded to it. Put differently, international institutions are particularly efficient means by which rising powers can measure the distance between their major-power identity and externally recognized role. Institutions are, unsurprisingly, key sites in the struggle for recognition.[121]

Different types of rules and procedures can impact the status aspirations of states differently. Membership rules (the categorization function of institutions) decide which political entities are to be even counted as states, and which states have legitimate standing to negotiate outcomes. For example, the willingness of a high-status actor to sit across a table and negotiate is itself an equalizing act, granting standing to the other party. The Soviet Union saw the Strategic Arms Limitation Talks (SALT) as "a visible cherished symbol of equality" that "helped to ease an acute ... complex of inferiority with regard to its wealthy, powerful, and envied geopolitical rival."[122] China similarly viewed civil repatriation negotiations following the Korean War as a way of establishing symbolic equality with the United States, a country that did not officially recognize the People's Republic at the time.[123] More generally, the UN since World War II has formally recognized the sovereign equality of all states, a membership rule that, coupled with a one-country-one-vote procedural rule, has made statehood a prestigious club to many who lack it.[124] In the words of Abram and Antonia Chayes, "Sovereignty, in the end, is status."[125]

Membership of prestigious institutional clubs is a significant source of symbolic equality for aspirants. Japan, for example, viewed the Organization for Economic Cooperation and Development's (OECD) club of rich democracies as a "salon of advanced countries" without

---

[121] Fehl and Freistein, "Organising global stratification," 289.

[122] Sergei Fedorenko, "Russia and arms control: The trials of transition to a post-Soviet era," *Naval War College Review*, 46:2 (1993), 45–58.

[123] Raymond Cohen, *Negotiating across Cultures: International Communication in an Interdependent World* (Washington, DC: United States Institute of Peace, 1998), 64.

[124] Raymond Cohen, "Reflections on the new global diplomacy: Statecraft 2500 BC to 2000 AD," in Jan Melissen (ed.), *Innovation in Diplomatic Practice* (Basingstoke: Palgrave, 1999), 1–18.

[125] Abram Chayes and Antonia Handler Chayes, *The New Sovereignty: Compliance with International Regulatory Agreements* (Cambridge, MA: Harvard University Press, 1995), 27.

whose membership Japan would be "treated as a second-rate power."[126] Once within clubs, procedural rules (the distribution function of institutions) impact a state's status through decision-making rules, special privileges, and the distribution of costs and benefits of institutional outcomes. Rules such as equal voting, rotating presidencies, and participatory decision-making promote inclusion and symbolic equality between club members.[127] As the next chapter discusses, those who are treated as "lesser" by an institution will resist rules that they see as unfair or procedurally unjust.

A small but growing literature has begun to systematically consider the question of rising powers and international institutions. Almost exclusively focused on the contemporary international order, this research has found variation across issue areas in terms of rising-power strategies (more on this in Chapter 7).[128] Most works in this vein, however, assume exclusively material interests on the part of rising powers, look only at one side of the satisfaction/dissatisfaction question, and focus on outcomes such as mutual adjustment and strategic co-optation rather than strategies.[129] A handful of works on status in world politics have pointed to the importance of institutions as elite clubs and the desire of rising powers for representation rather than normative contestation.[130] Other scholars, drawing on

---

[126] Shogo Suzuki, "Europe and Japan," *Review of European Studies*, 4:3 (2012), 54–63, quoting Hironao Suzuki.

[127] See Paul and Shankar, "Status accommodation," 168; Sophie Vanhoonacker, Karolina Pomorska, and Heidi Maurer, "The presidency in EU external relations: Who is at the helm?" *Dans Politique Européenne*, 35:3 (2011), 139–164.

[128] See Andreas Kruck and Bernhard Zangl, "The adjustment of international institutions to global power shifts: A framework for analysis," *Global Policy*, 11:3 (2020), 5–16; Stephen, "Rising regional powers."

[129] See Andreas Kruck and Bernhard Zangl, "Trading privileges for support: The strategic co-optation of emerging powers into international institutions," *International Theory*, 11 (2019), 318–343; Matthew D. Stephen and Kathrin Stephen, "The integration of emerging powers into club institutions: China and the Arctic Council," *Global Policy*, 11:3 (2020), 51–60; Bernhard Zangl, Frederik Heußner, Andreas Kruck, and Xenia Lanzendörfer, "Imperfect adaptation: How the WTO and the IMF adjust to shifting power distributions among their members," *Review of International Organizations*, 11 (2016), 171–196.

[130] See Larson, "New perspectives"; Edward Newman and Benjamin Zala, "Rising powers and order contestation: Disaggregating the normative from the representational," *Third World Quarterly*, 39:5 (2018), 871–888; Paul and Shankar, "Status accommodation."

sociological conceptions of status, have addressed the manner in which international institutions produce and reproduce hierarchies by restricting access to key rights and resources.[131] IST builds on these latter literatures of status – social and psychological – to explain both satisfaction and dissatisfaction in rising-power strategies toward an international order and its core institutions.

* * *

[131] Fehl and Freistein, "Organising global stratification," 288; Edward Keene, "Social status, social closure and the idea of Europe as a 'normative power'," *European Journal of International Relations*, 19:4 (2012), 939–956; Tristen Naylor, *Social Closure and International Society: Status Groups from the Family of Civilised Nations to the G20* (London: Routledge, 2018); Viola, *The Social Closure*, 25. For a similar sociological approach using practice theory, see Vincent Pouliot, *International Pecking Orders: The Politics and Practice of Multilateral Diplomacy* (Cambridge: Cambridge University Press, 2016).

3 | *Institutional Status Theory*

As discussed in the previous chapter, Institutional Status Theory (IST) assumes a unitary state represented by national leaders who experience status opportunities and threats to the state personally and act on its behalf. Status has intrinsic value and derives from traits as well as roles a state plays in the international order. Rising powers accumulate traits associated with great-power status such as advanced military capabilities and wealth. As they rise, they also develop the identity of a major power – a power that is not yet a great power but plays an important role in managing the international order.[1] This role entails membership of the great-power club, which is instantiated in symbolic equality between a rising power and the great powers as per the rules and institutions of the international order. IST explains the strategies rising powers follow to have their internally held major-power identity affirmed in terms of externally recognized roles in international institutions.

The fundamental quandary of a rising power, as posed by Robert Gilpin, is correct at one level: The global hierarchy of status (or prestige) becomes misaligned with the hierarchy of power as a state rises.[2] Status, however, is not simply a reputation for power. Because status is intersubjective, no matter how many status markers a rising power accumulates, its status aspirations will remain unmet until the members of the great-power club treat it as an equal. In other words, "If material resources determined status, the status order would collapse into class relations, and the nouveau riche would have access to the same privileges as old money."[3] Recognition matters, because the kind of status rising powers seek relative to the great powers pertains to membership of an identity group and can only be instantiated in

---

[1] This conceptualization draws on Murray, *The Struggle for Recognition*, 54–57.
[2] Gilpin, *War and Change*, 14.
[3] Duque, "Recognizing international status," 580.

relations with that group and its institutions. Membership of the great-power club is an association good. Status comes not only from being rich and powerful but also from being associated with others who already possess great-power status.

Social Identity and Status-Seeking

Social identity theory offers a framework within which to think about the status-seeking behavior of rising powers. It studies "the group in the individual,"[4] on the understanding that individuals, aside from having sources of identity that are unique to themselves, also draw their identity from the groups to which they belong. Individuals have an innate desire for self-esteem, or a "positive self-concept."[5] They bolster their self-esteem by categorizing the world into groups (such as nations), identifying strongly with their own group, and comparing their group favorably with others.[6] When groups are of equal status, their respective members tend to be biased in favor of their own group and against other groups.[7] When groups are of unequal status, lower-ranked groups engage in various strategies to enhance their self-esteem in the face of inequality.[8] The social hierarchy stands separately from the material hierarchy, though the two may be empirically correlated.[9]

Three types of strategy are prominent in settings of social inequality. First, lower-ranked groups may *cooperate* to climb the status hierarchy. This strategy, also known as social mobility, involves trying to become more like a higher-status group by adopting the latter's rules,

---

[4] Michael A. Hogg and Dominic Abrams, *Social Identifications: A Social Psychology of Intergroup Relations and Group Processes* (London and New York: Routledge, 1998), 3.

[5] Gérard Lemain, "Social differentiation and social originality," *European Journal of Social Psychology*, 4:1 (1974), 17–52.

[6] Hogg and Abrams, *Social Identifications*, 21.

[7] John C. Turner, "Social comparison and social identity: Some prospects for intergroup behaviour," *European Journal of Social Psychology*, 5:1 (1975), 5–34.

[8] Henri Tajfel and John Turner, "An integrative theory of intergroup conflict," in W. G. Austin and S. Worchel (eds.), *The Social Psychology of Intergroup Relations* (Monterey, CA: Brooks-Cole, 1979), 33–47.

[9] Michael Kalin and Nicholas Sambanis, "How to think about social identity," *Annual Review of Political Science*, 21 (2018), 239–257.

habits, and norms.[10] In effect, lower-status groups draw on higher-status group identities as the source of their social identity (while retaining the unique bases of their own identity). Second, lower-status groups may *challenge* the status hierarchy. This strategy, also known as social competition, involves clinging more closely to one's own social identity and rejecting the rules, habits, and norms of higher-status groups.[11] Social competition aims to overturn the status quo by challenging the very basis on which certain groups are ranked higher than others.

Third, and finally, lower-status groups may seek to cultivate a positive evaluation of their social identity by trying to *change* the criteria by which status is measured, through either (1) reframing negative evaluations of one's identity claims as positive or (2) introducing new criteria by which groups should be ranked.[12] This strategy, also known as social creativity, does not seek to overthrow the status quo, but rather to change it in ways that enhance the self-esteem of the lower-ranked group. (A common third tactic is comparing one's group to less high-ranking groups. This is excluded here as it does not apply to power shifts, where nothing short of symbolic equality with the great powers will achieve a rising power's status ambitions.)

In the case of rising powers, major-power identity is a social identity; it exists by virtue of a rising power's position in the hierarchy of the international order. Rising powers strive to maintain a positive evaluation of this identity in the eyes of significant Others such as the great powers. Status, in the form of symbolic equality with members of the great-power club, signals recognition of major-power identity. To attain this status, a rising power may engage in one of the four strategies described in Table 3.1.

Social identity theory's application in international relations is not without controversy. Steven Ward argues that the theory has been misapplied in international relations because it puts social mobility, an individual-level strategy, on the same plane as group-level strategies, such as social creativity and social competition.[13] However, this

---

[10] Itesh Sachdev and Richard Y. Bourhis, "Status differentials and intergroup behaviour," *European Journal of Social Psychology*, 17 (1987), 277–293.
[11] Hogg and Abrams, *Social Identifications*, 24–25.
[12] Tajfel and Turner, "An integrative theory," 43.
[13] Steven Ward, "Lost in translation: Social identity theory and the study of status in world politics," *International Studies Quarterly*, 61:4 (2017), 821–834. For a

Table 3.1. *Status-seeking strategies*

Strategy	Motivation	Behavior
Cooperate	Alter social identity to become more like higher-status group	Adopt rules, habits, and norms of higher-status group; accept the social status quo
Challenge	Reassert social identity to differentiate from higher-status group	Reject rules, habits, and norms of higher-status group; overturn the status quo
Change (reframe)	Alter the criteria by which groups are judged to have low or high status	Reframe negative evaluations of one's identity claims as positive
Change (expand)	Alter the criteria by which groups are judged to have low or high status	Expand the set of criteria used for status comparisons

interpretation holds social identity theory to its earliest and narrowest version. Research since the 1970s shows that entire groups coordinate their actions based on the collectively felt need for social mobility through "cooperation, hard work and participation within the current system."[14] In the context of states in particular, which are hierarchically organized, national leaders can engage in efforts to shift the basis of their nation's social identity by adopting great-power habits, practices, and norms.[15]

response, see Deborah W. Larson and Alexei Shevchenko, "Lost in misconceptions about social identity theory," *International Studies Quarterly*, 63 (2019), 1189–1191.

[14] Joseph Sweetman, Colin Wayne Leach, Russell Spears, Felicia Pratto, and Rim Saab, "'I have a dream': A typology of social change goals," *Journal of Social and Political Psychology*, 1:1 (2013), 293–320. See also Henri Tajfel, *Differentiation between Social Groups: Studies in the Social Psychology of Intergroup Relations* (London: Academic Press, 1978), 93–94; Mathias Blanz, Amélie Mummendey, Rosemarie Mielke, and Andreas Klink, "Responding to negative social identity: A taxonomy of identity management strategies," *European Journal of Social Psychology*, 28 (1998), 697–729; Diana Onu, Joanne R. Smith, and Thomas Kessler, "Intergroup emulation: An improvement strategy for lower status groups," *Group Processes and Intergroup Relations*, 18:2 (2015), 210–224.

[15] Larson, "How identities form," 61.

Explaining Status-Seeking Strategies

Social identity theory suggests two variables that influence a lower-status group's choice of strategy: the permeability of social groups and the legitimacy of the social hierarchy.[16] At the individual level, permeability has to do with the belief that the boundaries between groups are sufficiently porous such that actors can move into higher-status groups "through talent, hard work, good luck, or whatever other means."[17] At the group level, this is analogous to "the degree to which [a group's members] believe that the group's social value can be improved by collective efforts within the current social system."[18] Permeability enables lower-status groups to take on higher-status social identities in the hope of recognition.[19] When groups are impermeable, lower-status groups are more likely to challenge the status hierarchy or try to change the terms on which it is based.

Members of lower-status groups are also influenced by their perceptions of a hierarchy's legitimacy. Legitimacy, or "the normative belief by an actor that a rule or institution ought to be obeyed,"[20] can be a function of substantive outcomes produced by a particular social arrangement, or the procedures by which these outcomes are reached, or both.[21] Although substantive outcomes are not irrelevant, people rely primarily on procedural fairness as a criterion for judging the legitimacy of institutions.[22] In the context of social identity, "receiving

---

[16] A third variable, the hierarchy's stability, is commonly used in place of legitimacy. IST focuses on legitimacy because theoretically, stability is the product of legitimacy, and empirically, perceptions of stability are found to be highly correlated with perceptions of legitimacy. See B. Ann Bettencourt, Nancy Dorr, Kelly Charlton, and Deborah L. Hume, "Status differences and in-group bias: A meta-analytic examination of the effects of status stability, status legitimacy, and group permeability," *Psychological Bulletin*, 127:4 (2001), 520–542.

[17] Tajfel and Turner, "An integrative theory," 35.

[18] Sweetman et al., "'I Have a Dream'," 300.

[19] Naomi Ellemers, Ad van Knippenberg, Nanne de Vries, and Henk Wilke, "Social identification and permeability of group boundaries," *European Journal of Social Psychology*, 18 (1988), 497–513.

[20] Ian Hurd, "Legitimacy and authority in international politics," *International Organization*, 53:2 (1999), 379–408.

[21] Tom R. Tyler, "The psychology of legitimacy: A relational perspective on voluntary deference to authorities," *Personality and Social Psychology Review*, 1:4 (1997), 323–345.

[22] See Tom R. Tyler, "Psychological perspectives on legitimacy and legitimation," *Annual Review of Psychology*, 57 (2006), 375–400.

fair procedures is intertwined with being treated with respect and dignity, feeling that authorities are neutral, and trusting the motives of the authorities with whom one is dealing."[23] Fair procedures establish and maintain favorable social identities, and favorable social identities are correlated with rule-following behavior.[24] The legitimacy of a social order – frequently measured in terms of procedural fairness – has been repeatedly found to render lower status more acceptable.[25] Conversely, when lower-status groups view the status hierarchy as illegitimate, they are more likely to try and challenge it or change its standards.[26]

Although international relations scholars have not systematically investigated the form and impact of permeability and legitimacy as variables, it is possible to isolate their effects in an institutional setting, where states meet at the negotiating table instead of the battlefield. When it comes to military conflict, the link between the international order, status concerns, and state behavior is difficult to establish because war can break out for a number of other reasons related to security or economic anxieties. By contrast, we should expect to see satisfaction or dissatisfaction with the international order manifest primarily in the order itself. IST shows that status (dis)satisfaction is a function of institutional features pertaining to permeability and legitimacy, and develops two new variables – institutional openness and procedural fairness – that transpose these concepts into the study of rising powers and international order.

Institutional Openness

Institutional openness is a function of formal and informal membership rules that recognize some subjects as worthy of taking on

---

[23] Tom R. Tyler, "A psychological perspective on the legitimacy of institutions and authorities," in John T. Jost and Brenda Major (eds.), *The Psychology of Legitimacy: Emerging Perspectives on Ideology, Justice, and Intergroup Relations* (Cambridge: Cambridge University Press, 2001), 416–436.

[24] Ibid.

[25] Naomi Ellemers, Henk Wilke, and Ad van Knippenberg, "Effects of the legitimacy of low group or individual status on individual and collective status-enhancement strategies," *Journal of Personality and Social Psychology*, 64:5 (1993), 766–778; Deborah J. Terry and Anne T. O'Brien, "Status, legitimacy, and ingroup bias in the context of an organizational merger," *Group Process & Intergroup Relations*, 4:3 (2001), 271–289.

[26] See Bettencourt et al., "Status differences," 533.

institutional leadership and others as not. A relatively open institution is one with low barriers to entry for its leadership ranks. This means that one of three conditions is met: (1) institutional rules stipulating who gets to lead the institution do not exist; (2) institutional rules stipulating who gets to lead the institution are liberal, that is, it is possible for rising powers to take on a leadership role by virtue of their growing capabilities and willingness to shoulder managerial responsibilities; and (3) the great powers invite a rising power to join the leadership ranks of the institution. Conversely, high barriers entail stringent leadership criteria or the deliberate exclusion of a rising power from an institution's leadership ranks.

Although IST does not explicitly theorize the "fit" between a rising power's individual identity (i.e., not its social identity) and the norms of an institution, issues of fit come into play in the inclusion or exclusion of a rising power in an institution's leadership ranks. A great-power club dominated by a certain political ideology may be unwelcoming to a rising power of a contrary ideology. This was the case with the United States in the early nineteenth century, whose revolutionary republicanism was at odds with the conservative basis of the great-power club embodied in the Concert of Europe. Normative fit thus only matters if it impacts institutional openness, since a rising power's first priority with regard to the international order is to gain symbolic equality with the great powers rather than to live in harmony with international norms.[27] Indeed, symbolic equality with the great powers is necessary if a rising power seeks the political resources to alter unpalatable international norms.

Institutional openness affects a rising power's access to the great-power club. At a psychological level, the need for social connection is fundamental,[28] and a club with relatively open boundaries facilitates a sense of inclusion among those who would seek to join it. Inclusion itself has positive effects, affirming an individual's social identity and increasing self-esteem.[29] For rising powers, inclusion facilitates connectedness with the great powers, thus conferring status by

---

[27] See Newman and Zala, "Rising powers and order contestation."

[28] Jean M. Twenge and Roy F. Baumeister, "Social exclusion increases aggression and self-defeating behavior while reducing intelligent thought and prosocial behavior," in Dominic Abrams, Michael A. Hogg, and José M. Marques (eds.), *The Social Psychology of Inclusion and Exclusion* (New York: Psychology Press, 2005), 27–46.

[29] Fiona M. Begen and Julie M. Turner-Cobb, "Benefits of belonging: Experimental manipulation of social inclusion to enhance psychological and physiological health parameters," *Psychology & Health*, 30:5 (2015), 568–582.

association.[30] A relatively open institutional architecture signals to a rising power that it can play a role in the great-power club commensurate with its social identity as a major power. Consequently, its leaders will try to align their state's behavior with the role expectations of the great-power club and will generally harbor favorable views of the great powers.

The great-power club does not make it easy for new members to join. As Edward Keene has shown in the case of the EU, elite clubs use exclusion as a strategy to maintain social closure or an attempt to restrict access to social power.[31] Lora Anne Viola similarly argues that inclusion and exclusion are "central dynamics of the international system and its institutions."[32] Dominic Abrams et al. further conclude that at the international level, groups are likely to have membership rules that invoke ideology, moral conventions, and principles rather than strictly material criteria, for the purpose of social exclusivity.[33] To join the OECD, for example, a country must satisfy the official conditions of "like-mindedness, significant player, mutual benefit and global considerations."[34] Conditions of this nature make openness contingent on the subjective judgments of the great powers, which in turn opens up institutions to contestation over membership and the recognition it bestows.

Exclusion has a range of negative psychological effects,[35] including "the loss of important parts of the self."[36] This is not simply an issue of access to material resources. Citizenship, for example, is valued not just as a path to security and prosperity but also as an institutionalized source of symbolic equality with other members of a nation – so much so that even quasi-citizenship can strengthen bonds between a nation

---

[30] Duque, "Recognizing international status," 585.

[31] Keene, "Social status," 947.   [32] Viola, *The Closure*, 5.

[33] See Dominic Abrams, Michael A. Hogg, and José M. Marques, "A social psychological framework for understanding social inclusion and exclusion," in Abrams et al., *The Social Psychology of Inclusion and Exclusion*, 18.

[34] "Report of the Chair of the Working Group on the future size and membership of the Organisation to Council: Framework for the consideration of prospective members," meeting of the Organisation for Economic Cooperation and Development (OECD) Council at ministerial level, Paris, June 7–8, 2017, 5.

[35] C. Nathan DeWall and Jean M. Twenge, "Rejection and aggression: Explaining the paradox," in C. Nathan DeWall (ed.), *The Oxford Handbook of Social Exclusion* (Oxford: Oxford University Press, 2013), 114–121.

[36] Abrams et al., "A social psychological framework," 14.

and its overseas diaspora.[37] At the domestic level, a variety of disciplinary perspectives have emphasized that those who are excluded from groups lose both opportunities for consumption and production, as well as opportunities for political participation and social connection.[38] These effects are particularly damaging to individual identity in vertical hierarchies where exclusion means being prevented from climbing the social ladder (versus being excluded by peers).[39] Exclusion by subjectively important groups, with whom an actor seeks symbolic equality, is a greater denial of recognition than exclusion by other groups.[40] A rising power's exclusion from the great-power club, a subjectively essential group in the vertical hierarchy of the international order, signals the absence of any roles in the great-power club for a state with claims to major-power identity. This denial of desired status devalues the state's social identity. States will respond to exclusion by engaging in identity management or finding ways to reassert their social identity as major powers.

While rising-power responses to exclusion also depend on other factors, such as the procedural fairness of an institution, at minimum we can say that an excluded rising power's leaders will be less willing to emulate great-power practices and instead may choose to challenge the status hierarchy or try to reform it. For example, in the contemporary international order, the United Nations Security Council is more exclusive than the International Monetary Fund. The UN Charter sets a very high bar for permanent UNSC membership, whereas voting rights at the IMF change (albeit slowly) according to the relative economic weight of member countries. Consequently, rising powers

[37] Szabolcs Pogonyi, "The passport as means of identity management: Making and unmaking ethnic boundaries through citizenship," *Journal of Ethnic and Migration Studies*, 45:6 (2019), 975–993.

[38] Jane Millar, "Social exclusion and social policy research: Defining exclusion," in Dominic Abrams, Julie Christian, and David Gordon (eds.), *Multidisciplinary Handbook of Social Exclusion Research* (Chichester: John Wiley & Sons, 2007), 1–15.

[39] Ann Taket, Beth R. Crisp, Annemarie Nevill, Greer Lamaro, Melissa Graham, and Sarah Barter-Godfrey, "Introduction," in Ann Taket et al. (eds.), *Theorising Social Exclusion* (Abingdon: Routledge, 2009), 3–11.

[40] Michael J. Bernstein, Donald F. Sacco, Steven G. Young, Kurt Hugenberg, and Eric Cook, "Being 'in' with the in-crowd: The effects of social exclusion and inclusion are enhanced by the perceived essentialism of ingroups and outgroups," *Personality and Social Psychology Bulletin*, 36:8 (2010), 999–1009.

such as India and Brazil have focused their critique of the international order and institutional reform efforts far more on the UNSC than on the IMF.

Procedural Fairness

Procedural fairness is a function of formal and informal decision-making rules that allocate resources and privileges across different categories of states. It affects an institution's legitimacy, or the extent to which a rising power thinks the rules set by the great powers should be obeyed. The more legitimate an institution, the more likely a rising power will identify with it, thereby internalizing its rules and customs.[41] Most international relations scholars have treated legitimacy either as simple "agreement" between major powers[42] or as a "normative appellation" framed by shared understandings of an international society.[43] The first conception confuses an effect of legitimacy with the thing itself; the second renders legitimacy context-dependent and difficult to theorize across international societies or historical time periods. The latter is not a weakness per se, since legitimacy is, after all, "a subjective quality, relational between actor and institution, and is defined by the actor's perception of the institution."[44] For the sake of historical and cross-cultural comparison, however, it makes sense to focus on the procedural aspect of legitimacy, which is independent of contextual factors, especially when viewed through the psychological lens of procedural fairness.

Cooperation between actors typically requires each actor to give up some private gain for a better collective outcome – this "fundamental social dilemma"[45] is at the heart of the game theoretic conceit of the prisoner's dilemma. In order to trust an institution (and thereby cooperate with its rules), its members need to know that the institution will not exploit them. While economic losses are a concern, the more

---

[41] Ian Hurd, *After Anarchy: Legitimacy and Power in the United Nations Security Council* (Princeton: Princeton University Press, 2007), 41.
[42] Kissinger, *A World Restored*, 1.
[43] Reus-Smit, "Power, legitimacy, and order," 345.
[44] Hurd, *After Anarchy*, 7.
[45] E. Allan Lind, "Fairness heuristic theory: Justice judgments as pivotal cognitions in organizational relations," in Jerald Greenberg and Russell Cropanzano (eds.), *Advances in Organizational Justice* (Stanford: Stanford University Press, 2001), 56–88.

fundamental concern is a loss of identity: "To be taken advantage of is resented so much because it implies that one is the sort of person ... that can be taken advantage of."[46] Experimental evidence shows that cooperation by lower-status groups rests on a feeling of admiration for higher-status groups that are seen as competent and "warm," a cognate of "fair" in the literature.[47] In the case of global power shifts, the implication is that unfair international rules and procedures devalue a rising power's major-power social identity by treating it as lesser than the great powers. State leaders, therefore, use fairness judgments as a heuristic for the degree of exploitation involved in an institution. Judgments about procedural fairness are a critical part of this process.

Fairness is often equated with justice in the social sciences.[48] Both concepts involve the gap between self-perceived entitlement and actual procedures/outcomes for an individual or group relative to significant Others.[49] Like the desires for status and social connection, the evidence suggests that fairness is an innate and universal human concern.[50] People certainly care about the outcomes of institutional processes, but they assign independent value to procedural fairness and are even willing to tolerate unjust outcomes if they are arrived at by fair processes.[51] In international relations, scholars have found procedural justice (or fairness) to be a decisive factor in the success and durability of agreements in a host of areas ranging from ending civil wars to regulating international environmental hazards and negotiating

---

[46] Ibid., 63.

[47] J. Sweetman, R. Spears, A. G. Livingstone, and A. S. Manstead, "Admiration regulates social hierarchy: Antecedents, dispositions, and effects on intergroup behavior," *Journal of Experimental Social Psychology*, 49:3 (2013), 534–542.

[48] David A. Welch, *Justice and the Genesis of War* (Cambridge: Cambridge University Press, 1993), 18–19.

[49] Harald Müller, Daniel Müller, and Carsten Rauch, "Just a concert or a just concert: The role of justice and fairness considerations," in Harald Müller and Carsten Rauch (eds.), *Great Power Multilateralism and the Prevention of War: Debating a 21st Century Concert of Powers* (Abingdon: Routledge, 2018), 144–159.

[50] E. Allan Lind, "Exclusion, exploitation, and the psychology of fairness," in E. Allan Lind (ed.), *Social Psychology and Justice* (New York: Routledge, 2020), 75–92.

[51] Rebecca Hollander-Blumoff and Tom R. Tyler, "Procedural justice in negotiation: Procedural fairness, outcome acceptance, and integrative potential," *Law & Social Inquiry*, 33:2 (2008), 473–500.

multilateral trade agreements.[52] Most recently, in 2020, a survey of political and societal elites in both rising and established powers found their assessments of the legitimacy of key international institutions, such as the IMF and UNSC, to be correlated not with perceptions of their own country's influence in the institutions but with perceptions of good governance, of which fairness was the most important component across institutions.[53]

The concern for fairness is intimately connected to the desire for status. Experimental evidence shows that people are more concerned about fairness and more willing to accept fairly obtained results when they are primed to think about status compared to non-status issues,[54] a frame of mind comparable to that of states in the institutionalized hierarchy of the international order. More directly, individuals view fair treatment as a sign of their standing in a group, and fair treatment by recognized authorities in a hierarchical setting as a sign of being valued and respected.[55] For rising powers, procedural fairness in international institutions constitutes fair treatment and provides information about the extent to which their major-power social identity is recognized by the great powers. Fair treatment, by aligning reality with self-perceived entitlement, narrows the gap between a rising power's internally held identity and externally recognized role.

Scholars from diverse fields, including psychology, law, and political science, have offered various schema for what constitutes judgments of fair procedure. Three factors are most commonly cited: participation in decision-making; equality before the law (the "implicit promise to treat like with like"); and neutrality.[56] Keeping these in mind, for the

---

[52] See Cecilia Albin, "Rethinking justice and fairness: The case of acid rain emission reductions," *Review of International Studies*, 21:2 (1995), 119–143; Cecilia Albin and Daniel Druckman, "Equality matters: Negotiating an end to civil wars," *Journal of Conflict Resolution*, 56:2 (2012), 155–182; Ethan B. Kapstein, "Fairness considerations in world politics: Lessons from international trade negotiations," *Political Science Quarterly*, 123:2 (2008), 229–245.

[53] Jonas Tallberg and Soetkin Verhaegen, "The legitimacy of international institutions among rising and established powers," *Global Policy*, 11:3 (2020), 115–126.

[54] Jan-Willem van Prooijen, Kees van den Bos, and Henk A. M. Wilke, "Procedural justice and status: Status salience as antecedent of procedural fairness effects," *Journal of Personality and Social Psychology*, 83:6 (2002), 1353–1361.

[55] Ibid., 1354; Lind, "Exclusion," 77.

[56] Thomas M. Franck, *Fairness in International Law and Institutions* (Oxford: Oxford University Press, 1995), 10. See also Lisa Maria Dellmuth, Jan Aart Scholte, and Jonas Tallberg, "Institutional sources of legitimacy for

purposes of IST, procedural fairness exists when one or more of three conditions is met: (1) an institution's decision-making procedures are *consultative*; (2) an institution's rules are *consistent* in their application across members, that is, the great powers are not given special treatment; and (3) an institution's rules are *unbiased*, in that they do not unreasonably single out a rising power for lesser treatment or punishment. The criterion of fairness involved in all three conditions is of a rising power enjoying the same "constitutional" privileges as the great powers. Access to the great-power club does not by itself guarantee equal treatment relative to club members; procedural fairness does.

Because status is a scarce good, a rising power values fair procedures with regard to itself, irrespective of how any other state is treated by the institution. Evaluations of fairness also increase as more of the above three conditions are met. An institution that is consultative, consistent, and unbiased is preferable and more likely to elicit a rising power's cooperation than an institution that has only one or two of these attributes. Conversely, if an institution is lacking in fairness, a rising power is less likely to identify with it, and hence be less willing to cooperate with it. Legitimacy is ultimately a matter of "right process."[57]

Predicting Status Strategies in International Institutions

IST is a theory of how social identity in a hierarchy depends on social connectedness and procedural justice. As a state rises, it develops the social identity of a major power. In other words, a part of the state's identity depends on its improving position in the global status hierarchy. Its leaders seek recognition of this identity in the form of symbolic equality for their state with members of the great-power club. Symbolic equality obtains when core institutions of the international order recognize a rising power's claim to equal club membership (as a

international organisations: Beyond procedure versus performance," *Review of International Studies*, 45:4 (2019), 627–646; Caroline Fehl, Dirk Peters, Simone Wisotzki, and Jonas Wolff, "Introduction: The role of justice in international cooperation and conflict," in Caroline Fehl, Dirk Peters, Simone Wisotzki, and Jonas Wolff (eds.), *Justice and Peace: The Role of Justice Claims in International Cooperation and Conflict* (Wiesbaden: Springer VS, 2019), 3–28.

[57] Thomas M. Franck, "Legitimacy in the international system," *American Journal of International Law*, 82 (1988), 705–759.

Table 3.2. *Institutional openness and procedural fairness*

Institutional openness	Procedural fairness
An institution is relatively open if *one of three* conditions is met: 1. No formal rules about who gets to lead the institution (no barriers to entry) 2. Liberal rules about who gets to lead the institution (low barriers to entry) 3. Great powers invite a rising power to join the institution's leadership	An institution increases in procedural fairness as *one or more* of three conditions is met: 1. Decision-making procedures are consultative 2. Rules are consistently applied across members and over time 3. Rules and procedures are unbiased, i.e., do not single out a state

major power). Open leadership ranks and fair procedures are individually necessary and jointly sufficient for recognizing the status claims of a rising power (though empirically, complete openness and fairness are difficult to find). On this point, IST departs from existing theories of status and rising powers, in which "discerning the specific words and behaviors that will signal major power recognition is an empirical question" contingent on particular historical moments.[58] By contrast, as shown in the previous section, IST allows us to theorize the conditions under which recognition will or will not obtain. Recognition produces satisfaction with the status quo order, and, all else being equal, satisfaction produces cooperative behavior on the part of rising powers, whereas dissatisfaction is likely to have other effects, including challenging the hierarchy or trying to change it. Table 3.2 lays out the conditions for institutional openness and procedural fairness from the preceding discussion.

Openness and fairness are independent of each other. Having access to a club says nothing about the constitutional privileges one may enjoy in the club. Similarly, a club may be egalitarian for its members without any option for outsiders to join. Within an international institution, having a pathway to leadership along with a sense of equal treatment ensures that a rising power will feel symbolically equal to the great powers. We can imagine four scenarios representing

---

[58] Murray, *The Struggle for Recognition*, 56.

Table 3.3. *Strategies of rising powers toward the international order*

		INSTITUTIONAL OPENNESS	
		High	Low
PROCEDURAL FAIRNESS	High	Cooperate	Expand
	Low	Reframe	Challenge

combinations of openness and fairness that can predict the status-seeking strategies of rising powers within the institutional hierarchy of the international order. They are depicted in Table 3.3.

When faced with an international institution that is relatively open and procedurally fair, a rising power will feel more satisfied with the prevailing status hierarchy and thus *cooperate* with its rules and procedures. For the rising power, openness provides access to or potential inclusion in the leadership ranks of the institution (the great-power club); while procedural fairness lends legitimacy to the institution in the eyes of the rising power's leaders. Therefore, the rising power will adopt the institutional rules, habits, and norms of the great powers, because cooperation is the most effective way to have its major-power identity recognized.

Cooperation involves acceptance of the existing hierarchy and a good faith attempt to rise up within it by aligning one's behavior with the role expectations of the great powers. A small number of international relations scholars have studied this type of status-seeking behavior. Deborah Larson argues that "states may be willing to moderate their objectives in return for the prestige of belonging to an elite group."[59] In the case of states seeking "legitimate great power" status, Shogo Suzuki argues,

States which aspire to this status do not axiomatically seek to challenge the status quo. Rather, they can improve their standing in the "hierarchy" of international society by seeking "social recognition" from their peers. The result is that [they] actually end up reproducing the social structures of international society, rather than overturning them.[60]

[59] Larson, "New Perspectives," 250.
[60] Suzuki, "Seeking 'legitimate' great power status," 46.

Suzuki further notes that a "newcomer's recognition" as a member of the club occurs when it is treated as a social equal by the existing members and is accorded the same constitutional privileges as other legitimate great powers.[61] Courtney Fung's work on China in the UNSC shows that China's desire to not be isolated or singled out in its peer group on any particular case of multilateral intervention at the UNSC influences China's decision to cooperate.[62]

At the opposite end of the spectrum from cooperation is a rising power that chooses to *challenge* an international institution as a way of earning or maintaining status. A rising power will be most dissatisfied with, and will therefore challenge, an institution that is relatively closed and pro-cedurally unfair. Both denied access to the great-power club and faced with rules that are non-consultative, inconsistent, or biased, the rising power has little chance of attaining or maintaining symbolic equality with the club's members. In such a situation, challenging the institution and the hierarchy it represents remains the only way to maintain major-power identity. The rising power chooses to become an "outlaw state."[63] It rejects the rules, habits, and norms of the great powers, thereby seeking to overturn the institutional status quo. In practical terms, a challenge could involve one of three actions: (1) exiting or refusing to join an institution, (2) trying to set up an alternative institution that undermines the existing institution, or (3) willfully disobeying the rules of the existing institution as a sign of protest. All these actions serve to weaken the international order and reassert the status claims of the rising power.

Challenging an international institution through acts of noncompli-ance is not a mindless act of protest. Scholars have observed the rationality inherent in "fighting" for one's position in a hierarchy.[64] In an institutional setting, noncompliance can serve as a strategy to compel other actors to renegotiate the terms of a deal.[65] Noncompliance also serves as a signal of an alternative legitimacy, and those who enact it genuinely do so out of a sense of normative conviction.[66] Challengers, even states, often see themselves as

[61] Ibid., 48.   [62] Fung, *China and Intervention*.
[63] Simpson, *Great Powers*, xi.   [64] Renshon, *Fighting for Status*, 20.
[65] Timothy Meyer, "Shifting sands: Power, uncertainty and the form of international legal cooperation," *The European Journal of International Law*, 27:1 (2016), 161–185.
[66] Nicholas Kittrie, *Rebels with A Cause: The Minds and Morality of Political Offenders* (Boulder, CO: Westview, 2000), cited in Hurd, *After Anarchy*, 8.

conscientious objectors who are responding to being locked out and treated unfairly by the rules of the game. This is perhaps the best description of Japan's perspective on its treatment at the hands of the Western powers in the interwar period, which eventually led Tokyo to exit the Washington system.

In between the two extremes of cooperation and challenge are situations where a rising power will attempt to *change* the rules and procedures of an institution in order to earn status. These are situations where institutional design and functioning allow only partial symbolic equality with the great powers, and institutional reform to attain full equality is seen as a real possibility. In one scenario, an institution may be relatively open to the rising power joining its leadership ranks but may not treat that rising power in a fair manner. This means that while the pathway to joining the great-power club is open, the rising power does not enjoy the kinds of privileges the great powers do. The state may not be consulted as an equal in decision-making, institutional rules may apply double standards, or the state may be singled out as a problematic actor. The rising power thus has access to the great-power club without much reason to accept its legitimacy.

The most effective strategy for attaining status in this situation is to try and *reframe* institutional rules to make them fairer. Reframing is designed to alter evaluations of a rising power's identity claims such that it is accorded the same level of institutional deference as the great powers. In the contemporary international order, China's and India's projection of their respective identities as responsible nuclear powers in the international order is an example of rising powers trying to reframe existing categorizations that separate them from other major powers in terms of responsible nuclear behavior. Both states have engaged in "strategies of innovation" to promote alternative meanings of nuclear restraint – such as no-first-use pledges and small and de-alerted nuclear forces – to encourage positive valuations of their claims to symbolic equality as "nuclear responsibles."[67]

A final scenario is one in which a rising power is faced with a procedurally fair but relatively closed international institution. Institutional rules place high barriers to entering its leadership ranks; thus, there is little or no access to the great-power club. Nonetheless,

---

[67] Leveringhaus and Sullivan de Estrada, "Between conformity and innovation," 493–501.

the institution is run fairly. The great powers consult other states, especially rising powers, before making decisions; they follow rules just like other states; and there is little or no bias against the rising power itself. A rising power thus identifies with the institution but does not have access to the great-power club that manages it. The most effective strategy for attaining full symbolic equality with the great powers in this situation is to try and amend rules to *expand* the leadership ranks of the institution. Contrary to a strategy of reframing, which relies on altering the significance of existing evaluations of a state's identity claims, expansion is a strategy of introducing *new* criteria for formal leadership. This strategy is made more attractive by the existence of fair procedures, which permit a rising power to put forward its case for leadership expansion and be heard by the great powers.

An appeal to higher principle, or an overarching international goal that states have not yet attempted to achieve, is an effective means of trying to dilute existing criteria for high status. Again, in the contemporary international order, the approach of countries such as India, Brazil, Germany, and Japan – not all rising powers, but major regional powers nonetheless – to the UNSC represents an expansion strategy. In lobbying for an increase in the number of veto-wielding permanent members on the UNSC to include themselves, these states have justified their demand for reform on the basis of new leadership criteria such as representation and contributions to the UN, in contrast to the founding rationale of the UNSC, which assigned permanent veto-wielding membership to countries based on their importance in the aftermath of World War II.

Research Design

The potential universe of relevant cases in which to test IST's hypotheses throughout history is large; therefore, certain scope conditions are necessary in order to make the task of empirical analysis more tractable and its results more robust. Three are relevant here. First, IST is most applicable in the period following the Industrial Revolution. Since the early nineteenth century, the spread of industrial technology, democracy, and capitalism has transformed the nature of world politics, making systematic comparisons with the pre-nineteenth-century world difficult. The same applies to the nature of international order, which has, since 1815, developed a combination of formal sovereign equality, on the one hand, and material and status inequality, on the other hand.[68] This contradiction has made possible the rise of institutionalized cooperation, international law, and the need for great powers to manage the international order while also vying for supremacy over it.

Second, IST is applicable to large-scale power *shifts* and not transitions per se. Power transitions are situations where one state approaches or overtakes another in terms of capabilities. Power shifts, by contrast, refer to "predictable, long-run changes in relative capabilities," which often result in power transitions.[69] These shifts are consequential not just for war and peace, but also in terms of shaping the institutional architecture of the international order, which impacts the likelihood of war and peace.

Third, and lastly, IST is not a theory of great-power behavior. It cannot predict the conditions under which great powers will recognize rising powers' identity claims or accommodate their status concerns. IST concerns itself with great powers to the extent that their decisions impact international institutional variables, such as openness and procedural fairness, which in turn impact the strategies of rising powers. Although great powers are motivated to keep their circle small, they do recognize rising powers that they perceive as "responsible" or "willing to play by the 'rules of the game'."[70] IST predicts that the willingness to play by the rules depends on the nature of the rules themselves.

International Order, Great Powers, and Rising Powers

In keeping with scholarly practice, the period between 1815 and 1990 can be divided into three distinct international orders punctuated by the two World Wars: the Concert of Europe (1815–1914), the interwar period (1919–1939), and the Cold War (1945–1990).[71] Each of these orders was comanaged by two or more great powers. As discussed in Chapter 2, international order exists at multiple levels, from deep institutions such as diplomacy and contractual international law to concrete international organizations. IST operates at the latter level,

---

[68] Simpson, *Great Powers*, ix–x; Reus-Smit, *The Moral Purpose*, 3–4.
[69] Kim and Morrow, "When do power shifts," 896.
[70] Goddard, *When Right Makes Might*, 3.
[71] See Ikenberry, *After Victory*; Holsti, *Peace and War*.

focusing on the voluntary multilateral agreements between states – for convenience, these are labeled "international institutions" in this book – that rely on basic institutions for their functioning.

Great powers possess three features: extraordinary military capabilities, global geopolitical interests, and general recognition of their status by other states.[72] Although multiple great powers may manage the international order, some are more influential than others and can be termed "leading states" for their ability to decisively alter rules and norms. As the Concert of Europe weakened during the course of the nineteenth century, Britain and France emerged as leading states. During the interwar period, the United States and Britain were leading states and took the initiative to convene a series of conferences designed to manage the postwar order. Similarly, the United States and the Soviet Union were leading states during the Cold War.

A rising power is by definition not a great power, yet it must possess a minimum level of capabilities for its rise to be globally consequential. A rising power is thus a state that has already crossed a minimum threshold of power and is experiencing a sustained long-term increase in capabilities. In addition, a rising power develops a major-power identity in the process of its rise. Its leaders see it as a *future* great power – they benchmark their country's position in terms of capabilities and status to that of the leading states in the international system. Other states in the international system also begin to recognize a rising power as an important global actor (though the great powers may or may not recognize the rising power in this way). Details on the measures and method used to identify great powers and rising powers for this study are included in the Appendix.

Case Selection

Given that rising powers in the time period under consideration are small in number, qualitative case-study methods are best suited to testing IST's predictions. There are three possible ways in which to proceed. The first is to examine multiple rising powers within a single institution at a given point in time. Although this method avoids the difficulties of comparing institutions across different issue areas, it risks

---

[72] Vesna Danilovic, *When the Stakes Are High: Deterrence and Conflict Among Major Powers* (Ann Arbor: University of Michigan Press, 2002), 225–230.

introducing bias in the results due to unobservable differences between rising powers with different cultures, histories, and political systems.

The second method is to examine a single rising power across multiple institutions at a given point in time. This method holds constant unobservable differences between countries but runs into the problem of potential bias due to unobservable differences between issue areas. For example, it is harder to strike bargains over security issues than over economic issues, where national survival is not directly implicated.[73]

The third method avoids both the above problems. It is to focus on multiple cases within an issue area of a single rising power within a single international institution over time. By holding country and issue characteristics constant, and instead studying variation in state behavior over time, it is possible both to address concerns about unobservable factors and to trace in detail the process by which state decision-making changes in response to changes in institutional variables. If IST is correct, then at points when institutional openness and/or fairness change for exogenous reasons, that is, not being directly caused by the rising power itself, we should expect the state to alter its status-seeking strategy in response to the new conditions.

The next three chapters focus on the core security institutions of an international order, which have received insufficient attention in the literature.[74] These are multilateral institutions at the center of an international order, whose goal is to promote peace "as the normal condition ... to be breached only in special circumstances and according to principles that are generally accepted."[75] These institutions are of two types: those that aim to prevent war and those that aim to regulate the conduct of war when it breaks out. The former can be called *managerial* institutions and the latter *regulatory* institutions. Managerial institutions focus on the management of international disputes and crises, and require extensive great-power involvement. Since 1815, the managerial security institutions of international order have included the Concert of Europe, the League of Nations, and the United Nations Security Council. By contrast, regulatory institutions

[73] Robert Jervis, "Security regimes," *International Organization*, 36:2 (1982), 357–378.
[74] M. Patrick Cottrell, *The Evolution and Legitimacy of International Security Institutions* (New York: Cambridge University Press, 2016), 3.
[75] Bull, *The Anarchical Society*, 17.

aim to regulate war when it does break out. They do not require intense great-power involvement and take the form of agreements or treaties that stipulate rules and procedures to be followed. Historically, these institutions have dealt with the laws of war and arms control.

From a researcher's perspective, regulatory institutions have an advantage: The costs and benefits of compliance and noncompliance can be measured more consistently when there are specific actions that an institution regulates. By contrast, when an institution is designed to deal with the gamut of state-level threats to international security – as in the case of the League of Nations or the United Nations Security Council – costs and benefits become context-specific, making rigorous comparison difficult if not impossible. This book, therefore, draws its cases from the universe of regulatory security institutions since 1815. Three stand out as being central to their respective international orders: the 1856 Declaration of Paris, the 1922 Washington Naval Treaty, and the 1970 Nuclear Non-Proliferation Treaty. The Declaration of Paris was the centerpiece of the Atlantic system, the international order led by Britain and, to a lesser extent, France in the mid-nineteenth century. The Washington Naval Treaty was the central pillar of the Washington system, the interwar order led by the United States and Britain. The Nuclear Non-Proliferation Treaty was a major contributor to international stability in the Cold War order negotiated by the United States and the Soviet Union.

The rising power in each case is selected based on having the longest and most sustained rise within the order. The resulting candidates are: the United States in the Atlantic system, Japan in the Washington system, and India during the Cold War. Unsurprisingly, each of these countries played a pivotal role in the fate of the security institution it faced and in the international order more broadly. Table 3.4 summarizes the historical cases in this book.

The respective literatures on each of these cases continue to grapple with puzzles that existing approaches based on material interest cannot fully answer. Why did the United States initially advocate for treaties protecting private property at sea during war, and then reject the Declaration of Paris, which enshrined much of the same principle in international law? Why did Japan initially endanger its security by agreeing to build warships at a lower ratio than the great powers in the Washington Naval Treaty, only to renege on the agreement a decade later? Why did India initially renounce nuclear weapons and

Table 3.4. *Case studies*

International order	Concert of Europe/ Atlantic system	Interwar period/ Washington system	Cold War
Security institution	1856 Declaration of Paris	1922 Washington Naval Treaty	1970 Nuclear Non-Proliferation Treaty
Attempt to regulate	Maritime warfare	Naval armaments	Nuclear weapons
Great-power sponsors	Britain, France	United States, Britain	United States, Soviet Union
Rising power	United States	Japan	India

support nonproliferation despite a growing Chinese nuclear threat, only to repudiate the NPT and test its own nuclear bomb after the treaty took hold? We cannot convincingly answer these questions without considering the desire of each of these rising powers for symbolic equality with the great powers. At certain moments, the core security institutions these states were facing changed in terms of their openness and/or procedural fairness. In response, the leaders of these states changed their status-seeking strategies to better suit the new institutional environment. In doing so, they were willing to undertake risks to their security and economic well-being, and paid significant costs in the pursuit of status.

Methodology and Sources

Four questions structure the analysis of each case. First, what was the rising power's approach to the international order prior to the introduction of the new institution? This question establishes whether the rising power did in fact seek recognition of its major-power identity from the great powers, thus validating one of IST's central assumptions and a criterion used to define rising powers.

Second, what were the rising power's material (economic and/or security) interests with regard to the aspect of war that the international institution sought to regulate? This question allows us to compare IST's predictions with standard international relations approaches based on material interests (both domestic and international).

Third, how did the rising power approach negotiations over the security institution under consideration? Of particular importance here are the official positions taken by state negotiators in conferences and communications with the great powers, as well as the behind-the-scenes deliberations and communications between state leaders and officials involved in the rising power's diplomacy.

Fourth, and finally, how do we explain the rising power's compliance or noncompliance with the international institution's rules and procedures? This is a question of whether IST or materialist theories do a better job of explaining the course of negotiations and the behavior of the rising power, which can be categorized into four strategies: cooperate with the institution, challenge the institution's rules, reframe evaluations of one's identity claims, or expand the leadership ranks of the institution by adding new criteria. Any change in strategy must be investigated for preceding institutional changes (versus changes in the balance of power or domestic politics) and traced back to the deliberations of decision-makers as articulated in official and unofficial documents. In this manner, it is possible to study the causal process by which leaders made their decisions, and thereby identify the theory or framework that best explains these decisions.

The empirical analysis in the following chapters relies on both primary and secondary sources. Archival documents, official documentary collections, memoirs, and contemporary accounts in journals and periodicals offer insight into how a state's leaders viewed an institution, and the considerations that impacted their decision-making. Secondary sources are used to triangulate the information gleaned from primary sources.

Alternative Explanations and Observable Implications

In order to address alternative explanations in the case studies, available data are used to critically examine whether material considerations played a role in the decision-making of state leaders. The cases also identify domestic groups with an interest in the issue covered by the institution and examine their interests and influence on the decision-making process. Leaders and negotiators may reference security or economic concerns, but IST expects that they will give priority to status concerns. Importantly, the research design emphasizes change over time. If IST is correct, then moments of institutional change or opportunities to earn status will cause changes in a rising power's strategy, be this in the absence of any change on the economic or security front or independently of any such change.

What precisely should we expect to see in the empirical record if IST is correct? Determining the causes of state behavior when dealing in the realm of how actors perceive institutional features such as openness and fairness is challenging.[76] Nonetheless, evidence in favor of IST could potentially be found in three places: first, in the public statements and actions of a rising power's leaders with regard to the international order and its core institution; second, in the semi-private statements of a rising power's leaders to the leaders of the great powers; and, third, in the private (often secret) statements of a rising power's leaders to each other, as well as in their personal views recorded in diary entries, private notes, and other documentation.

The public arena is where a rising power can enact its strategies to attain symbolic equality with the great powers. Since status relies on the beliefs of other states, a rising power must demonstrate its efforts at cooperation, challenge, or change openly. The private arena of intra-leadership communication is where we can expect leaders to frankly discuss their motivations for making certain decisions. The semi-private arena of communication between the leaders of different states contains elements of both the public enactment of strategy and the private justification of it. All three arenas are thus of equal importance as sources of evidence for the effects of institutional openness and procedural fairness on the status-seeking strategies of rising powers.

A state that *cooperates* will publicly avow to do so and will seek to demonstrate its support for the institution, often accepting significant costs or risks in the process. This support should also be visible in discussions with leaders of the great powers. The innermost arena of intra-leadership debate is where we should expect to see the justifications for cooperation. If IST is correct, the dominant justifications will focus on the possibility of becoming a leader within the international order (a result of institutional openness), and on the impartial

---

[76] Suzuki, "Seeking 'legitimate' great power status," 48.

application of institutional rules and a sense of "fair play" by the great powers (a result of procedural fairness).

By contrast, a rising power that decides to *challenge* an institution will do so openly in public statements and actions, often going to the extent of incurring significant costs to undermine or break the rules of the institution. Private discussions with the leaders of great powers will also be antagonistic, as the rising power's leaders challenge the basis on which the great powers enjoy their social superiority. Private justifications among the rising power's leaders will focus on the lack of any means by which their state can ever be a leader in the international order. They will also criticize the biased and inconsistent nature of institutional rules and procedures, citing discrimination on the part of the great powers.

A rising power that seeks to change institutional rules to make them fairer or more open will actively lobby the great powers for institutional reform. If the strategy is one of *reframing* evaluations of one's identity claims, the rising power will publicly try to alter shared understandings of its claims or actions; for example, by casting "irresponsible" behavior as motivated by a just cause such as the interests of lower-ranked states. If the strategy is one of *expanding* the leadership ranks of the institution, the rising power will emphasize new criteria for measuring status or will appeal to higher (often unattainable) principles, such as international peace or universal disarmament, as a way of occupying higher moral ground. The state may also try to demonstrate competence in areas not regulated by the institution, in order to develop new metrics on which to assert symbolic equality with the great powers. When pursuing strategies of institutional change, the rising power's leaders in their private communications will criticize either the closed nature of the institution or its unfairness (depending on the situation), and will devise ways in which to alter rules and procedures in order to attain full symbolic equality with the great powers. The observable implications of each status strategy are summarized in Table 3.5.

IST does not assume or expect that the leaders of rising powers will uniformly hold the same views of the international order or their country's place in it. Nonetheless, in moments when a clear opportunity to earn status through a particular strategy emerges, IST expects that status-based arguments will carry the day. This is true for both cooperative and noncooperative strategies – those who advocate for

Table 3.5. *Observable implications of status strategies*

Strategy	Public statements/behavior	Private justifications
Cooperate	Follow rules, publicly support the institution, seek compromise	Possibility of leadership in the international order; consultation, fair play by great powers
Challenge	Publicly disobey/denounce rules, exit institution, try to set up an alternative	Impossibility of leadership in the international order; lack of consultation; bias; inconsistency
Change (reframe)	Amend rules to recognize alternative interpretations of status criteria	Possibility of leadership in international order but institution lacks consultation and fair play
Change (expand)	Promote new leadership criteria; appeal to higher principle(s)	Institution is consultative and great powers play fair, but no pathway to leadership ranks

either position based on the potential for symbolic equality with the great powers are likely to convince their compatriots of the soundness of their preferred strategy. On conflict, Ann Hironaka argues that "warmongering will be more successful if based on appeals to increased status and prestige of the state in the Great Power hierarchy."[77] IST predicts that appeals to status will also be effective when domestic actors advocate cooperative strategies. Conflict is costly. If an opportunity exists to attain status through a less expensive route – that is, when symbolic equality is substantially possible – it stands to reason that state leaders will come around to it.

As the next three chapters show, IST offers a superior explanation for rising-power decisions in the international order when compared to purely materialist accounts. This is not to say that material factors are irrelevant, but that rising powers rationally pursue both material and

[77] Hironaka, *Tokens of Power*, 22.

symbolic ends. When extraordinary opportunities arise to make their mark on the international order and claim symbolic equality with the great powers, rising powers will trade material gain for status. IST offers a systematic account of what these opportunities look like, and how rising powers respond to them.

* * *

4 | The United States and the Atlantic System in the Nineteenth Century

Among political scientists, American isolationism remains one of the most persistent myths about the United States' history before the twentieth century.[1] Historians, by contrast, have long shed the "tendency to reduce the American foreign policy tradition to a legacy of moralism and isolationism."[2] As Walter McDougall points out, the term "isolationist" itself emerged in the 1890s as a rhetorical cudgel in the hands of interventionists and expansionists in domestic debates.[3] Prior to that, it signified a reality entirely geographic and not political. From the very early days of the republic, the United States was engaged in building a vast commercial empire that required not just engagement but *integration* with Europe and its colonies.[4] Politically, the United States formed alliances with European powers – the 1778 alliance with France being the earliest example – when deemed to be in the national interest.[5] Even George Washington, while counseling against permanent alliances in his farewell address, endorsed the importance of "temporary alliances for extraordinary emergencies."[6] Such emergencies were in no short supply in the decades after independence. Walter Russell Mead observes that the period between the Revolutionary

[1] David Dunn, "Isolationism revisited: Seven persistent myths in the contemporary American foreign policy debate," *Review of International Studies*, 31 (2005), 237–261; Hilde Eliassen Restad, "Old paradigms in history die hard in political science: U.S. foreign policy and American exceptionalism," *American Political Thought*, 1:1 (2012), 53–76.
[2] Walter Russell Mead, *Special Providence: American Foreign Policy and How It Changed the World* (New York: Alfred A. Knopf, 2001), 7.
[3] Walter A. McDougall, *Promised Land, Crusader State* (New York: Houghton Mifflin, 1997), 39.
[4] Jay Sexton, *The Monroe Doctrine: Empire and Nation in Nineteenth-Century America* (New York: Hill and Wang, 2011), 29.
[5] Peter S. Onuf, *Jefferson's Empire: The Language of American Nationhood* (Charlottesville: University Press of Virginia, 2000), 60.
[6] George Washington, "Washington's farewell address 1796," The Avalon Project, https://avalon.law.yale.edu/18th_century/washing.asp

War and the Civil War saw the United States in "a permanent war atmosphere," with "American fighting forces ... found in every ocean and on every continent."[7]

The myth of isolationism entails another myth, also pervasive among political scientists, that the United States had no great-power pretensions prior to the late nineteenth century.[8] Historians have done much less to directly puncture this consensus. This chapter takes up the task, and more, by applying Institutional Status Theory to the case of the United States and the Atlantic system, or the international order led by Britain in the mid-nineteenth century.[9] It focuses on the US approach to the maritime laws of war, the only issue for which codified international law existed during this period.[10] Shifting the focus from power and wealth to status reveals an entirely new dimension of US grand strategy in the Atlantic system. The United States emerges as a rising power enamored of its own future greatness and potential to be a world player among the ranks of the great powers; a growing republic that sought symbolic equality with the foremost European states.

International maritime law offered American leaders a shot at greatness as major contributors to the community of "civilized" nations. From the 1820s onward, as the United States began its long rise, its leaders started proposing ambitious reforms to maritime law as a way of joining the great-power club. Although these efforts initially went nowhere, in the aftermath of the Crimean War, Britain and France crafted the 1856 Declaration of Paris, which adopted some of the very principles the United States had promoted. The Declaration, however, contained one crucial addition: the abolition of privateering, or the commissioning of private vessels in times of war. This came as a major blow to US leaders and the American public, for whom privateering had been a source of national pride and the only source of a claim to naval power at the time. Feeling isolated and unjustly singled out, the United States sought to undermine the Declaration with an alternative agreement and framed its challenge as activism on behalf of lesser states in the international order. Later, during the Civil War, the

---

[7] Mead, *Special Providence*, 18.
[8] For example, Ward, *Status and the Challenge*, ch. 6.
[9] Goddard, *When Right Makes Might*, 64.
[10] Ted L. Stein, "The approach of the different drummer: The principle of the persistent objector in international law," *Harvard International Law Journal*, 26:2 (1985), 457–482.

Union came close to signing the Declaration to preempt Confederate privateering, but negotiations once again failed due to US assessments of unfair dealings on the part of Britain and France. The US rejection of the international maritime order was costly, since the Declaration as a whole promised great benefit to the United States as a commercially oriented and relatively secure nation that was mostly neutral in European wars. American leaders were willing to pay the cost of challenging the Atlantic system's core security institution. To do otherwise would have relegated the United States to second-tier status relative to the great powers.

This chapter begins with an account of the early years of the republic, when the United States developed its major-power identity and sought symbolic equality with the great powers. It then provides background to the maritime order of the Atlantic system and derives the expected US position toward the pivotal 1856 Declaration of Paris through the lens of (domestic and international) material interests. It proceeds to test IST's predictions, delving into the status-seeking strategies pursued by the United States over time – first, cooperation, then expansion, followed by challenge – in response to the changing institutional openness and procedural fairness of the international maritime order. The analysis demonstrates the superiority of IST to a purely materialist account.

The Major-Power Identity of the Early Republic

As a new nation in the midst of European colonies in the New World, the United States had to engage in all manner of Old World politics in order to build itself up internally and externally. These efforts were not accidental, but rather the result of a grand strategy aimed at one overarching goal: national greatness. In a now famous speech to Congress, George Washington argued that the United States could not "for ever keep at a distance those painful appeals to arms" in which every other nation had historically indulged.[11] The reason, however, was not ultimately security. "There is a rank due to the United States among nations," he argued, "which will be withheld, if

---

[11] George Washington, "Speech to both Houses of Congress, December 3, 1793," in Worthington Chauncey Ford (ed.), *The Writings of George Washington, Vol. XII, 1790–1794* (New York and London: G. P. Putnam's Sons, 1890), 350–356.

not absolutely lost, by the reputation of weakness."[12] A young John Quincy Adams, writing around the same time, declared what he claimed to be the clearest article of his political creed: "[W]e shall proceed with gigantic strides to honor and consideration, and national greatness, if the union is preserved."[13]

The greatness of the United States depended on recognition of its major-power identity. Robert Kagan observes that most early American leaders expected their nation to eventually "take its rightful place among the world's great powers."[14] Eliga Gould shows that "the drive to be accepted as a treaty-worthy nation in Europe" was as instrumental as liberal and republican ideologies in shaping early US foreign policy.[15] According to the country's second Secretary of State, Edmund Randolph, "Although the United States be without the European circle," its "frequent correspondence with Europe" and its handful of treaties with European countries entitled it to the same treatment the great powers accorded each other.[16]

The desire for symbolic equality with the great powers fundamentally shaped US decision-making. While negotiating the Treaty of Paris that ended the Revolutionary War, John Adams and John Jay were wary of French proposals that treated the United States as a junior partner, depriving it of "the equal footing that our rank demanded."[17] Had the United States not approached Britain and Spain directly as an equal, Adams reasoned, "[W]e should have sunk in the minds of the English, French, Spaniards, Dutch, and all the neutral powers."[18] During the Quasi-War against the French in 1798, Secretary of War James McHenry sought to "preserve character abroad" and called upon Congress to sanction additional naval forces, lest the United States "exhibit to the world a sad spectacle of national degradation and imbecility."[19]

---

[12] Ibid.

[13] John Quincy Adams to Charles Adams, June 9, 1796, in Worthington Chauncey Ford (ed.), *Writings of John Quincy Adams, Vol. 1, 1779–1796* (New York: Macmillan, 1913), 493–494.

[14] Robert Kagan, *Dangerous Nation* (New York: Vintage Books, 2006), 56.

[15] Eliga H. Gould, *Among the Powers of the Earth: The American Revolution and the Making of a New World Empire* (Cambridge, MA: Harvard University Press, 2012), 11.

[16] Quoted in ibid., 114.   [17] Ibid., 4.   [18] Ibid.

[19] James McHenry, "Additional naval force, communicated to the House of Representatives, April 9, 1798," *American State Papers, Class VI (Naval Affairs)*, vol. 1 (Washington: Gales and Seaton, 1834), 34–36.

In the run-up to the War of 1812, the impressment of American sailors into the Royal Navy was hardly a material threat. Rather, it was a matter of standing among the powerful nations of the world.[20] In Madison's words, "To have shrunk under such circumstances ... would have struck us from the high rank where the virtuous struggles of our fathers had placed us."[21] The War of 1812 was ultimately an assertion of symbolic equality. "The civilized world is astonished at what our navy has done," declared a Baltimore newspaper after the first year of fighting, arguing that American naval prowess "only augurs the future greatness of this rising nation."[22] Although the United States achieved none of its material aims in the war, at the end, the *Niles Weekly Register* proclaimed that the United States "now stands in the first rank of nations."[23] Madison in his annual message to Congress rejoiced "in the proofs given that our political institutions ... are equal to the severest trials of war" and observed his nation "possessed of a growing respect abroad and of a just confidence in itself."[24] US leaders expected not only to take their place among the great powers but also to do so on the basis of equality.

James Monroe, who inherited from Madison a country at peace and growing in prosperity, echoed Washington's beliefs about the importance of rank. "We must support our rights or lose our character," he declared in his inaugural address. "A people who fail to do it can scarcely be said to hold a place among independent nations."[25] The Monroe Doctrine was itself an assertion of status. In July 1823, Britain proposed a bilateral declaration with the United States against any potential interference by the Holy Alliance (Russia, Prussia, and Austria) in the New World. Although Monroe leaned toward accepting, Secretary of State John Quincy Adams proposed a unilateral

---

[20] Faye M. Kert, *Privateering: Patriots and Profits in the War of 1812* (Baltimore: Johns Hopkins University Press, 2015), 3–4.

[21] James Madison, "Fourth annual message to Congress, November 4, 1812," in Gaillard Hunt (ed.), *The Writings of James Madison, Vol. VIII, 1808–1819* (New York: G. P. Putnam's Sons, 1908), 221–231.

[22] Reprinted as "Privateering, etc.," in *The Investigator* (South Carolina), June 29, 1813, NewsBank: America's Historical Newspapers.

[23] Quoted in Steven Watts, *The Republic Reborn: War and the Making of Liberal America, 1790–1820* (Baltimore: Johns Hopkins University Press, 1987), 283.

[24] James Madison, "Seventh annual message to Congress, December 15, 1815," in Hunt (ed.), *The Writings*, 335–344.

[25] James Monroe, "First inaugural address of James Monroe," March 4, 1817, The Avalon Project, https://avalon.law.yale.edu/19th_century/monroe1.asp

declaration instead. "It would be more candid, as well as more digni-
fied," he argued, "to avow our principles explicitly to Russia and
France, than to come in as a cock-boat in the wake of the British
man-of-war."[26] The doctrine is all the more remarkable because two
weeks before they introduced it in Congress, the Monroe cabinet had
learned that Britain had lost interest in a joint declaration.[27] Backed by
neither domestic resources nor foreign commitment, the doctrine was
ultimately nothing more than an expression of major-power identity.

The doctrine of Manifest Destiny similarly appears as an ideology of
naked expansion at first glance, but it was in fact imbued with a sense
of American greatness that was entirely in keeping with the ambitions
of preceding generations of statesmen. John O'Sullivan, the columnist
who coined the term, believed that when it came to "the entire development of the natural rights of man ... our country is destined to be
the great nation of futurity."[28] Ralph Waldo Emerson, whose works
informed the substance of the doctrine, publicly stated, "In every age of
the world, there has been a leading nation ... Which should be that
nation but these States?"[29] For Congressman Caleb Cushing, a major
advocate of a greater role for the United States in world affairs,
American civilization and Christianity reinforced each other, making
the United States "the highest civilization of Christendom."[30] The
expansion implied by Manifest Destiny was intimately linked to
notions of national greatness. It was *because* America was great that
it would expand to the Pacific. Senator Stephen Douglas, a prominent
spokesperson for the doctrine, argued that it was impossible to "fix
bounds to the onward march of this great and growing country,"
which was destined to "extend civilization, Christianity, and liberal

---

[26] John Quincy Adams, November 7, 1823, in Charles Francis Adams (ed.),
Memoirs of John Quincy Adams, vol. VI (Philadelphia: J. B. Lippincott & Co.,
1875), 179.

[27] George Dangerfield, *The Awakening of American Nationalism, 1815–1828*
(New York: Harper & Row, 1965), 182.

[28] John O'Sullivan, "The great nation of futurity," *The United States Democratic
Review*, 6:23 (1839), 426–430, emphasis in original.

[29] Quoted in Robert W. Johannsen, "The meaning of Manifest Destiny," in Sam
W. Haynes and Christopher Morris (eds.), *Manifest Destiny and Empire:
American Antebellum Expansionism* (College Station: Texas A&M Press,
1997), 7–20.

[30] Quoted in John Belohlavek, "Race, progress, and destiny: Caleb Cushing and
the quest for American empire," in Haynes and Morris (eds.), *Manifest Destiny
and Empire*, 21–47.

principles."[31] For Senator William Henry Seward, expansion would serve as proof of the success of republican government, the furtherance of which was America's "messianic mission."[32]

Europe, while serving as a standard of civilization and greatness, was also seen as actively trying to thwart America's rise, exhibiting "a spirit of hostile interference" aimed at "limiting our greatness," according to O'Sullivan.[33] The claim to membership of the "civilized" community of great powers and the impact of European non-recognition of US rights and privileges were major themes in American engagement with the Atlantic system from the 1820s onward. These themes set the context in which the United States approached questions of maritime law, and eventually the Declaration of Paris.

The Maritime Order of the Atlantic System

Prior to the nineteenth century, war at sea was conducted on the basis of a loosely defined and often contradictory set of rules that states chose to follow or abandon at their convenience. Britain, being the dominant naval power, pursued a unilateral policy of targeting the commerce of its adversaries in wartime, irrespective of the nationality of the ship in which it was conveyed.[34] This policy meant that if Britain was at war with another country, the commercial goods of that country were open to seizure by the Royal Navy upon the high seas even if the goods were in the ships of countries that were neutral in the conflict. Any goods belonging to neutral states inadvertently seized as a result would subsequently be returned to their owners. Nonetheless, the British search and seizure of neutral ships in its frequent wars with other powers was a major irritant and impediment to commerce, especially for countries that did not have large navies to protect their merchants on the high seas.

---

[31] Robert W. Johannsen, *The Frontier, the Union, and Stephen A. Douglas* (Urbana, IL: University of Illinois Press, 1989), 79.
[32] Quoted in Walter G. Sharrow, "William Henry Seward and the basis for American empire, 1850–1860," *Pacific Historical Review*, 36:3 (1967), 325–342.
[33] Quoted in Johannsen, "The meaning," 10.
[34] H. A. Munro-Butler-Johnstone, *Handbook of Maritime Rights, and the Declaration of Paris Considered* (London: W. Ridgway, 1876), 26–27.

It was hardly surprising, therefore, that neutral countries were the first to create a new set of rules for maritime warfare. In 1780, Russia declared the Armed Neutrality, setting principles that belligerents and neutrals would be expected to follow in the American Revolutionary War. Among other things, the principles declared: "[T]he effects belonging to subjects of the ... Powers at war shall be free on board neutral vessels, with the exception of contraband merchandise."[35] The Neutrality lasted till the end of the war, with France and the United States endorsing its principles and Britain largely staying clear of violating it. Although another Armed Neutrality in 1800 during the Napoleonic Wars was much less successful, the two attempts to assert the rights of neutrals laid the foundation for significant changes in the subsequent Atlantic system.[36] The turning point came in the run-up to the Crimean War in 1854, when Sweden and Denmark issued identical declarations of neutrality to France, Britain, and Russia, seeking "respect for the neutral flag."[37]

At this point, Britain and France maintained contradictory policies. While France followed the principle advocated by the neutrals, that is, free (meaning neutral) ships made free goods, it also held that enemy ships made enemy goods, that is, the goods of neutrals captured in enemy ships belonged to the captors. Britain held the opposite on both counts: Enemy goods found on free ships were not free, and neutral goods seized from enemy ships would be returned. Fighting the Crimean War together required compromise. Both nations declared that for the duration of the war, free ships made free goods (Britain's concession) and neutral goods seized from enemy ships would be returned (France's concession).[38]

At the Congress of Paris that concluded the postwar settlement in April 1856, Britain and France introduced a new code of maritime warfare based on their wartime compromise and invited all nations to

---

[35] "Declaration of the Empress of Russia, February 28, 1780," reprinted in James Brown Scott, *The Proceedings of the Hague Peace Conferences: The Conference of 1899* (New York: Oxford University Press, 1920), 274.

[36] Thomas Gibson Bowles, *The Declaration of Paris of 1856* (London: Sampson Low, Marston and Company, 1900), 91.

[37] Francis Piggott, *The Declaration of Paris, 1856: A Study* (London: University of Warwick Press, 1919), 6.

[38] George I. Phillips, "The Declaration of Paris, 1856," *The Law Quarterly Review*, 133 (1918), 63–71.

ratify it. The Declaration of Paris was a brief document containing four principles:

(1) Privateering is and remains abolished. (2) The neutral flag covers enemy's goods, with the exception of contraband of war. (3) Neutral goods, with the exception of contraband of war, are not liable to capture under enemy's flag. (4) Blockades, in order to be binding, must be effective – that is to say, maintained by a force sufficient really to prevent access to the coast of the enemy.[39]

The second and third principles constituted major concessions of neutral rights by Britain and France, respectively. Belligerents and neutrals alike already generally accepted the fourth principle. However, the first principle, on privateering, became the source of considerable controversy between the great powers and the United States.

On April 16, 1856, seven European powers – Britain, France, Austria, Russia, Prussia, Sardinia, and Turkey – signed the Declaration of Paris. Another forty-two states acceded to it by the end of the year, making it virtually universal. Eventually it would claim a total of fifty-five members,[40] making it the first widely accepted instrument of international law in the Westphalian state system. The Declaration marked "the beginning of modern international law as we know it: multilateral treaties open for accession by all powers with the intention of creating new universal rules."[41] Only four countries refused to join: Spain, Mexico, Venezuela, and the United States. By 1907, the United States and Venezuela (due to US pressure) remained the only holdouts.

US Material Interests and the Maritime Order

It is not immediately obvious why any country would sign onto a declaration that had no binding provisions or enforcement mechanisms. Scholars of the laws of war working with rational choice models explain this phenomenon as a type of equilibrium behavior, whereby

---

[39] "Declaration of Paris; April 16, 1856," The Avalon Project, http://avalon.law .yale.edu/19th_century/decparis.asp
[40] International Committee of the Red Cross, "Treaties and states parties to such treaties," www.icrc.org/applic/ihl/ihl.nsf/States.xsp?xp_viewStates=XPages_ NORMStatesParties&xp_treatySelected=105
[41] Jan Martin Lemnitzer, "'That moral League of Nations against the United States': The origins of the 1856 Declaration of Paris," *The International History Review*, 35:5 (2013), 1068–1088.

self-interested states enter into mutually reinforcing public agreements in which enforcement is reciprocal.[42] In the present case, a state would concede the safety of neutral commerce during war if the state itself expected to be neutral in some future conflict involving the currently neutral parties, and in a position to demand the same concession from them at that point. The more likely a state was to be a neutral in major wars and the more dependent it was on maritime commerce, the more incentive it should have had to agree to laws that protected neutral rights; especially if the most belligerent states – the great powers – had agreed to such laws.

As a state whose rise depended on trade, which in turn depended on remaining neutral in European wars, the United States had every incentive to support the Declaration of Paris.[43] "Neutrality had made the United States rich" as European trade shifted to neutral American shipping in the course of the French Revolutionary Wars.[44] Keeping this in mind, since the late eighteenth century, the United States had sought to have the principle of "free vessels making free goods" incorporated into bilateral treaties with lesser powers.[45] As a belligerent during the Mexican-American War of 1846–1848, the Commander of the US Navy's Home Squadron ordered his officers to follow the same principle.[46] The Declaration of Paris offered the universalization not only of this principle but also that of neutral goods being protected on board enemy ships.

The US objection to the Declaration centered on the abolition of privateering, or the use of authorized private vessels to attack enemy commerce. For a country with a small navy and large merchant marine such as the United States, privateering was a potentially cost-effective wartime measure.[47] Citizens owned the vessels, with the only payment

[42] Eric A. Posner, "A theory of the laws of war," John M. Olin Law & Economics Working Paper no. 160 (2002); James D. Morrow, "When do states follow the laws of war?" *American Political Science Review*, 101:3 (2007), 559–572.

[43] Samuel Flagg Bemis, *John Quincy Adams and the Foundations of American Foreign Policy* (New York: Alfred A. Knopf, 1949), 437.

[44] Troy Bickham, *The Weight of Vengeance: The United States, the British Empire, and the War of 1812* (Oxford: Oxford University Press, 2012), 25.

[45] See Carlton Savage, *Policy of the United States toward Maritime Commerce in War*, vol. 1 (Washington: Government Printing Office, 1934), 60–64.

[46] Kenneth J. Hagan, *This People's Navy: The Making of American Sea Power* (New York: Free Press, 1991), 127.

[47] Gary M. Anderson and Adam Gifford, Jr., "Privateering and the private production of naval power," *Cato Journal*, 11:1 (1991), 99–122.

being a share of the prize on board any captured vessels.[48] In strategic terms, privateering promised offensive power, especially in wars with trading states. Persistent attacks on enemy commerce put adversaries under domestic pressure to end wars sooner. In both the Revolutionary War and the War of 1812, privateers had imposed costs in the tens of millions of dollars on the British.[49]

The Costs of Privateering

On balance, however, privateering was costly and mostly ineffective, for three reasons. First, in any war, the other side also had recourse to privateers. In the War of 1812, a quarter of American captures of British merchant ships took place in the first three months while the British were busy fighting Napoleonic France.[50] The picture changed dramatically once the Royal Navy and British privateers got involved – by the end of the war in 1815, they had captured 20,961 American sailors and 1,407 American merchant ships.[51]

Second, privateering was not very effective against a superior naval power. In the War of 1812, the Royal Navy retook nearly half the total number of vessels captured by American privateers.[52] As the Royal Navy began blockading the US northeastern seaboard from December 1812, US trade fell dramatically.[53] Without much commerce to raid, privateers were rendered useless, a fate made worse by the Royal Navy's use of convoys to protect British merchant ships.[54] By mid-1813, the acting Secretary of the Treasury reported to Congress,

---

[48] Ibid., 101.
[49] Bickham, *The Weight of Vengeance*, 129; Thomas Clark, *Sketches of the Naval History of the United States* (Philadelphia: M. Carey, 1813), 13–14; Jerome R. Garitee, *The Republic's Private Navy: The American Privateering Business as Practiced by Baltimore during the War of 1812* (Middletown, CN: Mystic Seaport, 1977), 243–244; Hagan, *This People's Navy*, 17.
[50] Kert, *Privateering*, 7.   [51] Bickham, *The Weight of Vengeance*, 129.
[52] Henry Adams, *History of the United States of America during the Administration of James Madison* (1891; repr. New York: The Library of America, [1986]), 850.
[53] Douglas A. Irwin and Joseph H. Davis, "Trade disruptions and America's early industrialization," NBER Working Paper no. 9944 (2003), 4; Gordon S. Wood, *Empire of Liberty: A History of the Early Republic, 1789–1815* (Oxford: Oxford University Press, 2009), 689.
[54] Kert, *Privateering*, 88.

"[P]rivateering is nearly at an end."[55] Ultimately, privateers were not decisive for the war's outcome.

Third, and finally, privateering as a general practice had many negative externalities for the United States. Privateers did not exercise great discernment regarding the national origin of vessels and the appropriate protocols of search and seizure. The system thus "invited abuses approximating piracy at sea," its indiscriminate nature hurting both American and neutral commerce.[56] Many American privateers who participated in the War of 1812 subsequently shifted to the Caribbean, aiding colonial rebels in their wars against Spain. In response, the Spanish government authorized its own privateers against American commerce. As Spain's authority in the region declined, "the erstwhile Spanish privateers became outright pirates."[57] In 1823, the United States had to authorize naval action against Puerto Rico, by then a pirate hub.[58] Adams (then Secretary of State), who prior to the War of 1812 had supported privateering, grew to despise these "piratical privateers" – many of them American citizens – for bringing "the whole body of the European allies upon us in the form of remonstrances."[59]

US Opposition to Privateering before 1854

Given these costs, the United States sought to limit privateering in law and practice. A treaty with Prussia in 1785 banned privateering and guaranteed the safety of both nations' commerce during war.[60] When the National Assembly of France sent missives to various countries suggesting negotiations on the abolition of privateering and free

---

[55] Quoted in *New Bedford Mercury*, August 6, 1813, NewsBank: America's Historical Newspapers.
[56] Garitee, *The Republic's Private Navy*, 4. See also *American State Papers* (1834), 807.
[57] Hagan, *This People's Navy*, 95.
[58] J. Fenimore Cooper, *History of the Navy of the United States of America* (New York: G. P. Putnam & Co., 1853), 24.
[59] Quoted in David Head, *Privateers of the Americas: Spanish American Privateering from the United States in the Early Republic* (Athens: University of Georgia Press, 2015), 13.
[60] Article 23, "Treaty of Amity and Commerce Between His Majesty the King of Prussia, and the United States of America; September 10, 1785," The Avalon Project, https://avalon.law.yale.edu/18th_century/prus1785.asp.

navigation of commerce in 1792, the United States was one of the few countries to respond favorably.[61] Treaties with France in 1778 and Britain in 1795 placed numerous restrictions on the commissioning, outfitting, and conduct of privateers.[62] As the War of 1812 commenced, the Madison administration instructed privateers to "pay the strictest regard to the rights of neutral powers and the usages of civilized nations," and to follow the "rights of war" when engaging enemy vessels.[63] A newspaper out of Baltimore, a major hub of privateering, complained a year later, "[P]rivateering has not found much favor in the sight of Congress; for never was any permitted business so heavily clogged with duties and discouragements."[64]

Domestic opinion in the United States was also in favor of neutral rights and overwhelmingly against privateering. After the War of 1812, a number of peace societies that targeted privateering as a particularly abhorrent practice sprung up around the country. Massachusetts, which had supplied the largest share of private vessels in both wars with Britain,[65] was the epicenter of this movement. Peace societies petitioned the government, wrote letters to prominent statesmen, and published articles in journals and periodicals against privateering.[66] American newspapers were also generally against

---

[61] Francis Raymond Stark, *The Abolition of Privateering and the Declaration of Paris* (New York: Columbia University Press, 1897), 28.

[62] "Treaty of Amity and Commerce between the United States and France; February 6, 1778" and "The Jay Treaty; November 19, 1794," The Avalon Project, https://avalon.law.yale.edu/subject_menus/18th.asp.

[63] Stark, *The Abolition*, 128.

[64] "Privateering," *Baltimore Patriot*, June 16, 1813, NewsBank: America's Historical Newspapers.

[65] See Edgar Stanton Maclay, *A History of American Privateers* (New York: D. Appleton and Company, 1899), 506.

[66] See "Letter from the Hon. Mr. Jay, Bedford, State of New York, 12th Nov, 1817," *Friend of Peace*, No. XI (1817), 29–31; Committee of Foreign Relations, "Application to abolish privateering in time of war, communicated to the House of Representatives, January 4, 1820," *American State Papers* (1834), 628; Plainfield Peace Society, "Application to abolish privateering in time of war, communicated to the House of Representatives, January 11, 1820," *American State Papers* (1834), 643–644; "Notices of a 'proposed memorial' on privateering," *Friend of Peace*, vol. II, no. V (1821), 29–31; William Phillips et al., "Application to abolish privateering in time of war, communicated to the House of Reprsentatives, January 26, 1821," *American State Papers* (1834), 723–732; John Gallison, *A proposed memorial to the Congress of the United States* (Boston: publisher unknown, 1819), 4 (footnote); "Fifth Annual Report of the M.P.S.," *Friend of Peace*, vol. II, no. XI (1821), 11–18.

privateering. A survey of articles in the America's Historical Newspapers database published between 1789 and 1854 with the word "privateering" in their title shows 63 percent (55 articles) against privateering and 25 percent (22 articles) in favor.[67] Notably, 17 of the 22 articles in favor of privateering appeared during the War of 1812, when privateering was a recognizably unprofitable enterprise and ineffective strategy. Americans were thus against privateering except when it served as an instance of "American valor" undermining the "maritime pride of England."[68]

Influential statesmen such as Benjamin Franklin were outspoken critics of privateering as the "ancient relic of piracy."[69] American newspapers published extracts from Franklin's writings on the subject well into the 1840s. Although he had favored the use of privateers in the Revolutionary War, Franklin viewed the practice as the "most mischievous Kind of Gaming mixed with Blood."[70] Later statesmen such as John Quincy Adams found the practice "a relic of the barbarous warfare of barbarous ages."[71] By mid-century, privateering was a dishonorable, unchristian, and disreputable enterprise in American eyes. George Coggeshall, a former privateer of the War of 1812, in his history of American privateers published in 1856, bemoaned the "neglect, and even obloquy" that the "brave and patriotic" privateers of the war had encountered in the decades that followed.[72]

The War of 1812 was in fact the last time the United States ever used privateers.[73] Although Congress authorized letters of marque and reprisal against Algerian merchant shipping in 1815, there was little

---

[67] Calculated from NewsBank: America's Historical Newspapers.

[68] "Privateering," *Columbian*, April 7, 1814, NewsBank: America's Historical Newspapers.

[69] Quoted in Ethan A. Nadelmann, "Global prohibition regimes: The evolution of norms in international society," *International Organization*, 44:4 (1990), 479–526.

[70] "Benjamin Franklin to David Hartley, May 8, 1783," unpublished, *The Papers of Benjamin Franklin*, American Philosophical Society and Yale University. See also "Benjamin Franklin to Benjamin Vaughan, March 14, 1785," unpublished, *The Papers of Benjamin Franklin*, American Philosophical Society and Yale University.

[71] John Quincy Adams to the British Minister in Washington, June 24, 1823, quoted in Savage, *Policy of the United States*, 46.

[72] George Coggeshall, *History of the American Privateers, and Letters-of-Marque, during Our War with England in the Years 1812, '13 and '14* (New York: C. T. Evans, 1856), v.

[73] Bemis, *John Quincy Adams*, 447.

interest among American privateers given the paltry size of the target.[74] Fear of Mexican privateers in the war of 1846 caused President James Polk to recommend that Congress authorize US privateers to recapture American ships.[75] Congress did not oblige. By the time the great powers decided to codify the maritime laws of war in the Atlantic system through the Declaration of Paris, it had been four decades since the last US privateer had sailed.

Institutional Status Theory and the US Approach to the Atlantic System

Despite strong material interests in neutral rights and against privateering at the state and domestic levels, the United States refused to accept the new maritime order embodied in the Declaration of Paris and sought to actively undermine it. IST explains this counterintuitive behavior. As shown in Figure 4.1, there are three major periods in the timeline of the United States' approach to the maritime order of the Atlantic system: the 1820s, when the United States began its rise and the Atlantic system took shape; the mid-1850s when the Declaration of Paris was negotiated and implemented; and the early stages of the Civil War, in 1861, when the Union contemplated signing the Declaration of Paris to preempt international recognition of the Confederacy.

The first period coincided with the closure of the great-power club, as the great powers of Europe formed the Congress system of diplomacy and the Holy Alliance emerged as a concert of religious autocracies. The United States, not satisfying the membership rule of being a conservative monarchy, decided to try and join the ranks of the great powers by asserting its own status as a republican power destined for greatness – in IST's terms, a strategy of *expansion*. It did so by propagating the Monroe Doctrine and proposing radical reforms to the maritime laws of war in the name of civilization and Christianity.

In the second period, Britain and France dominated the Atlantic system and devised a new maritime order that effectively excluded the United States. Feeling unfairly denied of a major-power role by the great powers, US leaders undertook a major diplomatic *challenge*

---

[74] Garitee, *The Republic's Private Navy*, 247.
[75] James Polk, "State of the Union address 1846 – 8 December 1846," www.let.rug .nl/usa/presidents/james-knox-polk/state-of-the-union-1846.php

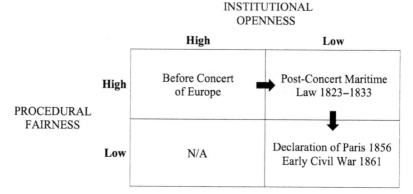

Figure 4.1 Institutional Status Theory and the United States in the Atlantic system

to the order. The challenge failed, as the great powers prevailed on smaller states to stay in line. Despite considerable risk, the United States still refused to sign onto the Declaration of Paris.

In the third period, during the Civil War, the Union offered to sign the Declaration if Britain and France would refrain from recognizing the Confederacy and would treat Confederate privateers as pirates. Indignant at British double-dealing on this question, the Lincoln administration soon withdrew its offer, and the United States remained a highly consequential outlier till the Declaration was superseded by the Second Hague Convention of 1907. The rest of this chapter traces the institutional evolution of the international order and the United States' approach to it from the 1820s to the early 1860s, and the manner in which IST's variables fit the case.

Seeking Status through Institutional Reform, 1823–1833

Before the 1820s, as a weak power that was yet to start rising, the United States simply followed the maritime laws of war out of a desire to be recognized as an independent member of the civilized world. However, the maritime order itself was not settled. The main axis of disagreement lay in the domain of neutral shipping: while most nations sought to establish the rule of "free ships, free goods," the British sought to confiscate enemy goods even if found in free, or neutral, ships. The United States followed both principles in its treaties with

European powers, treating the British approach as the law of nations, and the "free ships, free goods" principle as a justifiable exception.[76] American lawmakers and judges also based a number of maritime legal practices on those of the great powers, such as the rules and procedures of Prize Courts.[77] John Fabian Witt argues, "The aim of the [American] Revolution was to establish the membership of the United States in the club of civilized nations," and American leaders understood that "by displaying respect for the club's bylaws Americans would move that much closer to an independent seat at the table of nations."[78] Early America's respect for international law was thus driven by the need to not make new and more enemies, and the need to be recognized as an independent member of the civilized (i.e., European) world. The international order as it existed embodied the notion of war needing to be civilized, and the United States agreed wholeheartedly with this proposition. Although American statesmen had their own conception of what maritime law should do – provide immunity to all private property at sea – they were in no position to attempt changing the rules of the international order.

The Closure of the Great-Power Club

Two momentous changes took place after the 1815 Treaty of Ghent ended the war between Britain and the United States. First, the United States began to gradually recover from the war and lay the foundation for the rapid economic growth it would experience from the 1820s till the rupture of the Civil War. When James Monroe took office in 1817 and by the time he left office two terms later, the United States was still a "lightweight," but one that "no longer felt threatened by European governments in its neighborhood."[79] Second, the end of the Napoleonic Wars brought about a new structure of great-power relations in Europe and a fundamental shift in the international order. Through the Concert of Europe, Austria, Russia, Prussia, Britain, and (soon) France established a "collective hegemony," based on a

[76] Bowles, *The Declaration of Paris*, 191.
[77] Frederic Thomas Pratt, *Notes on the Principles and Practice of Prize Courts, by the Late Judge Story* (London: William Benning & Co., 1854), 13.
[78] John Fabian Witt, *Lincoln's Code: The Laws of War in American History* (New York: Free Press, 2012), 27.
[79] Gould, *Among the Powers*, 216.

conservative doctrine of "dynastic legitimacy," and "the practical desire to manage the [international] system."[80] Britain, although a member of the concert, was already pulling ahead in economic and naval power, thus inaugurating the Atlantic system.[81] After the early 1820s, the United States existed in a "Britain-centered global order" that was comanaged by a club of European great powers.[82]

From the American perspective, the concert meant exclusion from the great-power club. The United States was neither present at the Congress of Vienna in 1814–1815 nor part of the compact that emerged from the Congress. "All the restored governments of Europe are deeply hostile to us," wrote John Quincy Adams – perhaps the most important and influential American leader of this era – while serving as US Minister in London in 1816.[83] Support for monarchy and counterrevolution as membership rules of the great-power club were diametrically opposed to American political ideology: "The Royalists everywhere detest and despise us as Republicans."[84] So long as the concert was alive, leaders such as Adams saw no pathway to the top ranks of the international order for their rising country. The American political system was "essentially extra-European," argued Adams, and "as the importance of the United States as one of the members of the general society of civilized nations increases in the eyes of the others, the difficulties of maintaining this system, and the temptations to depart from it increase and multiply with it."[85]

Had the club been more welcoming, American leaders might have felt differently. The United States faced a double exclusion, however, not just on grounds of political ideology but also due to Britain's very public antipathy toward America's major-power pretensions.[86] Although Russia had invited the United States to join the Holy Alliance, Adams reasoned that "the organization of our government is such as not to admit of our acceding formally to that compact"[87]

---

[80] Adam Watson, *The Evolution of International Society* (London: Routledge, 1992), 239.
[81] Goddard, *When Right Makes Might*, 62.   [82] Mead, *Special Providence*, 82.
[83] Quoted in Charles N. Edel, *Nation Builder: John Quincy Adams and the Grand Strategy of the Republic* (Cambridge, MA: Harvard University Press, 2014), 125.
[84] Ibid.
[85] John Quincy Adams to Henry Middleton, July 5, 1820, in Ford (ed.), *Writings* Vol. 7, 46–52.
[86] See Goddard, *When Right Makes Might*, ch. 3.
[87] Adams to Middleton, in Ford (ed.), *Writings Vol. 7*, 50–51.

because in exercising its voice as a member of the alliance, the United States would inevitably disagree on matters of principle with "any European member of the bond."[88] Regarding Britain, Adams complained that "after vilifying us twenty years as a mean, low-minded, peddling nation, having no generous ambitions and no God but gold," Britain had now changed its tone and was "endeavoring to alarm the world at the gigantic grasp of our ambition."[89]

US Efforts to Expand the Great-Power Club

Excluded from the great-power club due to its political system, a rising United States nonetheless did not feel unfairly treated by the great powers. Even while rejecting the Russian offer to join the Holy Alliance, Adams noted that the United States supported the alliance's principles of keeping territorial aggrandizement in check and promoting Christian principles of interstate interaction.[90] In this sense, the United States held the rules and institutions of the international order to be legitimate. As predicted by IST, the United States responded to this new situation with a strategy of *expansion*, or an effort to have new criteria count toward the measure of greatness in the international order.

The American response unfolded along two distinct tracks. The first was to assert an alternative liberal and republican standard of greatness, most prominently in the form of the Monroe Doctrine. In correspondence with Russia in November 1823, the Monroe administration received a diplomatic note lauding the "new political system ... a new phase of European civilization" established by the conservative monarchies of the Holy Alliance.[91] Adams took it as an insult: The tsar was "bearding [the] U.S. to our faces upon the monarchical principles of the Holy Alliance."[92] Despite any evidence of a real threat of the Holy Alliance intervening in South American affairs, Monroe and his cabinet decided to issue their doctrine as a way of asserting the United States' claim to symbolic equality with the great powers. Dexter Perkins notes that in response to the Old World order based on "the

---

[88] Ibid. [89] Quoted in Edel, *Nation Builder*, 143.
[90] Adams, in Ford (ed.) *Writings Vol. 7*, 50.
[91] Albert Bushnell Hart, *The Monroe Doctrine: An Interpretation* (Boston: Little, Brown, and Company, 1917), 51.
[92] Quoted in Kagan, *Dangerous Nation*, 164.

doctrines of absolutism," the Monroe Doctrine offered the vision of a new world order "based on the right of the peoples of the world to determine their own destiny, and to govern themselves."[93] It was a move driven not by trade or security concerns, but by "profound political antagonism."[94]

The second track was to show the great powers that the United States, despite being a republican state and outsider to the club, could contribute significantly to the improvement of civilization, the sine qua non of club membership. A visible and impactful way to do this, reckoned American leaders, would be to lead in the development of international law. In an age in which "the progress of civilization" was becoming the "supreme guideline" for international legal reform,[95] the United States framed its efforts in terms of "moral principle and Christian precepts," which, with the rise of Britain's antislavery movement, were increasingly recognized as "considerations imperative upon the consciences of sovereign states."[96] In the realm of maritime law, whereas in previous decades the United States had largely accepted the terms of the great powers, it now began a diplomatic campaign for the protection of private property at sea. If successful, a proposal of this nature would be nothing short of a "profound revolution in the laws of warfare at sea," as it would not only end privateering but also prevent national navies from attacking maritime commerce during war.[97]

In April 1823, France invaded Spain and soon after declared that it would not harm Spanish and neutral commerce during the war. Sensing an opportunity, in July 1823, Adams "put forward possibly the most far-reaching propositions regarding commerce in war ever made by a Secretary of State of the United States."[98] He issued letters to US Ministers in London, Paris, and Moscow, instructing them to begin negotiations on draft treaties concerning maritime rights. Although Secretary of War John C. Calhoun was doubtful the British

---

[93] Dexter Perkins, *A History of the Monroe Doctrine* (1941; repr. London: Longmans, Green and Co., [1960]), 63.

[94] Dexter Perkins, *The Monroe Doctrine, 1823–1826* (Cambridge, MA: Harvard University Press, 1927), 81.

[95] Jan Martin Lemnitzer, *Power, Law and the End of Privateering* (New York: Palgrave Macmillan, 2014), 44.

[96] Savage, *Policy of the United States*, 50.   [97] Bemis, *John Quincy Adams*, 437.

[98] Savage, *Policy of the United States*, 46. See also Samuel B. Crandall, "Exemption of private property at sea from capture," *Columbia Law Review*, 5:7 (1905), 487–499.

would accept such a treaty, Adams was thinking more ambitiously. He had "no hope" that England would agree, but the goal was international recognition of the United States as a civilized and progressive nation.[99] "My plan involves nothing less than a revolution in the laws of war, a great amelioration in the condition of man," wrote Adams in his diary. "Should it even fail, it will be honorable to have proposed it."[100]

The desire for the United States to be counted among the civilized great powers was evident in Adams' letter to Richard Rush, the US Minister in London, in which he observed that "the pervading principle" of the Holy Alliance and Britain's "persevering efforts ... for the suppression of the African slave trade" suggest that "it is among the most indispensable duties of the rulers of mankind to combine their exertions for the general amelioration of the condition of man."[101] He reasoned that the great powers were increasingly engaged in their true Christian duty, which was to mitigate "the laws and usages of war."[102] It was, therefore, an opportune moment for the United States to urge the great powers, in the true spirit of Christianity, to take steps toward "the abolition of private war upon the sea."[103] Adams was, of course, aware that such a measure carried the potential of depriving the United States of an instrument – privateering – that had been useful in past wars. Quoting Benjamin Franklin, he advised Rush to emphasize to the British that although the United States was in a better geographical position to profit from privateering than any European nations, it was pursuing the abolition of privateering and immunity for private property "for the sake of humanity."[104] British leaders were unmoved. Rush reported that they were willing to negotiate on all matters proposed by the United States except the question of maritime rights.[105] The chargé d'affaires in Paris reported a similar sentiment among the French.[106]

On December 2, 1823, in his annual message to Congress – which also presented the Monroe Doctrine – James Monroe referred to

---

[99] Adams, in Adams (ed.), *Memoirs*, Vol. 6, 164.   [100] Ibid.
[101] Adams to Rush, July 28, 1823, *Documents Relating to the Foreign Relations of the United States with Other Countries during the Years from 1809 to 1898: Vol. 39* (Washington, DC: Department of State, 1854), 735–742.
[102] Ibid.   [103] Ibid., 736.   [104] Ibid., 738.
[105] Rush to Adams, October 9, 1823, *Documents*, 749–750.
[106] Sheldon to Adams, November 5, 1823, *Documents*, 750.

France's unilateral declaration from earlier in the year and affirmed that it concurred with "principles proclaimed and cherished by the United States from the first establishment of their independence, [and] suggested the hope that the time had arrived when the proposal for adopting it as a permanent and invariable rule in all future maritime wars might meet the favorable consideration of the great European powers."[107] Monroe and Adams remained hopeful that by suggesting a radical improvement in the law of nations, they could make a uniquely American mark on the world, introducing a new source of status that would facilitate US inclusion in the great-power club. Later that month, as Adams brought the new US Minister in Paris up to speed on the bilateral relationship, he highlighted the importance of the final suppression of the slave trade and "improvements in the general code of international law," specifically the maritime laws of war. "These two subjects are most intimately connected together," he wrote. "They both originated in the United States, and both are destined to exhibit memorable examples of their influence upon the history of mankind."[108]

The Great-Power Club Remains Closed

Despite US efforts, the Concert of Europe remained an important constraint on the great powers. Each was unwilling to venture into improvements upon international law without firm assurances that the other great powers would do the same. As the Russian foreign minister, Count Nesselrode, informed the US Minister in St. Petersburg, "as soon as the powers whose consent [the Russian Emperor] considers as indispensable shall have shown the same dispositions, he will not be wanting in authorizing his minister to discuss the different articles of an act which would be a crown of glory to modern diplomacy."[109] By August 1824, in the face of British intransigence, US status-related motives became even clearer. Rush reported his conversation with British diplomat Stratford Canning in London:

I said that the United States were not behind any of the powers of Europe in wishes, and, moving in their proper sphere, would never be behind them in

---

[107] Quoted in Stark, *The Abolition*, 40.
[108] Adams to Brown, December 23, 1823, *Documents*, 751.
[109] Nesselrode to Middleton, February 1, 1824, *Documents*, 757.

endeavors to bring about a general melioration in the condition of mankind; that such a principle [abolishing private war at sea] was eminently congenial to [US] political institutions, and had always been a maxim of [US] policy in the whole system of their external relations.[110]

Unfortunately for Rush, a different issue of national honor, impressment, got in the way. In negotiations with the British, Rush chose to prioritize impressment over neutral rights. The British were unwilling to discuss impressment, and Rush would not discuss anything if he could not discuss impressment.[111] Sensing American desperation to seek the high ground, the British simply stood firm and the negotiations reached an impasse.

Upon replacing Adams as Secretary of State in 1825 (while Adams became president), Henry Clay decided to not press the issue further. Yet he too felt that a treaty on maritime rights would allow the United States to set an example of highest civilization for the world. In a note to the US Minister in London, he wrote, "It cannot be doubted that, if Great Britain and the United States were to agree to the abolition of privateering, and no longer to consider private property on the high seas as lawful prize of war, their humane example would be generally followed."[112] Eventually, Clay had to suspend his efforts due to "the discouraging reception" from the British.[113] Clay's successor, Martin Van Buren, similarly believed that a US treaty with Russia would provide the example that America hoped to set for the world. In a letter to the US Minister in St. Petersburg, he spoke on behalf of President Andrew Jackson:

[The President] flatters himself that the adoption of these enlightened views by two powers [Russia and the United States] exercising in different hemispheres the degree of influence over the councils of their neighbors which necessarily attaches itself to their respective preponderance in the affairs of the two continents, may afford an example which will not be lost upon other nations.[114]

Russia prevaricated for months. Finally, in 1832, Nesselrode's response to the US Minister, James Buchanan, boiled down to a simple

---

[110] Rush to Adams, August 12, 1824, *Documents*, 760.
[111] Bemis, *John Quincy Adams*, 443–444.
[112] Clay to Gallatin, June 19, 1826, *Documents*, 768.
[113] Quoted in Savage, *Policy of the United States*, 53.
[114] Van Buren to Randolph, June 18, 1830, *Documents*, 778.

question: "What will England say to that?"[115] None of the great powers was willing to upset the delicate balance of the Concert of Europe by pursuing radical reform of international law. Meanwhile, the United States continued belaboring under the presumption that a bilateral treaty on maritime warfare secured with one of the great powers, which would find its way into the law of nations purely by example, was the best method of being recognized as a major power. Although Buchanan was skeptical of these treaty efforts on material grounds – he believed a treaty abolishing private war at sea would constrain US naval power[116] – he stuck to the official line. By 1833, the United States modified its original proposal to Russia by dropping the abolition of private war at sea and emphasizing the more limited "free ships, free goods" principle instead. Buchanan used the same argument as his predecessors. In an informal note to Nesselrode, he wrote,

At the first view there is force in the objection that it would be useless for Russia and the United States alone, without the concurrence of other powers, to establish the principle, by treaty, that "free ships shall make free goods." But, would the example of two such nations produce no effect upon the rest of the civilized world? Would it not have great influence in finally rendering this principle universal?[117]

Despite repeated attempts, Russia did not yield. In the end, after spending over a decade trying to convince the great powers – Britain, France, and Russia – to enter into bilateral treaties that would lead to a fundamental change in international maritime law, the United States accepted the futility of this enterprise. The great-power club remained closed, but not unfair – the European powers were as unwilling to conclude treaties on maritime law with each other as they were with the United States. The international order in this period remained unchanged. The next opportunity for the United States would arise two decades later, as Britain and France prepared to go to war with Russia.

Asserting Status by Challenging the International Order, 1854–1856

As Britain and France inched closer to entering the Crimean War on the side of the Ottoman Empire against Russia, the kingdoms of

---

[115] Buchanan to Livingston, June 29, 1832, *Documents*, 790.
[116] Buchanan to Livingston, October 19, 1832, *Documents*, 794.
[117] Buchanan to Nesselrode, May 18, 1833, *Documents*, 799–800.

Sweden and Denmark issued a declaration of neutrality to the great powers in January 1854. The declaration demanded that enemy goods (except war contraband) on neutral vessels be exempt from capture and that neutral goods found on enemy ships be returned to their owners.[118] Britain and France agreed, and Britain additionally sought a ban on privateering. British leaders were afraid that Russia, with its weaker navy, would commission American privateers and that Russian privateers would be welcomed in American ports, jeopardizing British commerce in North America.[119] France, however, vetoed the additional proposition.[120]

A New Opportunity for Institutional Reform

Meanwhile, Secretary of State William L. Marcy acknowledged that events in Europe would have "a most important ulterior bearing upon the United States."[121] He wrote to John Mason, the US Minister in Paris, "The United States have two things to do, or rather one thing to do, and, another not to do. We must take care of 'neutral rights', and not get involved in the conflict."[122] Buchanan, now US Minister in London, urged upon British foreign secretary Lord Clarendon the practical benefits to British-American relations that would accrue from adopting the principle of "free ships, free goods" during the war.[123] Mason was blunter about why the United States preferred the "free ships, free goods" principle. He conveyed to the French that due to the United States' vast commercial empire, "it was impossible that my country could submit to any practical exercise of the rights of war which would subject her citizens, their business, and their vessels to vexatious searches, captures or detentions."[124]

---

[118] Lemnitzer, "That moral League," 1072.
[119] See Buchanan to Marcy, February 24, 1854, *Documents*, 50–51; Crampton to Marcy, April 21, 1854, *Documents*, 44; Buchanan to Marcy, June 15, 1855, Private and Confidential, William L. Marcy papers, container 79, vol. II, Library of Congress (LOC).
[120] Lemnitzer, "That moral League," 1072.
[121] Marcy to Bille, February 14, 1854, reprinted in Piggott, *The Declaration*, 230.
[122] Marcy to Mason, April 17, 1854, Private and Confidential, William L. Marcy papers, container 80, vol. III, LOC.
[123] Buchanan to Marcy, February 24, 1854, *Documents*, 51.
[124] Mason to Marcy, March 22, 1854, *Documents*, 56.

Contrary to the pleadings of American diplomats in Paris three decades earlier, Mason's statement came across as a veiled threat. US leaders of the 1850s were far more self-conscious than before of their rise and were "confident that the time had arrived for the United States to join the ranks of the world's powers."[125] Britain's Minister in Washington, John Crampton, attributed "the threatening tone they [the Americans] hold to all the world" to a "reliance on the power of swagger" more than actual capabilities.[126] In fact, he observed, a sudden war "even with a Second-rate Power, would expose their Coasts and Commerce in an almost defenceless condition to an enterprising enemy."[127] Nonetheless, it was clear that the United States would at least diplomatically challenge any attempt by the great powers to establish a principle contrary to the protection of neutral rights, and that the challenge would be framed in terms of standing up for weaker powers. Mason wrote to Marcy that the circumstances of the war were "most auspicious to the establishment of our cherished principles of neutral rights – the rights of the weaker powers against the aggressive pretensions of the strong."[128]

By mid-March 1854, Britain and France had arrived at a compromise for the duration of the war. On March 16, a fortnight before the official announcement was made, Clarendon met with Buchanan in London and discussed, among other things, the issue of privateering. Buchanan sensed the British apprehension that American privateers would accept Russian commissions in the coming war. He reported to Marcy, "[A]lthough his lordship [Clarendon] did not propose a treaty between the two governments for the total suppression of privateering, it was evident that this was his drift."[129] Buchanan's response to Clarendon constitutes the earliest official statement of the eventual US position on the Declaration of Paris. It would not be possible, he said, "for the United States to agree to its [privateering's] suppression, unless the naval Powers would go one step further, and consent that war against private property should be abolished

---

[125] Sexton, *The Monroe Doctrine*, 126.
[126] Crampton to Clarendon, June 5, 1853, in James J. Barnes and Patience P. Barnes, *Private and Confidential: Letters from British Ministers in Washington to the Foreign Secretaries in London, 1844–67* (Selinsgrove: Susquehanna University Press, 1993), 75.
[127] Ibid.   [128] Mason to Marcy, March 22, 1854, *Documents*, 57.
[129] Buchanan to Marcy, March 24, 1854, *Documents*, 52.

altogether."[130] He painted a picture for Clarendon of a future war between Britain and the United States in which Britain, possessing a vastly superior navy, would destroy American commerce unless the latter had recourse to privateers who could do the same to British commerce. In the tradition of his predecessors who had appealed to what they understood to be the higher principles the United States shared with the great powers, he argued that it was "the genuine dictate of Christianity and civilization" that private war on the ocean be abolished and only public navies fight each other in wartime.[131]

The Stirring of US Dissatisfaction

On April 13, 1854, Marcy replied to Buchanan's note regarding the conversation with Clarendon on privateering. He observed that while the United States had treaties with other countries that explicitly prevented American citizens from privateering for foreign powers, the president would be unwilling to enter into any new treaties on the subject. "Our laws go as far as those of any nation – I think further – in laying restraints upon them [American citizens] in regard to going into foreign privateer service. This government is not prepared to listen to any proposition for a total suppression of privateering."[132] This was a remarkable position for a country for which the use of privateers was a net loss, whose citizens routinely deplored the practice as unprofitable and immoral, and that had not used privateers since 1815. Marcy's reasoning was the same as Buchanan's; that the United States would need its privateers in a future conflict. Lacking a large navy, which was a major attribute of being a great power, US leaders were unwilling to give up the only instrument – privateering – that could keep them in the running to be taken seriously as a maritime power.

Setting aside the question of privateering for the moment, Marcy took the opportunity to have neutral commerce protected in perpetuity. He wrote to the British Minister in Washington that "the United States are desirous to unite with other powers" to declare the "free ships, free goods" principle "as a rule of international law."[133] At the

---

[130] Ibid.   [131] Ibid., 53.
[132] Marcy to Buchanan, April 13, 1854, *Documents*, 54–55.
[133] Marcy to Crampton, April 28, 1854, *Documents*, 47.

same time, he initiated a period of hectic diplomacy with Russia and a number of minor powers to sign bilateral treaties echoing the two principles conceded by Britain and France.[134] Underlying this effort was a strand of status-seeking similar to that evinced by Adams in the 1820s. In his note to the US Minister in St. Petersburg, Marcy observed, "Should Russia, Great Britain, and France concur with the United States in declaring this [free ships, free goods] to be the doctrine of the law of nations, I do not doubt that the other nations of the world would at once give their consent and conform their practice to it."[135] Unlike in the 1820s, Russia was now keen to endorse a principle that went against British policy, and concluded a treaty with the United States on July 22, 1854.[136] However, US attempts to bring other countries on board yielded little – most consulted Britain and were advised not to accede unless the United States was willing to give up privateering as well.[137]

By the end of 1854, events in Europe began to gradually erode the legitimacy of the international order in US leaders' eyes. Attempts to universalize the principle of "free ships, free goods" were going nowhere. Instead, Britain sought to permanently abolish the United States' right to use privateers in wartime. Decades of followership and patient attempts at institutional reform of the maritime order had brought few results. In his annual message to Congress that year, President Franklin Pierce bristled at the overweening attitude of the European powers:

One or another of the powers of Europe has from time to time undertaken to enforce arbitrary regulations contrary in many respects to established principles of international law. That law the United States have in their foreign intercourse uniformly respected and observed, and they can not [*sic*] recognize any such interpolations therein as the temporary interests of others may suggest. They do not admit that the sovereigns of one continent or of a particular community of states can legislate for all others.[138]

---

[134] Lemnitzer, "That moral League," 1075.
[135] Marcy to Seymour, May 8, 1854, *Documents*, 65.
[136] Lemnitzer, *End of Privateering*, 46.
[137] Lemnitzer, "That moral League," 1079.
[138] Franklin Pierce, "Message of the President of the United States, on the Opening of Congress. – Washington, December 4, 1854," *British and Foreign State Papers*, vol. XLIV, 1853–1854 (London: James Ridgway and Sons, 1854), 266–287.

Pierce concluded by reiterating what US leaders had been proposing since the 1820s, but in a tone that was remarkably different from his predecessors: "Should the leading powers of Europe concur in proposing as a rule of international law to exempt private property upon the ocean from seizure by public armed cruisers as well as by privateers, the United States will readily meet them upon that broad ground."[139] Gone was the delicately conveyed hope of Monroe for the "favorable consideration of the great European powers."[140] In its place was an assertive leadership that chafed against the perceived inequity of the Atlantic system, in which a handful of great powers sought to deprive the United States of one of its primary pathways to great-power status.

The Crimean War ended with the Congress of Paris and a peace treaty signed on March 30, 1856. In the days that followed, the world witnessed an unprecedented event: the emergence of a multilateral agreement, open to all sovereign states in the international system, codifying universal principles governing interstate conduct. One of its main backers was, surprisingly, Britain. Longtime opponents of free ships making free goods, Britain's leaders concluded that their opposition was no longer tenable having conceded the principle during the war.[141] In exchange, the British won a concession of their own: the universal abolition of privateering.

The Declaration of Paris and the US Challenge

In the first week of April 1856, while the Congress of Paris was still underway, Clarendon (the British foreign secretary) wrote to Prime Minister Lord Palmerston, asking if he would object to a resolution against privateering in the Congress.[142] Palmerston replied that given the scale of British maritime commerce, the abolition of privateering would certainly be helpful. He then turned on its head the very logic that the United States had used in the past to try and expand the great-power club: "The United States have hitherto declined, but if all the Powers of Europe, and those not represented in [the Paris] Congress [that] might be invited to join were to unite in such an agreement the United States could scarcely refuse to accede, and the Engagement

---

[139] Ibid., 269–270.   [140] Quoted in Stark, *The Abolition*, 40.
[141] Lemnitzer, *End of Privateering*, 13.
[142] Lemnitzer, "That moral League," 1079.

might ultimately … become universal among all maritime states."[143] Clarendon concurred. If the United States chose to oppose such an agreement, they would "be left alone in their system, and have the world against them if the [Paris] Congress adopts the Resolution."[144] In their calculations, British statesmen were ultimately banking on the well-known US desire for international recognition and standing among the great powers.

On April 16, the Declaration of Paris came into effect, with two critical provisos. First, the principles of the Declaration were *indivisible*, that is, parties to the Declaration could not pick and choose principles of their liking but rather had to implement the Declaration in its entirety. Second, the Declaration was *universal*, that is, a country that signed the Declaration could not enter into any agreements pertaining to the maritime rights of neutrals during wartime that did not rest on the Declaration's four principles.[145] The Declaration was open to all states for accession, and the French foreign minister, Count Walewski, wrote to his Minister in Washington that he attached "peculiar value to the concurrence of the United States."[146]

The United States, having not been invited to the Congress of Paris, had no representatives at this gathering and was not consulted regarding the content of the Declaration prior to its announcement. On May 6, George Dallas, the US Minister in London, had a private meeting with Baron Brunow, the Russian Minister in London, in which he reproached his counterpart for signing the Declaration when the Baron "perfectly knew that it was aimed exclusively at the great defensive weapon of the United States against British disposition to go to war with us."[147] The American feeling of exclusion was palpable, particularly after decades of seeking the moral high ground on questions of neutral rights. Referring to their treaty of July 1854, in which the United States and Russia had effectively agreed to the second and third principles of the Declaration – free ships make free goods, and

[143] Palmerston to Clarendon, April 5, 1856. Quoted in ibid.
[144] Quoted in H. W. Malkin, "The inner history of the Declaration of Paris," *British Yearbook of International Law*, 8 (1927), 1–44.
[145] Department of State, *Correspondence Relative to Neutral Rights between the Government of the United States and the Powers Represented in the Congress at Paris* (Washington: A. O. P. Nicholson, 1856), 3.
[146] Walewski to de Sartiges, May 1856. Ibid., 2.
[147] George Mifflin Dallas, *A Series of Letters from London* (Philadelphia: J. B. Lippincott & Co., 1869), 32–33.

protection for neutral goods on enemy ships – Dallas bemoaned the futility of "having sympathized with Russia for two years" when "at the very first occasion Russia throws her weight into the scale of our adversary [Britain], and enables her claim to be backed by all Christendom!"[148] The weight of all Christendom was precisely what the United States had relied on in past years to stake a claim to symbolic equality with Britain, France, and Russia. To now hear those claims ring hollow struck a particularly discordant note.

The United States responded with a diplomatic offensive aimed at undermining the Declaration by convincing smaller powers not to sign it. Marcy issued instructions to this end to his Ministers in Brussels, Naples, Madrid, Stockholm, Copenhagen, Lisbon, Mexico, Nicaragua, Bogota, Caracas, Rio de Janeiro, Buenos Aires, Santiago, Lima, Quito, La Paz, and Hawaii.[149] He pointed out that the Declaration would "as a necessary consequence, defeat the negotiations of the United States" with these countries on neutral rights that were already underway.[150] The indivisibility and universality of the Declaration were particularly offensive, requiring nations to surrender an "important attribute of sovereignty," which was the right to negotiate neutral rights with any nation in an unconstrained fashion.[151] This meant the United States could not undermine the Declaration by negotiating separate treaties with its signatories. Although US leaders were greatly in favor of the second and third principles of the Declaration, the indivisibility clause meant they could not follow it selectively. Referring contemptuously to the "declaration" using quotation marks, Marcy reminded his envoys that the mutual surrender of the right of a state to employ privateers – especially one as heavily engaged in commerce as the United States – would inevitably place weaker nations at the mercy of the strong.

Shortly thereafter, Marcy wrote a famous note to Count de Sartiges, the French Minister in Washington, outlining the US position. Starting with the same arguments he had made to his envoys, he added that if the Declaration's signatories were to act on its dictates, they would be unable to conclude any agreements on neutral rights with the United States without surrendering "*a principle of maritime law which has*

---

[148] Ibid.
[149] Marcy to Seibels, July 15, 1856, Department of State, *Correspondence*, 6.
[150] Ibid., 5.   [151] Ibid.

never been contested – the right to employ privateers in time of war."[152] Backed into a corner, the United States was now arguing in favor of a practice that it had long sought to abolish. Nonetheless, Marcy was technically correct in noting that there had been no *successful* arrangements in the preceding half-century to abolish privateering,[153] which made its inclusion in the Declaration all the more unexpected and galling. Faced with an international order that seemed geared to undermine the United States, Marcy – like his predecessors – alluded to "[t]he prevalence of Christianity and the progress of civilization" and called on the great powers to amend the first principle of the Declaration to add exemption for all private property (except contraband of war) from seizure on the seas during wartime[154] – a proposal that has come to be known as the Marcy Amendment. "The reasons in favor of this doctrine," he argued, "are considered in this enlightened age so controlling as to have secured its partial adoption by all civilized nations" (partial because it applied on land but not at sea).[155] Marcy offered that the United States would sign the Declaration if his proposed amendment were adopted. If not, he sought clarification on how American privateers would be treated if they arrived in the ports of signatory states.

The Material Calculus

The US decision to challenge the Atlantic system by trying to undermine its central security institution makes little sense from a material point of view. As noted previously, the United States had much to lose by not becoming part of an institution that outlawed attacks on neutral shipping and protected neutral goods in belligerent ships. The United States also had little to gain from opposing the abolition of privateering. Since the Declaration of Paris only bound its signatories in their dealings with each other, great powers such as Britain and France – indeed, any party to the Declaration – could still legally use privateers in a war with the United States.[156] When Spain and Chile went to war in 1865, Chile as a party to the Declaration claimed the right to deploy

---

[152] Marcy to Sartiges, July 28, 1856, Department of State, *Correspondence*, 8, emphasis added.
[153] Ibid.   [154] Ibid., 12.   [155] Ibid.
[156] Hisakazu Fujita, "Commentary on the 1856 Paris Declaration respecting maritime law," in N. Ronzitti (ed.), *The Law of Naval Warfare: A Collection of*

privateers against Spain, which had refused to join.[157] The situation was the same in the case of neutral rights. When France declared war on the Austrian empire in defense of Sardinia in 1859, the French navy's official instructions restricted the application of the Declaration only to states that had joined the agreement. US leaders learned that as a neutral non-party to the Declaration, their country would be treated according to French maritime law and not the Declaration,[158] which meant that American goods found in belligerent ships would be confiscated.

Not only was rejecting the Declaration costly, there were no good reasons to oppose privateering even on grounds of military or economic disadvantage. The primary threat, of a war with a superior naval power – most likely Britain – was a distant and low-probability event. By mid-century, European powers were giving the United States a wide berth, leading a young Illinois legislator named Abraham Lincoln to proclaim that "all the armies of Europe, Asia and Africa combined ... could not by force, take a drink from the Ohio [river]."[159] Even if war were restricted to the seas, the US Navy would not be utterly incapable of defending the national interest. Between 1816 and 1856, the ratio of British to US warships had steadily declined from sixty-five British ships for every US ship to thirteen British ships for every US ship.[160] In terms of naval expenditure, whereas Britain spent fourteen times more than the United States in 1816, it spent four times more by 1856.[161] These odds improved dramatically were the United States to ally with either France or Russia in a war against Britain. Even if the US Navy was found wanting, experience from the War of 1812 showed that privateers had limited strategic value.

War would also be immensely costly for the United States. Crampton, the British Minister in Washington, concluded in early

Agreements and Documents with Commentaries (Dordrecht: Martinus Nijhoff, 1988), 61–76.

[157] Janice E. Thomson, *Mercenaries, Pirates, and Sovereigns: State-Building and Extraterritorial Violence in Early Modern Europe* (Princeton: Princeton University Press, 1994), 76.

[158] Lemnitzer, *End of Privateering*, 97.

[159] Quoted in Sexton, *The Monroe Doctrine*, 120.

[160] Calculated from George Modelski and William R. Thompson, *Seapower in Global Politics, 1494–1993* (Basingstoke: Macmillan Press, 1988), 71.

[161] Calculated from Modelski and Thompson, *Seapower*, 80.

1853 that US presidents would not risk war with Britain because it would threaten "real injury to the material and commercial interests" of US citizens, who were "a practical and money-making people."[162] Rapidly increasing trade between the United States and Europe, especially Britain, bolstered the incentives for peace. Between 1829 and 1856, the share of US imports carried by British ships increased from 8.6 percent to 31.3 percent.[163] The monetary value of US imports from Europe as a whole increased four times over between 1821 and 1856, and the value of US exports to Europe increased six times over during the same period.[164] Crampton concluded, "Nothing but the most wanton attack by us upon some point in which either the Interests of all the States were involved or which should enlist the general pride of the Country" could lead the United States into war with Britain.[165]

It was economics that drove many powers with navies smaller than the United States to enthusiastically support the Declaration of Paris, which would end the British practice of seizing neutral vessels.[166] These states also supported the abolition of privateering as a way of lowering shipping insurance rates and "keeping the lawlessness associated with privateering away from their doorsteps."[167] As shown earlier, these were considerations that had motivated the US leadership and public to oppose privateering as well. Yet, when the time came, the United States refused to give up the *right* to use privateers. By this decision, the United States became a major outlier. The three other countries that refused to sign the Declaration all did so because of apprehensions about the United States – Spain worried about US privateers in a future conflict over Cuba, Mexico was skeptical after Polk's attempt to commission privateers in the Mexican–American

---

[162] Crampton to Clarendon, February 7, 1853, in Barnes and Barnes, *Private and Confidential*, 64.

[163] *Statistics of the Foreign and Domestic Commerce of the United States Communicated by the Secretary of the Treasury in Answer to a Resolution of the Senate of the United States* (Washington: Government Printing Office, 1864), 18.

[164] Ibid., 28.

[165] Crampton to Clarendon, February 7, 1853, in Barnes and Barnes, *Private and Confidential*, 64.

[166] Lemnitzer, *End of Privateering*, 55; Thomson, *Mercenaries*, 72.

[167] Lemnitzer, *End of Privateering*, 42.

War, and Venezuela was the only country to succumb to US diplomatic pressure not to sign the Declaration without the Marcy Amendment.[168]

A Closed and Unfair Great-Power Club

IST predicts that a rising power will challenge an international order when the great-power club that dominates it is both institutionally closed and procedurally unfair. In the 1820s, US statesmen faced a closed yet procedurally fair great-power club founded on political principles antithetical to their own. They consequently sought to introduce new criteria into the collective understanding of what makes a great power. By the 1850s, the great powers themselves were much less cohesive, and it seemed the United States might be able to take its place among them. The 1856 Congress of Paris blindsided US ambitions in two critical ways. First, by abolishing privateering, the Declaration of Paris closed off a vital pathway by which the United States could claim the naval prowess necessary to join the great-power club. Second, by creating a situation where the United States was forced to be the only defender of an uncivilized practice, the Declaration seemed aimed specifically at singling out and isolating the United States diplomatically and morally in the community of civilized nations.

The importance of the Declaration in closing off access to the great-power club becomes clear when privateering is understood not as a complement to naval power for the United States, but as a *substitute* (albeit an imperfect one).[169] US leaders had always viewed naval power as integral to national greatness and international standing. According to Kagan, Alexander Hamilton had believed "a peacetime standing navy was necessary for a nation aspiring to greatness."[170] During the Virginia State Convention debate over the Federal Constitution, Madison had made the case for a standing navy on the same grounds as George Washington had for military preparedness: "Weakness will invite insults."[171] While serving as US Minister to

---

[168] Crandall, "Exemption of private property," 495; Lemnitzer, *End of Privateering*, 93.
[169] Anderson and Gifford, "Privateering," 104.
[170] Kagan, *Dangerous Nation*, 127.
[171] James Madison, responding to Edmund Pendleton, in Jonathan Elliot (ed.), *The Debates in the Several State Conventions, on the Adoption of the Federal*

Russia, John Quincy Adams had confided to his father, John Adams, that if the United States could form a "respectable navy" and maintain peace with England, "it would certainly tend to raise our national character in the estimation of the rest of the world."[172] Henry Knox, the first US Secretary of War, maintained that "a navy for the United States should be worthy of their national character," and despite the United States' limited strategic needs, had advocated building ships that would be "equal, if not superior, to any frigates belonging to any of the European Powers."[173] Although some, such as Thomas Jefferson, had disagreed with the need to match the Europeans in scale, they too were pleased when the US Navy earned the respect of European audiences through its exploits abroad.[174]

Reflecting this long-standing tradition of thought, the Secretary of the Navy's annual report for 1854 reiterated:

The protection of our wide-spread commerce, the guarding of our extended coast, *the preservation of our rank as a nation* demand that we should not be entirely stationary, and with inactive indifference behold the progress of other powers in naval strength. And it is hardly unwise to glance at the various national navy registers and compare the size of our navy, not merely with that of the mighty nations *with whom we claim equal rank*, but with that of other nations whom we esteem to be far, far behind us in the race of national greatness.[175]

Despite these ambitions of their statesmen, many Americans "looked with suspicion on the naval branch," fearing that a standing navy may become too powerful and draw the United States into unnecessary and expensive wars.[176] The navy was thus seen as "another menace to our republican institutions"[177] and a drain on the national treasury in

Constitution as Recommended by the General Convention at Philadelphia in 1787, vol. III (Washington: Jonathan Elliot, 1836), 309.

[172] John Quincy Adams to John Adams, October 14, 1811, in Worthington Chauncey Ford (ed.), *Writings of John Quincy Adams, Vol. IV, 1811–1813* (New York: Macmillan, 1914), 240–245.

[173] Henry Knox, "Construction of Frigates under the Act of March 27, 1794, communicated to the House of Representatives, December 29, 1794," *American State Papers*, 6.

[174] Kagan, *Dangerous Nation*, 100.

[175] 1854, 1855 Naval Reports for the President, publication no. M472, microfilm roll no. 5, National Archives and Records Administration (NARA), College Park, MD, emphases added.

[176] Willis J. Abbot, *The Naval History of the United States* (New York: Peter Fenelon Collier, 1886), 536.

[177] Senator William Maclay, quoted in Edgar Stanton Maclay, *A History*, 157.

peacetime.[178] While successive US presidents and secretaries of the navy lobbied Congress in vain for a larger naval program, privateers had to fill the gap in American power and status. Privateering thus became "the characteristic style of maritime warfare" in the New World,[179] and the navy struggled to recruit sailors, who typically preferred the higher wages and shorter cruises on privateering ships.[180]

As the Royal Navy was for the British and the French navy for the French, privateers were a source of national pride for Americans.[181] The War of 1812 had left an indelible memory of how American privateers – even if they achieved few material gains on balance – had "prevented a complete erosion of morale at home"[182] and forced the British to adopt the "mortifying expedient" of turning to French vessels for their trade.[183] To abolish privateering, therefore, would be to demolish a critical pillar of the United States' claim to symbolic equality with the great powers. "The right to resort to privateers, is as clear as the right to use public armed ships," declared Marcy.[184] He found it "extremely difficult to perceive why" if ships of the navy could still seize the vessels of belligerents, privateers, "which are in fact but another branch of the public force of the nation commissioning them," could not.[185] Without privateers, the United States had little access to the club of great powers, who all flaunted large and powerful navies.

The abolition of privateering alone may not have prompted an American challenge to the international order if the Declaration of Paris had affected all major powers equally. In fact, the United States felt uniquely singled out precisely because of its status aspirations. From the earliest years of the republic, American statesmen had been urging reform of international law to protect neutral rights. After decades of ignoring US pleas and prevaricating on the issue of maritime law, the great powers had devised an agreement that adopted the very principles the United States had advocated, with the crucial addition of a clause (on privateering) that seemed to have only one purpose: to deny the United States its rightful place among the great powers. Britain's Secretary of War astutely observed, "If the Americans stood

[178] Garitee, *The Republic's Private Navy*, 245; Hagan, *This People's Navy*, 2.
[179] Garitee, *The Republic's Private Navy*, 5.
[180] Adams, *History of the United States*, 852; Kert, *Privateering*, 12.
[181] Adams, *History of the United States*, 840.
[182] Garitee, *The Republic's Private Navy*, 241.   [183] Clark, *Sketches*, 37.
[184] Marcy to de Sartiges, July 28, 1856, *Correspondence*, 9.   [185] Ibid., 12.

out on a question of privateering against a Resolution adopted by the [Paris] Congress, they will be isolated on a point in which the whole civilized world will be against them."[186] Indeed, all of the states Marcy approached during the Crimean War for treaties on neutral rights declined the invitation, mostly out of fear of irritating Britain.[187]

Worse yet, the great powers devised and ratified the Declaration of Paris without once consulting the United States. After proposing the Declaration, France's foreign minister, Walewski, asked Mason, the US Minister in Paris, if the United States might be interested in signing on. Mason responded angrily that Walewski knew how much the United States valued privateering and that the French foreign minister should have at least inquired in advance if the United States had any opinion on the Declaration.[188] Jan Martin Lemnitzer argues that American leaders "perceived the Declaration of Paris as a slap in the face."[189] From their perspective, adds John Fabian Witt, "[t]he laws of war suddenly seemed a body of rules for strong European states to manipulate at the expense of the weaker military forces of the United States."[190] This feeling of being singled out and isolated cast the international order in a deeply biased light. In the aftermath of Marcy's note to the great powers, Dallas (the US Minister in London) wrote in a private note to a senator back home:

It is barely possible, however, that the late Congress at Paris intended their declaration abolishing Privateering as the ground work of a coercive movement by a confederacy of European sovereigns against America. If so, have at ye all, my lads! Governor Marcy's letter to [de] Sartiges is unanswerably conclusive, and is a fine platform upon which to fight till doomsday.[191]

Domestic opinion was equally sensitive to the unfairness of the great powers. Since the Treaty of Ghent, the US press had been overwhelmingly against the practice of privateering. This stance changed overnight upon the announcement of the draft Declaration in Paris in April 1854. The change was palpable in the reports of the British Minister in Washington. On March 27, 1854 – ten days before Britain and France would surprise the world with a draft declaration – he assessed that "the general feeling of the country is pretty strong against

---

[186] Quoted in Malkin, "The inner history," 27.
[187] Lemnitzer, *End of Privateering*, 50.   [188] Ibid., 76.   [189] Ibid., 76.
[190] Witt, *Lincoln's Code*, 136.   [191] Dallas, *A Series of Letters*, 75.

privateering."[192] Exactly five weeks later, he reported, "So far from countenancing any change in the law of nations by which the practice should be abolished, it is now the fashion to cry it up as a truly national and pre-eminently American mode of carrying on warfare: Privateers are spoken of as the 'noble militia of our seas'."[193]

The American press came out in support of the administration's position, and especially of the Marcy Amendment. "In every thing related to maritime freedom it [the United States] has been a leader, where other nations have been content to follow," wrote one newspaper.[194] Another declared that the American people were always "ready to meet, and honestly to respond to, any fair proposition emanating from other maritime Powers."[195] France and England had only to "show their sincerity, by disarming and dismantling their numerous superfluous ships not needed for peace purposes ... then America will be, if not on an equal, at least on a fair footing with them."[196] *The New York Times* supported the Marcy Amendment:

The great marine powers ... tell us, "reserving always the right to make what havoc our overgrown navies may choose to inflict upon your tempting commerce, we demand that you exempt our commerce from the only means of retaliation you possess ..." ... We reply, "The terms are unfair. Equalize them by declaring your public and our private armed vessels under the same prohibitory rule, and we are with you."[197]

Like the American public, US leaders now saw the international order as institutionally closed and procedurally unfair. They reacted accordingly by reasserting a claim to symbolic equality with the great powers in these changed circumstances. Simply refusing to sign the Declaration of Paris would lead to complete isolation. Instead, to salvage some amount of esteem in the world's eyes, the United States chose to play the role of a conscientious objector. The diplomatic

---

[192] Crampton to Clarendon, March 27, 1854, in Barnes and Barnes, *Private and Confidential*, 98.
[193] Crampton to Clarendon, May 1, 1854, in ibid., 100.
[194] "Privateering," *North American and United States Gazette*, June 2, 1856. NewsBank: America's Historical Newspapers.
[195] "Ought privateering to be abolished?" *The New York Herald*, May 17, 1856. NewsBank: America's Historical Newspapers.
[196] Ibid.
[197] "Privateering – Secretary Marcy's manifesto," *The New York Times*, August 12, 1856. NewsBank: America's Historical Newspapers.

challenge to the order was thus framed in terms of advocacy on behalf of weaker powers and in favor of a higher principle. Mason urged Marcy to propose an amendment adding the abolition of private war at sea as the precondition for US assent. "It may not be adopted," he reasoned, "But if rejected ... the United States, isolated though she be ... will stand justified before the world, for maintaining her rights, which she is willing to surrender, if other nations will agree with her."[198]

Marcy, initially hesitant, later agreed, observing, "Had we declined concurrence in the declaration simply because it abolished privateering, we should have been placed in a state of isolation."[199] Standing on principle was the only way to ameliorate the "embarrassment in which we were placed by the Paris declaration."[200] A British diplomat and interlocutor of Marcy's in Washington observed that the Marcy Amendment was intended "to place the United States' Government in the light of a protector or advocate of the rights of the secondary and third rate Powers, as opposed to the great maritime Powers."[201] Marcy's letter to de Sartiges had the desired effect, restoring some of the status the United States saw itself losing due to the Declaration. In the decades that followed, various smaller powers would return to the Marcy Amendment as the template for a truly progressive reformation of international maritime law (see below). Looking back four decades later, scholar Francis Raymond Stark observed, "This letter of Mr. Marcy's, at one stroke, took the United States out of the unpleasant position of appearing to obstruct progress, and enabled it, instead of being left an unwilling straggler, to pose as the leader of the van."[202]

In fact, secondary powers were far from the minds of US leaders when it came to the Declaration of Paris. US outrage was largely about the treatment of the United States itself. O'Sullivan, the inventor of the term Manifest Destiny, was posted as US Minister to Portugal at the time of the Congress of Paris. His reaction to the changed maritime order perhaps best encapsulated US sentiment:

---

[198] Mason to Marcy, April 25, 1856, quoted in Lemnitzer, *End of Privateering*, 76.
[199] Quoted in ibid., 92.   [200] Ibid.
[201] John Savile, Secretary of the British Legation in Washington, quoted in ibid., 81.
[202] Stark, *The Abolition*, 148.

I feel no small degree of indignation at this attempt, made by the great naval powers at Paris, to combine the community of nations in a sort of moral league against the United States, which shall thrust us outside of the circle of their general agreement upon *our own principles* in regard to neutral maritime rights, and which shall create an atmosphere of universal opinion to stigmatize as piratical a weapon of maritime self-defence *peculiarly our own*, & peculiarly indispensable to us, unless we shall succumb to their dictation on the subject, and consent thereby to redouble their effective naval preponderance against us.[203]

Decades of rule-following and attempting to expand the great-power club by contributing to the advancement of civilization had been repaid with a denial of the very status that the United States had sought all along. The great powers had admitted cherished American principles without admitting America itself into their midst. It soon became obvious that the great powers would not budge and that most other states had acceded to the Declaration. In February 1857, Dallas submitted to the British government what would be the final US proposal, reiterating the Marcy Amendment.[204] The following month, a new US president, James Buchanan, suspended negotiations.

Settling into Noncooperation, 1861

Buchanan's presidency (1857–1861) was marked by skepticism of the international order and a more domestic orientation. Secretary of State Lewis Cass briefly sought to revive the Marcy Amendment, when French naval instructions in the war of 1859 against Austria stated that non-signatories to the Declaration of Paris would not enjoy its protections. Cass viewed the indivisibility clause of the Declaration, which prevented states from being selective in their adherence to the Declaration's principles, as "an invidious one" that "ought not to have been adopted, directed as it was principally against the United States."[205] Cass's proposal to add further riders to the Marcy Amendment, specifying which types of ports could be blockaded and

---

[203] O'Sullivan to Marcy, June 12, 1856, quoted in ibid., 79, emphases added.
[204] Dallas to Clarendon, February 24, 1857, reprinted in Piggott, *The Declaration*, 404–408.
[205] Cass to chargé d'affaires in France, December 31, 1859, quoted in Savage, *Policy of the United States*, 86.

what should count as contraband of war, received a lukewarm response from the European powers.[206]

Maritime law emerged on the international agenda again for the United States due to the American Civil War, in which the international order and the great powers played an unexpected and important role. The Lincoln administration initially offered to sign the Declaration of Paris in order to preempt international recognition of the Confederacy and to outlaw the latter's use of privateers. Subsequent events, however, compelled the United States to reevaluate its stance and further entrenched the unfairness of the Atlantic system from the US perspective, pushing Washington from wanting to join the Declaration to abandoning negotiations within a span of four months.

The US Offer of Cooperation

Five days after attacking Fort Sumter and initiating the American Civil War, on April 17, 1861, the Confederacy invited applications from privateers. Possessing no navy of its own, the Confederacy saw privateering as a natural course of action. Nonetheless, in keeping with American tradition, Southern privateers were directed to "pay the strictest regard to the rights of neutral powers and the usages of civilized nations."[207] Two days later, President Abraham Lincoln announced a naval blockade of the ports of Southern states that had joined the Confederacy. Soon thereafter, Secretary of State William Henry Seward issued a remarkable circular to US Ministers in all major European capitals. He wrote that Lincoln had decided the time had come to bring negotiations over the Declaration of Paris to "a speedy and satisfactory conclusion," and to this end, instructed his envoys to begin negotiations with their respective counterparts in foreign governments.[208] Seward added that while "it would be eminently desirable for the good of all nations" for the parties to the Declaration to adopt

---

[206] Lemnitzer, *End of Privateering*, 98.

[207] "Instructions issued by the President of the Confederate States to Private Armed Vessels," *British and Foreign State Papers, 1864–1865*, vol. LV (London: William Ridgway, 1870), 584–586.

[208] Seward to Ministers of the United States in Great Britain, France, Russia, Prussia, Austria, Belgium, Italy, and Denmark, April 24, 1861, *Foreign Relations of the United States (FRUS), 1861*, vol. 1 (Washington: Government Printing Office, 1861), 34–36.

the Marcy Amendment, the impending wars in Europe and the ongoing insurrection in the United States suggested that "the right season seems to have passed" and "it is wise to secure the lesser good offered by the Paris Congress, without waiting indefinitely in hope to obtain the greater one offered to the maritime nations by the President of the United States."[209] The United States was effectively willing to sign the Declaration as it had been presented in 1856, without any amendments, "pure and simple."[210]

The motivation behind this turnaround was clear. The United States was willing to swallow its status concerns due to the exigencies of state survival. Lincoln's overriding concern was to preclude any form of external intervention in the Civil War.[211] Intervention meant not only material or moral assistance, but also any sort of recognition accorded to the Confederacy by other governments. Seward put it in no uncertain terms: "British recognition [of the Confederacy] would be British intervention, to create within our territory a hostile State by overthrowing this republic itself."[212] Given that the Confederacy had declared its intent to use privateers and that the United States had rejected the Declaration of Paris to protect the right to use privateers, Union leaders were afraid that the European powers would recognize the South as a belligerent in order to claim neutrality from any privateers that either the Confederacy or the Union might decide to commission. As Seward pointed out to the US Minister in Paris, "[T]he danger of such a case of depredation upon commerce equally by the [Union] government itself, and by its enemies, would operate as a provocation to France and other commercial nations to recognize the insurrectionary party in violation of our national rights and sovereignty."[213] If the Civil War were an internal matter, there would be no belligerents to speak of and hence no question of neutral rights. However, the Civil War could only be kept an internal matter if it did not threaten the interests of the great powers. The Confederacy, by employing privateers, posed a threat to the great powers and thereby invited them to recognize it as a belligerent, an outcome that the Union sought to avoid at all costs. Lincoln and Seward reasoned that by signing the Declaration of Paris as representatives of the United States, they could

---

[209] Ibid., 36.   [210] Seward to Adams, June 19, 1861, FRUS (vol. 1), 108.
[211] Seward to Dayton, June 17, 1861, FRUS (vol. 1), 224.
[212] Seward to Adams, May 21, 1861, FRUS (vol. 1), 89.
[213] Seward to Dayton, July 6, 1861, FRUS (vol. 1), 232.

bind both North and South to the first principle of the Declaration: "[P]rivateering is and remains abolished."

Intimations of Procedural Unfairness

Unfortunately for Lincoln and Seward, while Britain and France did not recognize the Confederacy as a state, they did accord it belligerent rights, thereby frustrating the underlying objective behind Lincoln's offer to sign the Declaration of Paris. In the first week of May 1861, John Russell, the British foreign secretary, announced in Parliament that the Queen's law officers had recommended the South be treated as a belligerent.[214] A week later, the day the new US Minister, Charles Francis Adams (son of John Quincy Adams), arrived in Britain to join his post, the British government issued a formal declaration of neutrality with regard to the Civil War that effectively accorded the South the status of a belligerent. Seward wrote to Adams, "This government considers that our relations in Europe have reached a crisis, in which it is necessary for it to take a decided stand."[215] Especially galling for the Union was the fact – learned from the American legation in St. Petersburg[216] – that Britain and France had decided to coordinate their policies toward the United States,[217] reviving the diplomatic isolation that American leaders had experienced in connection with the Declaration of Paris. Seward noted the unfairness of the approach the great powers had taken: "The United States have been impartial and just in all their conduct towards the several nations of Europe. [We] will not complain, however, of the combination now announced by the two leading powers, although [we] think [we] had a right to expect a more independent, if not a more friendly course, from each of them."[218]

The Union fell back on an alternative strategy: Even if the great powers chose to recognize the Confederacy as a belligerent, the Union could accede to the Declaration of Paris and legitimately expect that the great powers would uphold the Declaration's commitment to

---

[214] Adams to Seward, May 17, 1861, FRUS (vol. 1), 85.
[215] Seward to Adams, May 21, 1861, FRUS (vol. 1), 87–88.
[216] Seward to Dayton, June 17, 1861, FRUS (vol. 1), 225.
[217] For evidence of this decision from British documents, see Lyons to Russell, June 4, 1861, reprinted in Piggott, *The Declaration*, 419.
[218] Seward to Adams, May 21, 1861, 88–89.

abolishing privateering "everywhere in all cases and forever,"[219] which would make the Union blockade more effective. Any sign of unwillingness to accept the accession of the United States could only be construed as an inconsistent application of the rules of the international order: "If she [Britain] refuse it, it can only be because she is willing to become the patron of privateering when aimed at our devastation."[220]

Still, a number of American statesmen sought to introduce the Marcy Amendment in negotiations. William Dayton, US Minister in Paris, proposed to the French that the United States would sign the Declaration *with* the amendment. "I should very much regret an opportunity lost to obtain such a treaty provision, if possible," he wrote to Seward, "before we give up that species of volunteer marine by which we are enabled in some degree to affect the commerce of other nations, having a heavier naval marine, while they are destroying our own."[221] Seward himself backed Dayton's approach for a time, as did Adams in London (though Adams himself had not proposed the amendment to the British). Adams, however, noticed further signs of British hypocrisy, creating a growing feeling among American leaders that when it came to questions of maritime law, the great powers espoused one set of rules for themselves and another for the United States. Citing criticism of the Union blockade in the British press, he observed, "Great Britain, so long known and feared as the tyrant of the ocean, is now to transform herself into a champion of neutral rights and the freedom of navigation, even into the ports of all the world, with or without regard to the interests of the nations to whom they may belong."[222]

The Union government's disappointment with the great powers deepened in mid-June 1861, when the Ministers of Britain and France met with Seward in Washington to present him with dispatches from their respective governments. Breaking diplomatic protocol, Seward asked to first unofficially read the dispatches in the presence of the Ministers. The documents turned out to be declarations of neutrality that officially recognized the Confederacy as a belligerent. Both Britain and France also demanded that the Union government

---

[219] Ibid.   [220] Ibid.
[221] Dayton to Seward, May 22, 1861, FRUS (vol. 1), 211.
[222] Adams to Seward, May 31, 1861, FRUS (vol. 1), 96.

agree to ensure that its naval ships and privateers (none of which had actually been commissioned) follow the second, third, and fourth principles of the Declaration of Paris.

Having read the dispatches, Seward refused to accept them officially, for a number of reasons related to the unfair treatment he felt was being meted out to the United States by the great powers. First, as had already been made clear by Union diplomats in Europe, the very act of recognizing the South as a belligerent was an "abridgement" of US sovereignty that his government was unwilling to even debate with any other nation.[223] Second, echoing a complaint that Dallas had made with regard to the Declaration of Paris in 1856, Seward felt that his government had not been adequately consulted before the great powers had arrived at a momentous decision affecting its sovereignty.[224] Third, as reported by the British Minister, Richard Lyons, Seward made it clear that "he did not think that two European Powers ought to consult together upon the course to be pursued towards a great nation like the United States, and announce that they were acting in concert on the subject."[225] Finally, had the great powers paid closer attention to diplomatic correspondence from the United States, they would have noted that Seward had offered to sign the original Declaration of Paris in April, which granted more than the demands made by Britain and France in June.[226]

Despite this setback, Union leaders continued to pursue a conciliatory line in the hope that once they signed the Declaration, they could at a future date propose the Marcy Amendment. The locus of negotiations shifted back to London and Paris. Adams and Dayton renewed their respective offers to open negotiations on the accession of the United States. Seward instructed Dayton in particular to drop his insistence on the Marcy Amendment and agree to accede to the original Declaration. At the same time, both envoys were instructed to remind their interlocutors that although the United States' first preference was to have the Marcy Amendment, they were willing to put it off

---

[223] Seward to Dayton, June 17, 1861, FRUS (vol. 1), 226.
[224] Seward to Adams, June 19, 1861, FRUS (vol. 1), 106–107.
[225] Lyons to Russell (no. 14), June 17, 1861, reprinted in Piggott, *The Declaration*, 421.
[226] Lyons to Russell (no. 15), June 17, 1861, reprinted in Piggott, *The Declaration*, 422.

until "whenever there shall be any hope for the adoption of that beneficent feature by the necessary parties."[227]

Breakdown of Negotiations

While the United States resumed its overtures to the great powers, two critical events supervened. First, keen on securing its commercial shipping interests in the region, in early July 1861 – unbeknownst to the Union – the British government decided to open a channel of communication with the Confederate government regarding the proper treatment of neutrals.[228] Second, the first major battle of the Civil War – at Bull Run on July 21 – saw Union forces suffer a major reversal. For the first time, both domestic and international observers realized that the upheaval in the American South was not going to be a short-term insurrection. Consequently, Britain and France redoubled their efforts to deal directly with the Confederates to secure neutral rights based on the second, third, and fourth principles of the Declaration of Paris. At the same time, responding to a Union proposal that Britain and the Union sign a convention by which the latter would join the Declaration, Britain maintained its coordinated approach with France by insisting that an identical convention be concluded with France simultaneously on a predetermined day.[229]

The Marcy Amendment remained a sticking point among US statesmen. They viewed the Declaration's most far-reaching provision – the "free ships, free goods" principle – as American diplomacy's contribution to the world (even though France had urged this principle on a reluctant Britain during the Crimean War), and rued their inability to make an even greater impact on the world stage by having the Marcy Amendment included in the Declaration. Adams wrote to Seward, "The declaration of the leading powers of civilized Europe, made at Paris in 1856, engrafted upon the law of nations for the first time great principles for which the government of the United States had always contended against some of those powers, and down to that time had contended in vain."[230] He then pointed out that the "free ships, free goods" principle had reversed many decades of British policy, a

---

[227] Seward to Dayton, July 6, 1861, FRUS (vol. 1), 234.
[228] Lyons to Bunch, July 5, 1861, reprinted in Piggott, *The Declaration*, 424.
[229] Russell to Adams, July 18, 1861, FRUS (vol. 1), 116.
[230] Adams to Seward, July 26, 1861, FRUS (vol .1), 122.

"virtual triumph" for US diplomacy "all over the globe."[231] However, it was precisely this reversal that had made the British jealous of the Americans, contended Adams, and their reluctance to subsequently admit the Marcy Amendment "was calculated only to wither the laurels gained by our victory."[232] At no point in the history of international diplomacy over the Declaration of Paris is it clearer that the diplomatic tussle over the maritime laws of war in the minds of US leaders was chiefly a battle for America's place in the top ranks of the international order. The consistent denial of this place had now built up a sense of resentment at the unequal treatment given to the United States by those who dominated the system and its rules.

The British and the French, however, remained deeply skeptical of US intentions, viewing the offer to sign the Declaration as a ploy by the Union to get them to recognize Confederate privateers as pirates. While this was undoubtedly initially true, there was a clear legal loophole – the recognition of the Confederacy as a belligerent that was not a party to the Declaration – that Britain and France could have exploited to avoid this outcome (as Dayton himself had noted to Seward).[233] Nonetheless, to be doubly sure, Russell (the British foreign secretary) added a line at the end of a letter to Adams at the end of July 1861: "I need scarcely add that on the part of Great Britain the engagement will be prospective, and will not invalidate anything already done."[234] This line perplexed both Adams and Seward. After a long analysis of what Russell could have meant, Seward concluded, "[T]he 'thing' which 'has been done already,' and which Great Britain desires shall not be invalidated by the convention, must be something which she herself has done."[235]

What Britain had done became clearer in mid-August, when a colonel of the Confederate army was arrested in New York trying to leave the country on a British passport and carrying a number of letters and pamphlets addressed to British citizens. Among these items was a sealed consular bag containing "voluminous papers" addressed to Russell from the British consul at Charleston. Choosing not to open the bag, Seward sent it to Adams, asking him to hand it over to Russell with a demand that if any of its documentary contents were found to

---

[231] Ibid.   [232] Ibid.
[233] Dayton to Seward, June 7, 1861, FRUS (vol. 1), 220.
[234] Russell to Adams, July 31, 1861, FRUS (vol. 1), 126.
[235] Seward to Adams (no. 61), August 17, 1861, FRUS (vol. 1), 130.

be "treasonable," the foreign minister should hand them over to Adams.[236] Subsequently, Seward also found a number of letters that clearly implicated the British consul, especially in facilitating the recognition of the Confederacy and laying the groundwork for direct relations with Britain.[237]

Seward immediately demanded the consul's expulsion and an explanation from the British government, and wrote to Dayton in Paris to pause negotiations over the Declaration of Paris as "our negotiation in England has taken a new phase."[238] The latter step turned out to be unnecessary, because the British and French governments, meanwhile, submitted to the US Ministers in London and Paris, respectively, a declaration that they sought to make *in addition to* the conventions marking US accession to the Declaration of Paris. Both great powers declared that by accepting the accession of the United States, they did not intend "to undertake any engagement which shall have any bearing, direct or indirect, on the internal differences now prevailing in the United States."[239] In other words, Britain and France would not treat Confederate privateers as pirates. The French foreign minister went as far as to say that Britain and France would rather not have the United States join the Declaration than get involved in its domestic controversies.[240]

A Procedurally Unfair Great-Power Club

In Washington, this stance smacked of hypocrisy. Britain for one was already involved in the Civil War and preparing to deal directly with the Confederates. Moreover, through their addendum, the great powers were imposing unequal conditions on the United States' accession to the Declaration of Paris relative to the conditions imposed on all its other signatories. The United States had sought the cover of international law in the expectation that it would be treated as other major powers were. Instead, the international order continued to be biased, even when the United States was willing to give up privateering

---

[236] Seward to Adams (no. 63), August 17, 1861, FRUS (vol. 1), 132.
[237] Seward to Adams (no. 64), August 17, 1861, FRUS (vol. 1), 133.
[238] Seward to Dayton (no. 41), August 17, 1861, FRUS (vol. 1), 240.
[239] Russell to Adams, August 19, 1861, FRUS (vol. 1), 134.
[240] Dayton to Seward, August 22, 1861, FRUS (vol. 1), 242.

in perpetuity by acceding to the Declaration without the Marcy Amendment.

If the United States was willing to accept this unequal treatment, it could have signed the modified Declaration and called on other signatories to close their ports to Confederate privateers. In fact, this is precisely what European countries later did once it became clear that the Civil War was neither a brief nor minor rebellion. The decision of European countries to abide by the principles of the Declaration of Paris, along with the Union blockade, led to the decline and eventual demise of Confederate privateering.[241] Rejecting the modified Declaration thus carried significant material risks and lost opportunities to rein in Confederate privateers. Nonetheless, the United States chose to call off negotiations with the great powers. Given the delays in correspondence with Washington, both Adams and Dayton took the initiative to reply to their respective counterparts' proposals. To Britain, Adams wrote,

Rather than that such a record should be made, it were a thousand times better that the declaration remain unsigned forever. If the parties to the instrument are not to sign it upon terms of perfect reciprocity, with all their duties and obligations under it perfectly equal, and without equivocation or reservation of any kind, on any side, then [it is] plain that the proper season for such an engagement has not yet arrived.[242]

Dayton, in his reply to the French, was more circumspect:

I can scarcely suppose [the United States] will assent to the execution of a convention adopting the declaration of Paris, except upon terms of entire reciprocity, and subject to no other condition than those existing by and between the original parties ... It will ... exact no more and be content with no less than it would have been entitled to had the convention been executed in advance of its present internal controversy.[243]

At the end of August 1861, Adams pronounced the negotiations a failure.[244] Seward reported to his envoys that the president considered the addendum proposed by the great powers "inadmissible," adding that this view was "in harmony equally with a prudent regard to the

[241] Hagan, *This People's Navy*, 174; Garitee, *The Republic's Private Navy*, 248; Lemnitzer, *End of Privateering*, 14.
[242] Adams to Russell, August 23, 1861, FRUS (vol. 1), 138.
[243] Dayton to Thouvenel, August 26, 1861, FRUS (vol. 1), 246–247.
[244] Adams to Seward, August 30, 1861, FRUS (vol. 1), 135.

safety of the republic and a just sense of its honor and dignity."[245] One of Seward's primary objections was that the addendum was not reciprocal:

It proposes a special rule by which her Majesty's obligations shall be meliorated in their bearing upon internal difficulties now prevailing in the United States, while the obligations to be assumed by the United States shall not be similarly meliorated or at all affected in their bearing on internal differences that may now be prevailing, or may hereafter arise and prevail, in Great Britain.[246]

While a situation of insurrection in Britain may not have presented itself at any time in the near future, the point was one of principle and a way for the United States to put itself in the same category as Britain. At other points in correspondences with his envoys, Seward had emphasized that Britain's recognition of the Confederacy was akin to the United States recognizing Scotland, Ireland, or any other part of the British empire that might choose to rise up in insurrection.[247] American statesmen cared as much about being treated as equals of the great powers as they did about the substantive outcomes of the negotiations in which they were engaged. As before, they felt unfairly singled out. By imposing the addendum on them, the great powers were denying the United States the same status as themselves and all the other parties to the Declaration of Paris. Consequently, Seward decided that "the United States must accede to the declaration of the congress of Paris on the same terms with all the other parties to it, or … they do not accede to it at all."[248]

Given the circumstances, accession was impossible. However, the Union was too preoccupied to openly challenge the international order again. Seward chose to wait for "a happier time" when "the important objects of the proposed convention may be fully secured," including the Marcy Amendment.[249] Importantly, although the United States once again rejected the Declaration due to the unequal footing on which it was invited to join,[250] American leaders this time claimed *all* the principles in the Declaration. Seward wrote to Dayton,

---

[245] Seward to Adams, September 7, 1861; Seward to Dayton, September 10, 1861, FRUS (vol. 1), 142, 249.
[246] Ibid., 142.
[247] For example, Seward to Adams, April 10, 1861, FRUS (vol. 1), 79.
[248] Seward to Adams, September 7, 1861, FRUS (vol. 1), 143.   [249] Ibid.
[250] Seward to Dayton, September 10, 1861, FRUS (vol. 1), 250.

We have always practiced on the principles of the declaration. We did so long before they were adopted by the congress of Paris, so far as the rights of neutrals or friendly States are concerned. While our relations with France remain as they now are we shall continue the same practice none the less faithfully than if bound to do so by a solemn convention.[251]

The Perennial Outlier

After having tried and failed to undermine the Atlantic system (in 1856), a country embroiled in civil war could do nothing but protest the unfairness of the international order. Claiming to be the de facto originator and longtime practitioner of the laws in the Declaration of Paris allowed the United States to reassert a kind of symbolic equality with the great powers that had officially signed the agreement. The United States would follow the maritime laws of war because it was a civilized and great country, not because the great powers tried to unfairly arm-twist it into doing so.

In subsequent years, the United States consciously did not outlaw privateering in its bilateral treaties, which were typically with weaker states, such as Bolivia, Haiti, and the Dominican Republic.[252] Yet, the United States did not commission a single privateer. After the Civil War, Italy approached the United States, suggesting that the time was ripe for a universal agreement on the immunity of private property at sea, that is, the Marcy Amendment. Seward, who had earlier hoped for such a time, declined the offer. The United States, wrote Seward, in its "hour of trial" had "looked to the maritime powers of Europe for equal justice and magnanimity," while asking for "neither partiality nor friendship."[253] Instead, the great powers had declined to help and allowed Confederate privateers access to their ports (a reference to Britain).[254] "The remembrance of this great wrong still lingers in the memory of the United States, and weakens their disposition to confide in treaty stipulations as a security for their national commerce," he concluded.[255]

---

[251] Ibid., 251.   [252] Savage, *Policy of the United States*, 82.
[253] Seward to Cerruti, December 11, 1867, reprinted in ibid., 479.
[254] House of Representatives, "Insurgent privateers in foreign ports: Message from the President of the United States," 37th Congress, Second Session, Executive Document no. 104, April 12, 1862, Library of Congress.
[255] Seward to Cerruti, reprinted in Savage, *Policy of the United States*, 479.

US policy remained in this mold for the remainder of the nineteenth century. So long as the international order did not fully incorporate the Marcy Amendment, the United States would abide by the Declaration of Paris but refrain from signing it. This stance remained ingrained even though privateering became virtually impossible over time, as almost all states adhered to and internalized the laws of the Declaration. American privateers, had they sailed, would have found hardly any hospitable ports for supplies or prizes in the Americas and Europe. US opposition to the international maritime order persisted even as the United States became much more powerful – with a much larger navy – by the end of the nineteenth century. In advance of war with Spain in 1898, President William McKinley announced that the United States would not resort to privateering and would adhere to the rules of the Declaration of Paris.[256] To this day, the United States and Venezuela (due to US pressure) are the only two countries that never joined the agreement.

* * *

---

[256] William McKinley, "Proclamation 413 – Standards of Conduct and Respect of Neutral Rights in the War with Spain," April 26, 1898, The American Presidency Project, www.presidency.ucsb.edu/documents/proclamation-413-standards-conduct-and-respect-neutral-rights-the-war-with-spain

5 | Japan and the Washington System in the Interwar Period

Various studies of international order between the two World Wars have emphasized the central role of the Washington Naval Conference of 1921–1922, in which the three foremost naval powers – the United States, Britain, and Japan – agreed to a system of limitation on naval armaments and resolved a number of geopolitical controversies in the Far East.[1] Following on the heels of the Paris Peace Conference and the formation of the League of Nations, the conference and its resulting treaties famously capped the construction of capital ships – a navy's primary and largest warships – using a ratio of 5:5:3 for the United States, Britain, and Japan, respectively. The three countries, along with France, also signed an entente that sought to maintain the status quo in the Far East. Finally, there was broad agreement in principle regarding the territorial and administrative integrity of China. Altogether, the Washington Conference inaugurated a framework of diplomacy and a set of rules and institutions governing international security that historians have labeled the Washington system.[2]

The Washington Conference also cemented "a new order of sea power."[3] World War I had revealed America's vast industrial potential

---

[1] See, for example, Erik Goldstein, John Maurer, and Ernest R. May (eds.), *The Washington Conference, 1921–22, Naval Rivalry, East Asian Stability and the Road to Pearl Harbor* (London: Routledge, 1994); David W. Kearn, *Great Power Security Cooperation: Arms Control and the Challenge of Technological Change* (Lanham: Lexington Books, 2005), 49–86; Cecelia Lynch, *Beyond Appeasement: Interpreting Interwar Peace Movements in World Politics* (Ithaca: Cornell University Press, 1999), 125–148.

[2] Most prominently, Akira Iriye, *Japan and the Wider World: From the Mid-Nineteenth Century to the Present* (New York: Addison Wesley Longman, 1997), 51–53.

[3] Harold Sprout and Margaret Sprout, *Toward a New Order of Sea Power: American Naval Policy and the World Scene, 1918–1922* (1940; repr. New York: Greenwood Press, [1969]), ix–x.

and US leaders themselves sought to build "a navy second to none,"[4] a development that potentially threatened both British naval primacy worldwide and Japanese interests in the Far East. The fear of major conflict was heightened in all three capitals by the Anglo-Japanese Alliance. The Washington Conference, held at the behest of both Britain and the United States, allayed the specific fear of a trilateral conflict, though it did less to address bilateral sources of friction, especially between the United States and Japan. Historians have generally viewed the conference as a positive development, even in the trajectory of US–Japan relations in the early twentieth century. Asada Sadao describes it as a "happy interlude," one that temporarily dispelled fears of a Pacific war and created a framework for naval arms reduction and control.[5] Iriye Akira labels the period from the end of World War I till 1931 "the brief period of peace between the U.S. and Japan."[6]

The Washington system was in the end just an interlude. Subsequent naval conferences in Geneva in 1927, London in 1930, and again London in 1935 were but a shadow of the original, eliciting little cooperation, much recrimination, and general bitterness between the powers. In 1931, Japanese soldiers in China engineered the Mukden incident and used it as a pretext to take control of Manchuria. The diplomatic fallout eventually caused Japan to leave the League of Nations in 1933. The following year, Japan gave notice of its abrogation of the Washington Naval Treaty. The brief window of cooperation that had opened in Washington in 1921 was decisively closed.

Japan's initial extensive cooperation and subsequent costly challenge to the international order are difficult to explain through a purely materialist lens. This chapter takes on the task using Institutional Status Theory. It begins with an account of Japan's status aspirations from the Meiji Restoration onward. It then provides the background to the Washington Conference, and Japan's material interests with regard to the evolving order. The chapter proceeds to test IST's predictions based in part on previously unseen archival evidence: English-language

---

[4] George Theron Davis, *A Navy Second to None: The Development of Modern American Naval Policy* (Westport: Greenwood Press, 1971).
[5] Sadao Asada, *From Mahan to Pearl Harbor: The Imperial Japanese Navy and the United States* (Annapolis, MD: Naval Institute Press, 2006), ix.
[6] Akira Iriye, *Pacific Estrangement: Japanese and American Expansion, 1897–1911* (Cambridge, MA: Harvard University Press, 1972), 252.

translations of secret telegrams sent and received by the Japanese embassy in Washington in the 1920s, which were intercepted by US intelligence. The analysis delves into the status-seeking strategies pursued by Japan between 1919 and the early 1930s – first reframing, then cooperation, expansion, and finally challenge – in response to the changing institutional openness and procedural fairness of the international order. It demonstrates the superiority of IST to a purely materialist account in explaining Japan's approach to the Washington system.

Japan's Major-Power Identity

The great-power club in the nineteenth century was exclusively European, and it was European countries that established the rules of membership for joining the international order, or the so-called family of nations.[7] As shown in Chapter 4, this standard was one of "civilization," and those outside the order were by implication barbaric or uncivilized.[8] The impact on Japan of its first encounter with Western naval power in 1854 is well documented.[9] In the ensuing five decades, Japanese leaders deliberately emulated Western political institutions, social customs, economic policies, and military techniques in order to not only join the international order but also become an equal member of the great-power club. Ito Hirobumi, four times the prime minister of Japan between 1885 and 1901, observed that Meiji Japan strove "to attain among the nations of the world the status of a civilized nation and to become a member of the comity of European and American nations which occupy the position of civilized countries."[10] Throughout this period, Japanese leaders were "openly determined to 'catch up and surpass' the West and become a 'first-class nation'."[11]

---

[7] George Grafton Wilson, "The family of nations idea and Japan," *The Journal of Race Development*, 2:3 (1912), 246–255.

[8] Gong, *The Standard of 'Civilization'*.

[9] See W. G. Beasley, *The Meiji Restoration* (Stanford: Stanford University Press, 1972).

[10] Quoted in Erica Brenner, "Japanese national doctrines in international perspective," in Naoko Shimazu (ed.), *Nationalisms in Japan* (London: Routledge, 2006), 9–40.

[11] Richard J. Samuels, *Machiavelli's Children: Leaders and Their Legacies in Italy and Japan* (Ithaca: Cornell University Press, 2003), 12.

Using the "advantages of followership," in a very short period of time Japan accomplished what had taken European nations centuries to do – create a modern bureaucratic state, industrial economy, and powerful military.[12] These achievements enabled the revocation of the unequal treaties with which the great powers had bound Japan since the 1850s. After Britain became the first nation to renounce extraterritoriality through the Anglo-Japanese Treaty of Commerce and Navigation in 1894, diplomat Aoki Shuzo, who signed the agreement, observed that Japan could now "disregard the insults we have suffered over the last thirty years and at one go enter the 'Fellowship of Nations'."[13] Having acquired the material trappings of "civilization," Japan now began a new period of followership focused on emulating the external practices of the great powers. This objective entailed following international laws and conventions, building an empire, and demonstrating Japan's military prowess.

The international order by this time had taken on an "explicit juridical character."[14] Having assiduously followed the laws of maritime warfare as a neutral in the Franco-Prussian War of 1870–1871, Japan was a keen participant at the international conferences in the Hague in 1899 and 1907 that the great powers convened in an effort to "civilize" warfare. Referring to Tokyo's by-the-book prosecution of the 1895 Sino-Japanese War, a Japanese diplomat famously remarked to his Dutch counterpart prior to the first Hague Conference, "We show ourselves at least your equals in scientific butchery and at once are admitted to your council tables as civilized men."[15] Japanese leaders were also "scrupulous in their adherence to international humanitarian law" with regard to Russian prisoners in the war of 1905 and German and Austrian prisoners during World War I.[16]

---

[12] Kenneth B. Pyle, "Advantages of followership: German economics and Japanese bureaucrats, 1890–1925," *The Journal of Japanese Studies*, 1:1 (1974), 127–164.

[13] Quoted in Ian Nish, *Japanese Foreign Policy 1869–1942* (London: Routledge and Kegan Paul, 1977), 270–271.

[14] Gong, *The Standard of 'Civilization'*, 5.

[15] Quoted in Geoffrey Best, *Humanity in Warfare* (London: Weidenfeld and Nicolson, 1980), 141.

[16] John Hickman, "Explaining the interbellum rupture in Japanese treatment of prisoners of war," *Journal of Military and Strategic Studies*, 12:1 (2009), 1–20.

In their studies of the West's sources of power, Japan's leaders saw economic expansion as a key factor.[17] Japan began its expansion with the acquisition of the Ryukyu Islands and the opening of Korea to Japanese trade and influence in the 1870s. The 1895 Sino-Japanese War brought Korea more firmly within Japan's orbit while also giving Japan control over Formosa (Taiwan). The driving ideational force behind Japanese imperialism in Asia was the notion that Japan could only be an equal of the great powers if, as leading Meiji intellectual Fukuzawa Yukichi put it, Japan "left Asia."[18] This meant adopting Western civilization wholesale and acting toward Asian nations in the manner that Western countries did.

Leaving Asia also meant not being treated by the West as an Asian country, and this meant possessing the military strength to stake a claim to global recognition. In the eyes of Japanese elites, the victory over China in 1895 was the crowning achievement of the Meiji Restoration, establishing "Japan's imperial prestige in a great war."[19] Following the war, an editorial in the *Mainichi* newspaper declared, "[H]itherto Europe was blind to Japan's true greatness and apt to slight her ... [This] is the beginning of a new era of Japanese greatness."[20] External recognition did not take long to follow in the form of an alliance with Britain. Scholar Kemuriyama Sentaro noted that the Anglo-Japanese Alliance of 1902 "came upon the whole world as a surprise ... especially when it is considered that Japan had so far been generally regarded as a contemptible upstart in the East."[21] The alliance itself had little material value – Britain was not obliged to aid Japan in the event of war. Kawakami Kiyoshi, a prominent English-language Japanese journalist in the United States, wrote two decades later, "As far as Japan was concerned, the value of the alliance was moral rather than material ... for it was the first recognition of the fact that an Asiatic nation was capable of rendering assistance to a foremost Power of the West."[22]

---

[17] Iriye, *Pacific Estrangement*, 19.
[18] Quoted in Akira Iriye, *Across the Pacific: An Inner History of American-East Asian Relations* (New York: Harcourt, Brace & World, Inc., 1967), 65.
[19] Fukuzawa quoted in Samuels, *Machiavelli's Children*, 103.   [20] Ibid.
[21] Sentaro Kemuriyama, "Diplomacy," in Y. Takenob (ed.), *The Japan Year Book: Complete Cyclopedia of General Information and Statistics on Japan and Japanese Territories for the Year 1921–22* (Tokyo: The Japan Year Book Office, 1921), 316–370.
[22] Kiyoshi K. Kawakami, *Japan's Pacific Policy, Especially in Relation to China, the Far East, and the Washington Conference* (New York: E. P. Dutton & Company, 1922), 43.

The Russo-Japanese War of 1904–1905, in which Japan successfully demonstrated its military prowess against a great power, heralded yet another "new era" in Japanese history and is often taken as the point at which Japan became a great power.[23] However, Japan's capabilities were far below those of the United States and Britain, and it was not widely recognized as a great power in the sense of the term used in this book – Japan did not have preponderant capabilities, it did not have global interests, and it was not involved in the management of the international order. It was not a member of the great-power club. In fact, the war's main impact was on Japan's psyche. Iriye notes, "The glory [of victory in 1905] ... did not end the quest for great-power status abroad and social order at home that would be commensurate with each other. If anything, a new search began almost instantaneously after the end of the war, a search that in many ways would continue for several more decades."[24]

Emergence of the Washington System

Japan used World War I as an opportunity to expand its empire in East Asia at the expense of Germany and Russia. The great powers (the United States and Britain) viewed this expansion with suspicion, and the United States in particular began maneuvering to counter Japan's growing footprint.[25] American antipathy did not go unnoticed in Japan. A working paper prepared by the Japanese Naval Staff College in 1918 described the United States as Japan's "foremost hypothetical enemy," one that was following a "policy of intimidation in the Orient."[26]

Two years after the Paris Peace Conference of 1919, the great powers – the United States and Britain – proposed a conference in Washington on naval arms limitation and the Pacific. Two factors contributed to this proposal. First, since the early stages of World War I, Japan and the United States had been engaged in tit-for-tat

---

[23] Iriye, *Pacific Estrangement*, 126.
[24] Akira Iriye, "Japan's drive to great-power status," in Marius B. Jansen (ed.), *The Cambridge History of Japan, Volume 5, The Nineteenth Century* (Cambridge: Cambridge University Press, 1989), 721–782.
[25] Sprout and Sprout, *Toward a New Order*, 88.
[26] Quoted in Asada, *From Mahan to Pearl Harbor*, 53.

announcements of ever more ambitious naval construction plans.[27] While mostly on paper, this trend gave pause to politicians, planners, and strategists on both sides, who feared an escalating naval race. Second, given growing tensions between the United States and Japan, and Britain's wary eye on American naval expansion, Washington felt it might soon become the target of the Anglo-Japanese Alliance.[28] In May 1920, Washington instructed its ambassador in London to suggest changes to the alliance – which was up for renewal in 1921 – that would secure US interests in China.[29] The British themselves were lukewarm toward the alliance's renewal. A secret memo prepared by the British Foreign Office noted a number of areas of conflict between Britain and Japan, including conflicting goals in China and Japanese expansionism.[30] Despite these misgivings, the British government decided it would be best to maintain the alliance, lest Tokyo choose Berlin or Moscow instead.

Japan saw continued utility in the alliance. According to historian Kajima Morinosuke, there were four reasons behind this position. First, Japan would benefit from British assistance in a dispute with a third country (except the United States, as per an amendment to the alliance in 1911). Second, abrogating the alliance would invite a stronger British naval presence in the Far East, which was undesirable for Japan. Third, since Japan was the only non-white major power, "foreign countries might manifest anti-Japanese sentiments more plainly" in the absence of the alliance.[31] Fourth, and finally, given that Britain's designs in the Far East were mainly economic, maintaining the alliance would promote peace in the region. Writing in 1922, Kawakami suggested a deeper reason: "[Japanese leaders] know that Japan's continued association with the foremost Power of Europe will be an asset to her yet uncertain prestige among the nations. To put it

---

[27] David C. Evans and Mark R. Peattie, *Kaigun: Strategy, Tactics, and Technology in the Imperial Japanese Navy 1887–1941* (Annapolis, MD: Naval Institute Press, 1997), 166–167.

[28] William R. Braisted, "The evolution of the United States Navy's strategic assessments in the pacific, 1919–31," *Diplomacy & Statecraft*, 4:3 (1993), 102–123.

[29] Quoted in John S. Galbraith, "The Imperial Conference of 1921 and the Washington Conference," *The Canadian Historical Review*, 29:2 (1948), 143–152.

[30] Ibid., 144.

[31] Morinosuke Kajima, *The Diplomacy of Japan 1894–1922*, vol. III (Tokyo: Kajima Institute of International Peace, 1980), 442.

plainly, Japan is afraid of isolation."[32] As the Washington negotiations would bear out, fear of isolation – being unfairly singled out, in terms of IST – was perhaps the most important factor driving Japanese cooperation with the great powers.

Japan's Material Interests and the Washington System

Japan's material interests in the interwar period were straightforward: preserving room for economic expansion and maintaining security from external threats. To achieve these ends, Japan had to hold onto its recently acquired possessions in China and minimize the US naval presence in the Western Pacific. Japan's approach to the Washington system thus raises two related puzzles. First, if the United States was Japan's primary strategic threat, why did Japan make numerous concessions at the Washington conference and thereby acquiesce in an international order that was manifestly inimical to its rise? Aside from accepting an unequal ratio on naval limitation, Japan agreed to the replacement of the Anglo-Japanese Alliance with a loose four-power entente, the preservation of the United States' Open Door policy in China, and the withdrawal of Japanese troops from Shantung in China.

Scholars have generally explained Japan's cooperation in materialist terms. Accordingly, the conference succeeded because "it improved the security of the three powers by decreasing the probability of conflict through formal negotiation and the settlement of difficult issues that could have, if left unaddressed, precipitated a war in the Pacific."[33] The United States was considerably more prosperous and powerful than Japan; therefore, arguably, it made sense for Tokyo to avoid direct conflict and cooperate instead.[34] However, if the goal was to avoid a potential conflict spiral, Tokyo's naval strategy after the conference did not suggest so. Although Japan's naval budget did decrease considerably after 1922, the navy energetically launched into the construction of ships not covered by the Washington naval treaty[35] and invested in qualitative advancements that could make up for quantitative limits.

---

[32] Kawakami, *Japan's Pacific Policy*, 47.
[33] Kearn, *Great Power Security Cooperation*, 49.
[34] Dudley W. Knox, *The Eclipse of American Sea Power* (New York: American Army & Navy Journal, Inc., 1922), 33–45.
[35] Leo Marriott, *Treaty Cruisers: The World's First International Warship Building Competition* (Barnsley: Pen & Sword, 2005), 58–68.

The second puzzle arises from Japan's decision in the early 1930s to renege on its commitments. After the London Naval Treaty of 1930, Japanese decision-makers began a steady process of unraveling the Washington system. The Manchurian crisis, withdrawal from the League of Nations, and abrogation of the Washington Treaty itself are all puzzling if one considers the security environment facing Japan, which if anything was *worse* than the one facing it in 1921 given the significant increase in US military power and the deterioration of US–Japan relations during the 1920s. Pulling out of the Washington system all but guaranteed renewed and fiercer naval competition with the United States, a competition that Japan could scarcely afford. The Great Depression had created economic conditions in Japan that called for curtailing military expenditure, yet Japan's naval budget increased by 49 percent between 1931 and 1932, and by the following year was higher than pre-Washington Conference levels.[36]

In both 1921 and 1931, Japan faced a depressed economy at home, the threat of war with the United States, and a navy that considered the United States its primary adversary. The material cost of challenging the international order at both times was high. Yet, in 1921, Japan chose to cooperate with the Washington system, and in 1931, it began systematically violating the order's rules. What changed? As many scholars have noted, domestic politics in interwar Japan veered increasingly to the right and public opinion became increasingly anti-American.[37] However, political scientists often focus on the 1930s as the period of increasing militarism, and historians writing about the 1920s have focused on civilian and military rivalries and intrigues without explicitly linking them to external events.[38] In all accounts, the role of the Japanese bureaucratic and military elite is uncontested. As Richard Samuels notes, unlike German or Italian fascism that originated from outside established politics via a social movement led by a charismatic leader, "Japanese authoritarianism was built from the inside out – by a strong military with powerful bureaucratic allies."[39]

---

[36] Asada, *From Mahan to Pearl Harbor*, 297.
[37] For example, Akira Iriye, *After Imperialism: The Search for a New Order in the Far East 1921–1931* (Cambridge, MA: Harvard University Press, 1965), 36.
[38] For example, Peter Duus, *The Rise of Modern Japan* (Boston: Houghton Mifflin Company, 1976), 189–205; Ian Nish, *Japanese Foreign Policy in the Interwar Period* (Westport: Praeger, 2002), 33–84; Snyder, *Myths of Empire*, 112–152.
[39] Samuels, *Machiavelli's Children*, 27–28.

While these accounts are undoubtedly valid, by focusing on the 1930s as the key period of revisionism, they tend to conflate the rise of authoritarianism at home with the rise of militarism in Japan's external relations. They miss the deeper sources of Japan's growing disenchantment with the international order of the interwar period. Key questions remain unanswered or only partially answered. For example, what gave right-wing groups and militarists the upper hand? Why did that type of thinking emerge in the first place? Why did some political and naval leaders who took a relatively sanguine approach to the Washington system – such as Fleet Admiral Togo Heihachiro – dramatically change their opinions by the time of the Geneva (1927) and London (1930) conferences? The roots of Japanese behavior of the 1930s lie in the 1920s, and the Washington system played a vital but traditionally underappreciated role in shaping Japan's internal politics and external policies during this period.

Institutional Status Theory and Japan's Approach to the Washington System

IST's predictions fit the Japan case, as summarized in Figure 5.1. From the mid-nineteenth century till at least the Sino-Japanese War of 1895, Japanese leaders viewed the global order as institutionally open and procedurally fair. They saw the pursuit of "Rich Nation, Strong Army" as a worthy cause,[40] and believed that victory in war would definitively establish Japan's status as an equal of great powers such as Britain, Germany, France, Russia, and the United States. To their disappointment, neither victory against China in 1895 nor the even greater victory against Russia a decade later brought them the recognition they sought. While the world certainly considered Japan to be a major power following the Russo-Japanese War, the great powers looked down on Japan's rise as a non-European and non-Anglo-Saxon great power and displayed varying degrees of racial antipathy toward the "plucky little island nation" that had managed to defeat Russia.[41]

[40] Richard J. Samuels, *"Rich Nation, Strong Army": National Security and the Technological Transformation of Japan* (Ithaca: Cornell University Press, 1994), ix.
[41] Everis Anson Hayes, "Japanese exclusion: Speech of Hon. E.A. Hayes of California in the House of Representatives, Tuesday, March 13, 1906," Washington (1906), 3.

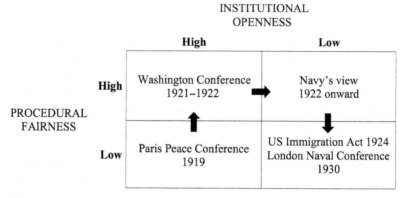

Figure 5.1 Institutional Status Theory and Japan in the Washington system

World War I shook up the international order, further opening it up for a rising power such as Japan to enter its leadership ranks. Although Japanese leaders found the order to be institutionally open, the 1919 Paris Peace Conference showed them that it was not entirely fair. Decision-making procedures at the conference were consultative, but the great powers were inconsistent in the way they treated Western (i.e., white-skinned) nations and non-Western nations. Consequently, Japan sought to *reframe* the rules of the international order to recognize all races as equal. Although this effort failed, soon the great powers proposed another conference in Washington that reassured Japan, as it joined the "Big Three," along with the United States and Britain, at the conference.

Afraid of jeopardizing their nation's newfound international standing in what seemed like an institutionally open and (now also) procedurally fair order, Japanese leaders went out of their way to *cooperate* with the great powers in negotiating the rules and institutions of the Washington system. However, the unequal ratio in capital-ship tonnage resulting from the Washington Conference caused some Japanese naval leaders to perceive the system as permanently relegating Japan to second-tier status. They compensated with a strategy of *expansion*, emphasizing new criteria for naval prowess, qualitative improvements in naval armaments and tactics, and the construction of auxiliary vessels not covered by the naval treaty. In this manner, they reasoned, Tokyo would be able to claim an equal tonnage ratio in a future negotiation.

Disagreements in the Japanese navy were greatly exacerbated by a singular event that poisoned Japan's relations with the Washington system and its principal guarantor, the United States. In 1924, the anti-Japanese movement on the US Pacific coast scored a major victory by having included in a federal immigration law a clause that in effect banned Japanese nationals from immigrating to the United States. Not only did the top ranks of the Washington system suddenly appear closed for a most deserving non-white nation, a perception of the entire system being also rigged to unfairly restrain Japan's growth emerged and grew over the following years, permeating Japanese assessments of the concessions Tokyo had made at the Washington Conference. By the early 1930s, this perception mixed with Japan's reaction to US sympathy for growing nationalism in Japan's colonies in China and Korea to produce a feeling that the great powers had closed off the international order to Japan's rise and harbored deep racial antipathy toward the Japanese.

While some influential civilians – led by foreign minister Shidehara Kijuro – still sought a modus vivendi with the great powers, the military and large sections of the media and the public increasingly took an antagonistic stance toward the international order and the United States in particular. They came to realize that "Japan's claims to equality of status with Western great powers could not be fulfilled within the constraints of a Western-dominated status hierarchy premised upon racial considerations."[42] Increasing resentment boiled over and led Japan to eventually *challenge* the Washington system by exiting it. The rest of this chapter traces the evolution of the international order and Japan's place in it during the 1920s, and the manner in which IST's variables fit the case.

Seeking Status through Institutional Reform, 1919

Japan joined the Paris Peace Conference in 1919 against a postwar backdrop of mutual suspicion with the United States. At the conference, Japan's status was unclear – as Margaret MacMillan has noted, Japan was a regional power that had contributed marginally to the Allied effort, yet it had emerged from the conflict greatly enriched and possessing one of the world's largest navies. Although Japan received

---

[42] Ward, "Race, status, and Japanese revisionism," 623.

the same number of delegates as Britain at the conference, in the Supreme Council – composed of the senior-most representatives of the United States, Britain, France, Italy, and Japan – MacMillan observes that "the Japanese were generally ignored or treated as something of a joke."[43] This confused status was reflected in the thinking of the Japanese as well, who viewed themselves as a "have-not" nation that had to compete for resources, territory, and recognition with the "have" nations such as Britain and the United States.[44] Despite their successes, the Japanese felt insecure about their place in the world.

Senior leaders in Tokyo had misgivings prior to Paris, worrying that it might turn out to be a ploy by the great powers to arrive at agreements that would lock in Japan's second-rank status.[45] They were deeply aware of the racial divide between Japan and the great-power club. In the instructions given to the Japanese delegates attending the conference, they worried that "the racial prejudices which have not yet entirely been banished from among the nations" could prove "gravely detrimental" for Japan in the League of Nations.[46] The delegates were directed to "secure suitable guarantees against the disadvantages to Japan which would arise as aforesaid out of racial prejudice."[47] One of Japan's chief goals at the conference, therefore, was to have a clause on racial equality included in the League's Covenant. In the face of a potentially unfair institution, Japan sought to *reframe* institutional rules to alter evaluations of its major-power identity claims and secure the same level of institutional deference as the great powers.

In February 1919, the Japanese delegates, Makino Nobuaki and Chinda Sutemi, circulated a draft proposal to this effect at a meeting of the League of Nations Commission: "Equality of nations being a basic principle of the League of Nations, the High Contracting Parties agree to accord, as soon as possible, to all alien nationals of States members of the League equal and just treatment in every respect, making no distinction, either in law or fact, on account of their race or nationality."[48] Makino argued that since the members of the League "constitute a great family of nations" that undertake to defend each

---

[43] Margaret MacMillan, *Paris 1919: Six Months That Changed the World* (New York: Random House, 2001), 306.
[44] Nish, *Interwar Period*, 13–14.   [45] MacMillan, *Paris 1919*, 317.
[46] Quoted in Naoko Shimazu, *Japan, Race and Equality: The Racial Equality Proposal of 1919* (London: Routledge, 1998), 113.
[47] Ibid.   [48] Quoted in Kajima, *The Diplomacy of Japan*, 398.

other with armed force if necessary, "each national would like to feel and in fact demand that he should be placed on an equal footing with people he undertakes to defend even with his life."[49]

Although a number of countries responded positively to the Japanese proposal, Britain remained opposed, largely due to Australian Prime Minister Billy Hughes' fear that the clause would open the floodgates of Asian immigration to Australia.[50] British delegate Arthur Balfour thought that "[none] of the English-speaking communities would tolerate a great Japanese flow of immigration."[51] Immigration was in fact far from the minds of the Japanese delegation, and Makino and Chinda emphasized to Hughes that Japan cared about the *principle* of racial equality and was happy to let the League's members work out the practicalities according to their respective domestic political constraints.[52] After being repeatedly rebuffed by Hughes, the Japanese watered down their proposal to one that would simply include the words "by the endorsement of the principle of equality of nations and just treatment of their nationals" in the Covenant's preamble.[53] Presenting this proposal to the League in April, Makino stated, "If this reasonable and just claim is now denied, it will, in the eyes of those peoples with reason to be keenly interested, have the significance of a reflection on their quality and status. Their faith in the justice and righteousness, which are to be the guiding spirit of the Covenant, may be shaken."[54]

The proposal went to a vote and secured the support of eleven out of sixteen members of the Commission. However, Woodrow Wilson, presiding over the session, declared that the importance of the motion required it to have unanimous support in order to pass, even though there had been cases in the past when matters in the Commission had been decided by a majority vote.[55] Defeated, Makino made a closing speech on the subject at the plenary session of April 28, in which he lamented the "poignant regret" felt by the Japanese people at the failure of the Commission to "approve of their just demand for laying down a principle aiming at the adjustment of this long-standing

---

[49] Ibid., 399.
[50] A. Morgan Young, *Japan in Recent Times 1912–1926* (New York: William Morrow & Company, 1929), 160–161.
[51] Quoted in Shimazu, *Japan, Race and Equality*, 19.
[52] Kajima, *The Diplomacy of Japan*, 401.   [53] Quoted in ibid., 411.
[54] Quoted in ibid., 412.   [55] Ibid., 414.

grievance, a demand that is based upon a deep-rooted national conviction."[56] It was evident that the great powers had used unfair methods to block Japan's legitimate desire for the principle (not substance) of racial equality to be acknowledged officially.

The Japanese public saw this outcome as a defeat, despite the fact that Japan had largely achieved its material goals at the conference by retaining the German islands in the Western Pacific as League Mandates and deferring the question of withdrawing from Shantung. When the Japanese delegation arrived back in Tokyo, it found a crowd protesting their inability to secure the racial equality clause.[57] Many saw this failure as confirmation of their original fears, that the great powers would use the League to continue treating Japan unfairly. Even the delegation's inability to secure outright ownership of the Pacific islands and a firm resolution of the Shantung question was attributed to the failure to secure equal status with the great powers.[58]

Although Japan's strategy of reframing the rules of the international order failed, the great powers had done enough to give Japan reason to believe it might be able to secure racial equality in the future. Hirobe Izumi notes, "While the failure of the Versailles Conference to insert a racial-equality clause into the League of Nations Covenant shocked the Japanese, they nevertheless gained confidence in their position as one of the great world powers by securing status as a permanent member of the Council of the League."[59] In his final words on the issue of racial equality to the conference, Makino stated that the Japanese government "will continue in their insistence for the adoption of this principle by the League in future."[60]

Racial bias in Paris was undoubtedly linked to the racism and discrimination that Japanese immigrants had been facing in the American West for decades. Goto Shinpei, a senior statesman and public figure, wrote in January 1921, "At bottom, the California question is one of principle. Nothing less than the principle of equality

---

[56] Quoted in ibid., 418.   [57] MacMillan, *Paris 1919*, 342.

[58] Lee Arne Makela, "Japanese attitudes towards the United States Immigration Act of 1924," unpublished PhD thesis, Department of History, Stanford University (1973), 15–16.

[59] Izumi Hirobe, *Japanese Pride, American Prejudice: Modifying the Exclusion Clause of the 1924 Immigration Act* (Stanford: Stanford University Press, 2001), 5–6.

[60] Quoted in Kajima, *The Diplomacy of Japan*, 418.

is involved, and no other solution than the one that will preserve this principle in its essential features will satisfy us."[61] The double standard applied to Japan's desire for symbolic equality rankled him. Goto observed, "In all such [Far Eastern] questions America is applying to us the most perfect and saintly canons of international dealings, which are observed nowhere else in this troubled world and which America herself failed to observe in almost everything that concerns her."[62] Okuma Shigenobu, another highly respected politician, argued that despite the best efforts of the white races to diminish Japan's achievements, Japan had proved that non-white races could "rank with the white peoples if only they exert themselves."[63] He warned, however, that even though most Asiatic nations were "fully peers" of the Europeans, they were discriminated against because of "the color of their skin" due to the "perverted feeling of racial superiority entertained by the whites."[64] He concluded that if things were to continue in this manner, "there is every likelihood that the peace of the world will be endangered."[65]

Japan's Status Anxieties over the Washington Conference, 1921

Soon after the Paris Peace Conference, another major opportunity for Japan to assert symbolic equality with the great powers presented itself in the form of the Washington Conference. In his inaugural address on March 4, 1921, President Warren G. Harding announced that the United States would consult other nations in order "to recommend a way to approximate disarmament and relieve the crushing burdens of military and naval establishments."[66] In April 1921, the Japanese navy issued a statement containing an interview given by Minister of the Navy, Admiral Kato Tomosaburo, to the Tokyo correspondent of the Associated Press of America, in which the minister said that although

---

[61] Shinpei Goto, "The Japanese question in America," reprinted in Kiyoshi K. Kawakami, *What Japan Thinks* (New York: The Macmillan Company, 1921), 189–203.
[62] Ibid., 200–201.
[63] Shigenobu Okuma, "Illusions of the white race," *Asian Review* (January 1921), reprinted in Kawakami, *What Japan Thinks*, 160–170.
[64] Ibid., 170.   [65] Ibid.
[66] Quoted in Paul Dukes, *The USA in the Making of the USSR: The Washington Conference, 1921–1922, and 'Uninvited Russia'* (New York: RoutledgeCurzon, 2004), 1.

current naval construction plans were essential for Japan's security, "Japan is nevertheless prepared to carry out the limitation of arma- ments to a certain extent in case any reliable agreement is concluded among the leading Powers for the restriction of armaments."[67] Meanwhile, Secretary of State Charles Evan Hughes pressured Britain to abrogate the Anglo-Japanese Alliance. Given that Washington was already keen on naval limitation, the British proposed a conference on both limitation and Pacific questions.[68]

Tokyo was initially skeptical of what it viewed as an Anglo- American effort to curtail Japan's rise and territorial expansion.[69] Japanese naval leaders had been quick to point out the double stand- ards of the great powers when it came to Japan's growing naval capability. Vice Admiral Sato Tetsutaro was critical of those who had clubbed Japan with Germany during World War I as a "militarist" country. Now that the war was over, Sato wrote, "[T]he ill-wishers of Japan are haunted with another bugbear. This time it is not militarism, but navalism."[70] He added,

It must be remembered that Japan is not the only nation constructing warships. England and America, too, are building warships. In spite of the fact that they have far stronger navies than Japan. Therefore, if any nation in the world is guilty of navalism, it is not Japan, but rather England and America .... So it is preposterous to say nothing against the big navies of England and America, and to hold up Japan's small navy, and accuse her of aggressiveness.[71]

Many Japanese military leaders saw their country as a rising power in an Anglo-American order, in which there was one set of rules for the great powers and another for Japan, which had developed many of the attributes of a great power but was not accorded corresponding roles.

Civilian leaders shared this concern. Hayashi Gonsuke, the Japanese ambassador to Britain, observed the "hatred of Japan" that existed

---

[67] Quoted in Y. Takenob, "The Army, Navy and Aviation," in Y. Takenob (ed.), *Japan Year Book*, 287–315.

[68] George Riddell, *Lord Riddell's Intimate Diary of the Peace Conference and After* (London: Victor Gollancz Ltd., 1933), 305.

[69] Sadao Asada, "Japan's 'Special Interests' and the Washington Conference," *The American Historical Review*, 67:1 (1961), 62–70.

[70] Tetsutaro Sato, "Japan's navalism," *Asian Review* (March 1920), reprinted in Kawakami, *What Japan Thinks*, 93–103.

[71] Ibid., 94–95.

among Americans who opposed the Anglo-Japanese Alliance, a hatred that he saw as "unavoidably a national condition."[72] Tokyo's worry was that the conference would be used by anti-Japanese sections of the US and British establishments for "defaming and censuring us."[73] Yamato Ichihashi, secretary to Minister of the Navy Kato Tomosaburo, explained Tokyo's hesitation:

Japan was a new international power and as such she had been subjected to severe criticisms by the more established nations. Her activities had been looked upon with suspicion. Her recent blunders had been magnified beyond their merit. In short, Japan had been made the "goat" of all international ills in the Pacific region . . . . In these circumstances it was but natural for her to manifest anxiety to a degree unwitnessed either in England or America when the American proposal for a Pacific conference was proclaimed.[74]

While some Japanese leaders worried that the conference would treat Japan as a second-rank power the way the Paris Peace Conference had, others were convinced that avoiding the conference would produce the same result. The politics of status dictated that Japan should at least take a seat at the table. Hayashi argued that since all the powers involved in Pacific and Far Eastern questions were already invited, any hesitation on Japan's part "may merely bring useless embarrassment to ourselves."[75] He added that a swift acceptance of the invitation would "quickly display the magnanimity of Japan" and produce "a great influence on our future national destiny."[76] In Tokyo, the Advisory Council on Foreign Affairs (*Gaiko Chosakai*) made two observations. First, the limitation of naval

---

[72] London to Washington, June 18, 1921, unnumbered, doc. 153, box 63, RG 457, NARA. Telegrams in this collection are often unsigned. In these cases, authorship is determined from the content of the telegram, the context provided by other telegrams, and the fact that only ambassador-level officials were involved in these very confidential exchanges on high politics. See Herbert O. Yardley, *The American Black Chamber* (Indianapolis: Bobbs-Merrill, 1931), 283–317. Yardley was the founder and head of the US government cryptographic unit that generated these documents.

[73] Tokyo to Washington, July 23, 1921, no. 303, Very Confidential, doc. 153, box 64, RG 457, NARA.

[74] Ichihashi Yamato, *The Washington Conference and After: A Historical Survey* (Stanford: Stanford University Press, 1928), 20–21.

[75] London to Washington, July 9, 1921, no. 230, Very Confidential, doc. 153, box 63, RG 457, NARA.

[76] London to Washington, July 13, 1921, no. 313, doc. 153, box 63, RG 457, NARA.

armaments was an increasingly popular issue with the governments and publics of the United States and Britain. Second, as paraphrased by Kajima, "should Japan not comply with the United States proposal, she could not escape responsibility for interrupting a plan to secure international peace."[77]

Through a series of exchanges and meetings with Ambassador Shidehara Kijuro in Washington, US Secretary of State Hughes assured him that the United States would not use the conference to "drive Japan into a corner."[78] It soon emerged that in addition to naval limitation, the great powers intended to discuss "Far Eastern questions" such as access to cabling rights on Yap Island and the status of Japanese troops in Shantung.[79] While this was not ideal from Tokyo's perspective, the government agreed to discuss these questions so long as they were restricted to "general principles such as mutual respect for territory, the open door, equal opportunities, etc." and not "accomplished facts and questions of sole concern to particular Powers."[80] Shidehara argued that Japan could not expect the United States to adhere to this caveat, which would additionally "react on the public opinion of the world and deepen the suspicion against us."[81] From London, Hayashi counseled that if Japan could "make clear our real intentions and show that we have a spirit of compromise," the great powers would undoubtedly develop "a favorable disposition towards us."[82]

The Japanese government relented, and officially accepted the US invitation in July 1921 with a watered-down proviso: "[I]ntroduction [in the agenda] of problems such as are of sole concern to certain particular Powers or such matters that may be regarded as accomplished facts should be scrupulously avoided."[83] With this exception, Japan sought to sideline discussion of the Anglo-Japanese Alliance,

---

[77] Kajima, *The Diplomacy of Japan*, 445.
[78] Shidehara quoted in Asada, "Japan's 'Special Interests'," 64.
[79] London to Washington, July 21, 1921, no. 329, doc. 153, box 64, RG 457, NARA.
[80] Tokyo to Washington, July 23, 1921, no. 303.
[81] Washington to Tokyo, July 25, 1921, no. 429, Urgent, doc. 153, box 64, RG 457, NARA.
[82] London to Washington, July 21, 1921, no. 329.
[83] Nish, *Interwar Period*, 27.

Shantung, Siberia, and the Pacific islands: issues that would "mischievously complicate the situation."[84]

Japanese leaders continued to debate Japan's ideal strategy for maintaining its standing with the great powers. In early August 1921, in a long summary of negotiations with the great powers, Hayashi sought to assuage Tokyo's concern that the conference was a plan concocted by Britain and the United States "to agree to oppress Japan."[85] Although Japan should look out for its material interests "with a suspicious eye" at the conference, he did not recommend "carrying this attitude too far in each thing that happens."[86] Shidehara stressed a similar point: Refusing to discuss matters outside the agenda "for trifling reasons of procedure" would give the impression of "bad conscience" on Japan's part and "afford strong pretexts for anti-Japanese agitators."[87] Japan had to be careful not to jeopardize the status benefits it was already enjoying by agreeing to participate. Shidehara noted that although Japan's excess caution had initially "led to some misunderstanding in America," Japan's subsequent willingness to cooperate had reversed this sentiment, "and the marked importance attached to the prestige of Japan compared with the European Powers was a very pleasant phenomenon."[88]

Although Tokyo came around to this view, Foreign Minister Uchida Kosai remained concerned about the "prejudices of various degrees about Japan's national policy in the past" and instructed Japan's conference delegates to "strive at this juncture to make clear Japan's true intention and to enhance Japan's reputation among nations."[89] Regarding Pacific questions, the Japanese government softened its stance and instructed the delegates to be open to discussing *faits accomplis* or issues concerning specific countries but in a way as "not

---

[84] Tokyo to Washington, July 13, 1921, no. 287, Very Secret, doc. 153, box 63, RG 457, NARA. See also London to Washington, July 15, 1921, no. 321, Very Confidential, doc. 153, box 64, RG 457, NARA.

[85] London to Washington, August 4, 1921, no. 353, Very Confidential, doc. 153, box 64, RG 457, NARA.

[86] Ibid. The Japanese Ambassador in Paris took a similar view. See Paris to Washington, July 11, 1921, Very Confidential, unnumbered, doc. 153, box, 63, RG 457, NARA.

[87] Washington to Tokyo, September 13, 1921, no. 608, doc. 153, box 64, RG 457, NARA.

[88] Washington to Tokyo, August 1, 1921, no. 458, doc. 153, box 64, RG 457, NARA.

[89] Quoted in Kajima, *The Diplomacy of Japan*, 459.

to give rise to a situation where Japan's past actions and policies alone are likely to be criticized."[90] Japan's top priority was to be treated as an equal member of the great-power club and not be unfairly singled out for any reason.

Seeking Status through Institutional Cooperation, 1921–1922

The opening day of the Washington Conference – November 12, 1921 – is well documented. Although all the delegations were vaguely aware that Hughes had a bold proposal in mind, he surprised everyone by offering a detailed and ambitious plan for the reduction of naval armaments in the opening plenary session itself. The plan required that all capital-ship-building programs be abandoned for ten years; that the three foremost naval powers – Britain, the United States, and Japan – scrap their older ships in order to arrive at a specific ratio of 5:5:3 for the United States, Britain, and Japan, respectively, in capital-ship tonnage; that the existing strength of the three powers be used to determine the appropriate tonnage ratio; and that the same ratio be applied to auxiliary vessels.[91] Hughes went on to propose scrapping specific numbers of capital ships built, being built, or authorized for building: 30 ships for a total of 845,740 tons for the United States, 23 ships for a total of 583,375 tons for Britain, and 25 ships for a total of 448,928 tons for Japan.[92]

For Minister of the Navy Kato Tomosaburo, the chief Japanese delegate, the concrete ambition of Hughes' plan landed like "a clap of thunder."[93] A British journalist at the conference noted, "Mr. Secretary Hughes sunk in thirty-five minutes more ships than all the admirals of the world have destroyed in a cycle of centuries."[94] Despite their prior fears, the Japanese delegates adopted a surprisingly cooperative approach toward Hughes' plan of capping Japan's capital-ship tonnage at 60 percent of US and British levels (via the 5:5:3 ratio). Kato stated in the opening plenary that, though the

---

[90] Ibid., 460; Nish, *Interwar Period*, 27.
[91] Sprout and Sprout, *Toward a New Order*, 154.   [92] Ibid., 154–156.
[93] Washington to Tokyo, November 23, 1921, no. 70, doc. 153, box 65, RG 457, NARA.
[94] Charles à Court Repington, *After the War* (Cambridge, MA: Houghton Mifflin Company, 1922), 432.

details may need adjustment, he agreed in principle with Hughes.[95] The following day, at a reception hosted by the Japanese embassy for the press, he stated, "It has never been the policy or intention of Japan to attempt to rival the two greatest navies of the world."[96] He reiterated this claim at the second plenary session on November 15, 1921, and followed it up with three proposed revisions to the Hughes plan. First, the ratio of capital-ship tonnage ought to be 10:10:7 (a 70 percent ratio) and not 5:5:3 (a 60 percent ratio). Second, Japan would retain the ships *Mutsu* and *Aki*, which would have been scrapped under the Hughes plan. Third, and finally, Japan desired parity in aircraft carriers, then a very new and untested technology.[97]

Japanese leaders uniformly viewed a 70 percent ratio as "absolutely necessary for the national defence of Japan."[98] Senior naval leaders reasoned that it would give the Japanese navy a 50–50 chance in a defensive battle against the United States.[99] According to Asada, "The notion of the 70 percent ratio ... was reinforced by war games, tabletop maneuvers, and fleet exercises, and it crystallized into a firmly held consensus – even an obsession – within the Japanese navy."[100] It was further entrenched when, in October 1920, the Japanese navy had obtained a copy of a US war plan that made exactly the same assessment.[101] Consequently, prior to the Washington Conference, a naval research committee set up by Kato had stated that "there can be absolutely no room whatsoever for compromise on this ratio."[102]

Japan's Concessions at the Washington Conference

In Washington, the United States and Britain were unyielding on their desired 60 percent ratio. Technical negotiations between naval experts

---

[95] Ibid., 161.
[96] Quoted in Yamato, *The Washington Conference*, 40. See also Shidehara's report of the interaction: Washington to Tokyo, November 14, 1921, no. 22, doc. 153, box 65, RG 457, NARA.
[97] Kajima, *The Diplomacy of Japan*, 471.
[98] Washington to Tokyo, November 19, 1921, no. 49, doc. 153, box 65, RG 457, NARA.
[99] Kajima, *The Diplomacy of Japan*, 48.
[100] Asada, *From Mahan to Pearl Harbor*, 48.
[101] Sadao Asada, "From Washington to London: The Imperial Japanese Navy and the politics of naval limitation, 1921–1930," *Diplomacy & Statecraft*, 4:3 (1993), 147–191.
[102] Asada, *From Mahan to Pearl Harbor*, 61.

of the three powers yielded little. Theodore Roosevelt, Jr., assistant secretary of the US Navy, noted that his counterpart, Japan's chief naval adviser at the conference, Kato Kanji (no relation of Kato Tomosaburo), made Japan's case "on two thoughts: a) that each nation had the right to determine what was necessary for her defence; b) that this navy [of 70 percent] was her minimum requirement."[103] In a communication to Shidehara, the Japanese government supported this position, which Kato Tomosaburo himself had stated as "the limit" before leaving for Washington.[104] On November 28, 1921, less than two weeks after the conference's naval subcommittee was convened, Kato Kanji publicly declared, "Japan is unable to accept the ratio of 60 per cent, because she considers it impossible to provide for her security and defense with any force less than 70 per cent."[105]

Meanwhile, the chief delegates of the three powers – Charles Hughes, Arthur Balfour, and Kato Tomosaburo – held private meetings on the ratio question. Hughes was intransigent and Balfour agreed with Hughes.[106] After more than twenty such meetings,[107] Kato relented, securing approval from Tokyo for the 60 percent ratio in exchange for an important concession: The United States and Britain would maintain the status quo with regard to defensive fortifications on islands in the Western Pacific. The resulting Five-Power Treaty – which also included France and Italy and was the cornerstone of the conference – was eventually signed on February 6, 1922. Japan had ultimately made a major concession on the naval ratio. In addition, contrary to Kato's initial stipulations, Japan gave up one of the two ships it had wanted to retain (the *Aki*) and accepted the same unequal ratio in aircraft carriers.

The Washington Conference achieved a number of important outcomes in addition to naval arms control. One of them was the Four-Power Treaty, which superseded the Anglo-Japanese Alliance with an entente between Britain, Japan, the United States, and France that

---

[103] Quoted in Ian Gow, *Military Intervention in Pre-War Japanese Politics: Admiral Kato Kanji and the 'Washington System'* (London: Routledge, 2005), 113–114.
[104] Tokyo to Washington, November 22, 1921, no. 44, Very Confidential, Urgent, doc. 153, box 65, RG 457, NARA.
[105] Quoted in Yamato, *The Washington Conference*, 48.
[106] Kajima, *The Diplomacy of Japan*, 471.
[107] Yamato, The Washington Conference, 47.

pledged the four countries to consult with each other in the event of any controversies that may arise in the Far East. In these negotiations, too, the Japanese delegation – led by Shidehara – conceded to US and British demands. At issue was the membership and geographical jurisdiction of the treaty. It was no secret that Japan desired a tripartite agreement. In a meeting with Maurice Hankey, secretary general of the British delegation, Saburi Sadao, counselor at the Japanese embassy in Washington, stated that only a tripartite agreement could supersede the alliance, because a larger agreement would dilute the original purpose of the alliance and the Japanese would consider it equivalent to abrogation.[108] The United States, however, pushed for France to be included in the entente, and Japan agreed.

Negotiations on Pacific and Far Eastern questions took place in parallel with negotiations on naval arms control and the Anglo-Japanese Alliance in Washington. Going into the conference, the United States wanted to get Japan to withdraw from Siberia, return Shantung to China, scale down its presence in Manchuria, acknowledge the Open Door principle and China's territorial integrity, and cede communications cable privileges to the United States on the island of Yap.[109] Remarkably, Tokyo conceded almost all these demands. Japan agreed to withdraw from Siberia, agreed bilaterally with China to return Shantung, and granted the United States cabling privileges on Yap as well as commercial access to former German islands under Japanese mandate. While maintaining special economic rights in Manchuria, Japan scaled down its military presence there and signed the Nine-Power Treaty, which formalized Washington's Open Door policy in China and required signatories to respect China's territorial integrity.

The Material Calculus

Japan's primary material constraint was the growing naval arms race with the United States. An agreement on naval limitation would reduce the financial resources Japan was pouring into shipbuilding. Soejima Michimasa, a senior Japanese politician, put it bluntly prior to the conference: "It is preposterous for a nation like Japan to spend so much on arms ... . America's proposal to curtail armaments is a

[108] Kajima, The Diplomacy of Japan, 568.
[109] Sprout and Sprout, *Toward a New Order*, 252.

national blessing."[110] In Washington, Shidehara thought that pushing too hard for a 70 percent ratio would alienate the Americans and "cause future naval competition, so that in the end we would be reduced below a 60 percent ratio."[111] Although Japan had prospered during World War I, by 1920 its wartime industries were in a slump and the country was headed into economic depression.[112] Worse yet was the realization that Japan's postwar recovery would largely depend on expanding economic relations with the United States.[113] Kato Tomosaburo's message to Tokyo was simple: "[W]e cannot fight a war without money. The United States is the only country with which war is probable, but it is also the only country where we can float foreign loans. Therefore, the conclusion is that we cannot fight a war with the United States."[114]

The above arguments mirror existing theoretical work on the ability of arms control to reduce the risk, scope, and cost of war. As Thomas Schelling shows, arms control works best when it produces "stabilized mutual deterrence," and for this to occur, states must have a common interest in reducing the dangers of war.[115] This condition applies to the Washington Conference. However, it does not explain the extent or nature of Japan's concessions. As noted by the naval planners of both Japan and the United States, the 60 percent ratio was a recipe for failure. Avoiding war was one thing; mortgaging Japan's future security was another, especially when the US economy was thriving and could be turned toward naval construction at short notice. Japan's territorial concessions in the Pacific and in China are even more perplexing, given the value Japanese leaders placed on overseas territories as a source of economic security.[116] Finally, Japan acquiesced in the abrogation of its alliance with Britain, its only geopolitical hedge against future US expansion in the Far East.

If Japan's goal was to avert a naval arms race, it is hard to explain why in 1922, "almost as soon as the ink was dry on the treaty," its

---

[110] Quoted in Knox, *The Eclipse*, 6–7.
[111] Washington to Tokyo, December 1, 1921, no. 127, Very Confidential, doc. 153, box 65, RG 457, NARA.
[112] Nish, *Interwar Period*, 15–16.   [113] Iriye, *After Imperialism*, 7.
[114] Quoted in Asada, *From Mahan to Pearl Harbor*, 84.
[115] Thomas C. Schelling, "The future of arms control," *Operations Research*, 9:5 (1961), 722–731.
[116] Iriye, *Pacific Estrangement*.

navy began constructing heavy cruisers and submarines, which were not covered by the treaty and had considerable value in a defensive battle.[117] By mid-1928 the Japanese navy had twelve heavy cruisers while the British had seven and the United States had none.[118] As the decade progressed, Japan's submarines began losing their defensive character and acquiring cruising radiuses of up to 20,000 miles.[119] Although the ten-year shipbuilding holiday was extended by seven years at the London Conference of 1930, Japan's naval expenditure rose sharply in the years following 1931 – even earlier by some estimates[120] – again driven by the construction of non-treaty vessels.

Scholars have argued that Japan's concessions were made possible by the agreement on non-fortification of islands in the Western Pacific.[121] The inability of the United States to fortify the Philippines and Guam would weaken the thrust of a US attack from its base in Hawaii, and would render the territories vulnerable if hostilities were to break out.[122] However, the agreement also meant that Japan could not fortify its own islands in the region, which greatly diminished any potential advantage. Roosevelt, Jr., who negotiated for the United States, thought the agreement was a net *loss* for Japan. He wrote in his diary:

[The agreement] leaves us, in my opinion, in a slightly better position than Japan. We trade certain fortifications which we would never have completed, for fortifications which they would have unquestionably completed. We retain one outpost in the Pacific of great importance [Hawaii] and they give up all but their mainland.[123]

More importantly, an agreement on Pacific defenses was a distinct *third-best* option for Tokyo. Foreign minister Uchida's instructions to his delegates prior to the conference contained no mention of island fortifications. The issue first came up in a cable from Tokyo to Kato

---

[117] Marriott, *Treaty Cruisers*, 12.   [118] Ibid., 63.
[119] See Asada, *From Mahan to Pearl Harbor*, 108.
[120] See Cassady B. Craft, "An analysis of the Washington naval agreements and the economic provisions of arms control theory," *Defence and Peace Economics*, 11:1 (2000), 127–148.
[121] Nish, *Interwar Period*, 46; George W. Downs, David M. Rocke, and Randolph M. Siverson, "Arms races and cooperation," *World Politics*, 38:1 (1985), 118–146.
[122] Knox, *The Eclipse*, 53–54.
[123] Quoted in Sprout and Sprout, *Toward a New Order*, 251.

Tomosaburo on November 28, 1921. Facing consistent opposition from both Hughes and Balfour, Kato had asked Tokyo for flexibility on the ratio. The reply, while urging him to "redouble your efforts to carry out our policy [of a 70 percent ratio]," stated that "in case of inevitable necessity" Kato should fall back on a 65 percent ratio. If, "in spite of your utmost efforts," this too failed, only then could he accept a 60 percent ratio and "endeavor to obtain *a wording which will make it clear that we have maintained equilibrium with the American fleet* by limiting its power of concentration and maneuver in the Pacific through a guarantee of reducing, or at least maintaining in status quo, the Pacific defenses."[124] Non-fortification was more a face-saver than a strategic victory or compensation. Two days later, in a private meeting with Balfour, Shidehara for the first time linked island defenses to the question of naval armaments.[125] On December 10, 1921, once all three parties agreed on the non-fortification zone, Tokyo finally relented: "[T]here is nothing to do but accept the ratio proposed by the United States."[126]

Far from being an initial objective of the Japanese (let alone the primary one, as some have argued), island fortification only entered the equation when they realized that they would not get the ratio that they considered indispensable to their national security. It was also not the case that the non-fortification clause enabled Japan to feel secure in making other concessions. Japan went into the conference prepared to make concessions on various issues, such as the Open Door, Shantung, Yap, and Siberia.[127] The non-fortification clause, therefore, does not account for Japan's cooperation at the Washington Conference. Even General Tanaka Giichi, chief army adviser to the Japanese delegation, described the clause as "incidental to the naval treaty" and not something that should "destroy the conference."[128]

---

[124] Tokyo to Washington, November 28, 1921, no. 73, Very Confidential, doc. 153, box 65, RG 457, NARA. Emphasis added.
[125] Washington to Tokyo, December 2, 1921, no. 131, Very Confidential, doc. 153, box 65, RG 457, NARA.
[126] Tokyo to Washington, December 10, 1921, no. 155, Very Confidential, Urgent, doc. 153, box 65, RG 457, NARA.
[127] Tatsuji Takeuchi, *War and Diplomacy in the Japanese Empire* (Garden City: Doubleday, Doran & Co, 1935), 233; Tokyo to Washington, July 13, 1921, no. 313, doc. 153, box 63, RG 457, NARA.
[128] Tanaka to Chief of Staff, Tokyo, January 16, 1922, no. A47, doc. 156, box 68, RG 457, NARA.

Some authors have pointed to divisions within the Japanese leader-ship as an explanation for Japan's cooperation.[129] Indeed, the two most important Japanese delegates, Kato Tomosaburo and Shidehara, both favored rapprochement with the United States and used their authority to lobby Tokyo to accept concessions. Had different leaders represented Japan, the outcomes might have been different. This counterfactual is illustrated in the person of Kato Kanji, chief naval adviser to the Japanese delegation, who staunchly opposed a lower ratio at the conference and communicated to Tokyo his fundamental disagreement on this point with Kato Tomosaburo. However, his opposition to the ratio was precisely on grounds of institutional openness, that is, it was grounded in status concerns. Thus, while there was indeed a growing civil–military divide in Japan, the basis of the division lay in differing assessments of how open the Washington system was to Japan's rise. The very appoint-ment of Kato Tomosaburo and Shidehara to represent Japan shows the importance that Tokyo placed on earning status within the inter-national order in 1921. Domestic politics, therefore, did play a role in Japan's approach to the Washington Conference, but as a vehicle for differing assessments of Japan's symbolic equality with the great powers.

An Open and Fair Great-Power Club, 1921–1922

While material constraints and domestic politics clarify the context in which Japan came to the negotiating table, Japan's concessions are best understood through the lens of IST. As a rising power seeking symbolic equality with the great powers, Japan pursued a cooperative strategy when faced with an institutionally open and procedurally fair great-power club. Not only did the great powers invite Japan into their inner circle but the Japanese delegates were also consulted at every step, and the great powers went out of their way to be fair to Japan's positions and demands. Given its status anxieties prior to the conference, Japan welcomed this change in the international order and reciprocated with sincere cooperation.

---

[129] Kawakami, *Japan's Pacific Policy*, 25; Makela, "Japanese attitudes," 44; Nish, *Interwar Period*, 50–51.

Japan's Inclusion in the "Big Three"

That the great powers were willing to open up the order's top ranks to Japan was evident in the way in which they treated Japan at the conference. Although the Japanese were initially hesitant about the conference based on past experience, Hughes was quick to assure Shidehara in July 1921 that the most important powers at the conference would be Japan, Britain, and the United States. He added that although France and Italy had hardly any interests in the Far East, they were invited so as to not hurt their feelings.[130] This was a welcome change from Paris in 1919 – Shidehara observed that "part of the present American Government authorities" had declared that "this conference shall not follow the evil course of the other."[131]

In his opening speech at the conference, Hughes emphasized that his proposal "immediately concerns the British Empire, Japan and the United States" and deferred the discussion of tonnage allowances for France and Italy to "the later consideration of the Conference."[132] All the vital discussions on naval limitation took place in private between the chief delegates of the so-called Big Three.[133] Senior statesman Elihu Root of the US delegation emphasized in a secret conversation to Hanihara Masanao of the Japanese delegation that "ultimately the standpoint of Japan would have foremost consideration."[134] Such was the impression made on the Japanese by their inclusion in the top ranks of the conference that after a month of negotiations journalist Kawakami Kiyoshi reported, "The general feeling among [the Japanese delegation] is one of gratification and confidence. They are especially gratified that the American Government, as well as the American public, has been exceedingly generous towards them."[135] Shidehara remarked to Tokyo that the attitude of the American delegates on Far Eastern questions was "felt to be one of concern lest our

---

[130] Kajima, *The Diplomacy of Japan*, 448.
[131] Washington to Tokyo, September 13, 1921, no. 608.
[132] Quoted in *Conference on the Limitation of Armament: Subcommittees, Washington, November 12, 1921–February 6, 1922* (Washington, DC: Government Printing Office, 1922), 60.
[133] Ibid., 534.
[134] Washington to Tokyo, December 2, 1921, no. 128, Very Secret, doc. 153, box 65, RG 457, NARA.
[135] Kawakami, *Japan's Pacific Policy*, 56.

national susceptibilities or dignity should be wounded."[136] Even Kato Kanji, a vocal opponent of the lower tonnage ratio for Japan, remarked to the press upon his return to Tokyo in March 1922, "The adoption of the ratio, the status quo for the Pacific Islands and the Four Power Pact meant the placing of Japan among the leaders of twentieth-century civilization."[137]

The Spirit of Mutual Concession

The Washington Conference's procedural fairness in Japan's eyes came from the consistent application of the new order's rules to Japan and the great powers. Contrary to Japan's status anxieties, the great powers did not seek to isolate Japan but in fact made significant concessions themselves. Prior to the conference, Shidehara assessed that Hughes was "anxious to display a fair attitude towards all the participating powers" and Japan should in the same spirit not try to restrict the conference agenda.[138] Tokyo conceded that although Japan needed a minimum level of military power for national defense, if the great powers were to offer cuts in their militaries "in a spirit of mutual concession," then "Japan will not necessarily persist in this [military buildup]."[139]

The fairness of the Hughes proposal lay in the fact that it eliminated vastly greater tonnage for the United States compared to Britain and Japan. US naval analyst Dudley Knox observed that the United States could have easily insisted that the capital-ship ratio apply not just to auxiliaries but also to naval bases and other aspects of sea power. "But with noteworthy generosity America offered to give up a certain first place (with no close second) in sea power and a positive ability to safeguard American interests the world over – and furthermore volunteered to do so at stupendous financial loss to herself."[140] British correspondent Charles Repington noted that the Hughes plan,

---

[136] Washington to Tokyo, December 1, 1921, no. 127, Very Confidential, doc. 153, box 65, RG 457, NARA.
[137] Quoted in Gow, *Military Intervention*, 151.
[138] Washington to Tokyo, September 13, 1921, no. 608.
[139] Tokyo to Washington, October 20, 1921, no. 537, Very Confidential, doc. 153, box 64, RG 457, NARA.
[140] Knox, *The Eclipse*, 41–42.

"however drastic, seems fair and sincere, and America is offering to scrap ships upon which she has spent \$880,000,000 already."[141] Ambassador Hayashi cabled Tokyo: "As the United States was the first to take such decisive steps as to propose the reduction of world armaments, the best policy appears to be to approve the whole immediately from a general point of view without making too many technical reservations."[142] Root reminded Hanihara that "America had first of all indicated her resolve to limit actually the power of her own navy, which but made her sincerity clear."[143]

Kato Tomosaburo understood that the Hughes plan was unassailable and Japan had to accept it. "It is simply impossible to oppose the American plan," he said. "If we oppose it, we'll have to pay a heavy price. World public opinion would not allow it."[144] Kato Kanji later recalled that although Kato Tomosaburo "was extremely concerned because of the vast scale of the [Hughes] proposals and their influence not merely on Japan's material strength but on the personnel and the morale of the future navy," he "resolved to respond to the spirit of the proposal."[145] Even during difficult negotiations over the ratio with the great powers, Kato Tomosaburo wrote to Tokyo, "The American way is on the whole fair-minded."[146] Contrary to Japanese expectations, he confirmed, "Anglo-American oppression is something we delegates at Washington have never imagined."[147]

Attaining Procedural Fairness

In areas where the great powers were less willing to treat Japan consistently as an equal, Tokyo demanded and attained procedural fairness. In negotiations over the Four-Power Treaty between the United States, Britain, Japan, and France, the term "insular possessions" quickly became controversial because, according to Hughes and Balfour, it included the islands of Japan proper.[148] This interpretation

[141] Repington, *After the War*, 432.
[142] London to Washington, November 14, 1921, no. 463, doc. 153, box 65, RG 457, NARA.
[143] Washington to Tokyo, December 2, 1921, no. 128.
[144] Quoted in Asada, *From Mahan to Pearl Harbor*, 73.
[145] Quoted in Gow, *Military Intervention*, 109–110.
[146] Quoted in Asada, *From Mahan to Pearl Harbor*, 87.   [147] Ibid.
[148] Washington to Tokyo, December 9, 1921, no. 179, Very Confidential, doc. 153, box 65, RG 457, NARA.

technically obligated Japan, when facing a threat to its mainland, to first consult the other powers, but did not place the same obligation on any of them to consult Japan in a similar situation. Although Hughes and Balfour pointed out that substantively this would hardly rule out any actions Japan took in self-defense, Shidehara objected that "national feeling" in Japan would oppose the inclusion of only Japan's main territory and not those of the other powers.[149] Balfour argued that it would be hard to explain to the British public why Australia was included in the treaty and Japan proper was not. Shidehara immediately resented being equated to a British Dominion and turned the question around, asking if Washington and London would not mind having the continental US and Canada be covered by the treaty.[150] Hughes replied that doing so would necessitate expanding the entente to include many more countries, which the Japanese clearly did not want.

Finding themselves cornered, the Japanese delegates agreed to the text of the treaty, but subsequently faced considerable backlash from Tokyo. "The fact of Japan alone bearing this obligation must be stigmatized as an inequality," argued Tokyo.[151] Uchida was unmoved when the US ambassador in Tokyo approached him and suggested that the debate over the inclusion or exclusion of Japan proper was a "ridiculous question."[152] Uchida replied that it was "a most important question," for three reasons: the other contracting parties did not have their mainland included; Japan was being equated to British Dominions such as Australia and New Zealand; and "Japan could herself attend to the matter of the defense of Japan."[153] As negotiations proceeded, Tokyo chastised its delegates for their "desire to dispose of these questions now by hasty decisions and merely to convenience other countries."[154] The government refused to accept the treaty as signed and instructed its delegates to either renegotiate to exclude Australia and New Zealand in exchange for Japan proper's exclusion or "find some other means of saving the situation which we consider is

---

[149] Ibid.   [150] Ibid.
[151] Tokyo to Washington, December 17, 1921, no. 198, Very Confidential, Urgent, doc. 153, box 65, RG 457, NARA.
[152] Tokyo to Washington, December 27, 1921, no. 248, doc. 153, box 66, RG 457, NARA.
[153] Ibid.
[154] Tokyo to Washington, January 12, 1922, no. 306, Very Confidential, doc. 153, box 66, RG 457, NARA.

very serious."[155] Ultimately, the Japanese delegates were able to clarify in a supplementary treaty that the Four-Power Treaty did not include Japan proper.[156]

A similar situation arose in the negotiations over naval limitation. After agreeing on maintaining the status quo on island fortifications, Britain and the United States sought to exclude specific territories of their own and include specific territories belonging to Japan. Tokyo once again objected to the "extreme unfairness" of the great powers,[157] and in this, was joined by General Tanaka, the chief army delegate at the conference, who described the situation as "a grave matter affecting the dignity of Japan."[158] Tokyo admitted that from a purely military point of view, the great powers' proposal was not significant.[159] However, the proposal was "really a contempt of international good faith" and a matter of "national feeling and sentiment."[160] The government was clear that in the context of the overall treaty, Japan was being asked to make the greater sacrifice:

It is said that when the agreement was made the British and American plenipotentiaries consented to it with hardship in order to lessen the menace from Great Britain and the United States which was felt by Japan, but did not Japan herself in making the agreement undergo greater hardship than Great Britain and the United States by consenting to the 60% ratio?[161]

Negotiations came to the brink over the inclusion of the Amami-Oshima and Bonin islands in the zone where no further fortifications would be allowed. Tokyo pushed Kato Tomosaburo hard to have them excluded, and he threatened to resign. However, he confided to his assistant that resigning would be an easy way to save his own reputation, but it would not save the nation: "Japan must not invite isolation."[162] In the end, Japan conceded the two islands in return for the United States including the Aleutian Islands and Britain including its territories south of the Equator except for Australia and New Zealand.

---

[155] Quoted in Kajima, *The Diplomacy of Japan*, 588.
[156] Yamato, *The Washington Conference*, 124.
[157] Tokyo to Washington, January 15, 1922, no. 321, Very Urgent, Very Confidential, doc. 153, box 66, RG 457, NARA.
[158] Washington to Tokyo, January 11, 1922, no. A43, doc. 156, box 68, RG 457, NARA.
[159] Tokyo to Washington, January 15, 1922, no. 321.   [160] Ibid.   [161] Ibid.
[162] Quoted in Yamato, *The Washington Conference*, 90.

Cooperation or Isolation

Since the early twentieth century, Japanese leaders had felt increasingly isolated, despite their efforts to follow the rules and procedures of the international order.[163] The Washington Conference sought to create a new type of diplomatic system that offered Japan a golden opportunity to join the ranks of the great powers. Despite various ideological and political divisions among Japanese leaders, there was widespread agreement that Japan had to cooperate with the great powers in order to avoid isolation. Even those concerned about the security implications of an unrestricted naval race viewed security as a necessary condition of maintaining Japan's status among the great powers. As Soejima observed prior to the conference,

Whether Japan can keep her honorable position in the international intercourse, ranking, as she does, on an equal footing with any of the great powers of the world; or whether she will be relegated to a second or third rate nation after an unforeseen calamity that may possibly result if she continues her naval expansion unrestrictedly, all depends upon the enthusiasm and determination in which Japan will attend the Pacific Conference.[164]

At the conference, viewing the emergent Washington system as an international order that was open to Japan's inclusion in its top ranks, and one whose procedures were ultimately fair and unbiased with regard to Japan, Kato Tomosaburo and Shidehara engaged in a strategy of cooperation in order to attain and maintain symbolic equality with the great powers. The alternative was diplomatic isolation and international blame for destroying a good-faith attempt at international peace.[165] At the conference, while the chief delegates of the Big Three negotiated the naval ratio, the US government reached out to Japanese financiers through an American banker and learned that "the Japanese delegation would compromise, if necessary to avoid a rupture and the complete isolation of the Island Empire."[166] Meanwhile, Kato Tomosaburo cabled Tokyo, "it is crystal clear that our country must bear the sole responsibility if we should clash with the United States on

---

[163] Iriye, *Across the Pacific*, 114.   [164] Quoted in Knox, *The Eclipse*, 6.
[165] Tokyo to Washington, July 13, 1921, no. 289, Very Confidential, doc. 153, box 63, RG 457, NARA.
[166] Diary of Chandler P. Anderson, quoted in Sprout and Sprout, *Toward a New Order*, 169.

the question of naval armament limitation and lead the conference to failure."[167]

Even when it came to the Anglo-Japanese Alliance, Shidehara admitted that Japan's desire to continue the alliance or renegotiate it as a tripartite agreement with the United States was "not in expectation of any help from the contracting countries in time of war; *but solely to stand in a group with Great Britain, or with Great Britain and America,* to act in concert with them, and mutually promise moral support, thereby averting Japan's international isolation."[168] Tokyo agreed that not only was it important to stand in a group with these powers, but that – in response to an American suggestion – France could be included in the treaty, making it an exclusive club of "four Powers which have important interests in the Pacific, are great naval Powers and have hitherto had mutual relations of agreement or treaty."[169] (Italy did not meet these criteria and was, therefore, excluded from the treaty, despite repeatedly expressing a desire to join it.)[170]

Expanding the Criteria for Naval Prowess, 1922 onward

On balance, the treaties signed in Washington were well received in Japan. The public and a number of newspapers were pleased at the promised reduction in naval expenditure and potential resolution of various outstanding issues in the Far East.[171] The conference also had its critics. The *Hochi,* a widely circulated newspaper, declared, "Japan has sustained such a loss through the conference as she would have suffered had she been defeated in her desperate war with Russia."[172] The *Yorodzu* described the conference as "the handkerchief which a magician uses to spellbind the spectators" while its real purpose was to "submerge the Anglo-Japanese Alliance."[173] The loss of the

[167] Quoted in Kajima, *The Diplomacy of Japan,* 473.
[168] Washington to Tokyo, November 30, 1921, no. 120, Urgent, Very Secret, doc. 153, box 65, RG 457, NARA, emphasis added.
[169] Washington to London, December 1921, no. 608, Urgent, doc. 153, box 65, RG 457, NARA.
[170] See Washington to Tokyo, December 9, 1921, no. 179.
[171] Kawakami, *Japan's Pacific Policy,* 30–31.
[172] Toyokichi Iyenaga, "How Japan views the arms conference," *Current History,* 16:1 (1922), 22–25.
[173] Ibid., 22.

alliance – a major source of status for Japan – was felt keenly in various quarters. Frederick Moore, an American adviser employed by Japan's foreign ministry and member of the Japanese delegation at the Washington Conference, observed, "The Japanese were shocked by the [alliance's] termination. The readiness of the British to meet American wishes without serious contention altered their opinion of that Power [i.e. Britain]."[174]

Japanese military advisers at the Washington Conference had been less sanguine than their chief (civilian) delegates in their view of the emerging order. General Tanaka had offered an assessment at the end of December 1921:

As this conference advances the spirit of America with respect to it become[s] clear. In other words there is a feeling that it is step by step succeeding with its objectives of doing away with the Anglo-Japanese alliance which it dislikes, limiting the Japanese navy, cutting its power of maneuver in the Pacific, and expelling the influence of Japan from China and Siberia. This is very regrettable.[175]

After the conference, the unequal naval ratio provoked the ire of key figures in the navy.[176] The most vocal and influential among them was Kato Kanji. At the Washington Conference, while chief delegate Kato Tomosaburo negotiated the ratio with his counterparts, Kato Kanji had sent a secret telegram to Tokyo that presaged the changing views of what came to be known as the navy's "fleet faction" after 1921:

The United States and Great Britain are banding together in oppressing Japan. Mutual compromise and give-and-take are something these powers simply don't have in mind. In our view, their intention obviously is to deprive the Imperial Navy of its predominance in the Orient. They are threatening Japan by holding it responsible for wrecking the conference. To yield to such an overbearing attitude is an utter humiliation.[177]

Where Kato Tomosaburo and Shidehara saw an open and fair order with opportunities for Japan to be an equal member of the great-power

---

[174] Frederick Moore, *With Japan's Leaders: An Intimate Record of Fourteen Years as Counsellor to the Japanese Government, Ending December 7, 1941* (New York: Charles Scribner's Sons, 1942), 61.
[175] Washington to Tokyo, December 29, 1921, no. A34, doc. 156, box 68, RG 457, NARA.
[176] Sprout and Sprout, *Toward a New Order*, 261–262.
[177] Quoted in Asada, *From Mahan to Pearl Harbor*, 87.

club, Kato Kanji saw only hypocrisy and exclusion. In a second telegram, Kato Kanji had written, "The whole matter involves Japan's
right of self defense."[178] His was a view rooted primarily in status
considerations. He believed that Japan was entitled *in principle* to
equality with the great powers, that is, "a ratio of 10:10."[179] A 70
percent ratio was already a major concession; a 60 percent ratio
represented "inequality and fetters" that hurt Japan's "national
prestige."[180]

At no point in the 1920s did Kato Kanji actually undermine the
Washington system by breaking its rules. He publicly praised the
conference and believed in arms limitation as a legitimate goal.
However, as Ian Gow notes, "[Kato] saw the imposition of 'inferior
ratios' as a means of permanently relegating another power to an
inferior position on the basis of some transient superiority. Navies in
any case were important for prestige as well as conflict and an inferior
ratio effectively meant, for Kato and many others, second rank
status."[181] The fleet faction saw the Washington system as closing
off Japan's access to the great-power club. An inferior ratio would
permanently lock Japan into a category below the one that the United
States and Britain occupied in the Washington system. It was a point of
principle for Kato Kanji and his colleagues that even though Japan did
not have the resources to construct battleships at parity with the United
States and Britain, it should not be denied the right to do so.[182] What
stung the fleet faction even more was the diligence with which the
civilian leadership – under Kato Tomosaburo as prime minister from
June 1922 – followed the rules of the Washington system. Japan
abandoned fleet expansion plans, scrapped a number of older ships,
canceled plans for the construction of new ships, laid off 7,500 officers,
and retired nine out of ten vice admirals.[183] The navy was left with
only six battleships and four cruisers.

In the years that followed, the fleet faction became increasingly
powerful, partly because of changes in societal and elite evaluations
of the international order (see below). In the fleet faction's eyes, the
great powers had treated Japan unfairly at the Washington
Conference, thereby restricting it permanently to second-tier status –

---

[178] Ibid., emphasis added.   [179] Quoted in ibid., 86.   [180] Ibid.
[181] Gow, *Military Intervention*, 140.   [182] Ibid.
[183] Asada, *From Mahan to Pearl Harbor*, 99–100.

the international order was both unfair and closed. Although IST predicts that a state in this situation would challenge the international order, the fleet faction neither represented nor controlled the Japanese state. Instead, the fleet faction chose to set Japan up for equality in future negotiations within the international order. They followed the rules of the Washington system but strove to build capability in areas not covered by the treaty, so that when the time came for the Washington system to incorporate those areas, the definition of existing strength – the standard used by the United States to measure tonnage at the Washington Conference – would yield a more favorable ratio for Japan. This amounted to a strategy of *expansion*, or introducing new criteria by which Japan could claim symbolic equality with the great powers.

The navy worked not just on quantitative buildup but also on qualitative improvements. The heavy cruisers Japan built were "faster, had a greater cruising radius, and were more heavily gunned than their American counterparts."[184] To counter US naval superiority, the Japanese navy General Staff worked to perfect its strategy of "using a few to conquer many," which had proved advantageous in the asymmetrical war against Russia in 1905.[185] In the 1920s, this involved developing long-range submarines, night combat techniques designed for surprise attacks, and tactics for striking adversaries early and decisively at a distance from which they could not retaliate.[186] In addition, the navy focused heavily on training and repeated drills, including night drills.

In a manner typical of introducing new attributes of status to compensate for weakness in traditionally valued areas, Japanese naval leaders emphasized the spiritual and psychological qualities of their officers as a way of asserting superiority over the US navy. Kato Kanji argued that Japan must mobilize its "willpower" against the US navy's physical might, "turning an impossibility into a possibility."[187] All these efforts were designed to develop capabilities that could match those of the great powers, but not along the dimensions on which the great powers themselves were superior since those were forbidden by the rules of the Washington system.

---

[184] Ibid., 106.   [185] Evans and Peattie, *Kaigun*, 206.   [186] Ibid., 206–207.
[187] Asada, *From Mahan to Pearl Harbor*, 179.

Seen through the lens of IST, the navy's post-conference investment in heavy cruisers, submarines, torpedo boats, and other auxiliaries at a time when economic conditions were weak is less puzzling than a strictly materialist interpretation would suggest. Given that previous naval estimates had held that 70 percent of US tonnage would be the minimum requirement for Japan's defense, the gap between what Japan wanted and what Japan accepted (a 60 percent quota) came to approximately 50,000 tons, or two capital ships. However, the extent to which Japan invested in alternative aspects of naval power went well beyond the cost and organizational effort required to build and operate two capital ships. Clearly, the fleet faction's motivation was not defense alone but an effort to build capability in non-treaty areas so as to claim equal rank with the great powers.

Building up to an Institutional Challenge, 1924–1930

In parallel to changes in naval assessments, broader evaluations of the Washington system underwent a drastic change with the passing of the Immigration Act in the United States in May 1924. Those in the navy who saw the Washington system as already unequal in its treatment of Japan found support among many members of the elite and the public for whom the exclusion of Japanese from immigration to the United States dramatically altered the openness and fairness of the international order.

Race and the Washington System

Race was deeply implicated in Japan's uncertain position in the international order. Experiences of Western opprobrium in the wake of Japan's victories against China in 1895 and Russia in 1905 had led Japanese leaders to suspect that they would not be welcomed into the great-power club with open arms.[188] Ito Miyoji, a member of the emperor's Privy Council, spoke for many elites when he said to a German friend, regarding Western apprehensions over a Russo-Japanese war in 1904: "Of course, what is really wrong with us is that we have yellow skins. If our skins were as white as yours, the whole

---

[188] Iriye, *After Imperialism*, 6.

world would rejoice at our calling a halt to Russia's inexorable aggression."[189]

The emergence of a strong anti-Japanese movement on the US Pacific coast – mainly in California – at the turn of the twentieth century greatly shaped Japanese judgments of the Western-dominated international order. Anti-Japanese Californians had begun calling for the 1882 ban on Chinese immigration to be extended to all Asian peoples, including Japanese.[190] To preempt this outcome, Tokyo proposed to voluntarily restrict the flow of immigrants to the United States in exchange for no explicit restrictions on Japanese immigration. The United States agreed, and the diplomatic notes exchanged to this effect came to be known as the Gentlemen's Agreement. Although the agreement was bilateral, given the paucity of American emigration to Japan, it was in fact a face-saving measure for Japan.[191]

American racism mattered to Japanese elites because it directly undermined Japan's major-power identity as a civilized nation. "What stamp of civilization will these people bring to us when they come to our shores?" asked legislators on the floor of California House.[192] Given Japan's goal of "leaving Asia," it was particularly galling when the American press frequently portrayed the Japanese as equal to or worse than the Chinese.[193] Foreign minister Kato Takaaki observed, in 1915, "We would not mind disabilities if they were equally applicable to all nations. We are not vain enough to consider ourselves at the very forefront of enlightenment; we know that we still have much to learn from the West. But we thought ourselves ahead of any other Asiatic people and as good as some of the European nations."[194] The lumping together of the Japanese with other Asian nations, and the preferential treatment given by Americans to "third-rate southern and eastern European nations" were a direct blow to Japan's claim to be an equal member of the great-power club.[195]

---

[189] Duus, *The Rise of Modern Japan*, 134.
[190] Toyokichi Iyenaga and Kenoske Sato, *Japan and the California Problem* (New York and London: G. P. Putnam's Sons, 1921), 73.
[191] Hirobe, *Japanese Pride*, 4–5.   [192] Hayes, "Japanese exclusion," 4.
[193] Albert G. Burnett, "Misunderstanding of Eastern and Western states regarding Oriental immigration," *The Annals of the American Academy of Political and Social Science*, 34:2 (1909), 37–41.
[194] The New York Times, "Says Japan is moderate: Seeks her share in China, but no monopoly, Baron Kato asserts," March 19, 1915.
[195] *Nichibei Shimbun* editorial from 1913, quoted in Yuji Ichioka, "The early Japanese immigrant quest for citizenship: The background of the 1922 Ozawa case," *Amerasia*, 4:2 (1977), 1–22.

Although the immigration issue had taken a back seat during World War I, it did not go away. Less than two months before the Washington Conference, Shidehara raised the "California question" with Hughes, who reportedly suggested it would be best to wait until the conference was over, lest "the anti-Japanese agitators on the Pacific coast, in order to oppose a solution of that question ... used the Yap [Island] question to arouse popular feelings."[196] Shidehara agreed, and added prophetically, "If there were no progress towards a solution of this question there would be an outbreak of popular dissatisfaction which ... might no longer permit a postponement of the solution of this question."[197] At the conference, General Tanaka, who felt that Japan had made far too many concessions to the great powers, observed, "If the basis of failure in this conference is the conflict of races and the insufficiency of the national power of Japan there is no use indulging in vain indignation, but being actually here and seeing the actual facts it is really impossible not to say these things."[198]

Japanese Exclusion and the US Immigration Act of 1924

Since 1911, the US legislature had passed laws that increasingly restricted immigration from Asian countries, with the exception of Japan. Each law carefully omitted any mention of "immigrants ineligible to citizenship," choosing instead to designate geographical exclusion zones for non-European immigrants and quotas for Europeans.[199] In December 1923, for the very first time, it appeared that Congress intended to leave the controversial phrase in the bill. The Japanese press and elites were initially impassive, expecting that as per past practice, the US executive would pressure the legislature to keep Japanese sensitivities in mind.[200] Nonetheless, Ambassador Hanihara in Washington – who had also been present at the Washington Conference – wrote to Secretary of State Hughes that such a measure would be "arbitrary and unjust discrimination reflecting upon the

---

[196] Washington to Tokyo, September 17, 1921, no. 615, doc. 153, box 64, RG 457, NARA.
[197] Ibid.   [198] Tanaka to Chief of Staff, Tokyo, December 29, 1921, no. A34.
[199] Raymond Leslie Buell, "Again the Yellow Peril," *Foreign Affairs* (December 1923), reprinted in Julia E. Johnsen (ed.), *The Reference Shelf, Vol. III, No. 4: Japanese Exclusion* (New York: The H. W. Wilson Company, 1925), 33–50.
[200] Makela, "Japanese attitudes," 19–20.

character of the people of a nation, which is entitled to every respect and consideration of the civilized world."[201]

Hanihara reminded Hughes that Japan had scrupulously met the conditions of the Gentlemen's Agreement, and that although to suffer such discrimination despite cooperating with the United States was "mortifying," the Japanese were "exercising utmost forbearance" and relying on "the high sense of justice and fair-play of the American Government and people" to ensure that this law did not come to pass. He added that the question was not one of material interests but of Japan's status:

To Japan the question is not one of expediency, but of principle. To her the mere fact that a few hundreds or thousands of her nationals will or will not be admitted into the domains of other countries is immaterial ... The important question is whether Japan as a nation is or is not entitled to the proper respect and consideration of other nations.[202]

Hughes suggested that Hanihara address a letter to him clearly stating the Japanese position, which Hughes could then convey to Congress in an effort to lobby it to amend the bill. Hanihara complied, handing over a letter to Hughes on April 11, 1924, in which he warned of "grave consequences" that the law would create for US–Japan relations.[203] To the dismay of both statesmen, exclusionist members of Congress and the American press seized upon this phrase and portrayed it as a threat and an attempt by Japan to interfere in US domestic affairs. This interpretation galvanized both houses of Congress to pass the bill in a matter of four days after receiving the letter.[204]

Hughes found the exclusion clause "entirely unnecessary," especially in the context of "the attitude taken by Japan at the Conference on the Limitation of Armament held at Washington, and the spirit of friendship and mutual confidence then evoked."[205] On May 23, 1924, President Calvin Coolidge signed the bill into law and publicly regretted "the impossibility of severing from it the exclusion

---

[201] Hanihara to Hughes, January 15, 1924, *Foreign Relations of the United States (FRUS), Vol. II* (Washington: Government Printing Office, 1939), 335.
[202] Ibid., 336.   [203] Hanihara to Hughes, April 10, 1924, FRUS (II), 373.
[204] Hughes to Woods, April 15, 1924, FRUS (II), 375; "Memorandum of Conversation," April 15, 1921, FRUS (II), 379–380.
[205] Hughes to Coolidge, May 23, 1924, FRUS (II), 391–392.

provision which, in the light of existing law, affects especially the Japanese."[206] From Tokyo's perspective, Japan had followed all the rules laid out by Washington, and was still singled out for discrimination in the 1924 law. In effect, Japan was no longer a "Western" great power in Asia, having been grouped with other already excluded Asian nations. In a memorandum of protest, the Japanese government wrote, "The patient, loyal, and scrupulous observance by Japan for more than sixteen years, of these self-denying regulations [the Gentlemen's Agreement], in the interest of good relations between the two countries, now seems to have been wasted."[207] Years of cooperation with the United States out of a fear of isolation had ended in precisely what Japan had feared most: isolation. It was impossible to claim symbolic equality with the great-power club when its foremost member treated one's citizens with racial contempt and discrimination. Hughes presciently observed that the exclusion clause had "undone the work of the Washington Conference and implanted the seeds of antagonism which are sure to bear fruit in the future."[208]

Exclusion's Impact on Japanese Perceptions

The 1924 immigration law dealt a severe blow to Japan's major-power identity. Scholar Hori Mitsukame publicly stated that the law's effect "would be to take away Japan's position in the world, denying her right to international existence and to the pursuit of her own happiness as a respectable member of the family of nations."[209] The *Osaka Mainichi* declared, "In matters relating to material losses or gains, we might endure, according to circumstances. But when the honor and dignity of our nation are called into question, we cannot remain silent."[210] George Rea, a journalist intimately familiar with the Far East, warned of the momentous impact exclusion would have on Japan's approach to the international order:

It does not require any great political prescience to sense that if Japan is affronted and rejected by the west [sic] and the truth is brought home to her

---

[206] Hughes to Woods, May 26, 1924, FRUS (II), 396.
[207] Hanihara to Hughes, May 31, 1924, FRUS (II), 401.
[208] Quoted in Sean Brawley, *The White Peril: Foreign Relations and Asian Immigration to Australasia and North America 1919–1978* (Sydney: University of New South Wales Press, 1995), 88.
[209] Quoted in Makela, "Japanese attitudes," 98.   [210] Quoted in ibid., 1.

people that they can never hope for full recognition of their claim to equality, a revulsion of feeling will sweep over the empire that must inevitably lead to the formulation of new policies and a new outlook upon the future.[211]

Moore (American adviser to Japan's foreign ministry) witnessed the law have "a profound effect upon the nation" and severely hurt the sentiments of the government and the public, so much so that when Moore's contract came to an end in 1926, the Japanese government declined to renew it, under criticism "for having an American in its diplomatic service."[212]

The Japanese public reacted with considerable outrage. "Don't look down upon us as a small nation! We are the possessors of the Yamato Spirit (*Yamato Damashii*) which has been handed down for thousands of years," declared a letter delivered to the US consulate in Nagasaki in June 1924, signed "Blood and Iron."[213] The *Kokumin* newspaper wrote that the law rendered Japan "inferior even to Chinese bandits."[214] Various right-wing groups emerged in this moment, while existing groups received a shot in the arm via the sudden turn in public mood.[215] A mass movement emerged in mid-1924, peaking with protests in thirty-eight out of Japan's forty-six prefectures on July 1, labeled "National Humiliation Day," the date on which the law went into effect in the United States.[216]

Japanese elites, initially outraged, tried to discourage public protest in an effort to repair diplomatic relations with Washington. Shidehara, now foreign minister, was at pains to explain to Diet members that the issue was not one of Japan's racial inferiority. According to him, the American contention was that "the Japanese are to the Americans what oil is to water. Neither oil nor water can be said to be superior or inferior to the other, but the fact is that in no case can oil dissolve and merge in water."[217] This proved a tough sell. Diet member Hatoyama Ichiro asked Shidehara if he sincerely believed "that international relations, so far as Japan is concerned, are entering an era of cooperation with other countries, when Japan herself is subjected to all manner of humiliation, especially by America, which looks down upon

[211] George Bronson Rea, "Grave consequences," *Far Eastern Review*, 20 (1924), 199–200, reprinted in Johnsen (ed.), *The Reference Shelf*, 106–110.
[212] Moore, *With Japan's Leaders*, 1.
[213] Quoted in Makela, "Japanese attitudes," 159.   [214] Quoted in ibid., 99.
[215] Iriye, *After Imperialism*, 36.   [216] Makela, "Japanese attitudes," 161.
[217] Caffery to Hughes, July 8, 1924, FRUS (II), 409.

us as an inferior nation, as demonstrated by the abolition of the Gentlemen's Agreement."[218] Even the *Gaiko Jiho*, a semi-official publication associated with Shidehara's own ministry, severely criticized the exclusion of Japanese from America.[219] Japanese leaders were ready to admit that the issue was primarily "a sentimental matter,"[220] but that was precisely the point – as a survey of Japanese elites published by *The Japan Times and Mail* in October 1924 showed, sixty-two out of sixty-six respondents identified racial prejudice as a factor behind the US law.[221] Japan did not suffer any economic losses due to the law, nor was its security threatened. The matter was one of exclusion and unfairness, which called into question the entire purpose of trying to be counted among the great powers by cooperating extensively with the Washington system.

Changing Assessments of the Washington System

After 1924, the Washington system began losing its legitimacy in Japan. Legalized racial exclusion in America officially confirmed that Japan would never have a seat at the great-power table – the international order was effectively closed. From Japan's perspective, it was also unfair in the way it privileged smaller white European nations and clubbed Japan with the rest of Asia that Japan had sought to leave behind. As foreign minister Kato Takaaki had observed a decade earlier (see above), uniform exclusion of all immigrants would have been understandable, but preferential treatment given to immigrants from countries clearly inferior to Japan (from Japan's perspective) was unacceptable.

The assessment of the international order as closed and unfair gradually grew among elites and the public. The emergence of right-wing groups that denounced the United States' "white imperialism" was a potent counterweight to the attempts of moderates such as Shidehara to smooth things over.[222] Two related strands of thinking in particular were empowered by the events of 1924. Both proceeded from the view that the Washington system was a white-sponsored and white-dominated system designed to keep Japan suppressed. One strand concluded that instead of following the whites, Japan should

[218] Quoted in Makela, "Japanese attitudes," 252–253.
[219] Hirobe, *Japanese Pride*, 25–26.
[220] Prime Minister Kato Takaaki, quoted in Makela, "Japanese attitudes," 258.
[221] Makela, "Japanese attitudes," 247–248.   [222] Iriye, *After Imperialism*, 36.

build solidarity and alliances with Asian nations in order to shore up Japan's international stature.[223] The other argued that the West was able to bully Japan and exclude it because Japan was militarily weak; therefore, building a strong military would ensure that Japan could at least hold its own in an unjust and unequal international order.[224] Japan's postwar dilemma, described by MacMillan as "whether to trust the white powers, work with them in strengthening the international order, or assume that it had better look out for itself,"[225] had so far resolved itself in favor of cooperative diplomacy. Now, new and powerful voices began to speak of autarky, pan-Asianism, and militarism.

Japan's changing approach to the Washington system was evident at the International Opium Conference in Geneva in November 1924. When British delegates rejected a Japanese proposal, the Japanese delegates surprised their counterparts with an unusually strong reaction, accusing the British of discrimination and slandering Japan in front of the international community. British diplomats privately noted Japan's sensitivity at being treated as a second-class power, particularly its objection to concerns about verifying Japanese certificates of transshipment for opium raised by a "little island like Hong Kong."[226] In late 1924, word spread that the United States and Britain might soon organize a second arms limitation conference. The *Yamato* newspaper's reaction typified the manner in which the Washington system had started to lose its legitimacy in Japan. "It may be wrong to say that the chief motive of America for convening the Washington Conference was to reduce Japan to a position of isolation internationally," said the editorial, "but there is no doubt that this was one of the objectives she had in mind."[227]

In 1925, the Japanese navy produced a report on the lessons of the Washington Conference, which made three major observations. First, poor preparations ahead of the conference had relegated Japan to a passive role and resulted in failure. Second, public opinion needed to be united behind Japan's interests at any future conference. Third, and finally, "the utmost caution must be taken never again to be

---

[223] Iriye, *Across the Pacific*, 153; Makela, "Japanese attitudes," 207.
[224] Hirobe, *Japanese Pride*, 23. [225] MacMillan, *Paris 1919*, 313.
[226] Harumi Goto-Shibata, "The International Opium Conference of 1924–25 and Japan," *Modern Asian Studies*, 36:4 (2002), 969–991.
[227] Quoted in Makela, "Japanese attitudes," 261.

confronted by joint Anglo-American coercion."[228] In fact, Japan had been well prepared going into the Washington Conference, with a naval committee dedicated to studying arms limitation from June 1919 onward.[229] Japanese diplomats had played an active role in the conference, and according to some assessments, had won a major concession in terms of the non-fortification of islands. The experiences of 1924 had, however, deeply colored the navy's judgment of the legitimacy of the entire Washington system, and Japan's performance and achievements of just four years prior had begun to feel hollow. In the words of senior statesman Ishii Kikujiro, who would lead the Japanese delegation at the Geneva Naval Conference in 1927, "whether correct or not, the Japanese people resent the 'inferior ratio' allocated to Japan at Washington and considered it a slight against them."[230]

A Closed and Unfair Great-Power Club

By 1927, Japanese leaders were increasingly chafing against the Washington system and sought to firmly establish a 70 percent ratio for Japan in the category of auxiliaries, which were the subject of a conference in Geneva. David Carlton echoes the scholarly consensus on the Geneva Conference being "one of the most dramatically unsuccessful international gatherings of the twentieth century."[231] France and Italy rejected President Coolidge's invitation, alleging that the conference was too narrowly focused on naval limitation. The conference itself failed due to irreconcilable differences between the United States and Britain. Japan played a subdued role, though major divisions emerged within the Japanese delegation between the civilian negotiators and their naval advisers who opposed anything less than a 70 percent ratio in auxiliaries.[232] Tokyo did not help matters by bypassing the civilian delegates and issuing instructions directly to the chief naval adviser of the delegation. Vice Minister of the Navy Osumi Mineo was instrumental in this process. He regarded the Washington system "a most flagrant oppression" of Japan,[233] so much so that

---

[228] Quoted in Gow, *Military Intervention*, 161.
[229] Gow, *Military Intervention*, 79.   [230] Quoted in ibid., 164.
[231] David Carlton, "Great Britain and the Coolidge Naval Disarmament Conference of 1927," *Political Science Quarterly*, 83:4 (1968), 573–598.
[232] Asada, "From Washington to London," 163.   [233] Quoted in ibid., 164.

when the Japanese delegation at Geneva proposed accepting 65 percent as a compromise, Osumi called the offer "most deplorable" and demanded that the delegates "must persist to the bitter end in their demand for a 70 per cent ratio."[234] If the demand was not met, Osumi reasoned, "a worst case scenario might arise, ultimately forcing us to resolve to fight to the death."[235]

In September 1928, the navy's research committee on arms limitation put together a preparatory report for the next naval conference. The majority opinion viewed the Washington system, including the capital-ship ratio, as having benefited Japan. The minority view emphasized the imposition of the inferior ratio on Japan by the great powers. Both views, however, concurred that the 70 percent ratio was "absolutely necessary for the nation's defence, nay for its very existence," and called for it to be "adhered to without any bargaining at the next conference."[236] As the world headed into the Great Depression, in March 1929, Kato Kanji spearheaded a new and ambitious construction plan for various types of vessels to be completed by 1936, the year the Washington Naval Treaty was set to expire.[237]

Having learned from its mistakes at the Washington Conference, the fleet faction in the navy undertook a more coordinated and concerted effort to lobby the civilian leadership and public in the run-up to the next conference in London.[238] It was not difficult to convince a country still resentful of exclusion at the hands of the Americans that Japan had to fight for its rights. Every year on July 1, public protests would reiterate Japan's National Humiliation Day. The foreign ministry's civilian journal and the Japanese press would periodically publish articles critical of Japanese exclusion. In August 1928, for example, the *Hochi* editorialized that "exclusion places us on a par with half-civilized and inferior races."[239] Japanese diplomats raised the exclusion issue at every major meeting with the United States after 1924, but hesitantly, so as not to be accused of meddling in US domestic affairs.[240] The Washington system became impossible to separate from the unfair treatment meted out to the Japanese by Washington itself.

---

[234] Quoted in ibid., 167.   [235] Ibid.
[236] Quoted in Gow, *Military Intervention*, 177–178.   [237] Ibid., 184.
[238] Takeuchi, *War and Diplomacy*, 284.
[239] Quoted in Makela, "Japanese attitudes," 272.
[240] Hirobe, *Japanese Pride*, 12.

In this climate, it was not surprising that Tokyo's instructions to its delegates centered on "three fundamental claims" to be made at the London Conference: first, a 70 percent ratio in heavy cruisers; second, a 70 percent ratio for all auxiliary vessels; and third, parity in submarine tonnage.[241] Pre-conference negotiations soon revealed that unlike its approach to the Washington Conference, the United States this time did not intend to play fair. Whereas earlier the US definition of existing strength had been ships already built or under construction, this time its definition also included ships authorized – a critical change, given that the United States had delayed beginning the construction of heavy cruisers. The new definition changed the ratio at which Japan would possess heavy cruisers from 73 percent to 46 percent. After years of investing in heavy cruisers precisely so that Japan could claim a 70 percent ratio, "Japan found that once she had mastered the rules of the game to her advantage, the Western Powers changed the rules."[242]

Japanese naval leaders already viewed the Washington system as closing off Japan's access to the great-power club. Combined with American racism and self-serving procedural alteration, the system also lost its legitimacy in their eyes. In November 1929, Kato Kanji met with Prime Minister Hamaguchi Osachi to emphasize the unfairness of the new rule. He quoted Fleet Admiral Togo, who had supported conceding the 60 percent ratio in Washington in 1921. Based on the definition of existing strength at that time, Togo had believed Japan could not attain parity. At the London Conference, however, Togo knew Japan would "surpass Britain and America respectably in cruisers," and yet Japan was willing to compromise by accepting a 70 percent ratio.[243] "If Great Britain and the United States do not go along with us on this we should leave the conference," Kato quoted Togo as saying.[244] Kato himself added, "The reality exposes the huge contradiction in the position the U.S. takes, reflecting its intent of demonstrating its world superiority. This should open the eyes of anyone worried about the responsibility for abolishing the new treaty."[245] Japanese thinking had come a long way from its fear of isolation and resulting unwillingness to do anything to upset the status quo.

---

[241] Takeuchi, *War and Diplomacy*, 288.
[242] Gow, *Military Intervention*, 190–191.   [243] Quoted in ibid., 196–197.
[244] Ibid.   [245] Quoted in ibid., 197.

Japan's Final Straw: The London Naval Conference, 1930

At the London Conference, it quickly became evident that neither the United States nor Japan was willing to compromise. Chief naval adviser Sakonji Seizo reported that the US proposal almost totally disregarded Japan's position: "there is no room whatsoever for accepting the 'selfish' American proposal."[246] Kato Kanji did not attend the negotiations, but kept a close eye on them. He continued to believe that far from a 70 percent ratio, it was Japan's sovereign right to have parity with the great powers on all types of armaments. In a letter to the Lord Keeper of the Privy Seal (a senior and powerful adviser to the emperor), he warned that the more Japan gave up its sovereign right to parity, "the more flagrant the United States would become in flaunting its high-handed and coercive attitude of forcibly imposing the 60 percent ratio."[247] The issue was not one of security but of Japan being treated as a lesser power by the great powers. Kato wrote to Sakonji: "The real issue at stake is no longer our naval power per se but our national prestige and credibility."[248]

Kato's view of the Washington system was deeply colored by the US exclusion of Japanese immigrants. He wrote to Kaneko Kentaro, a member of the Privy Council, that Japan's "timid" diplomacy in 1921 had made the United States look down on Japan to the extent that it passed the immigration law in 1924.[249] Kaneko had himself strongly protested the immigration law, despite being a life-long advocate of better US–Japan ties. It increasingly seemed that asserting Japan's rights by breaking with the international order was the only way to attain symbolic equality with the great powers and stave off the kind of humiliation experienced due to the law.

In an effort to resolve the deadlock in London, US delegate David Reed and Japanese delegate Matsudaira Tsuneo hammered out a compromise agreement behind closed doors, without the knowledge of the Japanese naval advisers. The agreement gave Japan a 60.2 percent ratio in cruisers but the United States agreed to delay

---

[246] Quoted in Sadao Asada, "The London Conference and the tragedy of the Imperial Japanese Navy," in John Maurer and Christopher Bell (eds.), *At the Crossroads between Peace and War: The London Naval Conference in 1930* (Annapolis, MD: Naval Institute Press, 2014), 89–134.
[247] Quoted in Asada, *From Mahan to Pearl Harbor*, 130.   [248] Quoted in ibid.
[249] Quoted in ibid., 131.

construction, so that Japan would in fact have a ratio of 70 percent until the next conference in 1935. In addition, Japan would have parity in submarines, but at a significantly lower total tonnage.[250] The agreement meant that Japan could not construct new heavy cruisers until 1935, thereby losing the opportunity to make technological advancements. Meanwhile, the United States, with its altered definition of existing strength, could construct fifteen new heavy cruisers. Moreover, the lower submarine tonnage meant that Japan had to scrap one-third of its existing submarine tonnage and could not construct any new submarines until its existing ones reached replacement age.

The unveiling of the Reed–Matsudaira compromise sent shockwaves through the Japanese establishment. "The present American compromise plan offers us crumbs and tells us to like them," said Kato Kanji to another official. "This is extremely high-handed."[251] He cabled Japan's naval adviser at the conference, once again using Fleet Admiral Togo's authority and words to argue that "there is no way but to break up the conference and come home."[252] Breaking all manner of protocol, senior naval officers circulated an "Admiralty Statement" to the press in an attempt to rally public opinion against the compromise.[253] The civilians at the London Conference held fast, however, and were backed by Hamaguchi and Shidehara, both of whom feared the status repercussions of Japan torpedoing the conference. Prince Saionji Kinmochi, the last surviving *genro* (Meiji-era oligarch) after 1924, took a similar view, arguing that "Japan should lead other nations to recognize her earnest promotion of international peace by voluntarily accepting 60 per cent."[254] This line of reasoning, that "Japan will greatly increase her future international role if she takes a leading part in bringing this conference to a successful conclusion,"[255] was very much in keeping with the cooperative strategy that Japan had followed at the Washington Conference. Saionji, however, was out of touch with his compatriots, who had increasingly moved toward challenging

---

[250] Asada, "The London Conference," 106–114.
[251] Quoted in Kumao Harada, *Fragile Victory: Prince Saionji and the 1930 London Treaty Issue from the Memoirs of Baron Harada Kumao*, trans. Thomas Francis Mayer-Oakes (Detroit: Wayne State University Press, 1968), 97.
[252] Quoted in Asada, *From Mahan to Pearl Harbor*, 143.
[253] Takeuchi, *War and Diplomacy*, 295.
[254] Quoted in Harada, *Fragile Victory*, 85.   [255] Ibid.

the Washington system as the latter ceased to be institutionally open and procedurally fair.

Ultimately, those in favor of the compromise prevailed, and Japan signed the London Naval Treaty in April 1930. Hamaguchi did not want Japan to "place itself in isolation" and feared the financial implications of a renewed naval arms race.[256] Kato Kanji was unmoved: "It's as if we had been roped up and cast into prison by Britain and America," he argued to a colleague.[257] The next six months witnessed "the most vigorously contested [domestic] battle ever fought," not just between the navy and civilian leadership, but within the civilian leadership itself, particularly between the cabinet and the Privy Council over the ratification of the treaty.[258] Eventually, the Privy Council decided to back the cabinet and the treaty went through, leading Kato to resign as chief of the Navy General Staff. At the societal level, there were "widespread demonstrations of militant nationalism" against the treaty.[259] On November 14, 1930, a right-wing youth shot Hamaguchi at Tokyo Station in protest against the treaty and economic conditions in Japan.[260] The prime minister succumbed to his injuries a few months later. Japanese naval journalist Ito Masanori, who lived through the entire period and had close contact with many of its protagonists, later wrote that the London Conference was "one of the remote causes of the war with the Anglo-American powers."[261]

Japan Challenges the Washington System, 1931 onward

In his history of Japanese foreign policy from 1869 to 1942, Ian Nish marks 1931 as a watershed between the period of "Japan among the Powers" and the period of "Japan versus the Powers."[262] Iriye identifies the Manchurian Crisis of 1931 as inaugurating "the triumph of military thinking in Japan [which] marked the return of security considerations as the basic framework of national policy, and ... also

---

[256] Quoted in Asada, *From Mahan to Pearl Harbor*, 149.
[257] Quoted in Harada, *Fragile Victory*, 111.
[258] Takeuchi, *War and Diplomacy*, 336.
[259] Shigenori Togo, *The Cause of Japan* (New York: Simon & Schuster, 1956), 109–110.
[260] Nish, *Interwar Period*, 98.
[261] Quoted in Asada, *From Mahan to Pearl Harbor*, 126.
[262] Nish, *Japanese Foreign Policy*, 3.

signaled the emergence of pan-Asianism as an official ideology."[263] In the absence of IST, this move toward revisionism seems irrational from a purely security perspective. After all, as a rising power, Japan could have chosen to cooperate with the great powers and strengthen its economy and defenses – engaging in what might today be called a "peaceful rise" – instead of marching down the path to war.[264] However, IST shows that security was far from the only thing on the minds of Japan's leaders. As Ishii observed in 1933, "Ever since Japan's entrance into the family of modern nations in the middle of the nineteenth century her diplomacy has striven, and still strives, to attain two objectives – *equality* and security."[265]

In 1931, Japan decided that challenging the order was the only way to achieve equality. In the midst of the domestic crisis touched off by the London Conference, Hanihara, who as ambassador in Washington had failed to stave off the 1924 US Immigration Act, unexpectedly spoke up at a farewell dinner for the US Ambassador in Tokyo:

[The] resentment is felt now as it was then. Nor will it ever die out so long as the wound inflicted remains unhealed ... It is not so much a question as to whether one Nation should or should not exercise its sovereign rights in regulating matters relating to its domestic affairs as it is often represented to be. Rather it is a question of whether one people should treat another people sympathetically, fairly or unfairly.[266]

Hanihara's thoughts were shared not just by the fleet faction but also by many Japanese politicians and intellectuals previously sympathetic to the Washington system. Nitobe Inazo, an internationalist who had served as an under-secretary general of the League of Nations, wrote, "Each year that passes without amendment or abrogation only strengthens and sharpens our sense of injury, which is destined to show itself, in one form or another, in personal and public intercourse."[267] Ishii, himself a former president of the Council of the League of Nations, underscored the long-term reversal that Japan had

---

[263] Iriye, *Across the Pacific*, 172.
[264] Ward, "Race, status, and Japanese revisionism," 616.
[265] Kikujiro Ishii, "The permanent bases of Japanese foreign policy," *Foreign Affairs*, January 1, 1933, emphasis added.
[266] Quoted in Daily Boston Globe, "Says resentment in Japan remains: Ex-Ambassador Hanihara breaks silence," May 24, 1930, 1.
[267] Inazo Nitobe, *Japan: Some Phases of Her Problems and Development* (London: Ernest Benn Ltd., 1931), 167.

experienced as a result of exclusion: "Full appreciation of our disappointment ... is possible only when it is projected against the background of our unremitting toil of seventy years for the realization of our aspiration for equality."[268] The US immigration law, "the severest cut of all," was a fundamental denial of Japan's major-power identity.[269]

Developments in the Washington system only exacerbated the feelings of exclusion and injustice that had begun to permeate Japanese assessments of it, particularly in the navy. Vice Admiral Suetsugu Nobumasa – a prominent member of the fleet faction who had participated in the Washington Conference – came to view the "status quo" as "a stock phrase of the 'have-powers'" such as Britain and the United States, one that Japan "must destroy."[270] Unlike at the Washington Conference where the United States had acted in a fair and self-sacrificing manner, at the London meeting the United States appeared self-serving and inclined to shift goalposts in order to keep Japan in second-rank status. Faced with an inferior ratio and a fundamentally unfair international order, many Japanese leaders sought to break away from the London treaty, and almost did. Although those who supported cooperation as the optimal strategy for Japan still remained in important positions, they too eventually recognized that this strategy had not paid off.[271] Cooperation with the international order had earned Japan only further insult and exclusion. As the second London Naval Conference approached, the navy switched from demanding 70 percent to an outright common upper limit for all powers, emphasizing Japan's "equal right of armament" and "national right of survival."[272] The US ambassador in Tokyo observed that the conference would inevitably strain Japan's relations with the great powers, "with loud and angry vituperations against us for keeping Japan an 'inferior nation'."[273]

In the fall of 1934, a Japanese navy ministry memorandum predicted, "If by any chance the coming naval conference should

---

[268] Ishii, "The permanent bases."   [269] Ibid.
[270] Quoted in Asada, *From Mahan to Pearl Harbor*, 179.
[271] Ward, "Race, status, and Japanese revisionism," 619–620.
[272] Nish, *Interwar Period*, 97.
[273] Joseph C. Grew, *Ten Years in Japan: A Contemporary Record Drawn from Diaries and Private and Official Papers* (New York: Simon and Schuster, 1944), 116.

recognize the traditional discriminatory ratios, our Empire will forever be ordered around by the Anglo-American powers, and it is obvious that our Empire will go to ruin."[274] On December 30, 1934, Japan gave advance notice of its withdrawal from the Washington system upon the expiration of its treaties in 1936. At the second London Naval Conference in December 1935, when Japan's demands for parity and a common upper limit were not met, its delegates walked out.[275] Japan had completed its transition from seeking to reform the international order at Paris in 1919, to cooperation at the Washington Conference of 1921–1922, to attempting expansion of the great-power club after Washington, and finally challenging the international order in the aftermath of the London Conference of 1930. At critical points in this transition, the Washington system had changed in terms of its openness and fairness, which in turn impacted Japan's status-seeking strategy. IST shows that the roots of Japan's more aggressive policies in the 1930s can be traced back to the manner in which the Washington system evolved in the 1920s.

* * *

[274] Quoted in Asada, *From Mahan to Pearl Harbor*, 197.   [275] Ibid., 100.

6 | India and the International Order of the Cold War

Compared to previous international orders, the Cold War order was marked by three differences. First, geopolitical competition between the two leading states – the United States and the Soviet Union – played out along ideological lines. This made for a bifurcated order that intersected in various institutions but was ultimately premised on two distinct modes of domestic and international political organization. Second, new rules and institutions emerged in a number of areas, especially international trade, development, and finance. Whereas previous international orders had mostly focused on preventing and regulating war, the Cold War order had multiple components. Third, the international order was significantly enlarged as new states joined the international system. While the great powers clashed over the management of the order, the newly decolonized states of Asia and Africa clashed with the great powers over issues of international social and economic justice.[1]

Amidst these divisions, there was one subject on which the superpowers and many other countries found agreement, and that was nuclear weapons. The destructive potential of the growing arsenals of the two superpowers, as well as the emergence of Britain, France, and China as nuclear weapon states in the early Cold War, led to a lengthy period of multilateral diplomacy from the mid-1950s onward over the rules and institutions needed to govern the development, testing, and spread of nuclear weapons. The superpowers did not agree on much, but they did agree on the need to "increase their own, and the rest of the world's chances of survival."[2] The 1970 Nuclear Non-Proliferation Treaty (NPT), the centerpiece of the nuclear order, was "a pillar of global governance" representing "a grand bargain between states with

---

[1] Barry Buzan and Ole Wæver, *Regions and Powers: The Structure of International Security* (Cambridge: Cambridge University Press, 2003), 15–18.
[2] Cui and Buzan, "Great power management," 186.

and without nuclear weapons."[3] States possessing nuclear weapons committed to not transfer nuclear weapons to nonnuclear states or assist them in building nuclear weapons. Nonnuclear states committed to not building nuclear weapons in exchange for the right to develop nuclear energy for peaceful purposes, subject to safeguards under the International Atomic Energy Agency (IAEA). All signatories committed to pursuing negotiations in good faith toward nuclear disarmament.

The NPT stands out as one of the few examples of successful multilateral cooperation during the Cold War. It was the core security institution of an international order – which also included the IAEA, the Partial Test Ban Treaty (PTBT), and various multilateral groupings such as the Nuclear Suppliers Group (NSG) – that largely achieved its primary purpose of restricting the spread of nuclear weapons. Only four countries – India, Pakistan, Israel, and South Sudan – have never signed the treaty. Among them, India is the only country to have conducted an overt nuclear test during the Cold War, just four years after the NPT came into force. India's challenge to the international order was surprising given its extensive cooperation on nuclear non-proliferation and disarmament prior to the NPT, especially as a founding member of the IAEA in the mid-1950s and through the Eighteen-Nation Committee on Disarmament (ENCD) that met between 1962 and 1969 and eventually produced the NPT.

India's challenge to the international order is highly consequential. New Delhi's nuclear test of 1974 became Pakistan's justification for pursuing its own nuclear weapons program and spurred the great powers to establish the NSG to further control international nuclear commerce. Moreover, New Delhi took every opportunity to publicly criticize the great powers for designing an unequal and discriminatory order (from India's perspective). Indian leaders maintained nuclear disarmament on the international agenda at the United Nations for the entire Cold War, presenting a constant reminder to the great powers of failing to meet their own commitment under the NPT. After the Cold War, India, followed closely by Pakistan, shook up the international order by conducting a second round of nuclear tests in 1998.

---

[3] Richard Butler, "NPT: A pillar of global governance," *Penn State Journal of Law and International Affairs*, 2:2 (2013), 272–281.

India's relationship with the Cold War order (and beyond) is inter-twined with the history of India's nuclear tests and raises two import-ant puzzles. First, if the dominant approach in the literature on nuclear proliferation is correct and major security threats drive the pursuit of nuclear weapons,[4] China's first nuclear test in 1964 and repeated tests of nuclear and thermonuclear devices as well as short-range missiles in the 1960s should have prompted India to embark on a nuclear weapons program of its own. Indian leaders chose otherwise, focusing on nonproliferation and disarmament negotiations instead. At a time when India could have taken advantage of the loose rules and proced-ures around nuclear proliferation to address a major security threat,[5] its leaders instead cooperated with a great-power club that sought to close the door on future entrants.

Second, India undertook both its nuclear tests – in 1974 and in 1998 – at times when it was *more* secure from external threats than at most other times since World War II. In fact, it was likely that nuclear tests at those times would be perceived by India's adversaries – primarily China and Pakistan – as a provocation, thereby *worsening* India's security environment. Both tests were also conducted within international orders that were essentially facilitating India's rise, and doing so particularly rapidly in the 1990s. In 1998, at a time when India had no major external security threats to deal with and had much to lose by challenging the international order – for example, via economic sanctions – New Delhi chose to conduct nuclear tests in direct violation of the rules and institutions established by the great powers (though technically not in violation of international law, since India had not signed the NPT).

This chapter shows that standard materialist and even norms-based accounts of nuclear proliferation and of India's nuclear history cannot sufficiently explain the empirical record of India's nuclear tests and weapons development. Instead, we must turn to Institutional Status Theory (IST), which shows that India's nuclear decision-making was driven less by security considerations and more by India's status aspir-ations as they related to the evolving nature of the international order.

---

[4] See Alexandre Debs and Nuno P. Monteiro, *Nuclear Politics: The Strategic Causes of Proliferation* (Cambridge: Cambridge University Press, 2016).
[5] On the United States' sporadic attention to nonproliferation before 1974, see Nicholas L. Miller, *Stopping the Bomb: The Sources and Effectiveness of US Nonproliferation Policy* (Ithaca: Cornell University Press, 2018), chapters 2–3.

The rest of the chapter proceeds with an account of India's major-power identity in the two decades following independence in 1947. It then provides the background to the NPT, particularly the ENCD that negotiated it and other nuclear-related issues. Next, it examines existing explanations for India's nuclear decision-making. While these explanations are helpful for individual episodes or periods, they fail to provide a comprehensive account. The chapter then proceeds to test IST's predictions, focusing on the status-seeking strategies pursued by India from the mid-1950s to the early 1970s, namely, expansion, followed by cooperation, and finally challenge. Although IST applies to the 1990s as well, for reasons of space this chapter focuses on the former period, with some discussion of the latter by way of conclusion.

India's Major-Power Identity

Scholars of India's Cold War foreign policy have variously emphasized India's sense of "civilizational exceptionalism,"[6] "moral greatness,"[7] and "greater moral mission."[8] Others have highlighted India's belief in "the moral superiority of the Indian approach to international affairs"[9] or the desire for "a global leadership role" among the Indian elite.[10] According to Itty Abraham, "This grand objective, global recognition of India's importance, has been a continuous thread of India's foreign policy since independence."[11] Even in the early years following independence, before India began its gradual rise (see Appendix), Indian leaders were convinced of India's future greatness.

Jawaharlal Nehru, India's prime minister and foreign minister from 1947 till his death in 1964, was confident that India was "potentially a Great Power" that would in the future be "the pivot" around which

---

[6] Priya Chacko, *Indian Foreign Policy: The Politics of Postcolonial Identity from 1947 to 2004* (New York: Routledge, 2012), 3.

[7] Sreeram R. Chaulia, "BJP, India's foreign policy and the 'realist alternative' to the Nehruvian tradition," *International Politics*, 39 (2002), 215–234.

[8] Richard M. Fontera, "Anti-colonialism as a basic Indian foreign policy," *The Western Political Quarterly*, 13:2 (1960), 421–432.

[9] T. A. Keenleyside, "Prelude to power: The meaning of non-alignment before Indian independence," *Pacific Affairs*, 53:3 (1980), 461–483.

[10] Ramesh Thakur, "India after nonalignment," *Foreign Affairs*, 71:2 (1992), 165–182.

[11] Itty Abraham, "The future of Indian foreign policy," *Economic and Political Weekly*, 42:42 (2007), 4209–4212.

problems of Asian security would have to be considered.[12] It was "absurd for India to be treated like any small power in this connection."[13] Nehru was optimistic about India's military capabilities. As early as 1948, he was convinced that India was not a "weak or mean country" and that it would be "foolish for us to get frightened, even from a military point of view, of the greatest of the Powers today."[14] To Nehru, the great-power club was composed of "three big countries": the United States, the Soviet Union, and China.[15] "If you peep into the future," he said in a 1954 speech, "the obvious fourth country in the world is India."[16]

India's signature foreign policy doctrine in the Nehru era was non-alignment, according to which India would align with neither the United States nor the Soviet Union. It would instead "plough a lonely furrow,"[17] maintaining its distance from the power politics of the Cold War. For Nehru, nonalignment was "the natural consequence of an independent nation functioning according to its own rights."[18] India would not be dictated to by either of the superpowers. Nonalignment was at least in part a ploy for global recognition as a major power, and a way of turning weakness into strength. Kate Sullivan de Estrada and Rajesh Basrur describe the Nehru era as one in which India enjoyed "status without power."[19] Given its material weakness, India could have easily taken a back seat in international politics while it built up its economic and military capabilities. Instead, India chose nonalignment because it created a distinctive identity for India as a powerful yet peace-loving country. Scholar Stanley Heginbotham observed in 1972 that in a world where status was often accorded to powers with economic and military heft, "India has been powerfully influenced by a vision of a different founda-tion for its place among the world powers ... that the appearance of powerlessness can be a great asset in achieving a position of influence."[20]

---

[12] Quoted in Baldev Raj Nayyar and T. V. Paul, *India in the World Order: Searching for Major-Power Status* (Cambridge: Cambridge University Press, 2003), 133.
[13] Ibid. [14] Ibid., 130. [15] Ibid., 135. [16] Ibid.
[17] Extracts from Nehru's speech to the Constituent Assembly of India, 4 Dec. 1947, partially reproduced in A. Appadorai, *Select Documents on India's Foreign Policy and Relations 1947–1972*, vol. I (New York: Oxford University Press, 1982), 10.
[18] Quoted in Priyankar Upadhyaya, *Nonaligned States and India's International Conflicts* (New Delhi: South Asian Publishers, 1990), 7.
[19] Kate Sullivan de Estrada and Rajesh Basrur, *Rising India: Status and Power* (New York: Routledge, 2017), chapter 2.
[20] Stanley J. Heginbotham, "In the wake of Bangla Desh: A new role for India in Asia?" *Pacific Affairs*, 45:3 (1972), 372–386.

Nonalignment did not mean detachment from world politics, particularly within the institutions of the international order. Much as the United States in the nineteenth century thought itself exceptional while being deeply involved in routine world politics, India thought itself above the fray of the Cold War while being deeply enmeshed in its politics. Some of this involvement in the Nehru era was necessitated by India's military conflicts with Pakistan and growing rivalry with China. The rest was the result of a Nehruvian impulse to "achieve international stature through mediatory efforts and moral suasion."[21] During the Korean War, India sought to mediate between East and West, sending a field ambulance unit as part of the US-backed UN intervention while also declining to label China an aggressor in the UN's resolutions. After the war, India headed the Neutral Nations Repatriation Commission, which supervised the return of prisoners of war under UN auspices. India, along with Poland and Canada, served on the International Control Commission that monitored the implementation of the Geneva Accords of 1954, which oversaw the settlement of outstanding issues from the Korean War and the beginning of the end of the French empire in Southeast Asia. New Delhi also contributed the largest number of troops to peacekeeping missions in the Suez in 1956 and the Congo in 1960. Outside the UN, India was active in organizing the 1955 Bandung Conference of Asian and African nations.

When it came to global concerns over nuclear weapons, India once again sought to provide moral leadership through the multilateral route. On April 2, 1954, in a parliamentary speech, Nehru became the first head of state to call for a global "standstill agreement" on nuclear weapons testing.[22] He followed it up in July 1956 with an official submission from India to the UN Disarmament Commission.[23] Although international negotiations over disarmament floundered through the 1950s, things began to change in the early 1960s, just as India was beginning its economic and military rise.

The Nuclear Order of the Cold War

After years of failed United Nations resolutions, bilateral negotiations, and brief multilateral negotiations (in the form of the short-lived Ten-

---

[21] Ibid., 374.
[22] N. D. Jayaprakash, "Nuclear disarmament and India," *Economic and Political Weekly*, 35:7 (2000), 525–533.
[23] Ibid.

Nation Committee on Disarmament), the superpowers came to an agreement, via a common declaration on December 21, 1961, to set up the Eighteen-Nation Committee on Disarmament, which would include five members of the Western bloc (the United States, the United Kingdom [UK], France, Canada, and Italy), five members of the Eastern bloc (the Soviet Union, Czechoslovakia, Poland, Romania, and Bulgaria), and eight nonaligned nations (Brazil, Burma, Ethiopia, India, Mexico, Nigeria, Sweden, and the United Arab Republic).

The United Nations General Assembly initially charged the ENCD with arriving at a plan for general and complete nuclear disarmament. The ENCD first met on March 14, 1962, and spent the first two years of its existence on this question. Failing to make much headway, committee members decided to focus instead on "partial" disarmament, or goals that were more achievable than general and complete disarmament. These included a ban on nuclear testing, the designation of nuclear-free geographical zones, and nuclear nonproliferation. An early result of these efforts was the 1963 PTBT, which banned all forms of testing that were relatively easy to detect: in the air, under water, and in space. The harder question of underground testing was put off and remained unresolved.

As for general disarmament, fundamental differences between the positions of the United States and the Soviet Union precluded agreement. What did emerge as an area of great-power agreement was the need to prevent the spread of nuclear weapons to other countries. In July 1965, the superpowers each introduced a draft nonproliferation treaty. Negotiations over the following three years led to concessions on both sides and eventually agreement on the NPT. The treaty was opened for signature in the UNGA on July 1, 1968, and – subject to ratification by the United States, Soviet Union, UK, and forty other countries – came into force on March 5, 1970. Although the NPT was initially considered a weak treaty with no enforcement mechanisms and boycotted by two nuclear powers, France and China, it has, in retrospect, been described as "the only important agreement that emerged from the Eighteen-Nation Committee."[24] The NPT's

---

[24] Albert Legault and Michel Fortmann, *A Diplomacy of Hope: Canada and Disarmament 1945–1988*, trans. Derek Ellington (Montreal and Kingston: McGill-Queen's University Press, 1992), 198.

membership increased from 61 countries in 1970 to 139 in 1990, and today stands at 191 countries.[25]

The ENCD held its 430th and final meeting on August 26, 1969. The committee was subsequently expanded into the Conference on the Committee on Disarmament, which eventually became the Conference on Disarmament as it exists today. The ENCD was the first multilateral institution in which nonaligned states contributed to discussions on nuclear disarmament and nonproliferation alongside the superpowers and their allies. It was, therefore, an important venue for a country such as India, which had already earned considerable recognition as being both nonaligned and scientifically advanced relative to other countries of the Third World.

Existing Explanations for India's Nuclear Trajectory

To ask when and why India cooperated with or challenged the nuclear order of the Cold War is to ask why India tested nuclear devices when it did, in 1974 and 1998, and why India did not pursue nuclear weapons when it had strong material incentives to do so. Despite a voluminous literature, there has been no satisfactory single explanation of India's nuclear testing decisions. The best histories of India's tryst with the atom continue to grapple with three basic puzzles. First, why did India not respond to China's rapidly growing nuclear capability after 1964, waiting instead for a decade and then conducting only a "peaceful nuclear explosion"?[26] Second, after testing its first device in 1974, why did India not take any action toward building nuclear weapons until 1989? Third, why did India opt for a second round of nuclear tests in 1998 at a time when proliferation might have incurred heavy economic and social sanctions?

These puzzles become clearer through Scott Sagan's account of why states develop nuclear weapons, which describes three types of

---

[25] United Nations Office for Disarmament Affairs, "Treaty on the non-proliferation of nuclear weapons, Status of the Treaty," https://disarmament.un.org/treaties/t/npt

[26] Peaceful Nuclear Explosions (PNE) were in vogue during the 1960s and 1970s among the superpowers, who experimented with the idea of using nuclear explosions for large-scale projects such as dam building, gas stimulation for oil extraction, and harbor construction. They were abandoned by the United States in the late 1970s following evidence of adverse environmental consequences and the resulting public opposition to PNEs.

explanations for this monumental choice: security threats, domestic politics, and norms.[27] The first, and most common, explanation for India's nuclear decision-making rests on the constraining effects of the international system, specifically an overt Chinese nuclear capability after 1964 and a growing Pakistani capability, largely aided by China. Threat-based explanations conclude that India's nuclearization was structurally predetermined.[28] However, this line of reasoning cannot explain why India waited ten years after China's first test (and numerous subsequent tests) to break nuclear ground; or why India tested in 1998, when there were no major external threats either from China or Pakistan. While security was undoubtedly a necessary motive for India's nuclear weapons program, it cannot explain the pattern of India's nuclear decision-making.

A second set of arguments focuses on domestic and bureaucratic politics, contending that when a certain group with an interest in the bomb – either scientists driven by a modernist imperative or bureaucratic interest, or economically inward-looking nationalist political coalitions – is influential, they increase the likelihood that a country will at least test a nuclear device, if not build nuclear weapons.[29] By contrast, political coalitions that seek to liberalize the economy will be averse to pursuing nuclear weapons for fear of jeopardizing external economic relations. These types of arguments do not fully explain the Indian case. Neither scientists nor nationalists play a decisive *political* role in India's nuclear history. The direction of India's nuclear program has always firmly been in the hands of its political leadership. When it came to ruling coalitions, nationalist and economically inward-looking coalitions under Prime Ministers Lal Bahadur Shastri and Indira Gandhi in the 1960s and 1970s consistently abjured nuclear weapons, whereas liberalizing coalitions under Rajiv Gandhi, P. V. Narasimha Rao, and Atal Bihari Vajpayee in the 1980s and 1990s pursued weaponization and testing.

[27] Scott D. Sagan, "Why do states build nuclear weapons? Three models in search of a bomb," *International Security*, 21:3 (1996), 54–86.
[28] See Sumit Ganguly, "India's pathway to Pokhran II: The prospects and sources of New Delhi's nuclear weapons program," *International Security*, 23:4 (1999), 148–177.
[29] Etel Solingen, "The political economy of nuclear restraint," *International Security*, 19:2 (1994), 126–169.

A third set of arguments focuses not on interests but norms. At the domestic level, a "Gandhian moral impulse" and "moral aversion" to nuclear weapons allegedly led to nuclear disavowal during the 1960s, whereas the Hindu nationalism of Vajpayee led to the nuclear tests of 1998.[30] At the international level, the prestige surrounding nuclear weapons influences the value states place on them.[31] In the 1960s, prestige came from joining the nuclear club; in the 1990s, it came from joining the NPT.[32] Again, neither set of arguments fully explains India's nuclear trajectory. Domestic norms cannot explain why India's morals were jettisoned for its 1974 test and rediscovered shortly thereafter. Nor can norms explain why prime ministers who were not Hindu nationalists pursued nuclear weapons in the late 1980s and early 1990s. At the international level, if following norms unambiguously bestowed prestige on countries, India would have sought the bomb in the 1960s when international norms were in favor of joining the nuclear club, and abjured nuclear weapons in the 1990s when international norms were against proliferation. India did exactly the opposite.

Institutional Status Theory and India's Approach to the Cold War Order

IST's predictions fit the Indian case, as summarized in Figure 6.1. From independence onward, India invested in big science, especially nuclear technology, as a way of maintaining symbolic equality with the great powers. In the mid-1950s, as the great powers took steps to establish the IAEA, India lobbied to *expand* the elite club of advanced nations involved in the negotiations. The great powers obliged, and coupled with procedurally fair negotiations, India's inclusion in the negotiating

[30] Jacques E. C. Hymans, *The Psychology of Proliferation: Identity, Emotions, and Foreign Policy* (Cambridge: Cambridge University Press, 2006), 179; George Perkovich, *India's Nuclear Bomb: The Impact on Global Proliferation* (Berkeley: University of California Press, 1999), 3, 85.
[31] Barry O'Neill, "Nuclear weapons and national prestige," *Cowles Foundation Discussion Paper* no. 1560 (New Haven: Cowles Foundation for Research in Economics, 2006).
[32] Sagan, "Why do states," 76.

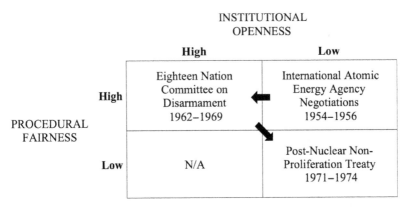

Figure 6.1 Institutional Status Theory and India in the Cold War

group satisfied its leaders' desire for recognition of their state's major-power identity. Although relations with China turned ugly in the 1960s, India adopted a *cooperative* stance with the international order that can be described as "nuclear ambiguity." On the one hand, this meant wholeheartedly supporting nonproliferation and nuclear disarmament in multilateral negotiations. On the other hand, it meant abstaining from nuclear weapons while publicly keeping the nuclear option open.

The international order signaled a shift to less openness after the superpowers introduced drafts of the NPT in the ENCD that revealed their plan to curb nuclear proliferation to nonnuclear countries while leaving the arsenals of the nuclear powers untouched. Furthermore, by stating that only countries that conducted nuclear tests prior to 1967 would count officially as nuclear powers, the NPT applied its rules inconsistently: it accommodated countries that openly rejected disarmament and nonproliferation, such as France and China, while penalizing a conscientious rule-follower such as India. India's response was to *challenge* the international order – just over a year after the NPT went into effect, Prime Minister Indira Gandhi began preparations for a nuclear test. The 1974 test restored India's status as a technologically advanced yet pacifist country. India was now a de facto nuclear-capable state, though its leaders still saw the international order as deeply unfair. They engaged in a strategy of reframing their position outside the order as being in the cause of justice and equality. India did nothing to develop nuclear weapons, while seeking to delegitimize the international order as a form of "nuclear apartheid" that separated the nuclear haves from the have-nots.[33]

After the Cold War, the international order began changing again through the negotiations for the Comprehensive Nuclear-Test-Ban Treaty (CTBT) and the permanent extension of the NPT in 1995, the latter coming as a major surprise to India. New Delhi decided to *challenge* the international order once again. Through a series of nuclear tests in May 1998, India established itself as a de facto nuclear weapon state, irrespective of the legal definition in the NPT. In 2005–2008, the United States concluded an agreement on civilian nuclear cooperation with India that recognized India's status as a responsible de facto nuclear power. Now, facing an institutionally open and procedurally fair international order that does not treat India differently from the great-power club, New Delhi has muted its criticisms and taken a cooperative approach to nuclear issues.

The rest of this chapter delves into the period from the 1950s to the 1970s, with some discussion of the rest of the period mentioned above.

Seeking Status through Big Science

India's desire for symbolic equality with the great powers drove Nehru's early decision to invest in big science, especially atomic energy. India's strategy at this point was one of emulation or catching up with the great powers in scientific achievement. Historians of Indian science have dealt extensively with how leaders such as Nehru and his chief nuclear scientist, Homi J. Bhabha, saw in this field the "modernist imperative"[34] of a postcolonial nation and benchmarked India's status to that of the great powers.[35] Raja Ramanna, the architect of India's first nuclear test and an associate of Bhabha's, observed an "inferiority complex" among those Indian scientists who were left out of international networks of researchers working on particle physics, quantum mechanics, and other new fields.[36] Bhabha himself was widely

---

[33] Perkovich, *India's Nuclear Bomb*, 138; Jaswant Singh, "Against nuclear apartheid," *Foreign Affairs*, 77:5 (1998), 41–52.
[34] Jahnavi Phalkey, *Atomic State: Big Science in Twentieth-Century India* (Ranikhet: Permanent Black, 2013), 11–12.
[35] Itty Abraham, *The Making of the Indian Atomic Bomb: Science, Secrecy, and the Postcolonial State* (London and New York: Zed Books, 1998), 19–34.
[36] Raja Ramanna, *Years of Pilgrimage: An Autobiography* (New Delhi: Viking, 1991), 59.

respected in these circles, and used his connections to encourage his Indian colleagues to "catch up with the front-runners."[37]

As early as 1945, in a speech at the Bombay branch of the Indian Council of World Affairs, Bhabha reportedly stated that "given proper education and facilities for work, the Indian mind was perfectly capable of keeping pace with the other scientifically advanced countries of the West."[38] Nehru highlighted this imperative when introducing the Atomic Energy Bill in the Constituent Assembly of India in 1948: "If we do not set about it now, taking advantage of the processes that go towards the making of atomic energy ... we will be left behind and we shall possibly only just have the chance to follow in the trail of others. That is not good enough for any country, least of all for a country with the vast potential and strength that India possesses."[39]

Nehru was clear that to be an equal of the great powers, India would need to cooperate with them on equal terms and not terms of dependence. While inaugurating a rare earths factory in Alwaye in 1952, he said, "[We] want to do this work ourselves – not to be helpless and dependent upon others, but to cooperate with others in this task. While our financial resources are nowhere near to other countries, we hope certainly to have scientific talent of the first order so that we may go ahead with this by ourselves or in cooperation with others."[40] He believed that, barring the great powers, India in the early 1950s was ahead of the vast majority of the world in the realm of atomic energy.[41]

In 1957, India launched the *Apsara*, a swimming pool reactor that Bhabha and his team designed using British blueprints and constructed using uranium fuel rods imported from the UK. With this achievement, in Ramanna's words, "[t]he Indian nuclear energy establishment was finally a force to reckon with."[42] Nehru was now confident even of outdoing the superpowers. He reminded fellow lawmakers of the need to stay ahead of the technological curve: "We cannot wait for America or Russia or some other country to achieve [technological advancements in nuclear power] and then try to imitate the benefits of that. We

---

[37] Ibid.

[38] Times of India, "Keeping abreast of scientific world: Dr. Bhabha stresses need for India." August 28, 1945, 4.

[39] Jawaharlal Nehru, *Pandit Jawaharlal Nehru on Atomic Energy* (Bombay: Bhabha Atomic Research Centre, 1989), 8.

[40] Ibid., 21.   [41] Ibid., 47–48.   [42] Ramanna, *Years of Pilgrimage*, 63.

have to build up in order to keep in the fore all the time."[43] By the early 1960s, India had developed theoretical and applied expertise in a number of advanced fields, such as atomic energy, oil and gas extraction, geological science, mining, water and power production, and agricultural research.[44]

In July 1960, the Canada India Reactor Utility Services (CIRUS) reactor, supplied by Canada with heavy water from the United States, became operational, boosting India's international status. According to Ramanna, "The CIRUS experience certainly gave India more confidence in its technological capabilities and our reputation for reaching proposed time-schedules gained credibility in scientific circles here [in India] and abroad."[45] In March 1964, barely two months before Nehru's death and a little over six months before China's first nuclear test, India completed Project Phoenix, its first plutonium separation plant at Trombay. The accompanying press release from the Department of Atomic Energy (DAE) emphasized that only four other countries in the world had operating plutonium plants – the United States, the Soviet Union, Britain, and France – and that India was now "among the first half of a dozen countries in the world in the utilisation of atomic energy."[46]

Securing Status through Expansion of the IAEA, 1954–1956

As India accumulated the traits of a major scientific power, it developed commensurate expectations of its role in the international order as well. The effects were clearest in India's approach to the negotiations over the IAEA in the mid-1950s. On December 8, 1953, US President Dwight D. Eisenhower delivered his historic "Atoms for Peace" speech at the United Nations, in which he proposed the establishment of an international organization that would regulate the spread of atomic energy for peaceful purposes. The IAEA was formed

[43] Jawaharlal Nehru, *Jawaharlal Nehru's Speeches: September 1957–April 1963*, vol. IV (New Delhi: Ministry of Information and Broadcasting, Government of India, 1964), 439.
[44] See M. S. Thacker, "Scientific research: Progress in India since independence," *India Quarterly*, 13:4 (1957), 287–307.
[45] Ramanna, *Years of Pilgrimage*, 71.
[46] Telegram from American Consul in Bombay, A-249, April 29, 1964, National Security Archive, 4, http://nsarchive.gwu.edu/NSAEBB/NSAEBB187/IN03.pdf

three-and-a-half years later, after extensive negotiations. India played a key role, making the nascent nuclear order more open and inclusive than the United States had originally intended. The great powers made a number of concessions to India, by supporting Bhabha's leadership of the prestigious International Conference on the Peaceful Uses of Atomic Energy; expanding the core group of countries negotiating the IAEA statute to include India; engaging widely in consultations over the statute with UN members; sharing valuable scientific information with the international community as well as key classified documents with India; and, above all, accepting a quasi-permanent place for India on the IAEA's Board of Governors.

As predicted by IST, when initially faced with a potentially closed but relatively fair institution, India lobbied for inclusion by appealing to a new principle: geographical representation. Subsequently, although the negotiations were procedurally fair from India's perspective, the nature of safeguards in the final IAEA statute put the great powers in a potentially advantageous position. Nonetheless, Indian leaders were satisfied with the result, expecting that future progress in the nuclear order and in India's own production of nuclear technology would address distributional issues.

India's Initial Skepticism

Eisenhower's speech envisaged a club of five countries that were the most advanced in nuclear technology – the United States, the Soviet Union, the UK, France, and Canada – negotiating the terms of the IAEA. Given this exclusivity, Indian leaders were initially skeptical of US intentions. In September 1954, after talks failed with the Soviet Union and the United States announced it would proceed in a group of eight advanced countries – adding Australia, South Africa, Belgium, and Portugal – V. K. Krishna Menon, India's ambassador to the UN and close friend and advisor to Nehru, wrote to the prime minister, "The role and interests of countries like ours in atomic matters has [*sic*] not even entered into the consideration of the powers that be."[47] An internal foreign ministry memo observed that "India's exclusion was unjustified, particularly when Australia was included," because India

---

[47] Menon to PM, October 4, 1954, Top Secret, National Archives of India (NAI), UII/54/4571/10004.

had "a better claim" based on a comparison of nuclear resources (especially thorium).[48]

Despite these concerns, Indian leaders decided the US proposal was "an important and valuable step" that left room for India to push for an open and fair institution.[49] At the UN, Menon approached his US counterpart, Henry Cabot Lodge, Jr., and conveyed India's "unofficial disapproval" at not being consulted.[50] Officially, India suggested that the negotiations "be broadened so as to include all states able and willing to participate."[51] In response to a draft resolution introduced by the eight nations in the UNGA in November 1954, India proposed amendments calling on the UNGA itself to nominate states to join the eight nations, and for the negotiating group to consult other states widely.[52] Pointedly, India did not press these amendments to a vote.

Lobbying for Inclusion

For most of 1955, as the eight nations got down to business, India kept up the pressure. Bhabha felt India should be a permanent member of the IAEA Board on the basis of its thorium deposits and position as "scientifically and technically the most advanced country ... possibly in the whole of Asia."[53] He proposed to Nehru that they "press on Washington to be included as a founder-member."[54] Bhabha envisioned a Board of a different set of eight permanent members – the United States, the Soviet Union, the UK, Canada, France, India, Brazil, and China (in future) – in addition to eight elected term members.[55]

---

[48] "Atoms for Peace" Resolution, Secret, November 24, 1954, NAI, UII/54/4571/10004.

[49] Ibid.

[50] Lodge, Jr., to Secretary of State, November 10, 1954, Confidential, NARA, NN3–326-93-004, box 1.

[51] Statement by Ambassador Henry Cabot Lodge, Jr., November 19, 1954, NARA, NN3–326-93-004, box 1.

[52] Report of the First Committee, Ninth Session, November 26, 1954, NAI, UII/54/4571/10004.

[53] Views on Proposed International Atomic Energy Agency, Memorandum of October 16, 1954, Secret, NAI, UII/54/4571/10004.

[54] Bhabha to Nehru, May 27, 1955, Confidential, NAI, 70-9/55-AMS.

[55] Hussain from Bhabha, September 13, 1955, Secret, Nehru Memorial Museum and Library (NMML), Jawaharlal Nehru Papers (JNP), file 381.

Nehru concurred, and officially sent word to India's representatives in Washington, Moscow, Paris, and London to advocate these terms.[56]

Meanwhile, Menon reported "little liking" among UN members "for the attitude of exclusiveness of the [eight] sponsors," and took the opportunity in debates to emphasize the "colonial aspects" of the emerging agency.[57] In a meeting with US Secretary of State John Foster Dulles, Menon warned that the IAEA should not look as though "it was an exclusive club dominated by a few big powers."[58] Faced with a potentially closed institution, Indian leaders appealed to a new principle for Board membership: geographical representation. In an aide memoire to US and Canadian negotiators, Bhabha argued that states did not deserve any "privileged position" on the Board "solely on grounds that they are actual or potential producers of uranium and thorium."[59] Instead, the Board should include, in addition to the five most technically advanced countries, "representatives from other large areas of the world."[60] In an official statement at the UNGA, Menon reiterated the need to create an agency that "does not breathe a sense of exclusion and which does not create a system of castes among sovereign states."[61] The IAEA, he added, "must be an agency that, by the text of its statutes, proclaims to the world that it is a good club to join."[62]

India's Scientific Status Recognized

In response to New Delhi's intense lobbying, the great powers initially sought to recognize India's major-power identity in other ways. Along with the IAEA, Eisenhower had proposed an unprecedented international conference on the peaceful uses of atomic energy. The

[56] Prime Minister for Ambassador/High Commissioner, October 7, 1955, Secret, NMML, JNP, file 390.
[57] Pillai from Krishna Menon, Personal, October 9, 1955, Secret, NMML, JNP, file 391.
[58] Note regarding discussion with Mr John Foster Dulles, October 15, 1955, Secret, NMML, JNP, file 392.
[59] Prime Minister from Bhabha, October 11, 1955, Top Secret, NMML, JNP, file 391.
[60] Ibid.
[61] Statement in the United Nations General Assembly, Tenth Session, First Committee, Verbatim Record of the 768th Meeting, A/C.1/PV.768, UN Meeting Records, October 25, 1955, 41–42.
[62] Ibid.

UNGA nominated India as a member of the preparatory committee for this conference, to serve alongside the United States, the Soviet Union, the UK, Canada, France, and Brazil, with UN Secretary-General Dag Hammarskjöld specifically requesting Bhabha's participation.[63] Once the committee's work was done, Hammarskjöld invited Bhabha to be president of the conference.

From India's perspective, the presidency was "a great tribute to Bhabha personally" and one that reflected "the sane attitude" of the UK and France, who supported Bhabha over initial US support for a Swiss candidate.[64] The conference, held in Geneva over twelve days in August 1955, was "the largest gathering of scientists and engineers the world had ever seen," with 1,500 delegates and over 1,000 scientific papers presented.[65] By all accounts, it was a highly prestigious and successful event. Bhabha was deeply impressed by the extent to which the great powers shared previously classified research in this setting. Writing to Nehru, he effusively noted that the United States, the UK, and the Soviet Union deserved "full credit" for the "immense amount of hitherto secret information which they freely made public, but for which the Conference could not have been the success it was."[66] As far as scientific discussions went, "all signs of the cold war [*sic*] appear to have disappeared," and he thought India should "take the opportunity of this excellent atmosphere to push forward with an enlarging of the areas of cooperation in this field."[67] As predicted by IST, Indian leaders were more cooperative when the international order was open to Indian leadership.

Bhabha was further pleased with India's "good showing" in terms of scientific papers, and India's ambassador to the United States, G. L. Mehta, observed that the way in which Bhabha led the conference had "deeply impressed leading scientists and public men in this country."[68] In a meeting with Bhabha and Mehta in October 1955, Lewis Strauss, chairman of the US Atomic Energy Commission (AEC), "expressed himself in full sympathy with our [Indian] attitude" and agreed that

---

[63] Lall to R. K. Nehru, December 9, 1954, NAI, UII/54/4571/10004.
[64] Lall to Pillai, January 31, 1955, NAI, UII/54/4571/10004.
[65] David Fischer, *History of the International Atomic Energy Agency: The First Forty Years* (Vienna: International Atomic Energy Agency, 1997), 31.
[66] Bhabha to Nehru, August 24, 1955, NMML, JNP, file 373.   [67] Ibid.
[68] Note regarding Dr. Bhabha's visit to Washington DC, October 15, 1955, Secret, NMML, JNP, file 392.

India should have a permanent seat on the IAEA.[69] Mehta reported the atmosphere at this meeting as one of "complete cordiality and friendship," with an evident desire on the part of the AEC to assist India's atomic energy plans.[70]

Toward an Open and Fair Great-Power Club

In an effort to address the sensitivities of countries outside the great-power club more generally, the great powers sought to put in place fair procedures of consultation and oversight. In his Atoms for Peace speech, Eisenhower had stated that the IAEA would be set up under the aegis of the United Nations, a commitment that Lodge, Jr., reiterated at the UNGA.[71] Although he rebutted Menon's proposal that the UNGA nominate additional states to the negotiations, Lodge, Jr., emphasized that this "emphatically does not mean that we are not eager actively to consult all governments," assuring them of "the most complete intention" among the IAEA's sponsors that there be "representatives of the underdeveloped countries" on its Board.[72]

Although the initial plan had been to agree on a statute among the group of eight and establish the agency before inviting other states to join,[73] by mid-1955 the chief US negotiator, Ambassador Morehead Patterson, believed it would be "political suicide" for the IAEA to have a Western-dominated Board that would essentially "have the appearance of a NATO uranium cartel."[74] Patterson further recommended scrapping the idea of formal permanent membership entirely, given that it was "intensely unpopular among most states."[75] In private meetings at the State Department, British and Canadian diplomats suggested India as a permanent member due to its "geographic position and role in Asia" and because, if the Soviets withdrew, India's

---

[69] Ibid.   [70] Ibid.
[71] Statement by Ambassador Lodge, Jr., November 15, 1954, NARA, NN3–326-93-004, box 1.
[72] Statement by Ambassador Lodge, Jr., November 19, 1954, NARA, NN3–326-93-004, box 1.
[73] Fischer, *History of the International Atomic Energy Agency*, 30.
[74] Statute of the International Atomic Energy Agency – Composition of the Board of Governors, June 20, 1955, Confidential, NARA, NN3–326-93-004, box 1.
[75] Ibid.

presence would avert the impression of the Board being "almost like a creature of NATO."[76] Consequently, when Ambassador Mehta met with Special Assistant to the Secretary of State for Atomic Energy, Gerard C. Smith, in July 1955, Smith "appreciated the importance of India" as a potential founder member of the IAEA and "hoped that India would play an important part in the proposed Agency."[77]

In the cooperative global atmosphere created by the scientific conference in Geneva, and wary of the need to consult widely, the United States soon circulated the eight-nation draft statute to all eighty-four states in the international system. More than thirty-five responded with comments.[78] In October 1955, largely as a result of pressure from developing countries in the UNGA, the United States invited the Soviet Union, Czechoslovakia, India, and Brazil to join negotiations and decided to convene a conference of all nations to discuss the statute, once drafted.[79] "The eight power monopoly has been broken," wrote Menon to Nehru.[80] According to him, India had also successfully "shifted the firmly held position of the Colonial powers" on issues such as the IAEA's relationship with the UN.[81] Most importantly, India was in the club: "[W]e will be present as one of the sponsors or negotiating group as it is now called."[82]

Indian leaders continued to be impressed by US even-handedness. In bilateral negotiations with New Delhi over nuclear cooperation, Washington proved willing to find creative ways to exceed the official limit on the amount of fissionable uranium transferable under existing US regulations.[83] When New Delhi learned that the scientists of Canada, Czechoslovakia, France, the UK, the United States, and the Soviet Union had held secret talks in Geneva in the week following the

---

[76] Memorandum of Conversation, April 19, 1955, Confidential, NARA, NN3–326-93-004, box 2; Memorandum of Conversation, May 11, 1955, Confidential, NARA, NN3–326-93-004, box 2.

[77] Mehta to Dutt, July 8, 1955, Secret, NAI, 70-9/55-AMS.

[78] Circular to all US Posts, September 18, 1956, Confidential, NARA, NN3–326-93-004, box 8.

[79] Chronology of IAEA Negotiations, December 3, 1956, Confidential, NARA, NN3–326-93-004, box 5.

[80] Prime Minister from Menon, November 4, 1955, Personal and Secret, NMML, JNP, file 397(I).

[81] Ibid.   [82] Ibid.

[83] Krishnamurti to Husain, June 2, 1955, NAI, 70-9/55-AMS.

scientific conference,[84] the Indian embassy in Washington requested copies of the record of discussions and the US State Department agreed to hand them over.[85] On the eve of the twelve-nation negotiations in February 1956, India's permanent representative to the UN, Arthur Lall, reported that the deputy chief of the US delegation, James Wadsworth, was "receptive to our suggestions" regarding a closer relationship between the UN and the IAEA, and the possibility of a larger board of governors based partly on geographic distribution.[86]

Securing Status in the Twelve-Nation Negotiations

Starting in February 1956, the group of twelve nations negotiated the IAEA's draft statute over seven weeks in Washington. Three points of contention stood out: the IAEA's relationship with the UN, the composition of the board of governors, and safeguards. India was able to achieve its preferred outcomes on the first two counts but not the third. Nonetheless, India's negotiators saw sufficient evidence to suggest that India was treated as a symbolically equal member of the great-power club, thus justifying further engagement with the nuclear order.

Regarding the UN, the United States wanted to establish the IAEA as a specialized agency, which would report – like other agencies – to the UN's Economic and Social Council. The Soviet Union, by contrast, wanted an IAEA reporting to the UN Security Council, where veto power would come into play.[87] Ultimately, the twelve nations agreed that the IAEA would do neither. It would be an autonomous agency reporting to the UNGA. This was in line with India's preferences,[88] and Menon credited the Indian delegation with making "substantial

[84] New Delhi to Indian Embassy in Washington, November 11, 1955, Secret and Immediate, NMML, JNP, file 399.
[85] Memorandum of Conversation, November 30, 1955, NARA, NN3–326-93-004, box 4.
[86] Lall to New Delhi, February 11, 1956, Secret, NMML, JNP, file 419.
[87] Elisabeth Roehrlich, "The Cold War, the developing world, and the creation of the International Atomic Energy Agency (IAEA), 1953–1957," *Cold War History*, 16:2 (2016), 195–212.
[88] United Nations General Assembly, Tenth Session, First Committee, "Verbatim record of the seven hundred and sixty-eighth meeting," A/C.1/PV.768, UN Meeting Records, October 25, 1955.

contributions" by brokering a compromise between the United States and the Soviet Union.[89]

On institutional membership, India was adamant about equality and inclusion. At the outset, India successfully proposed an amendment to the statute to have sovereign equality explicitly written into it.[90] Regarding the IAEA Board, Bhabha argued that cooperation in the peaceful uses of atomic energy was a service "to be rendered in a spirit of dedication and not in an arrogant take-it-or-leave-it manner."[91] It was vital "to carry the recipient countries with us as equal and enthusiastic partners in this enterprise."[92] This objective required "an equitable distribution in the composition of the Board of Governors."[93]

India now proposed a Board of twenty-three countries, of which ten would be quasi-permanent. These seats would be filled not by naming countries but according to a criterion that would ensure de facto permanence, namely, being advanced in nuclear technology and source materials, subject to a geographical distribution across eight world regions.[94] Institutional openness, above all, meant inclusion for India in the top ranks of the IAEA. Bhabha reported to Nehru that privately, both the Soviet and US delegations expressed their support for India's "inclusion in [the agency's] top category."[95] Nehru himself was pleased with India's growing status. He publicly declared back home that it was "very encouraging that people of other countries value our advice and more and more come to us to discuss matters."[96]

The twelve-nation discussion on safeguards proved a disappointment for India. During the negotiations, the United States proposed new and more extensive safeguards than previous drafts of the IAEA statute had contained. Western states supported the proposal, suggesting that they prioritized the control of nuclear materials far more than

[89] Prime Minister from Menon, March 7, 1956, Secret and Immediate, NMML, JNP, file 425.
[90] Working Level Meeting on the Draft Statute of the IAEA, April 27, 1956, Conference Confidential, NARA, NN3–326-93-004, box 10.
[91] Statement by Dr. H. J. Bhabha on Article VII, March 9, 1956, Attachment 4, doc. 12 (rev. 1), Working Level Meeting, April 27, 1956, NARA, NN3–326-93-004, box 10.
[92] Ibid.   [93] Ibid.
[94] Fischer, *History of the International Atomic Energy Agency*, 39.
[95] Prime Minister from Bhabha, March 19, 1956, Top Secret and Most Immediate, NMML, JNP, file 428.
[96] Address by the Prime Minister at the DIG, CID's Conference on March 13, 1956, NMML, JNP, file 426(II).

the peaceful uses of atomic energy. The West was trying to "corner all world production of uranium,"[97] Bhabha reasoned, and extensive safeguards would "divide States in the world into two categories, and place those States receiving aid from or through the Agency at a disadvantage."[98] Strict controls would penalize developing countries, which would depend on the IAEA, while advanced Western countries could rely on their own nuclear technology and materials not subject to IAEA controls.

India's objection was grounded not in procedural fairness – after all, the statute placed identical obligations on all states – but in distributional inequality. Bhabha believed that stringent safeguards would give the agency "power to interfere in [the] economy of States receiving aid," which would not be the case for advanced countries that could do without the IAEA.[99] Stringent safeguards, Bhabha argued in the meetings, would thus bring the world to "the brink of a dangerous era sharply dividing the world into atomic 'haves' and those dominated by them through the instrumentality of the Agency."[100] Combined with the dominance of atomic haves on the IAEA Board, this would result in "a colonial situation as bad or worse than any that has been experienced hitherto."[101] In the end, India was alone among the twelve nations in articulating its opposition.[102] Although the Soviet Union and Czechoslovakia voted in favor of India's proposed amendments on this issue, their gestures were symbolic given the cohesive support for the safeguards in the Western bloc.[103]

[97] Prime Minister from Bhabha, March 17, 1956, Secret and Immediate, NMML, JNP, file 427(II).

[98] Statement by Dr. H. J. Bhabha on Article XIII, Attachment 2, doc. 14 (rev. 1), Working Level Meeting, April 27, 1956, NARA, NN3-326-93-004, box 10.

[99] Prime Minister from Bhabha, September 24, 1956, Secret and Immediate, NMML, JNP, file 475.

[100] Statement by Dr. H. J. Bhabha on the Indian Amendment to the United States Amendment to Paragraph C-5 of Article XIII, Attachment 3, doc. 19 (rev. 1), Working Level Meeting, April 27, 1956, NARA, NN3-326-93-004, box 10.

[101] Statement by Dr. H. J. Bhabha on the Indian Amendment to the United States Amendment to Introduce a New Paragraph, A-6, to Article XIII, Attachment 4, doc. 19 (rev. 1), Working Level Meeting, April 27, 1956, NARA, NN3-326-93-004, box 10.

[102] Summary Report on 12-Nation Working Level Meeting on IAEA Statute, March 23, 1956, Confidential, NARA, NN3-326-93-004, box 8.

[103] See Summary of Developments Working Level Meeting Draft Statute IAEA Tenth through Sixteenth Sessions, March 23, 1956, NARA, NN3-326-93-004, box 8.

Despite this setback, the twelve-nation negotiations ended in April 1956 with significant wins for India: sovereign equality codified in the statute, an expanded Board to include India, an IAEA accountable to the UNGA, and substantial new powers for the IAEA's General Conference.[104] These changes ensured India's inclusion in the IAEA's top ranks as well as a more consultative and accountable decision-making framework for the agency. While the *outcome* on safeguards risked exacerbating global inequality, it was arrived at by a fair process in which India had extensive opportunity to press its position. Moreover, the IAEA statute did not recognize any differences between members when it came to the *application* of safeguards.

India's Satisfaction with the Evolving Nuclear Order

As predicted by IST, the procedural aspects of the negotiations significantly influenced the Indian delegation's overall assessments. India was seen to have played a major role in the discussions alongside the United States and the Soviet Union (partly because the Western bloc and Brazil chose to let the United States speak collectively for them on most occasions).[105] Due to the success of India's proposal regarding the composition of the board of governors, the meeting was "the first occasion on which the Statute of an international organisation provide[d] for the representation of geographical regions of the world."[106] Even on safeguards, the delegation noted with satisfaction that India had led the opposition to US amendments, resulting in "long and persistent arguments," which even managed to convince the Soviets to support India's position.[107]

As leader of the delegation, Bhabha himself evinced a nuanced view of the evolving nuclear order. He noted "a genuine desire" among the great powers to promote the peaceful uses of atomic energy, offset by "a strong desire to maintain their present privileged position."[108] The lesson for India was not to abandon the IAEA but to be the first country in Asia and Africa to "develop a vigorous atomic energy programme which does not depend upon help from any of the

---

[104] Report of the Indian Delegation on the Working Level Meeting for a Draft Statute of the IAEA, Washington, June 26, 1956, Secret, NMML, JNP, file 454 (I).
[105] Ibid.   [106] Ibid.   [107] Ibid.
[108] Bhabha to PM, April 20, 1956, Secret, NMML, JNP, file 439(II).

advanced countries."[109] This was essential not just for India's own use but for it to provide limited assistance to friendly African and Asian countries as well. After all, "[a]n active and developing atomic energy programme appears to give to a country an importance and position in international affairs," and India could only enjoy this status by having an independent program in the manner of other advanced countries.[110]

Menon agreed with Bhabha's assessment but was wary of the impression India might create among Asian and African countries by assuming "leadership or monopoly" on atomic energy.[111] The atom was becoming cartelized like oil, and India had to avoid looking like it was "tied up largely with foreign cartels and organisations mostly American."[112] Four years into his ambassadorship to the UN, Menon was more connected than Bhabha to India's identity as a leading anti-colonial nation. Therefore, while he welcomed India's inclusion in the great-power club, he was conscious of the politics of being associated with an agency he himself had publicly labeled neocolonial.

Nehru split the difference between his two top officials. He reminded them that it was already India's policy to "develop our atomic energy programme, if necessary, without any external aid."[113] India now had to progress "at least as fast as ... any Asian or African country receiving external aid."[114] Whereas Bhabha had sought to bestow India's nuclear largesse on the developing world and Menon was wary of the optics of doing so, Nehru was focused on ensuring that India remained ahead of any future claimants to membership in the great-power club. "We have at present a certain lead in regard to [the] atomic energy programme in Asia and Africa," he wrote. "We should maintain that lead."[115] To that end, he authorized six new positions in India's Department of Atomic Energy, a uranium mining program, and a uranium enrichment plant (in future), and recommitted to domestic heavy water production.[116] Nehru also agreed with Menon that India should be vigilant for any future attempts at "some kind of control of atomic energy by a few great Powers."[117] As an equal member of the club, India would try to mitigate the distributional effects of the club's

[109] Ibid. [110] Ibid.
[111] Menon to PM, May 3, 1956, NMML, JNP, file 439(II). [112] Ibid.
[113] Nehru to Secretary, Department of Atomic Energy, Finance Minister, and Cabinet Secretary, May 4, 1956, Secret, NMML, JNP, file 439(II).
[114] Ibid. [115] Ibid. [116] Ibid. [117] Ibid.

rules. As Bhabha noted in a radio broadcast from New Delhi a few
months later, although India was concerned with the severity of IAEA
safeguards, "fear and suspicion should not be allowed to throttle the
main objectives of the agency."[118]

In line with India's earlier demand for a world conference, a meeting
of eighty-two nations in New York took up the twelve-nation draft
over a period of five weeks starting in September 1956. Participating
countries submitted ninety-one amendments, of which thirty were
withdrawn, twenty-six were voted down, and thirty-five were voted
up.[119] None of the latter entailed substantial revisions. Both India and
France lobbied to minimize the statute's inspection and control clauses,
and to exempt source materials entirely.[120] Although these efforts
failed, India was able to secure a change that limited inspections to
chemical plants only and not the entire nuclear cycle. Bhabha reported
from New York that this amendment "completely changes [the] com-
plexion of safeguards and deprives [the] agency of power to interfere in
[the] economic life of States receiving aid."[121]

In the end, the entire statute was put to a vote and passed unani-
mously. In a briefing note to the Indian cabinet a few months later –
likely authored by Bhabha himself – the Department of Atomic Energy
described the final statute as "a great improvement over the original
draft," largely due to India's efforts.[122] India had secured almost
everything it had sought in the negotiations, especially "a *de facto*
permanent place on the Board of Governors of the Agency with such
other countries as U.S.A., U.K., France, Canada and U.S.S.R." and a
satisfactory relationship between the IAEA and the UN.[123] Even the
provisions on safeguards had incorporated some of India's views, and
India's remaining reservations were distributional and not procedural,

---

[118] American Embassy New Delhi to Department of State, September 14, 1956,
NARA, NN3–326-93-004, box 8.
[119] Paul C. Szasz, *The Law and Practices of the International Atomic Energy
Agency* (Vienna: International Atomic Energy Agency, 1970), 40.
[120] Analysis of International Atomic Energy Agency Statute, December 17, 1956,
NARA, NN3–326-93-004, box 9.
[121] Prime Minister from Bhabha, October 22, 1956, Secret and Immediate,
NMML, JNP, file 481.
[122] Ratification of the Statute of the International Atomic Energy Agency,
Summary for the Cabinet, March 30, 1957, Secret, NMML, JNP, file 516(I).
[123] Ibid.

that is, "concerned not so much with the present form of the Statute as with the manner in which it might be operated."[124]

Although India would have preferred the safeguards applied to states irrespective of whether they went through the IAEA or not, Indian leaders ultimately agreed to the provisions "for a limited period on the understanding either that during the next few years these measures will extend to all countries, whether they come to the Agency for aid or not, or that they cease to apply to all countries, because of progress in the sphere of disarmament."[125] Two years after the statute was approved, Bhabha revisited some of India's earlier concerns in a note to Nehru from an IAEA meeting in Paris. He noted that there was now a widespread feeling among IAEA members that the agency should build additional links to the UN. His assessment was that despite the IAEA's imperfections, India had secured gains in the agency that should be preserved. Most importantly, "India has a quasi-permanent seat on the Board of Governors, together with the five countries most advanced in the field of atomic energy," Bhabha concluded. "We should ensure that this position is not lost."[126]

Nuclear Ambiguity as Cooperative Strategy

"The idea of showing you can do something by not doing it" is, as Barry O'Neill argues, an important source of prestige when it comes to nuclear weapons.[127] India had anchored its nuclear policy exactly to this principle since the late 1940s. In an often-cited speech from 1946, Nehru said, "I have no doubt that India will develop her scientific researches and I hope Indian scientists will use the atomic force for constructive purposes. But if India is threatened she will inevitably try to defend herself by all means at her disposal."[128] A decade later, in the midst of the IAEA negotiations, Bhabha made the status-related motivations of this position explicit. In a secret note to Nehru, he argued that India should develop a "vigorous programme in developing atomic energy for peaceful purposes" because it was well known that "a country which can develop such a strong peaceful atomic programme

[124] Ibid.   [125] Ibid.

[126] Bhabha to PM, October 2, 1958, NAI, F.1(17)-UNII/58, vol. II.

[127] O'Neill, "Nuclear weapons," 3.

[128] M. V. Ramana, "India's changing nuclear policy," *Peace Magazine*, 14:1 (1998), 6–9.

could also produce atomic weapons, if it wished."[129] India's claim to symbolic equality with the great powers would lie in abstaining from building nuclear weapons despite possessing the capacity to do so. "The decision not to produce atomic weapons in these circumstances would immensely increase the country's moral prestige and political importance in the councils of the world, perhaps even more than if the same programme had been directed to military ends," Bhabha concluded.[130]

Although scholars such as Ashley Tellis have used the term "nuclear ambiguity" to describe India's posture after the Cold War,[131] the term also applies to India's approach to the international order in the 1950s and 1960s. It was a two-pronged strategy. First, India consistently pushed for general and complete nuclear disarmament through various international institutions, such as the disarmament conferences in Geneva and the UNGA, as well as the high-profile Bandung Conference of Asian and African countries.[132] Second, Indian leaders consistently kept the nuclear option open, insisting that while they could build nuclear weapons, they chose not to in the interest of international peace and disarmament.[133] If disarmament were successful, there would be no need for nuclear weapons. If disarmament decisively failed, India could build the bomb and join the nuclear club. Either way, India was assured of its symbolic equality with the great powers.

Nuclear ambiguity was a cooperative strategy, enabled by an international nuclear order that Indian leaders held to be open to India joining its top ranks as a nuclear power in the future and procedurally fair at this point, with no institutional distinctions between states with nuclear weapons and states without. Andrew Kennedy notes, "Nehru's nuclear diplomacy reflected a sense that India possessed a certain moral authority in the international system, particularly in the wake of its nonviolent independence struggle, and it aimed at nothing less than slowing the nuclear arms race between the superpowers."[134]

---

[129] Bhabha to PM, April 20, 1956, Secret, NMML, JNP, file 439(II).   [130] Ibid.
[131] Ashley J. Tellis, *India's Emerging Nuclear Posture: Between Recessed Deterrent and Ready Arsenal* (Santa Monica: RAND, 2001), 10.
[132] See Nehru, *Speeches*, 309, 318, 362–363, 394.
[133] See Perkovich, *India's Nuclear Bomb*, 20; Nehru, *Speeches*, 436.
[134] Andrew B. Kennedy, "India's nuclear odyssey: Implicit umbrellas, diplomatic disappointments, and the bomb," *International Security*, 36:2 (2011), 120–153.

Nuclear ambiguity allowed India to maintain a unique position in the international order as a scientifically advanced and potentially powerful but essentially pacifist country. As a rising power that was increasingly recognized as a major player in international institutions, India valued recognition of its major-power identity enough to be willing to sacrifice short-term security for it.

Cooperation despite Security Threats, 1964–1971

In October 1964, China conducted its first nuclear test, at Lop Nor in the southeastern region of Xinjiang province. The political fallout occurred over a thousand miles away, in New Delhi. "China blasted its way into the world's nuclear club today," proclaimed a front-page story in *The Times of India*.[135] Prime Minister Shastri was alarmed but not surprised – China's intention to go nuclear was well known.[136] Yet, memories of a humiliating military defeat at the hands of the Chinese just two years earlier were still fresh. Calls for an Indian atomic bomb, louder since the Sino-Indian war, intensified among the political elite. Despite this pressure, neither Shastri nor his successor, Indira Gandhi, came anywhere close to starting a nuclear program in the 1960s.

Existing accounts argue that India saw China as a nuclear threat but lacked the resources and technical know-how to develop the bomb as a potential deterrent.[137] Security undoubtedly mattered. Collusion between China and Pakistan, which to Indian minds had "even gone beyond a formal alliance," was especially troubling.[138] During the Sino-Indian War of 1962, Pakistan allegedly convinced its nationals working in shipping between West Bengal and Assam to go on strike, thereby severing communications and supply lines between two vital Indian regions.[139] In 1965, China issued India with an ultimatum

---

[135] Times of India, "Solemn pledge not to use it first: Main aim is to break nuclear monopoly," October 17, 1964.

[136] Frank E. Couper, "Indian party conflict on the issue of atomic weapons," *The Journal of Developing Areas*, III (1969), 191–206.

[137] Jayita Sarkar, "The making of a non-aligned nuclear power: India's proliferation drift, 1964–8," *The International History Review*, 37:5 (2015), 933–950.

[138] Confidential note (author not mentioned), NAI, Ministry of External Affairs (MEA), WII/104/16/66.

[139] Untitled file, NAI, MEA, WII/105/5/66.

threatening hostilities along their shared border if India did not cease hostilities in its war with Pakistan.[140] By 1966, Indian leaders interpreted the visit of Pakistani scientist Abdus Salam to Peking as "undoubtedly an indication of nuclear collaboration between the two countries in the military field."[141]

Despite these concerns, top policymakers in Delhi did very little through the 1960s except to sanction theoretical work that might someday result in a nuclear test.[142] While it is true that nuclear technology was not cheap, the deeper issue is that a political decision was made *not* to pursue the bomb. Had the opposite decision been made, the Chinese example shows that India could have assembled the required resources, especially given that India already possessed the basic civilian nuclear infrastructure and Indian nuclear scientists were far more globally networked than their Chinese counterparts.

Domestic Pressure versus International Status

Despite great pressure from opposition parties and members of his own party to launch a weapons program following the Chinese test, Shastri stuck to India's policy of ambiguity. *Time* magazine declared that while Indian nuclear physicists "could easily build an atomic bomb in a year to 18 months," India had "no real military use for it."[143] If anything, India's prestige was at risk. In a meeting with the director of the US Arms Control and Disarmament Agency in Washington, two weeks after the test, India's ambassador, B. K. Nehru (Jawaharlal Nehru's nephew), mentioned "strong pressures" at home for a nuclear test "to offset the genuine psychological advantages which the Chinese had obtained in Southeast Asia by virtue of their explosion."[144] To make matters worse, China was now suggesting a five-power nuclear conference, which would exclude India as a nonnuclear state. B. K. Nehru was clear on the implications: "In view of India's status in Asia and her peaceful nuclear achievements, such a

---

[140] NAI, WII/104/16/66.   [141] NAI, WII/105/5/66.

[142] M. V. Ramana, "*La trahison des clercs*: Scientists and India's nuclear bomb," in M. V. Ramana and C. Rammanohar Reddy (eds.), *Prisoners of the Nuclear Dream* (New Delhi: Orient Longman, 2003), 206–244.

[143] TIME, "India: Pride & reality," August 13, 1965, 5.

[144] Memorandum of Conversation, Washington, November 3, 1964, Foreign Relations of the United States (FRUS), vol. XXV.

meeting without her would be a disastrous blow psychologically and every other way to the Indian Government."[145] Any great-power meeting on nuclear weapons would have to include India.

Bhabha, meanwhile, sought to use the moment to secure greater cooperation on civilian nuclear technology. In a meeting with US State Department officials in Washington in February 1965, he highlighted the importance of India needing "some dramatic 'peaceful' achievement to offset the prestige gained by Communist China among Africans and Asians."[146] When Under Secretary of State George Ball replied that the United States was focused on getting "major non-nuclear countries to agree to forego nuclear weapons," Bhabha retorted that "it was not helpful to differentiate between members of the 'nuclear club' and non-nuclear nations," and reminded Ball that "India could quite easily have achieved China's capability" but had chosen not to.[147] In other words, symbolically, there was nothing distinguishing India from the members of the great-power club. Bhabha concluded the meeting with a summation of India's status calculation: "[W]ays must be found by which [India] can gain at least as much by sticking to peaceful uses as it could by embarking on a weapons program."[148]

India's political leadership in fact believed they gained substantial recognition as a major power from cooperating with the international order. During a heated debate at the annual meeting of the Indian National Congress party's central decision-making body, a month after China's nuclear test, Shastri emphasized India's ability to "give the lead in the maintenance of world peace," especially to newly independent African and Asian countries; a lead that would undoubtedly be jeopardized by nuclear tests.[149] His foreign minister, Swaran Singh, argued that at a time when "there was such increasing response to the policy of non-alignment and peaceful co-existence [championed by India]," it would be foolhardy if "India herself expressed doubts about the validity of its principles" by testing.[150] Menon, who had

[145] Ibid.
[146] Memorandum of Conversation (Secret), Indian Nuclear Energy Program, Washington, February 22, 1965, FRUS (vol. XXV).
[147] Ibid.   [148] Ibid.
[149] Times of India, "Nuclear bomb manufacture will be heavy burden: Shastri," November 9, 1964, 7.
[150] Ibid.

been defense minister during India's defeat at the hands of China in 1962, argued more pragmatically that nonalignment had "enabled India's voice to be heard in international councils" while allowing India to continue arming itself conventionally and being on good terms with both superpowers.[151] To conduct a test now would be to throw all of these achievements away.

Both Shastri and Bhabha died in January 1966, the former of natural causes and the latter in a plane crash, and Indira Gandhi took over as prime minister. In May 1966, after China had conducted its third nuclear test and Parliament was once again up in arms about the lack of an equivalent Indian response, Swaran Singh reiterated that India's "policy (of making a bomb) is kept under constant review." He added, "In the matter of peaceful development of atomic energy we are pushing ahead and giving it top priority ... [T]he world recognizes that we're one of the countries which are capable of being an atomic power within a reasonably short time."[152] Once again, India's leaders stressed the technical ability to produce a weapon and the desire not to do so. Singh's notes for parliamentary Question Hour in August 1966 made it clear that India was still not considering nuclear weapons:

After consideration of all security, political and other aspects of the question Government have decided that the answer to this threat does not lie in the development of a national nuclear deterrent. Government have, however, decided at the same time to continue all efforts to develop nuclear know-how and capability though nuclear energy would continue to be used exclusively for peaceful purposes.[153]

Singh's comments echoed an internal memo prepared by the foreign ministry's Historical Division, which stated that although China's test was "another challenge to India's policy of non-alignment" and India "has the potentiality of making a nuclear bomb," New Delhi had "no intention to change her policy" of trying to end the Cold War by renouncing nuclear weapons and thereby eliminating the balance of

---

[151] Ibid.
[152] A. G. Noorani, "India's quest for a nuclear guarantee," *Asian Survey*, 7:7 (1967), 490–502.
[153] Note for Supplementaries (On Lok Sabha Starred Question No. 734 for 29.8.1966), NAI, WII/104/5/66.

terror.[154] In June 1967, eight months after China's first test of a medium-range ballistic missile, Singh's successor, M. C. Chagla, while responding to questions in Parliament about a future Chinese intercontinental ballistic missile (ICBM) capability, recognized the elevated threat but reaffirmed that "we have no intention of exploding an atomic bomb."[155]

By maintaining this stance, India continued to emulate the peaceful technological achievements of the great powers without undermining an order that it found procedurally fair and that had so far allowed New Delhi to retain a pathway to future great-power status. Columnist A. G. Noorani noted at the time, "It is not so much that India, with her immense problems, wishes to embark on a nuclear weapons program as that she wishes anxiously, and one might add legitimately, to protect her option to do so."[156] Instead of building the bomb, India sought security guarantees from the superpowers, largely to assuage the domestic pro-bomb lobby.[157] The guarantees, however, seemed not to be forthcoming, partly because the superpowers were leery of a potential nuclear showdown with China, and partly because India's own pursuit of the guarantee conflicted with its nonaligned foreign policy and hence was half-hearted. Even the theoretical research sanctioned by Shastri barely served its purpose of being a token concession to pro-bomb groups. Almost two years after the research program had been authorized, Congress party Members of Parliament (MPs) such as K. C. Pant were still privately reminding their own leadership of the Chinese threat and requesting "a full-scale exercise on the time and resources necessary" to explode a nuclear device.[158]

Nuclear ambiguity was self-reinforcing. So long as international disarmament efforts did not bear fruit, India could retain the future option of building the bomb; and so long as the nuclear option was open, India could play an important role in disarmament negotiations.

---

[154] India's Policy on ending the Cold War, May 5, 1966, NAI, MEA, WII/125/46/66.
[155] Lok Sabha Starred Question No. 273, to be answered on the 5th June, 1967, Stationing of Nuclear Missiles on Indian Territory, NAI, MEA, U-IV/125/12/67.
[156] Noorani, "India's quest," 501.
[157] Ziba Moshaver, *Nuclear Weapons Proliferation in the Indian Subcontinent* (New York: Palgrave Macmillan, 1991), 33.
[158] Pant to Singh, Note on the International Assembly on Nuclear Weapons, August 15, 1966, NAI, MEA, UI/162/11/66.

The strategy was, however, not optimal from a security perspective. Maintaining the option to build nuclear weapons was a far cry from deterrence against potential nuclear coercion by China. That said, nuclear ambiguity was intended not for security but symbolic equality with the great powers in an international order that was institutionally open and procedurally fair.

An Open and Fair Great-Power Club

So long as the international order left a pathway open for India to eventually join the ranks of the great powers and treated India in a consultative and consistent manner, Indian leaders saw their status ambitions best served through cooperation. A cooperative strategy required observable good-faith investment in the institutions of the nuclear order. In April 1964, P. N. Haksar, India's ambassador to Vienna, wrote a note presumably intended for New Delhi, requesting that a junior officer from the Department of Atomic Energy be seconded to the office of India's permanent representative to the IAEA, a position he held *ex officio*. He wrote, "As a permanent member of the Board of Governors of the I.A.E.A., our country occupies a special position. We also occupy a special, even a leading, position among the developing countries." Haksar continued but later crossed out this part: "by reason of the fact that … we are the most advanced in the field of the development of nuclear energy. Indeed, my impression is that we are quite a leading country, even when compared to some of the West European countries." He went on to argue that given India's position, it should be well placed to take "detailed interest in the day to day functioning of the Agency [the IAEA]. Our participation should be well informed. We owe this not only to ourselves but to the large number of developing countries who look towards us for guidance and support." Haksar's predecessor, Lall, had been largely absent from his Vienna posting. As a result, India had been represented at the IAEA by the chargé d'affaires and, according to Haksar, "our reputation as effective members of the governing body slumped during this period."[159]

---

[159] Untitled draft note (April 1, 1964), P.N. Haksar Papers (PNHP), I&II installment, SF27, NMML. Final version not available.

Lall was absent from Vienna because he was involved alongside Menon in the negotiations of the ENCD in Geneva, another venue in which India sought recognition as an active and constructive member. Indian leaders saw their country as having "always stood at the fore-front of the movement for general and complete disarmament under effective international control."[160] The ENCD was the premier global stage on which India's leadership in this area could be demonstrated. The committee's proceedings opened in March 1962, with high-level delegates present from each country. Menon led the Indian delegation in the first six meetings and returned to Geneva from time to time.

Early in the proceedings, Menon strongly advocated positions that one would not expect from a country that many thought was flirting with nuclear weapons. He advocated general disarmament, reminding the committee that this was largely the responsibility of the nuclear powers. Nonnuclear nations could not "throw away atomic bombs" because "we have not got them – all that we can do is to commit ourselves not to make atomic weapons," he argued.[161] Remarkably, he also pushed for nonproliferation: "We have ourselves advocated for a long time that the spread of these weapons to other countries not only increases the area of danger but also places them ... in less responsible hands."[162] Finally, he called for a comprehensive test ban and a moratorium on testing as long as the ENCD was in deliberations: "[W]e are in favour of a treaty as sacrosanct as it can be made; we are in favour of any type of arrangements that can be made. But, pending those treaties, we are even more concerned to see to it that even the prospect of such a treaty is not jeopardised by explosions that may take place."[163] Menon's cooperative positions on all three issues (disarmament, nonproliferation, and testing) were unconditional and in stark contrast to positions that India would begin taking in the late 1960s.

Menon's rhetoric may have been insincere; talk that was essentially cheap for a middle power such as India so long as the great powers were deadlocked on these critical issues. However, one only has to

---

[160] Statement of Leader of the Indian Delegation to ECOSOC, NAI, MEA, UI/251/78/64.
[161] Conference of the Eighteen-Nation Committee on Disarmament (ENCD), "Final verbatim record of the fifth meeting," Private, ENDC/PV.5, March 20, 1962, 32, University of Michigan Digital Library.
[162] Ibid., 35.   [163] Ibid., 37.

look at the example of France to see the counterfactual case of a country that deliberately avoided the ENCD because of fears that the superpowers would curb its nascent nuclear weapons program.[164] India did not suffer from the same fears because at the time, it enjoyed the recognition of being an active and constructive member of the international order. Menon declared in the committee, "We do not take the view that we have come here as onlookers, merely to bear witness to what has been said and what has not been said, because war and its consequences make no exemptions based on race or creed or geography, or anything of that kind."[165]

Lall, who led the Indian delegation at the ENCD for the first two years, held similar views of India's role in the committee. Shortly after stepping down from his role, he wrote in an article in the *Bulletin of the Atomic Scientists*, "In the context of disarmament negotiations one is entitled to ask why the non-aligned nations are there at all." The answer, according to him, was that "[t]he non-aligned have ... come into a position of quite considerable parliamentary power in world councils to which the major power blocs are sensitive. The political philosophy of non-alignment in international affairs, though no older than about fifteen years, has already won the adherence of some forty-five member states of the United Nations."[166] He offered several reasons as to why the nonaligned nations – one can safely infer that he was thinking primarily of India in this context – had gained such influence. These included, among other things, the increasingly active and successful disarmament-related diplomacy by nonaligned countries in the UN since the mid-1950s; their role in major international peace conferences; and the fact that some nonnuclear powers, such as Sweden and India, would soon be able to manufacture nuclear weapons.[167]

The great-power club at this time, as instantiated in the nuclear order, was sufficiently open and procedurally fair for a rising power such as India to keep the door to nuclear weapons open while feeling

---

[164] Edward A. Kolodziej, "French disarmament and arms control policy: The Gaullist heritage in question," in William G. Andrews and Stanley Hoffmann (eds.), *The Fifth Republic at Twenty* (Albany: SUNY Press, 1981), 412–429.

[165] ENCD, "Fifth meeting," 42.

[166] Arthur S. Lall, "The nonaligned in disarmament negotiations," *Bulletin of the Atomic Scientists*, 20:5 (1964), 17–21.

[167] Ibid., 18–19.

duly consulted on the substance of the order itself. Lall viewed the role of India and other nonaligned countries as indispensable to the ENCD's mission. He argued that "it was virtually impossible for the two sides [United States and Soviet Union] to agree to sit down in negotiations without the presence of nonaligned representatives."[168] In a monograph he subsequently produced as a visiting professor of international relations at Cornell University, he noted,

For the first seven years or so of United Nations history, the non-aligned countries were a small insignificant minority ... But things suddenly changed. The success of the Indian resolution on Korea altered the status of the nonaligned at the United Nations ... In April 1954 Prime Minister Jawaharlal Nehru took a step which arose out of this new realization and made the world take note that the nonaligned were no longer going to remain on the side lines. He asked the United Nations to put on its agenda the question of the cessation of nuclear weapon tests ... Thus, it was a nonaligned initiative which brought to the United Nations the issue of nuclear tests.[169]

In April 1962, when American and Soviet negotiators had reached an impasse on whether inspections should be allowed in all testing environments, the eight nonaligned nations put forward a compromise proposal that would permit inspections only in the case of underground tests. The superpowers agreed, introducing two separate treaties: one on underground tests and one on all other environments, with the latter becoming the Partial Test Ban Treaty. Reflecting on this episode, Lall argued, "The weight of the Eight Nation memorandum ... increased the standing of the nonaligned at the Geneva Conference as partners in negotiation. The nonaligned, of course, entirely concede the primacy of interest of the nuclear powers in the matter of arms control and disarmament, but they do not at all accept [the] view that negotiations should involve nuclear powers alone."[170] Not every diplomatic intervention by India and the nonaligned nations was successful – a similar attempt, in early 1963, to break a deadlock on the number of inspections was "stillborn."[171]

---

[168] Ibid., 18.
[169] Arthur S. Lall, *Negotiating Disarmament: The Eighteen Nation Disarmament Conference: The First Two Years, 1962–64* (Ithaca: Center for International Studies, Cornell University, 1964), 2.
[170] Ibid., 23.   [171] Ibid., 25.

Nonetheless, the nuclear order formalized India's symbolic equality with the great powers as a partner in resolving thorny disagreements over nonproliferation and disarmament. This was reason enough to stay involved and cooperative.

India's Growing Disillusionment

From the mid-1960s onward, India's approach to the ENCD underwent a transformation due to the evolution of nonproliferation on the institutional agenda. Indian leaders had consistently advocated the non-dissemination of nuclear weapons and technology to nonnuclear states, but as a step toward nuclear disarmament. In July 1962, Menon had called on the nuclear powers to "declare unilaterally but simultaneously that here and now they will not pass on to any other country or group of countries nuclear weapons or the control of such weapons or the means and knowledge to manufacture them."[172] Vishnu Trivedi, Lall's successor in the ENCD, argued, in March 1964, for the nuclear powers to build on the momentum of the PTBT and introduce a similar treaty for nuclear nonproliferation: "The four nuclear Powers should commit themselves not to transfer nuclear weapons or weapon technology, and the non-nuclear nations should pledge not to manufacture, possess or receive these weapons."[173] Crucially, however, Trivedi argued that nonproliferation was necessary to increase the likelihood of disarmament at a future stage of negotiations.

China's nuclear test in October 1964 did not substantially change India's stance, except to add the proviso of a security guarantee for nonnuclear powers. In May 1965, Indian representative B. N. Chakravarty made a speech in the Disarmament Commission, outlining a five-point proposal for nonproliferation, which included the nontransfer of nuclear weapons and technology by nuclear powers; the nonuse of nuclear weapons against nonnuclear powers; a UN security guarantee for nonnuclear powers; tangible progress toward disarmament; and non-acquisition and non-manufacture of nuclear

---

[172] Times of India, "No supply of a-arms to others: Menon asks big powers to act," July 25, 1962, 1.

[173] Conference of the Eighteen-Nation Committee on Disarmament, "Final verbatim record of the one hundred and seventy-fourth meeting," ENDC/PV.174, March 12, 1964, 17, University of Michigan Digital Library.

weapons by nonnuclear powers.[174] Procedural fairness was India's main concern. Nonproliferation and disarmament measures *by all states* would not only allow India to maintain symbolic equality with the great powers, but, if successful, be a cheaper method – compared to an Indian nuclear deterrent – of constraining China's nuclear arsenal.

The Indian proposal was a tall order for the superpowers. In August 1965, the United States and the Soviet Union introduced separate initial drafts of the NPT in which there were *no* obligations on the nuclear powers to halt the further production of nuclear weapons and delivery vehicles, or to reduce existing stocks. India's leadership was taken aback. Trivedi decried "the unrealistic and irrational proposition that a non-proliferation treaty should impose obligations only on non-nuclear countries, while the nuclear Powers continue to hold on to their privileged status or club membership by retaining and even increasing their deadly stockpiles."[175] A decade earlier, India had cooperated in the IAEA negotiations because even though the agency risked producing distributional inequalities, it was procedurally fair and open. The NPT was shaping up to be neither. Trivedi coined the terms "horizontal" and "vertical" proliferation,[176] as well as "nuclear apartheid,"[177] as a means of criticizing the nuclear powers for engaging in double standards and excluding India from the nuclear club. India had publicly abjured the bomb and supported disarmament and nonproliferation in order to maintain symbolic equality with the great powers. The NPT threatened to subvert India's nuclear ambiguity by compelling it to give up the nuclear option while *also* relegating it to second-tier status relative to the great powers.

By late 1965, India was more concerned about the evolving nuclear order than the Chinese nuclear threat. Indeed, Indian leaders saw a nondiscriminatory institutional approach to nuclear testing and

---

[174] E. L. M. Burns, "Can the spread of nuclear weapons be stopped?" *International Organization*, 19:4 (1965), 851–869.

[175] Conference of the Eighteen-Nation Committee on Disarmament, "Final verbatim record of the two hundred and twenty-third meeting," ENDC/PV.223, August 12, 1965, 13, University of Michigan Digital Library.

[176] E. L. M. Burns, *A Seat at the Table: The Struggle for Disarmament* (Toronto/Vancouver: Clarke, Irwin & Co., 1972), 216.

[177] Conference of the Eighteen-Nation Committee on Disarmament, "Final verbatim record of the two hundred and ninety-eighth meeting," ENDC/PV.298, May 23, 1967, 10, University of Michigan Digital Library; Perkovich, *India's Nuclear Bomb*, 138.

proliferation as necessary for containing the threat. Questioned by members of his own party about the feasibility of security guarantees, foreign minister Swaran Singh stated the government's view: "[T]he only effective guarantee against the [Chinese] nuclear threat would lie in the elimination of nuclear weapons and their delivery vehicles."[178] He reiterated this view in Parliament in August 1966: "Chinese nuclear developments must make it all the more urgent that agreement should be reached on the prohibition of all nuclear weapon tests and of any further production of nuclear weapons."[179]

NPT negotiations revealed that the existing nuclear powers were unwilling to accept any limits on their nuclear stockpiles while seeking to stop nonnuclear states from acquiring nuclear technologies that might be deemed sensitive (which many technologies were, due to their suitability for both civilian and military purposes). This potential outcome threatened to leave India out of the great-power club for at least the treaty's twenty-five-year lifespan. India rallied by pushing hard for disarmament by the great powers in the ENCD, acknowledging that if these efforts failed, the government would "retain their option to reconsider their policy."[180]

An Increasingly Closed and Unfair Great-Power Club

As the decade wore on, India came under pressure from the great powers to sign the NPT, even though the great powers were themselves unwilling to modify the agreement to address India's concerns. In November 1966, Lord Chalfont, the British foreign minister, visited New Delhi to solicit India's support for the NPT. During a meeting with foreign secretary C. S. Jha, Chalfont argued that India's stance on disarmament should not get in the way of a "simple nonproliferation treaty" that did not require inspection and control.[181] After all, the nuclear powers could not be expected to relinquish their weapons in the face of "the developing Chinese nuclear threat."

---

[178] Lok Sabha Debates, Thirteenth Session, Third Series, vol. XLVIII, no. 18, Lok Sabha Secretariat, New Delhi, November 29, 1965, 4295.
[179] Lok Sabha Starred Question no. 734 to be answered on August 19, 1966, NAI, MEA, WII/104/5/66.
[180] Note for Supplementaries, NAI, MEA, WII/104/5/66.
[181] Summary record of discussions, Secret, November 8, 1966, PNHP (I&II), SF28, NMML.

Jha explained that India had been in favor of disarmament well before China went nuclear, and he was sanguine that "with the passage of time, China might adopt a more cooperative attitude to various disarmament proposals particularly after it assumes its place in the United Nations." India saw China as India saw itself – a state desiring recognition of its major-power identity through equal membership of the great-power club in the core institutions of the international order. It was "an unacceptable thesis," contended Jha, that China's nuclear capability justified the great powers rejecting disarmament. Jha also highlighted the growing feeling in India that "disarmament negotiations were being directed towards the preservation of the monopoly of smaller Powers," a direct barb at the British representative.

In March 1967, the nuclear strategist Albert Wohlstetter, visiting New Delhi for an academic seminar, requested an off-the-record meeting with Jha on the Chinese nuclear threat. In the meeting, Jha admitted that China's imminent ICBM capability was dangerous.[182] However, India was under no illusion that the United States would come to India's aid if China threatened nuclear use. Wohlstetter dismissed the notion of US unreliability and suggested that a security guarantee, coupled with India signing the NPT, would address India's concerns. Jha shot back that the NPT was unacceptable because it was unequal and placed nonnuclear powers "in perpetuity in positions of dependence on the nuclear Powers." India "would not be dictated to by other States, no matter how powerful." Under these conditions, "if we were expected merely to sign on the dotted line, it was expecting too much."

Indira Gandhi shared this view. According to her, India's "geographical position and resources" meant that it "cannot but play [a] fairly large part in international affairs" and be recognized as "a potential great power" by other countries.[183] The NPT belied this claim. Gandhi criticized the treaty for being discriminatory and unequal, while also advocating the exclusion of nuclear explosions for peaceful purposes from the ambit of the treaty (though she was

[182] Record of discussion (Secret), March 31, 1967, NAI, MEA, WII/110/2/67.
[183] Quoted in N. B. Sen, *Wit and Wisdom of Indira Gandhi: The Uncrowned Queen of India* (New Delhi: New Book Society of India, 1971), 159.

prepared to subject them to safeguards).[184] Although a fair and open nuclear order was her first priority, she desultorily explored security guarantees from the nuclear powers as a way of hedging against China. Thus, in April 1967, she sent her principal secretary, L. K. Jha (not related to C. S. Jha), to Moscow, Paris, Washington, and London. In London, he met with, among others, Lord Chalfont. During this meeting, Jha was clear that given the dual-use nature of nuclear technology, India would not agree to anything that only prevented non-nuclear states from acquiring nuclear technology and thereby diminished India's standing in the peaceful uses of atomic energy. "This was one field in which India was not under-developed and we proposed not to take a back seat in the advance of nuclear technology," wrote Jha in his report of the conversation.[185] As before, Indian leaders viewed their country's status as being tied to scientific advancement, and nuclear ambiguity remained New Delhi's preferred method of maintaining this status. Upon Jha's return, foreign minister Chagla stated in Parliament that Jha's trip was only exploratory. There was "no question of seeking any guarantee" from the superpowers.[186]

India's opposition to the NPT was entirely on grounds of institutional openness and procedural fairness. Not only did the treaty close off India's pathway to the great-power club, it also singled out and discriminated against India as a technologically advanced state that had deliberately foresworn nuclear weapons. Particularly galling was language in the draft treaty that counted only those countries that had tested a nuclear device prior to 1967 as nuclear powers. "Do these countries [the great powers] want India not to become a nuclear power?" asked Congress MP Siddheshwar Prasad in Parliament in June 1967.[187] Chagla sidestepped the question and focused on a more poignant source of inequality. If the draft became the treaty, "it would mean that China will be a nuclear nation and we, who have shown great restraint, will be a non-nuclear nation."[188] India could scarcely afford to let China waltz into the great-power club while it was excluded.

---

[184] Uncorrected draft of parliamentary debate, November 21, 1967, NAI, MEA, U-IV/125/41/67.
[185] Summary of Discussions in London, Secret, May 5, 1967. PNHP (III), SF110, NMML.
[186] Stationing of Nuclear Missiles, NAI, MEA, U-IV/125/12/67.
[187] Ibid. (Original in Hindi).   [188] Ibid.

Security vis-à-vis China was a secondary consideration, and one that would follow from an open and fair order. On more than one occasion, Chagla clarified in Parliament, "The question of security assurance for India and other non-nuclear weapon powers against nuclear attack is an issue *separate from* the non-proliferation treaty."[189] The NPT was only "bound up with security" insofar as it ought to "advance the cause of general and comprehensive disarmament by preventing proliferation, not merely by preventing non-nuclear countries from acquiring nuclear weapons, but also by compelling and obliging the nuclear Powers to freeze their stockpile, if not to reduce their stockpile."[190] India subordinated its own security concerns to the cause of a nondiscriminatory treaty.

Indian statesmen continued hoping to get their way while the NPT was debated at the UN. In June 1967, Chagla described the treaty as being at "a very preliminary stage."[191] In April 1968, barely ten weeks before the treaty was opened for signature, Haksar, now principal secretary to the prime minister, noted that India had not yet taken a decision "in respect of a Treaty whose final form has not yet emerged."[192] When it did emerge, the NPT denied India its status aspirations and consequently set off the process by which Indian decision-makers arrived at their decision to break with the Cold War order. In an address to the UNGA in October 1968, Indira Gandhi said, "The problems of insecurity cannot be solved by imposing arbitrary restrictions on those who do not possess nuclear weapons, without any corresponding steps to deal with the basic problem of limiting stockpiles in the hands of a few powers. How can the urge to acquire nuclear status be controlled so long as this imbalance persists?"[193]

The nuclear order began to steadily lose legitimacy in India's eyes after this point. Although some scholars have suggested that India rejected the NPT due to the need to "hedge" in a dangerous security

[189] Lok Sabha Starred Question no. 17, to be answered on the 22nd May, 1967, Nuclear Non-Proliferation Treaty, NAI, MEA, U-IV/125/9/67, emphasis added.
[190] Stationing of Nuclear Missiles, NAI, MEA, U-IV/125/12/67.   [191] Ibid.
[192] Note by P. N. Haksar regarding Starred Question D. no. 119, April 15, 1968, NMML, PNHP (I&II), SF36.
[193] Indira Gandhi, *Selected Speeches of Indira Gandhi, January 1966 – August 1969* (New Delhi: Ministry of Information and Broadcasting, Government of India, 1971), 359–360.

environment,[194] Indian decision-makers were clear that their opposition to the NPT was not grounded in security considerations. As Haksar himself noted in a note to Gandhi:

The Government of India have already stated that they do not intend to manufacture nuclear weapons. This is a unilateral decision taken many years ago and is unrelated to the Treaty on non-proliferation of nuclear weapons. We shall continue our efforts for nuclear disarmament because *it is only through nuclear disarmament that discrimination can be eliminated and equality between nations re-established.*[195]

India's struggle was not for security but for symbolic equality, and the great-power club was denying India the one policy instrument – disarmament – that would help attain equality. India had used its institutional status to get key provisions introduced into the NPT that provided UN-backed security guarantees for nonnuclear powers and permitted the pursuit of nuclear technology for peaceful purposes under international supervision.[196] However, New Delhi's main objective – to get the nuclear powers to concretely commit to halting production and reducing stocks of nuclear weapons and delivery vehicles – went unmet. The issue for Haksar was "essentially a political one," though it also had "serious implications" for India's security.[197]

Restoring Status through Institutional Challenge, 1971–1974

When the NPT came into force in March 1970, Article IX of the treaty contained the following definition: "a nuclear-weapon State is one which has manufactured and exploded a nuclear weapon or other nuclear explosive device prior to 1 January 1967."[198] There was no clearer demotion of India's status in the international system. The United States, the Soviet Union, and the United Kingdom were official nuclear weapon states. France and China, albeit non-signatories to the

[194] Jayita Sarkar and Sumit Ganguly, "India and the NPT after 50 years," *The Diplomat*, June 22, 2018.
[195] Haksar to PM, April 4, 1968, NMML, PNHP (I&II), SF36, emphasis added.
[196] George Bunn, "The Nuclear Nonproliferation Treaty," *Wisconsin Law Review*, 3 (1968), 766–785.
[197] Haksar to PM, April 4, 1968, NMML, PNHP (I&II), SF36.
[198] United Nations Office for Disarmament Affairs, "Treaty on the non-proliferation of nuclear weapons (NPT)," www.un.org/disarmament/wmd/nuclear/npt/text/

NPT, were de facto nuclear powers. India was neither. The carefully crafted strategy of nuclear ambiguity, designed to reinforce India's major-power identity, had resulted in disaster. The pre-eminent nuclear scientist Raja Ramanna later noted that the superpowers' proposals to India contained "neither a note of persuasion, nor an attitude of give and take ... [The NPT] was thrust upon us as though the superpowers were the chosen custodians to uphold the peace of the world."[199] India was relegated to the second tier of world powers.

The Indian elite began to consider ways in which to redress this status imbalance. In March 1968, the journalist G. S. Bhargava wrote, "The situation would have been different if two years ago we had gone ahead and launched a peaceful explosion. This would have left us capable of taking the next step [of not signing the NPT] without being immediately committed to making the bomb."[200] India would now have to demonstrate its nuclear capability. It was in these circumstances that Indira Gandhi gave in-principle approval for India's first nuclear test in the autumn of 1971, and formal approval a year later.[201] The fact that it took almost three years to produce a nuclear explosion suggests that India had not taken any significant prior steps toward a weapons capability, since US intelligence agencies had estimated a time horizon of one to three years for weaponization in 1965.[202] On May 18, 1974, India conducted a nuclear test in the Pokhran desert and labeled it a peaceful nuclear explosion in the vein of contemporaneous international ideas about the use of nuclear explosions for large-scale construction projects.

Security was once again a secondary concern. The China threat was now almost a decade old and India's decisive victory in the India-Pakistan War of 1971 – in which Islamabad lost territory (Bangladesh) containing 55 percent of Pakistan's population – had in fact made India *more* secure than at any time since independence. The absence of any efforts to build nuclear weapons after the test shows that India's decision-making was "not driven by events on the other

---

[199] Ramanna, *Years of Pilgrimage*, 94.
[200] G. S. Bhargava, "A non-policy on non-proliferation," *Economic and Political Weekly*, 3:12 (1968), 482–483.
[201] Perkovich, *India's Nuclear Bomb*, 172.
[202] See Director of Central Intelligence, SNIE 31-1-65, India's nuclear weapons policy, Secret, October 21, 1965, National Security Archive, https://nsarchive2 .gwu.edu/NSAEBB/NSAEBB187/IN09.pdf; Sagan, "Why do states," n. 22.

side of the Himalayas," that is, by China's nuclear program.[203] George Perkovich argues that India's decision had less to do with the India-Pakistan war than with "the Atomic Energy Commission's determination to prove its mettle and Indira Gandhi's sense that India would gain confidence in itself as a nation and in her as a leader."[204] Although status was a general and constant concern for Indian leaders since independence, it was status in terms of *symbolic equality* with the great powers that mattered, and a rising power such as India inferred its status from the institutional architecture of the Cold War order. When the rules changed in ways that threatened India's identity as a major power, the need to reassert symbolic equality with the great powers became urgent. Prior to this point, India was content to maintain its status by cooperating with the rules and institutions of an open and procedurally fair international order.

The official documentary record of India's decision to test is classified or perhaps nonexistent as key decisions were communicated orally.[205] Interviews, given mostly by nuclear scientists, offer a one-sided picture of events, which tends to place disproportionate importance on the scientific community as the motor of India's nuclear program.[206] The political story is underrepresented in existing scholarship. By setting the decision to test against the previous decision *not* to test, and by foregrounding the role of the evolving international order in India's nuclear calculus, IST offers the most plausible explanation of the 1974 test: It was driven by the need to reassert India's status following the NPT, and it was executed as soon as all the technical elements were in place. Itty Abraham calls the test "at best, a scientific experiment," which was officially termed a "demonstration," presumably of Indian achievements in nuclear science.[207] Faced with a great-power club that punished India for its cooperation and closed off any prospect of membership in the near future, India decided to challenge the international order. Looking back, Ramanna wrote:

---

[203] Hymans, *The Psychology of Proliferation*, 173.
[204] Perkovich, *India's Nuclear Bomb*, 168.   [205] Ibid., 12.
[206] See Raj Chengappa, *Weapons of Peace: The Secret Story of India's Quest to Be a Nuclear Power* (New Delhi: HarperCollins, 2000).
[207] Itty Abraham, "Contra-proliferation: Interpreting the meanings of India's nuclear tests in 1974 and 1998," in Scott Sagan (ed.), *Inside Nuclear South Asia* (Palo Alto: Stanford University Press, 2009), 106–135. See also Ramanna, *Years of Pilgrimage*, 96.

[The world] hadn't expected such an achievement from a developing nation ... The objections were predictable variations on a theme: who were we to upset the balance maintained by the superpowers, a privilege bestowed only upon those who had won the Second World War? ... [The test] exposed the hypocrisy of those nations who talked of non-proliferation and the peaceful use of nuclear energy. It was clear that these countries applied one set of standards to themselves and another to the rest of the world.[208]

Four months after the test, Trivedi presented a paper at a meeting in Divonne, France, organized by the Arms Control Association and the Carnegie Endowment. He offered a poignant summation of the Indian predicament:

[India] adopted the Atomic Energy Act in April 1948 and set up its Atomic Energy Commission in August 1948, one year after independence. Indian engineers and scientists designed, built and commissioned the first research reactor in Asia in 1956, built India's own fuel element fabrication plant in 1959 and her first plutonium separation plant in 1964. There was thus nothing to prevent India from exploding a nuclear explosive device before January 1, 1967, the date separating the era of nuclear-weapon powers from the nonnuclear-weapon powers under the Non-Proliferation Treaty.[209]

Encapsulated in Trivedi's statement was everything an observer needed to know about India's desire for status based on nuclear ambiguity in the pre-NPT world, and the sharp jolt that New Delhi had received in terms of status demotion that led to its peaceful nuclear explosion. The test was the demonstration that India's leaders had longed for the world to see. Looking back three years later, Indira Gandhi justified it in terms of the need "for our scientists to know what they're capable of."[210] Having restored its status, India then settled back into a posture of nuclear ambiguity for the next two decades.

---

[208] Ramanna, *Years of Pilgrimage*, 92.
[209] Vishnu C. Trivedi, "India's approach towards nuclear energy and non-proliferation of nuclear weapons," working paper presented at a meeting organized by the Arms Control Association and Carnegie Endowment for International Peace, Divonne, France, September 9–11, 1974, Permanent Mission of India to the Conference on Disarmament, MEA, http://meaindia.nic.in/cdgeneva/?pdf0592?000, 42–46.
[210] Interviewed in Shashi Tharoor, *Reasons of State: Political Development and India's Foreign Policy under Indira Gandhi, 1966–1977* (New Delhi: Vikas Publishing House, 1982), 71.

Delegitimizing the Nuclear Order, 1974–1995

Despite India's challenge, the international order remained closed. For twenty-five years – the lifespan of the NPT – India could not expect to count as an equal of the great powers. Indian decision-makers also continued to view the order as procedurally unfair for having permitted France and China to join the club while keeping India out. Although India did not challenge the order by conducting any further tests during the Cold War, Indian diplomats took every opportunity to delegitimize it through official channels and public international forums. Although this strategy was not one of reframing (within the IST framework), it did in part involve reframing India's noncompliance as activism on behalf of the nonnuclear powers of the world, as well as continued insistence on nuclear disarmament as the overarching goal of the international order.[211] By highlighting the great powers' inability to meet a standard they themselves had set, India assured for itself a distinct position in the international status hierarchy as a conscientious objector to the great-power club's status monopoly.

The NPT still stung Indian policymakers, not because it constrained their nonexistent nuclear program, but because it was a powerful symbol of India's inferior status. A fundamental challenge to the international order, however, would be costly and inadvisable. Therefore, India's optimal strategy was to play the conscientious objector. A secret policy planning paper in the foreign ministry by joint secretary A. K. Damodaran in 1976 reflected this thinking. Analyzing India's diplomatic priorities in concentric geographic circles, he wrote, "After the neighbours and near-neighbours ... our major interest would be the Superpowers with whom we have to co-exist in [*sic*] this planet under conditions of some equal relationship."[212] Being denied this equality, India was now neither votary nor revolutionary. "On the whole we are a status quo power," he wrote, "but we have by no means a vested interest in the United Nations structure as it is

---

[211] India's strategy was similar to the United States' strategy over a century prior of reframing its challenge to the Atlantic system as speaking up for lesser states and standing on a higher principle of universal protection for private property at sea (see Chapter 4).

[212] India's Diplomatic Objectives (Secret), MEA, Policy Planning Division, November 25, 1976, NMML, PNHP (I&II), SF89.

today." At the same time, India "would certainly not risk a confrontation to change it." On nuclear issues, he added:

Our peaceful nuclear explosion is an affirmation of the right of the poorer countries to develop their own technological expertise. It is also connected with our feeling that the resources of the world should be exploited under some reasonable international order and not merely by the present, small group of countries possessing the technical capacity to do so.[213]

India's decision-makers considered the foundations of the international order to be worth investing in; however, they wished to do so as equals with the great powers, and nuclear nonproliferation was a vital test of the good faith of the great powers and their treatment of India. What this meant in practice was that, in Damodaran's words, "only by behaving like an important and strong power can India become one,"[214] but the definition of importance and strength would be on India's terms. New Delhi would continue following the norms of the international order while seeking to delegitimize the inequality that the order had created between nuclear haves and have-nots. At an abstract level, the term "nuclear apartheid" contained the essence of India's complaint: a situation where inequality replaced equality as the ordering social principle.

In June 1988, Prime Minister Rajiv Gandhi undertook a major initiative by submitting to the UNGA an "Action Plan for Ushering in a Nuclear-weapon free and Non-Violent World Order," which called for the elimination of nuclear weapons in three stages over two decades. In keeping with India's nuclear activism, the plan prioritized global and universal disarmament. It served to remind the international community of the double standards of the great powers, and further entrenched India's position as a responsible nuclear-capable state whose noncompliance with the international order was morally justified. Gandhi's oratory at the UN was tailored to exactly this message. "History is full of such prejudices paraded as iron laws," he said, "that men are superior to women; that the white races are superior to the coloured; that colonialism is a civilising mission; that those who possess nuclear weapons are responsible powers and those who

---

[213] Ibid., 32.   [214] Ibid., 33.

do not are not."[215] It was in this manner that India "resignified" the meaning of responsibility such that it was "linked to nuclear disarmament and equality rather than nuclear non-proliferation and hierarchy."[216] In its new framing, responsibility meant (at least rhetorically) prioritizing the dignity of lesser states in the international order, as opposed to the oligarchic practices of the great powers. The empirical record shows that although India was not pursuing a nuclear program at this time, its leaders were loath to concede their *right* to do so.[217]

India's Second Challenge to the International Order, 1995–1998

The next break in India's relationship with the international order came in May 1998, when New Delhi tested five nuclear devices in the same location where it had conducted its first nuclear test twenty-four years earlier. The end of the Cold War and the demise of the Soviet Union dramatically altered India's strategic landscape. Some have argued that the 1998 nuclear tests were driven by security concerns, with India no longer able to rely on the 1971 Indo-Soviet mutual defense pact and faced with an increasingly rampant insurgency, backed by Pakistan, in the Kashmir valley.[218] However, security-driven arguments for the 1998 tests are weakened when one considers that although India was more vulnerable to US pressure after the demise of the Soviet Union, a priori the one way to worsen India's prospects in a unipolar world dominated by the United States was to conduct a second round of nuclear tests. Moreover, a second round of tests would undoubtedly set off an arms race or at least retaliation from Pakistan, if not China. As it turned out, Pakistan responded with nuclear tests of its own just two weeks later. Finally, India's relations with China, Pakistan, and the United States were not in jeopardy in the mid-1990s. Therefore, it is unlikely the decision to test

---

[215] Rajiv Gandhi, *Selected Speeches and Writings, Vol. IV, 1988* (New Delhi: Publications Division, Ministry of Information and Broadcasting, Government of India, 1989), 338.

[216] Priya Chacko and Alexander E. Davis, "Resignifying 'responsibility': India, exceptionalism and nuclear non-proliferation," *Asian Journal of Political Science*, 26:3 (2018), 352–370.

[217] The following year, with an eye on Pakistan's growing nuclear capability, and seeing no scope for progress on global disarmament, Rajiv Gandhi authorized the covert development of nuclear weapons.

[218] See Ganguly, "India's pathway."

was motivated primarily by security concerns, even though officially India pointed to security concerns over China as motivation.[219]

In terms of domestic politics, it is possible that the Bharatiya Janata Party's (BJP) ideology of a "macho national security state,"[220] or Prime Minister Vajpayee's "oppositional-nationalist" identity,[221] or his political vulnerability precipitated the need to test in 1998.[222] However, these arguments are contradicted by the fact that successive governments since the Narasimha Rao government of 1992–1996 had seriously considered, taken preparatory steps, and come very close to testing, only to be held back by some combination of US pressure and the fear of sanctions on India's post-1991-crisis economy. By 1998, the Indian economy had enjoyed four years of growth at approximately 6.5 percent per year on average.[223] Along this dimension, Vajpayee was less constrained than his predecessors.

Instead, as predicted by IST, two major changes in the international order played a greater role in motivating India's 1998 tests. The first was the negotiation of the Comprehensive Nuclear-Test-Ban Treaty, which began in 1993 and all but singled out India and Pakistan as potential problem states whose signature was required – along with forty-four other states that were less problematic – for the treaty to come into effect. Worse yet, the treaty itself embodied an inequality similar to the NPT in the 1960s. While it was a "comprehensive" test ban, it did not ban a new generation of tests, such as subcritical tests or computer simulated tests, which did not require a nuclear explosion but could still generate useful technical data for those with the capability to conduct them, that is, the great powers. Once again, the order was biased against India.

The second major event took place in May 1995, when the NPT was reviewed and permanently extended by all parties. This was a development that "stunned" India's foreign policy establishment,[224] which

[219] The Indian Express, "China is potential threat number one," May 4, 1998.
[220] Gaurav Kampani, "From existential to minimum deterrence: Explaining India's decision to test," *The Nonproliferation Review*, 6:1 (1998), 12–24.
[221] Hymans, *The Psychology of Proliferation*, 171–203.
[222] Kanti Bajpai, "The BJP and the bomb," in Sagan (ed.), *Inside Nuclear South Asia*, 25–67.
[223] The World Bank, World Development Indicators (WDI), http://wdi.worldbank.org/.
[224] Dinshaw Mistry, "Domestic-international linkages: India and the Comprehensive Test-Ban Treaty," *The Nonproliferation Review*, 6:1 (1998), 25–38.

had not expected other countries to go along with the US desire for a permanent extension. India's second-tier status was now irrevocable. After twenty-four years of trying to delegitimize a closed and unfair international order, India decided to mount a bigger challenge to definitively assert its symbolic equality with the great powers. In September 1995, Prime Minister Narasimha Rao authorized preparations for nuclear tests, which were ultimately carried out by the Vajpayee government in May 1998. After the tests, India's preeminent defense expert K. Subrahmanyam declared, "Nuclear weapons are not military weapons. Their logic is that of international politics and it is a logic of global nuclear order ... India wants to be a player in, and not an object of, this global nuclear order."[225]

Manjari Chatterjee Miller argues that taken together, the CTBT and NPT "convinced India of the systematic institutionalization of an unequal nuclear order."[226] India's tests were driven by a "sense of grievance against the 'nuclear club' led by the United States, which it believed was responsible for creating an unequal, unfair and racist nuclear order."[227] T. V. Paul similarly argues that the tests were "primarily the culmination of long-term ... processes that began in the 1960s," and "should be seen in the larger context of global power politics involving the great powers and India, especially the fact that the former remain[ed] unwilling to accept the latter's aspirations to join their ranks."[228] Following the test, defense minister George Fernandes said to a *New York Times* correspondent, "I would ask Bill Clinton only one question ... Why is it that you feel yourself so close to China that you can trust China with nuclear weapons, just as you can trust yourselves with nuclear weapons, and you can trust the Russians and the French and the British, but you cannot trust India?"[229]

---

[225] Quoted in Strobe Talbott, "Dealing with the bomb in South Asia," *Foreign Affairs*, 78 (1999), 110–122.

[226] Manjari Chatterjee Miller, *Wronged by Empire: Post-imperial Ideology and Foreign Policy in India and China* (Stanford: Stanford University Press, 2013), 83.

[227] Ibid.

[228] T. V. Paul, "The systemic bases of India's challenge to the global nuclear order," *The Nonproliferation Review*, 6:1 (1998), 1–11.

[229] John F. Burns, "India defense chief calls U.S. hypocritical," *The New York Times*, June 18, 1998.

After the tests, although India remained intransigent on the NPT, it began taking a more conciliatory approach toward other aspects of the nuclear order in the face of international opprobrium. New Delhi announced a voluntary moratorium on nuclear testing and proposed various measures to reduce the risk of nuclear war in South Asia, including a no-first-use policy. The BJP-led government signaled that it was ready to sign the CTBT and offered to join multilateral counter-proliferation efforts such as the Proliferation Security Initiative and the Container Security Initiative. New Delhi "began to downplay the notions of equity and equality" in discussing the international nuclear order, instead emphasizing India's role as a "responsible" nuclear weapon state.[230] Once again satisfied with its status relative to the great powers, India was more willing to engage with an international order that had proved unable to de facto exclude it from the great-power club.

India's Recognition as a Nuclear Power, 2005–2008

Following India's 1998 tests, the United States calculated that it was better to engage India than to leave it outside the nuclear order. Through several rounds of talks over more than two years, Deputy Secretary of State Strobe Talbott and Minister of External Affairs Jaswant Singh salvaged the US–India relationship, though India remained an outsider.[231] From India's perspective, an overt challenge to nuclear rules and institutions had brought a "unipolar power that could remake the international order" to the negotiating table.[232] The United States was now taking India's concerns seriously. Although conscious of the opportunity to claim their due recognition as a responsible nuclear power, Indian statesmen remained alert to the long history of technology denial and second-tier status to which their country had been subjected. As conversations with the United States about some form of civilian nuclear cooperation progressed, Shyam Saran, foreign secretary at the time and later the Prime Minister's Special

---

[230] C. Raja Mohan, "Rising India: Partner in Shaping the Global Commons?" *The Washington Quarterly*, 33:3 (2010), 133–148.

[231] See Strobe Talbott, *Engaging India: Diplomacy, Democracy, and the Bomb* (Washington, DC: Brookings Institution Press, 2004).

[232] Interview with Shyam Saran, New Delhi, May 28, 2018.

Envoy for Nuclear Affairs, conveyed India's red line: "[Y]ou cannot treat India both as a partner and as a target."[233]

In July 2005, President George W. Bush and Prime Minister Manmohan Singh issued a joint statement resolving to "transform the relationship between their countries and establish a global partnership."[234] The centerpiece of this document was the official recognition of India as a "responsible state with advanced nuclear technology" that deserved "the same benefits and advantages as other such states."[235] The United States committed to ensuring full civilian nuclear cooperation in return for India separating its civilian and military nuclear facilities and putting the former under IAEA safeguards. This statement laid the foundation for the US–India nuclear deal, which was signed in March 2006 and came into effect in October 2008. According to the agreement, the US modified both domestic and international law to create exceptions for India to be recognized as a de facto nuclear weapon state, thus granting it access to internationally controlled supplies of nuclear fuel and technology, despite it being a non-signatory of the NPT.

The agreement was unprecedented in all respects, essentially rewarding India with access both to nuclear materials and to the great-power club, despite its repeated challenges to the nuclear order since the 1960s.[236] The Bush administration went out of its way to convince Congress and domestic critics of the importance of integrating India fully into the international order, and to lobby the Nuclear Suppliers Group to make an exception for India without NPT membership. From India's perspective, the United States modified the international order to correct a historic wrong and to fairly accommodate India's major-power identity.

The terms of the NPT, however, ensured that India could never officially count among the nuclear powers. Under these conditions of

[233] Ibid.
[234] Department of State, "Joint statement by President George W. Bush and Prime Minister Manmohan Singh," July 18, 2005, https://2001-2009.state.gov/p/sca/rls/pr/2005/49763.htm.
[235] Ibid.
[236] Amrita Narlikar, "Reforming institutions, unreformed India?" in Alan Alexandroff and Andrew Cooper (eds.), *Rising States, Rising Institutions: Challenges for Global Governance* (Washington, DC: Brookings, 2010), 105–127.

a procedurally fair but closed order, IST predicts that India would adopt a strategy of expansion, or trying to introduce new criteria by which to claim symbolic equality with the great powers. Indeed, since 2008, India has emphasized its credentials as a "de facto nuclear power,"[237] and it has taken a cooperative approach to the international order on issues of nonproliferation and counter-proliferation.[238] This approach has helped India gain further access to international institutions dealing with export controls in the nuclear order, such as the Australia Group, the Wassenaar Arrangement, and the Missile Technology Control Regime.

Indian diplomats who negotiated the agreement clearly perceived the momentousness of their achievement. "With it [the agreement], India moves from being an outlier to an insider, just as China did in the 1970s," argued S. Jaishankar, who was joint secretary for the Americas in India's foreign ministry during the negotiations.[239] It was the United States that had facilitated China's entry into the international order through a permanent seat on the UNSC in 1971, and it was the United States that had now brought India into the nuclear fold. According to Shivshankar Menon, who was India's foreign secretary during a substantial part of the negotiations, the agreement served two purposes: to make partners out of the United States and India, and to help India "break out of nuclear apartheid."[240] For the first time since the 1950s, the international nuclear order had changed in India's favor. "It was an exception, and your exceptionalism was recognized by the international system," Menon observed. "That's a big step for a country like India, for an emerging country."[241]

* * *

[237] Ashley J. Tellis, "De facto, not de jure – India is the world's sixth nuclear power," *Mint – Wall Street Journal*, September 30, 2008.
[238] Kate Sullivan de Estrada, "Understanding India's exceptional engagement with the nuclear nonproliferation regime," in Johannes Plagemann, Sandra Destradi, and Amrita Narlikar (eds.), *India Rising: Ideas, Interests and Institutions in Foreign Policy* (New Delhi: Oxford University Press, 2020), 23–49.
[239] Interview with S. Jaishankar, New Delhi, May 27, 2018.
[240] Interview with Shivshankar Menon, Singapore, June 7, 2018.   [241] Ibid.

7 | China and the Liberal International Order

The Cold War was a bipolar system with two major centers of power; the world since 1990 has been unipolar. The international order of the post–Cold War era is often described as "liberal." It reflects the culmination of the growing power of liberal democracies as leading states, starting with British predominance in the nineteenth century down to US preponderance today. The resulting liberal international order is at least in theory based on "economic openness, multilateral institutions, security cooperation and democratic solidarity."[1] This chapter does not delve into the debate over whether the order is in fact liberal in all these respects. Rather – like the Atlantic system in Chapter 4, the Washington system in Chapter 5, and the Cold War order in Chapter 6 – the LIO is used as shorthand for the order maintained and expanded upon by the United States since the end of the Cold War.

At an institutional level, there is a good deal of continuity between the Cold War and the LIO.[2] Multilateral arrangements for peace and security, nuclear nonproliferation, international trade, development finance, foreign aid, monetary policy, the environment, human rights, and other issues have remained broadly the same. However, both the degree and type of cooperation within these institutions has changed since the end of the Cold War. For example, whereas UN peacekeeping in the Cold War was largely restricted to overseeing ceasefires in interstate conflicts, after the Cold War the UN took on increasingly complex and ambitious missions in civil conflicts around the world. For most of the Cold War, the number of active peacekeeping missions in a year rarely exceeded five. Between 1989 and 1994 alone the United Nations Security Council authorized twenty new missions, and as of August 2021, the UN has twelve active missions employing 87,000

---

[1] G. John Ikenberry, "The end of liberal international order?" *International Affairs*, 94:1 (2018), 7–23.
[2] Rosemary Foot and Andrew Walter, *China, the United States, and Global Order* (Cambridge: Cambridge University Press, 2010), 4.

246

personnel.[3] Institutionalized cooperation since the end of the Cold War has not only expanded within issue areas to take on new challenges, it has also taken on new issues such as climate change mitigation. The international order under unipolarity is wider and deeper than ever before.

Within the LIO, China has rapidly emerged as a potential challenger to the United States' hegemony in Asia and beyond. Scholars and analysts have spent three decades trying to ascertain how this longer-term global geopolitical shift will impact the international system. The probability of major war breaking out between the United States and China is attenuated by the former's global military primacy and the respective nuclear arsenals of both countries.[4] The more pertinent question, therefore, is how China will approach the myriad inter-national institutions that compose the American global order.[5] Will Beijing's rise be "responsible" and based on the norms of the existing order, or will it be marked by contestation, rule-breaking, and oppos-ition to these norms?[6] The answer has proved elusive. Since the late 1980s, the world has seen China go from the Tiananmen Square crackdown, multiple nuclear tests, and the Taiwan Strait Crisis, to the doctrine and policies of "peaceful rise," and back to a degree of assertiveness since the Global Financial Crisis of 2007–2008, which seemed to be dialed up amidst the outbreak of the COVID-19 pan-demic in 2020. At the same time, China remains engaged in almost all parts of the LIO, its stance cooperative in many instances. In the words of scholar Wu Xinbo, "Beijing is unlikely to seek to overturn the liberal hegemonic order as a whole, but likely to try to expand its liberal features while diluting its hegemonic nature."[7]

---

[3] United Nations Peacekeeping, "Peacekeeping operations fact sheet," August 31, 2021, https://peacekeeping.un.org/sites/default/files/peacekeeping_missions_fact_sheet_august_2021_en.pdf

[4] Schweller, "Emerging powers," 286. The same cannot be said for lower levels of militarized conflict. See Bear F. Braumoeller, *Only the Dead: The Persistence of War in the Modern Age* (New York: Oxford University Press, 2019).

[5] Mingjiang Li, "Rising from within: China's search for a multilateral world and its implications for Sino-US relations," *Global Governance*, 17:3 (2011), 331–351.

[6] See Robert Zoellick, "Whither China? From membership to responsibility," remarks to the National Committee on US-China Relations, September 21, 2005.

[7] Xinbo Wu, "China in search of a liberal partnership international order," *International Affairs*, 94:5 (2018), 995–1018.

While many uncertainties remain about the future of the LIO, it is
only by developing reliable explanations of Chinese conduct, based on
evidence from the last three decades of China's rise, that we can begin
to systematically contemplate the future. Existing theories cannot fully
explain why China cooperates with some aspects of the LIO and resists
others. Many explanations take an undifferentiated view of the international order and tend to conflate the LIO and US–China relations.[8]
Institutional Status Theory addresses these problems in two ways.
First, by disaggregating the order into its major component institutions, IST can explain empirical variation in China's cooperation and
resistance within the LIO. Second, by foregrounding China's major-
power identity and the importance of institutions as a source of symbolic equality with the great powers, IST more faithfully accounts for
the thick institutional environment in which China has been pursuing
great-power status.[9]

Three caveats are due here. First, according to the method used to
identify great powers and rising powers in this book (see Appendix),
China became a great power in 1974, shortly after becoming a permanent member of the UNSC. However, although China meets all the
criteria for being counted as a great power, there is broad agreement in
the literature that, in a unipolar world, it is a *rising* great power.[10]
Although in the post-2009 world there is increasing talk of China as a
great power,[11] this narrative is largely tied up in status ambitions
rather than an objective evaluation of China's position. For the purposes of this chapter, therefore, China is considered a rising power,
though one that is much further along in its rise compared to the
nineteenth-century United States, interwar Japan, and Cold-War
India. IST's ability to explain China's behavior within the LIO serves

---

[8] Alastair Iain Johnston, "China in a world of orders: Rethinking compliance and
challenge in Beijing's international relations," *International Security*, 44:2
(2019), 9–60; Huiyun Feng and Kai He (eds.), *China's Challenges and
International Order Transition: Beyond "Thucydides's Trap"* (Ann Arbor:
University of Michigan Press, 2020), ch. 1.

[9] Marc Lanteigne, *China and International Institutions: Alternate Paths to Global
Power* (Abingdon: Routledge, 2005).

[10] See David M. Edelstein, "Cooperation, uncertainty, and the rise of China: It's
about 'time'," *The Washington Quarterly*, 41:1 (2018), 155–171; Wang Jisi,
"China's search for a grand strategy: A rising great power finds its way,"
Foreign Affairs, (March/April 2011), 68–79.

[11] Shogo Suzuki, "Journey to the West: China debates its 'great power' identity,"
Millennium, 42:3 (2014), 632–650.

as a demonstration of the theory's applicability to late-stage rising powers as well. Although these powers are not the focus of this book, they can serve as fertile empirical terrain for future research.

Second, unlike previous chapters, this chapter examines the applicability of IST across issue areas. The method used to test IST's predictions in the preceding chapters relies on controlling for the confounding effects of intrinsic differences between issue areas by focusing on a single issue: security. This method was possible – indeed necessary – for previous international orders because security institutions were their central pillars (even during the Cold War, the overall order was centered on security, though the Western-led part of it had major economic components). The LIO does not allow for this kind of narrowing, because the international order since the 1990s has grown incredibly complex and multifaceted, relying on numerous interlinked core institutions for its successful functioning. At the same time, the political imprint of the hegemon, the United States, is much clearer across the board. Indeed, the very notion of a *liberal* international order (as opposed to one defined in reference to the great powers of the age) suggests a certain homogeneous political underpinning to various international institutions. The causal effects of institutional openness and procedural fairness are thus more likely than before to be found across issue areas, despite intrinsic differences between them.

Third, and finally, unlike previous chapters, this chapter relies entirely on secondary sources. The recency of the period in question, combined with the difficulties a nonspecialist would face attempting to access primary sources in China, rules out the use of archival or interview material as potential evidence. While the theoretical critiques and arguments of this chapter are vital to the question of China's place in the LIO, the empirical analysis should be read as an effort to identify broad patterns that can suggest avenues for future research by specialists. These three caveats taken together mean that this chapter should be read as a plausibility probe for the application of IST to the LIO. Although the chapter does not engage in deep empirical analysis within a single issue area over time, it is able to show that IST sheds valuable new light on existing puzzles surrounding China's rise.

The rest of this chapter first examines the nature of China's engagement with the international order, and poses the central puzzle of the book in this case: Why does China in some issue areas challenge an international order that has abetted its rise, and why does it in other issue areas accept the order even if it might constrain its rise? The chapter then considers existing explanations for this question, which point to a crucially under-theorized aspect of power shifts and international order: legitimacy. The chapter then demonstrates how IST can fill this gap. It discusses China's major-power identity and its influence on China's approach to the LIO as a whole and in parts. Ultimately, institutions that are more open and procedurally fair to China have witnessed greater cooperation from Beijing.

China's Approach to the Liberal International Order

The LIO has greatly benefited China. Core economic institutions such as the WTO, the IMF, and the World Bank have provided Beijing access to markets, monetary stability, and development finance, respectively, which have in turn spurred China's rapid economic growth. Core security institutions such as the UNSC and NPT have maintained international stability and given Beijing a veto on critical issues. On issues pertaining to the global commons, the LIO has helped China reduce the transaction cost of coordinating policies with countries by providing multilateral forums where countries can negotiate agreements en masse. This is particularly helpful on issues requiring coordination, where China benefits from participating in international standard-setting institutions governing global health, engineering, civil aviation, food safety, business practices, and other common goods. Despite these significant benefits, China has not uniformly embraced the international order; nor has it mounted an outright challenge. In some areas, Beijing has taken actions that serve to undermine preexisting rules and institutions. In other areas, Beijing has actively supported them.

China's challenges to the international order take three forms: rule-breaking, delegitimation, and institutional proliferation. Rule-breaking is a direct challenge, while delegitimation and institutional proliferation are indirect challenges, in that they are acts of resistance with the longer-term potential to unravel the international order. Rule-breaking and delegitimation have been most prominent in the area of maritime law. In the South China Sea, China has built artificial islands; tried to restrict the use of airspace; and engaged in numerous gray zone tactics, such as harassing ships of other countries, probing the territorial waters of littoral states, and conducting naval operations in contested waters.[12] Observers question if China will remain a party to the United Nations Convention on the Law of the Sea (UNCLOS), under which a tribunal ruled against Beijing's claims in 2016.[13]

Delegitimation is perhaps the most common form of China's opposition to the LIO. According to Randall Schweller and Xiaoyu Pu, delegitimation involves using rhetoric to undermine key rules and institutions, as well as "cost-imposing strategies that fall short of full-fledged balancing."[14] China has openly criticized prominent institutions of the order for being unrepresentative of non-Western countries, especially developing countries, and for acting as fig leaves for the pursuit of narrow American interests. Beijing has criticized the IMF and World Bank for not accurately reflecting the growing economic power of countries such as China, India, and Brazil. It has criticized international climate change mitigation efforts for not adequately accounting for the historical role of developed Western economies in contributing to global emissions through their early and sustained industrialization. China has also criticized international human rights institutions for espousing a particularly Western view of rights and freedoms. In all these areas, China has not challenged the need for cooperation per se, but rather the terms on which it has taken place.

Institutional proliferation involves the creation of new institutions that in many cases replicate the mandates and functions of existing US-led institutions. The New Development Bank (NDB) emulates the World Bank in its effort to promote development through public or private projects funded by loans, guarantees, and private investment. The Asian Infrastructure Investment Bank emulates the Asian Development Bank (ADB) in its focus on economic development and regional cooperation in Asia. The Shanghai Cooperation Organization (SCO) emulates the UN in its efforts to maintain international peace, develop friendship between member countries, and cooperatively solve international problems. The level of capitalization of new lending institutions established or backed by China is low, and their membership is far from universal. Yet, the very existence of duplicate institutions is

---

[12] Michael Green, Kathleen Hicks, Zack Cooper, John Schaus, and Jake Douglas, *Countering Coercion in Maritime Asia: The Theory and Practice of Gray Zone Deterrence* (Lanham, MD: Rowman & Littlefield, 2017).

[13] Mark J. Valencia, "Might China withdraw from the UN Law of The Sea Treaty?" *The Diplomat*, May 3, 2019.

[14] Schweller and Pu, "After unipolarity," 44.

not only puzzling from a purely materialist point of view (more on this below) but may also potentially undermine cooperation within the international order by creating a "fragmentation of global govern-ance" leading to "coordination problems, redundancy, and rule con-flict."[15] None of the new institutions constitutes a direct challenge to the international order. However, their existence and growth is likely to indirectly weaken global governance in the LIO.

While challenging the LIO in some core areas, China has chosen to cooperate with it in others, thus reinforcing some aspects of the order.[16] Most notable in this regard is China's support for the UNSC as the most desirable forum through which to address problems of peace and security in the international system.[17] Additionally, China has gradually "eased into accepting intervention" of the nonconsen-sual variety often advocated by the United States and its allies in the UNSC, even though such interventions tend to erode state sovereignty, a principle that China holds dear.[18] Since the 1990s, China has also become a cooperative member of the nuclear order. In East Asia, while China's contestation of the LIO has been "antihegemonic" in some respects, in others it has been "pro-order," seeking to "expand the scope of regional consensus on key strategic issues" and leveraging "values or norms that other regional states actually share."[19] For example, China's support for the Association of Southeast Asian Nations (ASEAN) Regional Forum and the ASEAN Plus Three dia-logue mechanism has sought to create an Asia-centric basis of security cooperation.

Existing Explanations for China's Behavior

The typology of theories of revisionism presented in Chapter 1 identi-fies two distinct paradigms based on whether the dominant motive for

[15] Tyler Pratt, "Angling for influence: Institutional proliferation in development banking," *International Studies Quarterly*, 65:1 (2021), 95–108.
[16] Yongjin Zhang, "China and liberal hierarchies in global international society: Power and negotiation for normative change," *International Affairs*, 92:4 (2016), 795–816.
[17] Joel Wuthnow, *Chinese Diplomacy and the UN Security Council: Beyond the Veto* (London: Routledge, 2013).
[18] Fung, *China and Intervention*, 1–2.
[19] Evelyn Goh, "Contesting hegemonic order: China in East Asia," *Security Studies*, 28:3 (2019), 614–644.

state behavior is material (wealth or security) or symbolic (status or recognition). Within each of these categories, theories may be further divided into those that prioritize causal processes at the level of the international system and those that do so at the level of domestic politics. Perhaps due to the high barriers in the way of studying contemporary China, the bulk of theorizing about China's potential revisionism in the international order locates causes at the international level. Those focused on the domestic level highlight contesting schools of thought, suggesting that China has "multiple international identities and a schizophrenic personality," which precludes reliable predictions of state behavior.[20] In keeping with IST's assumption of a unitary state, the discussion below focuses only on the international level.

Hegemonic War

Theories of hegemonic war derive from power transition theory and assume that China has purely material motivations. These theories imply that any cooperation on China's part is simply a tactic to buy time while China is relatively weak, so that it can enforce its preferred set of international rules and institutions when it is stronger. In a world where the unipolar power (the United States) can punish anything that looks like a direct challenge, delegitimation is a rational strategy.[21] However, by this token, these theories cannot explain costly cooperation of the kind that China has pursued in the UNSC or in the nuclear order.

There are three reasons for this theoretical blind spot. First, power transition approaches to China lack a conception of the LIO that is distinct from the distribution of power.[22] Accordingly, they make the untenable prediction that a change in the latter will necessitate a change in the former.

Second, they tend to view China's potential challenge as largely a military one, thus lacking any explanation for nonmilitary challenges

---

[20] David Shambaugh, "Coping with a conflicted China," *The Washington Quarterly*, 34:1 (2011), 7–27.
[21] Daniel W. Drezner, "Counter-hegemonic strategies in the global economy," *Security Studies*, 28:3 (2019), 505–531.
[22] See Kim and Gates, "Power transition theory."

or alternative strategies such as cooperation and reform.[23] In fact, in a world in which nuclear weapons make major war between great powers a low-probability event,[24] institutions are a far "less costly and risky choice for China" to pursue its international objectives.[25] Conflating challenge with war misses a great deal of what has actually been going on in the international order as China rises.

Third, and finally, these theories do not sufficiently theorize China's (dis)satisfaction, which is a key driver of international political change.[26] As a result, scholars often infer (dis)satisfaction from behavior that may have many other causes.[27] Without a robust theoretical foundation, various behaviors can be marshaled as evidence for either side of the argument. For example, China's presumed dissatisfaction (based on growing military power) makes the AIIB a challenge to "Pax Americana" and a rival of the IMF and World Bank.[28] Alternatively, China's presumed satisfaction (based on signing international treaties and rarely using its UNSC veto) makes the AIIB complementary to the IMF and World Bank.[29] These arguments are less persuasive without a proper theoretical account of (dis)satisfaction.

Hegemonic Peace

Theories of hegemonic peace take a more granular approach and draw on functional regime theory to explain China's behavior in the LIO. They do not assume an automatic desire on China's part to challenge the international order, which itself is more richly theorized in these accounts. Rather than asking how a state might react to the

---

[23] See David Rapkin and William Thompson, "Power transition, challenge and the (re)emergence of China," *International Interactions*, 29:4 (2003), 315–342; M. Taylor Fravel, "International relations theory and China's rise: Assessing China's potential for territorial expansion," *International Studies Review*, 12 (2010), 505–532.

[24] Schweller, "Emerging powers," 286.

[25] Lanteigne, *China and International Institutions*, 30.

[26] Avery Goldstein, "Power transitions, institutions, and China's rise in East Asia: Theoretical expectations and evidence," *Journal of Strategic Studies*, 30:4–5 (2007), 639–682.

[27] See Yves-Heng Lim, "How (dis)satisfied is China? A power transition theory perspective," *Journal of Contemporary China*, 24:92 (2015), 280–297.

[28] Christopher Layne, "The US-Chinese power shift and the end of the Pax Americana," *International Affairs*, 94:1 (2018), 89–111.

[29] Chan et al., "Discerning states' revisionist and status-quo orientations," 635.

international order as a whole, these theories focus on incentives for cooperation across different institutions and issue areas. Scholars such as Phillip Lipscy argue that rising powers such as China are more likely to cooperate when they have fewer outside options.[30] Scott Kastner et al. show that when sufficient outside options exist, China's cooperation hinges on whether the great powers find China indispensable to an institution or not.[31]

These explanations are incomplete in two respects. First, the range of behaviors that they predict remains within the realm of cooperation. At most, states threaten to exit international institutions or hold up negotiations. These models cannot account for China's aforementioned challenges to the international order. Second, like theories of hegemonic war, theories of hegemonic peace lack a theoretical account of China's (dis) satisfaction. Choosing whether to invest in, hold up, or accept an institution presumes an underlying preference for alternative arrangements that may not be realized due to insufficient outside options. But where does this preference originate? Scholars assume states "often grow dissatisfied with their representation or influence" in international institutions, and rapidly rising states in particular "may feel that existing arrangements do not sufficiently reflect their newfound power."[32] China is thus said to be building new institutions because existing institutions have failed to adapt to changes in the global distribution of power.[33]

These are problematic assumptions for theories of hegemonic peace. The paradigm within which these theories operate assumes that states will cooperate through institutions when institutions can deliver lower-cost cooperation compared to alternatives, and all else being equal, the cost of reforming existing institutions is lower than establishing new ones.[34] Within this framework, so long as an institution is providing net positive benefits to a state – in China's case substantially so – there is no reason why the state would want to incur *higher* transaction costs and create *greater* uncertainty by breaking institutional rules or setting

---

[30] Phillip Y. Lipscy, *Renegotiating the World Order: Institutional Change in International Relations* (Cambridge: Cambridge University Press, 2017).
[31] Scott L. Kastner, Margaret M. Pearson, and Chad Rector, "Invest, hold up, or accept? China in multilateral governance," *Security Studies*, 25 (2016), 142–179.
[32] Lipscy, *Renegotiating the World Order*, 2–3.
[33] Pratt, "Angling for influence."
[34] See Robert O. Keohane, *After Hegemony: Cooperation and Discord in the World Political Economy* (Princeton: Princeton University Press, 1984), 85–109.

up parallel institutions.[35] Indeed, these theories cannot tell us why a state experiencing increasing power would want more representation in an institution that is already delivering positive returns; all the more so when institutional leadership carries maintenance costs.[36] It must be that rising states desire something in addition to material benefits. It is not surprising, then, that international regime theorists studying China end up including some version of status or prestige in their assumptions to explain state motivations.[37]

Status/Recognition

Theories of status in world politics address head on the question of why a rising power that is benefiting from an international order would seek to challenge it. Rising powers seek recognition of their identity as major powers.[38] If the great powers are unable or unwilling to provide this recognition, a rising power seeks to "resist its social subordination and forcefully reassert its aspirant major power identity."[39] An international order that benefits a rising power materially may still be subject to challenge on grounds of status immobility.[40]

Status theories still fall short of explaining China's variable behavior with regard to the LIO. Although they adopt a thicker view of international order than theories of hegemonic war, they operate at a relatively high level of abstraction. Scholars in this vein define the LIO in terms of open and rule-based relations, universality, and American leadership[41]; or sovereignty, a global economy, and an institutional architecture of cooperation[42]; or simply "rules, norms, and institutions."[43] These descriptions are accurate but broad and amorphous. Asking what China thinks of universality or sovereignty is a less

---

[35] This is an argument based on absolute gains, which also holds when based on relative gains. Rising powers are by definition doing relatively better (growing at a higher rate) under existing institutional arrangements than the great powers.

[36] Schweller, "Emerging powers," 288–289.

[37] Lipscy, *Renegotiating the World Order*, 4; Pratt, "Angling for influence," 97; Kastner et al., "Invest, hold up, or accept," 170.

[38] Larson and Shevchenko, *Quest for Status*, 230.

[39] Murray, *The Struggle for Recognition*, 192.

[40] Ward, *Status and the Challenge*.   [41] Ibid., 184.

[42] Murray, *The Struggle for Recognition*, 211.

[43] Deborah Larson, "Will China be a new type of great power?" *The Chinese Journal of International Politics*, 8:4 (2015), 323–348.

reliable guide to China's behavior in the LIO than asking how China deals with specific institutions where sovereignty or universality is implicated.

Like theories of hegemonic war, status theories tend to conceive of the international order largely in terms of American leadership and a Chinese challenge largely in military terms. The answer to whether China will become revisionist ends up hinging on the state of US–China relations,[44] and given China's rapidly growing military capabilities and search for hegemony in East Asia, revisionism becomes a question of war and peace. This assumption does not shed much light on China in the LIO. The international order involves much more than American leadership or whether US leaders are pessimistic, optimistic, rejectionist, or integrationist about China's rise.[45] Going beyond questions of war and US–China relations can yield richer theoretical and empirical insights on a range of observed behaviors such as rule-breaking, delegitimation, and institutional proliferation.

The Role of Legitimacy

Taken together, existing theories struggle to fully explain the pattern of Chinese satisfaction or dissatisfaction with the international order, and China's decision to challenge some parts of the order while supporting others. These two phenomena – (dis)satisfaction and revisionism – are linked to a more fundamental question: What is it that makes an international order durable and less susceptible to challenges from rising powers? The answer, hidden in theories that often make no explicit room in their assumptions for it, is legitimacy. E. H. Carr famously observed, "[A]n international order cannot be based on power alone."[46] Nuno Monteiro argued that even the "preponderant power" of a unipolar state, such as the United States, "does not necessarily get states what they want."[47] Martha Finnemore identifies the crux of the problem: "Using power as more than a sledgehammer requires legitimation," which makes a powerful state dependent on

---

[44] See Larson and Shevchenko, *Quest for Status*, 195–197.
[45] See Murray, *The Struggle for Recognition*, 211; Ward, *Status and the Challenge*, 186.
[46] Carr, *The Twenty Years' Crisis*, 216.
[47] Nuno P. Monteiro, *Theory of Unipolar Politics* (Cambridge: Cambridge University Press, 2014), 7.

other states.[48] Writing about the LIO, Ian Clark observes, "A multitude of writers, working from quite different perspectives, is in agreement that it is this lack of legitimacy that threatens the very fabric of the [present] order."[49]

Theories of hegemonic war often rely on legitimacy to argue that dissatisfaction arises from contestation over "who has the authority to make the rules of the game."[50] Theories of hegemonic peace rely on legitimacy to explain why China might accept or threaten to exit certain institutional arrangements.[51] The frequent references to legitimacy in these literatures is surprising because materialist theories do not make room for ideational factors in their foundations. Status theories do, focusing on a rising power's attempt to either legitimate its own identity as a major power[52] or delegitimate the international order when experiencing status immobility.[53] However, they do not tell us what makes an international order legitimate or illegitimate. IST fills this gap.

The next few sections describe China's major-power identity, and demonstrate the applicability of IST to China's approach to the LIO and its behavior across institutions and issue areas of the order.

China's Major-Power Identity

Like the United States in the nineteenth century, Japan in the interwar period, and India during the Cold War, China's major-power identity is wrapped up in visions of greatness, exceptionalism, and a desire for symbolic equality with the great powers.[54] Chinese leaders are keen to

---

[48] Finnemore, "Legitimacy, hypocrisy," 60.

[49] Ian Clark, "Legitimacy in a global order," *Review of International Studies*, 29 (2003), 75–95.

[50] Xiaoyu Pu, "Socialisation as a two-way process: Emerging powers and the diffusion of international norms," *The Chinese Journal of International Politics*, 5 (2012), 341–367. See also Layne, "The US-Chinese power shift," 110; Schweller, "A tale of two realisms," 11.

[51] Lipscy, *Renegotiating World Order*, 32; Miles Kahler, "Rising powers and global governance: Negotiating change in a resilient status quo," *International Affairs*, 89:3 (2013), 711–729.

[52] Murray, *The Struggle for Recognition*, 66–70.

[53] Ward, *Status and the Challenge*, 10–32; Larson and Shevchenko, *Quest for Status*, 232–251.

[54] Hoo Tiang Boon, *China's Global Identity: Considering the Responsibilities of Great Power* (Washington, DC: Georgetown University Press, 2018), ch. 1.

see their state recognized on the international stage as a great power.[55] However, they are also certain that China will not be like the other great powers. Chinese exceptionalism originates from a self-perception of being "the most moral of the major states."[56] While other major powers practice *realpolitik* and engage in unethical foreign policies, China sees itself as "a uniquely principled actor."[57] Since the Maoist era at least, Chinese leaders have believed that their "moral superiority" entitles them to "great power status and moral authority."[58]

Although perceiving their state as great and exceptional, Chinese leaders still value symbolic equality with the great powers. While they recognize the gap in military capabilities between China and the United States, they are keen to effect a transformation of the international order from one "dominated or controlled by Western great powers to one in which the West, and especially the United States, accepts the need to coexist in an equal and reasonable manner with newly rising non-Western states."[59] China is often frustrated by the United States' unwillingness to pursue "a globalization based on equality and mutual respect," instead turning globalization into "Americanization" that seeks to impose on China.[60] Beijing has pushed this line more strongly since the Global Financial Crisis, arguing for a "two superpowers, several strong powers" world order.[61]

China's status aspirations have made its leaders acutely conscious of their country's reputation abroad and of how the world perceives China's leadership potential in the international order.[62] Chinese

---

[55] Rosemary Foot, "Chinese power and the idea of a responsible state," in Yongjin Zhang and Greg Austin (eds.), *Power and Responsibility in Chinese Foreign Policy* (Canberra: Australian National University Press, 2001), 21–47.

[56] Denny Roy, "The foreign policy of great-power China," *Contemporary Southeast Asia*, 19:2 (1997), 121–135.

[57] Ibid., 124.

[58] Feng Zhang, "The rise of Chinese exceptionalism in international relations," *European Journal of International Relations*, 19:2 (2011), 305–328.

[59] Rosemary Foot, "Chinese strategies in a US-hegemonic global order: Accommodating and hedging," *International Affairs*, 82:1 (2006), 77–94, citing the arguments of Shi Yinhong.

[60] Rosalie Chen, "China perceives America: Perspectives of international relations experts," *Journal of Contemporary China*, 12:35 (2003), 285–297.

[61] David Shambaugh, "Chinese thinking about world order," in Xiaoming Huang and Robert Patman (eds.), *China and the International System: Becoming a World Power* (Abingdon: Routledge, 2013), 21–31, quoted in Goh, "Contesting hegemonic order," 626.

[62] Roy, "The foreign policy," 123.

leaders have emphasized that playing a constructive role in multilateral institutions of the international order is a "touchstone for China's effort to join the ranks of the first-class powers in the world."[63] In terms of IST, recognition as an equal of the great powers matters to China. Typically, this means recognition *by* the great powers, which are the Western states in the international system.[64] Shogo Suzuki highlights a strand of "Occidentalism" in Chinese elite thinking about international affairs, according to which China's identity as a great power is "deeply connected to Western recognition."[65] Indeed, "becoming a member of the club of great powers has long been the most important theme of Chinese nationalism."[66]

It is worth noting here that China has frequently sought to downplay its major-power identity and emphasize the identity of a poor developing nation in order to maintain its status among the developing nations of the world.[67] However, China's desired position in the latter case is not that of an equal to the developing nations, but a leading nation among them.[68] By contrast, Chinese leaders have sought equality with the states in the great-power club. More generally, China's mixed status signaling is a function of its dual reality as a rising state and an imminent, if not already risen, great power. Ann Kent describes China's "complex identity" as an "incipient superpower": a permanent member of the UNSC and nuclear power, on the one hand, and a developing state and former victim of colonization, on the other hand.[69] For IST's purposes, it is safe to assume that China's primary concern is its major-power identity, which relies on recognition of its claim to symbolic equality with the great powers.

[63] Wang Yi, quoted in Evan S. Medeiros, *China's International Behavior: Activism, Opportunism, and Diversification* (Santa Monica, CA: RAND Corporation, 2009), 18.
[64] Yong Deng, *China's Struggle for Status: The Realignment of International Relations* (Cambridge: Cambridge University Press, 2008), 2.
[65] Suzuki, "Journey to the West," 634.
[66] Yongnian Zheng, *Discovering Chinese Nationalism in China: Modernization, Identity, and International Relations* (Cambridge: Cambridge University Press, 1999), 129, quoted in ibid., 637.
[67] Xiaoyu Pu, *Rebranding China: Contested Status Signaling in the Changing Global Order* (Stanford: Stanford University Press, 2019).
[68] Miller, *Wronged by Empire*, 55–81.
[69] Ann Kent, "China's participation in international organisations," in Zhang and Austin (eds.), *Power and Responsibility in Chinese Foreign Policy*, 132–166.

Institutional Status Theory and China

While it is difficult to decisively claim that China is either cooperative or uncooperative with regard to the LIO as a whole, it is possible to discern Chinese attitudes toward the LIO as a first step toward a more comprehensive theory of China's engagement with different institutions of the order. Experts may disagree on several aspects of Chinese foreign policy, but they seem to be in broad agreement that China seeks to advance its status within the international order. While bilateral relations may help Beijing address specific conflicts of interest with other countries, international institutions help confer "prestige, status and domestic legitimacy" on the Communist Party of China.[70] As social environments thick with diplomatic interactions and public forums, international institutions act as "effective theatres-in-the-round for China to demonstrate its developing greatness."[71] Ann Florini argues that the declining attraction of the Western model of economic growth and political management after the Iraq War and the Global Financial Crisis has only intensified China's status-seeking within the international order, leading to "a striking mood of Asian triumphalism."[72]

China's leaders continue striving for status because China has not yet been granted the recognition it seeks. In Western media, China is often simultaneously labelled a rising great power and a rogue state.[73] Chinese elites have frequently been frustrated at the United States' so-called containment strategy, which they see as an attempt to "deny China's entry into the great power club."[74] As a result, scholars describe China's position in the international order as "curious" and its membership of the great-power club as "at best contentious."[75] Despite formal membership in the upper echelons of the international

---

[70] Ibid., 135.   [71] Lanteigne, *China and International Institutions*, 28.
[72] Ann Florini, "Rising Asian powers and changing global governance," *International Studies Review*, 13:1 (2011), 24–33.
[73] See Sherman Katz, "How to tame China's rogue state capitalism," *Financial Times*, July 30, 2019; Brittany Gibson, "The biggest rogue states of the climate crisis," *The American Prospect*, October 9, 2019; BBC News, "China a 'rogue state', says ex Cameron adviser Steve Hilton," October 21, 2015.
[74] Chen, "China perceives America," 289.
[75] Yongjin Zhang and Greg Austin, "China and the responsibility of power," in Zhang and Austin (eds.), *Power and Responsibility in Chinese Foreign Policy*, 1–20.

order, China's "ambiguous status has persisted."[76] In many respects, China remains an outsider inside the great-power club.

Assessments vary as to how China's desire for symbolic equality with the great powers translates into behavior with regard to the international order. Some scholars argue that China complies with the order even against its own material interests, to avoid being "singled out for disapprobation."[77] Beijing is keen to promote its image as a responsible and trustworthy actor in the international order, lest other countries conclude otherwise and try to isolate China.[78] This position is reminiscent of interwar Japan's approach to the Washington system – the fear of being singled out and thereby falling in the esteem of the international community can be a powerful source of cooperation. Others argue that having been denied the voice it has sought in the international order – in spite of the assistance China provided the Western countries during the Global Financial Crisis – Beijing has adopted a more assertive stance in international affairs in order to reassert its claims to equality with the United States.[79] Barry Buzan admits China's status ambitions but argues that China is a "reformist revisionist" for purely instrumental reasons.[80] IST shows, however, that status-seeking is just as instrumental as the quest for security or wealth, and in fact international institutions enable the simultaneous pursuit of both material *and* symbolic goods.

China's preoccupation with fairness and justice in the international order shows that its leaders do not prioritize only material ends in this context. Yan Xuetong notes that the Chinese (presumably the elites) regard their country's rise as a "restoration of fairness rather than gaining advantages over others."[81] According to this logic, restoring fairness will give China a greater say in global governance and thereby restore China to its former status of being a globally recognized great power. China's demand within the international order has been more for "equal participation" than for a greater share of the benefits of

---

[76] Li, "Rising from within," 331.   [77] Foot, "Chinese power," 37.

[78] Shaun Breslin, "China's emerging global role: Dissatisfied responsible great power," *Politics*, 30:S1 (2010), 52–62.

[79] Nadège Rolland, "China's vision for a new world order," NBR Special Report #83 (January 2020); Maximillian Terhalle, *The Transition of Global Order: Legitimacy and Contestation* (Basingstoke: Palgrave Macmillan, 2015), 5.

[80] Barry Buzan, "China in international society: Is 'peaceful rise' possible?" *The Chinese Journal of International Politics*, 3 (2010), 5–36.

[81] Quoted in Deng, *China's Struggle for Status*, 9.

cooperation.[82] Chinese scholar Cai Tuo argues that "the existing international order [is] profoundly unjust," primarily because the power to make decisions is in the hands of the United States and its Western allies.[83] Beijing's support for a multipolar distribution of power and the democratization of global governance is ultimately shaped by a desire for fairer procedures that will give China its due as a great power. The Chinese example shows that a rising power expects greater influence in the international order, not necessarily because its material interests are at stake, but because it tends to perceive as biased institutional arrangements that were designed without its concurrence.[84]

Explaining Variation in China's Approach to the Liberal Order

Given China's status aspirations, IST expects that if the international order were to tend toward greater fairness, it would have greater legitimacy in Chinese leaders' eyes and hence be likely to elicit cooperation from Beijing. Rosemary Foot and Andrew Walter support this contention, arguing that China has increasingly cooperated with the LIO since the 1980s in part because "the process of norm creation and elaboration [in the order] is perceived [by China] as procedurally legitimate and, in substantive terms, provides for a reasonably fair distribution of material and social costs and benefits across countries."[85] This argument rests on both procedural and substantive legitimacy, whereas IST focuses primarily on the procedural features of an institution, alongside openness. Evelyn Goh argues that China plays "two simultaneous games": one of deferring to the United States in order to earn recognition as a great power, and the other of resisting parts of the international order it sees as "especially illegitimate."[86]

Given the complexity of the LIO, as noted earlier, disaggregating the order into its core institutions can provide greater analytical leverage

---

[82] Hu Jintao, quoted in Gregory Chin and Ramesh Thakur, "Will China change the rules of global order?" *The Washington Quarterly*, 33:4 (2010), 119–138.

[83] Quoted in Gerald Chan, Pak K. Lee, and Lai-Ha Chan, *China Engages Global Governance: A New World Order in the Making?* (Abingdon: Routledge, 2012), 32.

[84] Foot and Walter, *China, the United States, and Global Order*, 11.

[85] Ibid., 30.   [86] Goh, "Contesting hegemonic order," 627.

Table 7.1. *Institutional Status Theory and China in the liberal international order*

		INSTITUTONAL OPENNESS	
		High	Low
	High	**Cooperate**	**Expand**
		UNSC, WTO, NPT/	IMF, World
PROCEDURAL		CTBT, G20	Bank, Foreign
FAIRNESS			Aid (DAC)
	Low	**Reframe**	**Challenge**
		Climate Change	Human Rights
		(UNFCCC), Maritime	(UNCHR/
		Law (UNCLOS)	UNHRC)

on the variable pattern of China's cooperation.[87] This approach takes into account the fact that "emerging powers are conflicted states that may play all three roles – spoiler, supporter, or shirker – depending on the issue and the audience."[88] As the other empirical chapters in this book demonstrate, rising powers also cooperate at certain times and not at others, within the same international institution. Given the broad-based nature of the empirical analysis below, what follows will cover both variation across institutions and change over time, if any, within specific institutions. The findings are summarized in Table 7.1.

IST predicts that China is more likely to *cooperate* in international institutions in which it is already recognized – formally or informally – as an equal member of the great-power club. These include the UNSC, the WTO, the NPT/CTBT, and the G20. In institutions that exclude China from their top ranks but nonetheless apply their rules in a consultative and consistent manner, Beijing seeks to *expand* the top ranks of the institution in an effort to attain symbolic equality with the great-power club. These include the Bretton Woods institutions (the IMF and the World Bank), as well as the issue area of foreign aid in

---

[87] Xinyuan Dai and Duu Renn, "China and international order: The limits of integration," *Journal of Chinese Political Science*, 21 (2016), 177–197.
[88] Schweller, "Emerging powers," 287.

which the OECD's Development Assistance Committee (DAC) plays a central role and does not include rising powers such as China and India.

In institutions or issue areas that are open to Chinese leadership – and often welcome it – but apply their rules unfairly from China's perspective, Beijing lobbies for fairer rules by *reframing* its own attributes or behavior to achieve symbolic equality with the great-power club. These include the United Nations Framework Convention on Climate Change and the United Nations Convention on the Law of the Sea, in which China feels subject to inconsistent or biased institutional rules. Finally, in institutions or issue areas that are closed to Chinese leadership and also unfair from China's perspective, Beijing *challenges* the institution and openly chooses not to comply. The chief instance in this domain is the United Nations human rights system, which includes Charter-based bodies, such as the former UN Commission on Human Rights (UNCHR) and the UN Human Rights Council (UNHRC), and treaty-based bodies monitoring the implementation of UN human rights treaties. As a nondemocratic power, China can never claim leadership of this system, and Beijing is often singled out by the Western great powers in the system as a major violator of human rights.

Open and Procedurally Fair Institutions

Chinese decision-makers are willing to cooperate, sometimes at considerable material cost, with institutions that are open to China joining (or remaining in) their top ranks as a member of the great-power club and that treat China in an unbiased manner. The United Nations, and the UNSC in particular, is an institution that meets these criteria. Since 1971, China has had access to the great-power club through permanent membership of the UNSC. This access is all the more pertinent because it involved the great powers orchestrating Taiwan's replacement with the People's Republic of China in the institution. The UNSC is also procedurally fair from China's perspective – decisions are made in consultative fashion and the veto gives China equal power to block decisions it does not like.

Chinese leaders have praised the UN as the "most universal, representative, and authoritative international organization in the world."[89] Representation is certainly important to them. However, in keeping with IST's assumptions, they are typically concerned with their *own*

---

[89] Qian Qichen, quoted in Foot, "Chinese strategies," 91.

country's representation. China values the institutional privileges of the great powers relative to other member states, and while the UNSC's procedural fairness can help Beijing keep a check on American power, permanent membership carries its own intrinsic status benefits.[90] Zhang Yongjin argues that being a member of the P-5 (five permanent members) confers upon China "a socially recognized and accepted Great Power status," which then motivates China to defend the institution as "normatively sensible, morally defensible and politically viable."[91]

Faced with an open and procedurally fair institution, cooperation becomes the most efficient means of attaining and then maintaining symbolic equality with the great powers. China has no need to go against the UNSC because the institution recognizes China as an equal member of the great-power club. In fact, China has accepted increasing costs and risks associated with its support for the UNSC. Chief among these is Beijing's qualified acceptance of nonconsensual military intervention authorized under Chapter VII of the UN Charter,[92] a practice that has hurt Chinese interests in countries such as Libya and Syria. Courtney Fung shows how a concern for maintaining status within the UNSC has shaped Beijing's decision-making on questions of intervention.[93] President Xi Jinping has admitted that as a permanent member of the UNSC, China "has heavy responsibilities to assume" and is willing to do so.[94] China has contributed increasing numbers of troops and resources to UN peacekeeping missions, motivated both by an ideology that reinforces Chinese superiority relative to recipient states and by a desire to project the image of being a responsible great power.[95]

[90] Ibid., 92.   [91] Zhang, "China and liberal hierarchies," 801.
[92] Lise Morjé Howard and Anjali Kaushlesh Dayal, "The use of force in UN peacekeeping," *International Organization*, 72:1 (2018), 71–103.
[93] Fung, *China and Intervention*.
[94] Zhang, "China and liberal hierarchies," 812.
[95] Shogo Suzuki, "Why does China participate in intrusive peacekeeping? Understanding paternalistic Chinese discourses on development and intervention," *International Peacekeeping*, 18:3 (2011), 271–285; Courtney J. Richardson, "A responsible power? China and the UN peacekeeping regime," *International Peacekeeping*, 18:3 (2011), 286–297; Rosemary Foot, "'Doing some things' in the Xi Jinping era: The United Nations as China's venue of choice," *International Affairs*, 90:5 (2014), 1085–1100.

The WTO is another core institution of the LIO where institutional openness and procedural fairness have engendered cooperation on China's part, though the overall picture of China's trade policy is mixed.[96] Initially, Chinese leaders had to overcome a lengthy negotiation process and much domestic opposition from powerful government bureaucracies in order to join the institution.[97] According to former Premier Li Peng, WTO membership for China was primarily a political question and not an economic question.[98] China sought membership in order to obtain "a seat at the bargaining table to influence the rules of the game,"[99] thus establishing "its rightful place in the world's most important trading body."[100] Within the WTO, China's growing economy has made it a pivotal player over time. Cognizant of their country's membership in the great-power club and viewing the institutional rules of the WTO as broadly fair (in their design, if not their outcome), Chinese leaders have taken a partially cooperative approach. This approach is partial because even though China overhauled many aspects of its legal and regulatory regime in order to join the WTO, its centralized and authoritarian political system inhibits the kind of fundamental economic reform that would enable full compliance with WTO regulations.[101]

Partial cooperation also does not mean that China has scrupulously adhered to the letter and spirit of the WTO – few countries do – but that it has been compliant in some areas and willing to roll back unfair trade practices when challenged in others. China has in particular been sensitive to not take any actions that might harm its reputation in the WTO's dispute settlement system (DSS).[102] Beijing has over time become a frequent source and target of litigation in the DSS, and has displayed a strong track record of compliance with DSS rulings, at least

---

[96] Johnston, "China in a world of orders," 41–46.
[97] Hongyi Harry Lai, "Behind China's World Trade Organization agreement with the USA," *Third World Quarterly*, 22:2 (2001), 237–255.
[98] Li Peng, quoted in Schweller and Pu, "After unipolarity," 54, n. 51.
[99] Ibid., 51.   [100] Foot, "Chinese power," 36.
[101] Jessica Brum, "Technology transfer and China's WTO commitments," *Georgetown Journal of International Law*, 50 (2019), 709–743.
[102] Xiaojun Li, "Understanding China's behavioral change in the WTO dispute settlement system: Power, capacity, and normative constraints in trade adjudication," *Asian Survey*, 52:6 (2012), 1111–1137.

in part to preserve China's reputation as a "system builder."[103] This stands in stark contrast to China's rejection of third-party dispute resolution in other areas such as the law of the sea.[104]

Status concerns have also suffused China's engagement with the international nuclear order since the early Cold War. China's nuclear program, begun in the 1960s, was framed by Mao in terms of breaking the nuclear monopoly of the superpowers and thereby keeping a pathway open to the great-power club.[105] Despite being a de facto member of the nuclear club, China continued to advocate a more equal nuclear order through the UN and the Conference on Disarmament, which Chinese leaders saw as providing "small and medium sized countries with an important forum for participation."[106] After the Cold War, the United States and its allies began singling China out for its continued nuclear testing and proliferation of nuclear technology to countries such as Iran and Pakistan. Faced with the prospect of being treated as a lesser member of the club, Beijing decided to double down on international institutions for "a legitimate seat at the table."[107]

China signed the NPT in 1992 and the CTBT in 1996, participated in numerous multilateral conferences, reaffirmed its no-first-use pledge, and even submitted a draft international no-first-use treaty to the United Nations General Assembly in 1994.[108] The latter in particular earned China a "unique moral high-ground in the nuclear club."[109] Having secured its position as an equal in the nuclear order, China has since the 1990s defended the order even against American unilateralism and double standards, such as the George W. Bush administration's abrogation of the Anti-Ballistic Missile Treaty in 2002.[110] Over

---

[103] Xiaowen Zhang and Xiaoling Li, "The politics of compliance with adverse WTO dispute settlement rulings in China," *Journal of Contemporary China*, 23:85 (2014), 143–160.

[104] Gregory Shaffer and Henry Gao, "China's rise: How it took on the U.S. at the WTO," *University of Illinois Law Review*, 2018:1 (2018), 115–184.

[105] Morton Halperin, "Chinese nuclear strategy: The early post detonation period," *Adelphi Papers*, 5:18 (1965), 3–13; Jonathan D. Pollack, "Chinese attitudes towards nuclear weapons, 1964–9," *China Quarterly*, 50 (1972), 244–271.

[106] Forsburgh, *China and Global Nuclear Order*, 93.   [107] Ibid., 106.

[108] Ibid., 106.

[109] Ibid., 111, citing Shen Dingli, "Nuclear deterrence in the 21st Century," *China Security*, 1 (2005), 10–14.

[110] Chen, "China perceives America," 288.

the last two decades, China has maintained its status within the various institutions of the nuclear order by cooperating with other countries to manage nuclear threats (such as North Korea) and making sure that institutions and rules stay abreast of advances in nuclear technology.[111]

Perhaps no institution highlights the importance of openness and procedural fairness more than the G20. The Group of Eight (G8) was an exclusive club that had only one Asian member: Japan. The Global Financial Crisis, which hit the West hardest, made it evident that "the G8 or any other small exclusive club is not a legitimate or effective means of problem solving," given the interconnected nature of global finance and the complexity of economic interdependence in the LIO.[112] The formation of the G20 was a symbol of the declining relative economic power and prestige of the United States and the concomitant rise of Asia, especially China and India.[113] Unlike other institutions of the international economic order, which China had not helped design and instead joined as a latecomer, Beijing was now able to claim "historical ownership" over the construction of a pivotal new institution.[114] The transition from the G8 to G20 represented a dismantling of the barriers to entry, erected by the great powers, to China's membership of one of the most elite groupings of the LIO, and the creation of new institutional terrain on which China could participate as an equal. This "parity of voice,"[115] coupled with China's capacity as an economic heavyweight, motivated Beijing to cooperate with other G20 members as a way of maintaining its status as a member of the great-power club in a changing international order.[116]

Procedurally Fair but Closed Institutions

Institutions characterized by procedural fairness and (relative) institutional closure are those with rules that China has found to be

---

[111] Thomas J. Christensen, *The China Challenge: Shaping the Choices of a Rising Power* (New York: W. W. Norton, 2015), ch. 5.
[112] Andrew F. Cooper and Daniel Flemes, "Foreign policy strategies of emerging powers in a multipolar world: An introductory review," *Third World Quarterly*, 34:6 (2013), 943–962.
[113] Layne, "The US-Chinese power shift," 100.
[114] Zhang, "China and liberal hierarchies," 814.   [115] Ibid.
[116] See John J. Kirton, *China's G20 Leadership* (London: Routledge, 2016).

consultative, consistent, and unbiased, but that have not created avenues for the rise of new powers to their top ranks. Beijing's response has been to advocate institutional reform to expand the club of great powers that dominates these institutions. This category includes the Bretton Woods institutions – the IMF and the World Bank – as well as the OECD's Development Assistance Committee, which acts as the preeminent institution for coordinating the policies of industrialized donor countries. In the case of the DAC, China has not sought membership but rather sought symbolic equality with the great powers by emphasizing the unique and South-South nature of Chinese aid.[117]

The Bretton Woods institutions highlight the relative nature of openness and fairness. In the context of the broader international order, the IMF and World Bank are in fact quite open. New countries can join with relative ease, and institutional rules stipulate that a country's influence rises with its economic weight (through the purchase of voting shares).[118] From China's perspective, however, the Bretton Woods institutions are not as open as other institutions in the LIO, such as the ones mentioned in the previous section. Mario Carranza notes that the two key indicators of membership of the great-power club in the LIO are permanent membership of the UNSC and "real decision-making power in key International Political Economy Institutions" such as the IMF, World Bank, and G20.[119] This section focuses on the IMF, which experts regard as "the favored twin" and "primus inter pares" among the Bretton Woods institutions.[120]

The IMF's weighted system of voting, in which states are allotted voting quotas tied to their economic weight, has traditionally been the source of American primacy in the institution. Additionally, the IMF maintains a list of constitutional issues, such as the allocation of voting quotas, the method of calculating reserves, the sale of the IMF's gold stock, etc., on which special majorities of 70–85 percent of weighted

---

[117] See Emma Mawdsley, "Human rights and South-South development cooperation: Reflections on the 'rising powers' as international development actors," *Human Rights Quarterly*, 36 (2014), 630–652.

[118] G. John Ikenberry, "The rise of China and the future of the West," *Foreign Affairs*, 87:1 (2008), 23–37.

[119] Mario E. Carranza, "Rising regional powers and international relations theories: Comparing Brazil and India's foreign security policies and their search for great-power status," *Foreign Policy Analysis*, 13 (2017), 255–277.

[120] Devesh Kapur, "What next for the Bretton Woods twins?" *Project Syndicate*, October 18, 2019.

vote shares are required to make decisions.[121] The list of issues requiring this type of super-majority has grown over time as a result of amendments pushed by the United States, whose current vote quota of 16.52 percent is sufficient – with additional support from allies, if required – to exercise an effective veto over all major governance decisions at the IMF. Despite this structural dominance, during the Cold War, the United States "found it valuable to veil its power through conventions that convinced other countries that the rules of the game were reasonably fair."[122] One of these conventions was to rely on informal decision-making and consensus-building by the IMF managing director, who by convention was always from a European country and whose term renewal depended on American approval.[123]

The appointment of the top leadership posts in premier international financial institutions (IFIs) is an issue of institutional openness for China and other rising powers such as India and Brazil. The IMF has never had a non-European managing director or a non-American first deputy managing director; the World Bank has never had a non-American president; and the Asian Development Bank has never had a non-Japanese president. Equally significant at the IMF is the composition of the twenty-four-member Executive Board, which, while giving China a member of its own, overrepresents European countries.[124] Along with voting rights, China has lobbied for a more representative Executive Board and a more diverse selection of staff at the IMF (and the World Bank). Although the United States and its allies have committed to reform, the appointment of a Bulgarian managing director of the IMF in the most recent succession race, in October 2019, suggests that for the time being, these institutions remain closed to China joining their top ranks. Similarly, reforms promised to make

---

[121] International Monetary Fund (IMF), "Special voting majorities for selected financial decisions," *IMF Financial Operations 2015*, www.imf.org/external/pubs/ft/finop/2015/pdf/finop2015app2.pdf.

[122] Miles Kahler, "The United States and the International Monetary Fund: Declining influence or declining interest?" in Margaret P. Karns and Karen A. Mingst (eds.), *The United States and Multilateral Institutions: Patterns of Changing Instrumentality and Influence* (1992; repr. London: Routledge, [2003]), 62–77.

[123] Ibid., 64.

[124] Dries Lesage, Peter Debaere, Sacha Dierckx, and Mattias Vermeiren, "Rising powers and IMF Governance Reform," in Dries Lesage and Thijs Van de Graaf (eds.), *Rising Powers and Multilateral Institutions* (London: Palgrave Macmillan, 2015), 153–174.

the IMF's Executive Board more representative have gone nowhere.[125] Recent research shows that China's rise in global financial governance more broadly remains, at best, an "illusion."[126] Even at the UN more broadly, China remains far behind the United States, France, and Britain (but not Russia) in its occupation of executive leadership positions.[127]

The story of voting rights at the IMF also shows that when institutional closure is compounded by procedural unfairness, a rising power that was hitherto focused on institutional reform switches to a strategy of challenging the institution as a means of asserting its symbolic equality with the great powers. In the aftermath of the Global Financial Crisis, China and the leaders of the developing world perceived "a profound double standard in global economic governance" perpetrated by the IMF.[128] Whereas earlier lending to developing countries experiencing financial crises in the 1990s – including the Asian Financial Crisis – had imposed strict conditions requiring austerity on the part of borrowing governments, when the time came for Europe to borrow from the IMF, the institution's leadership began arguing against austerity. Although developing country leaders agreed in substance, "they found it infuriating that such arguments would be made by those in control of the purse strings on behalf of Greece or Portugal, but not in their own cases."[129] The only way to prevent this type of inconsistent application of IMF rules in future would be to push harder for institutional reform. The need for Chinese reserves to bolster IMF funds in the aftermath of the Global Financial Crisis offered the perfect opportunity.

Accordingly, China pursued a "hold up" strategy at the IMF, demanding concessions in return for helping bail out Western

---

[125] Ibid., 163–164.

[126] Falin Zhang, "Rising illusion and illusion of rising: Mapping global financial governance and relocating China," *International Studies Review*, 23:1 (2021), 1–29.

[127] Courtney J. Fung and Shing-Hon Lam, "Staffing the United Nations: China's motivations and prospects," *International Affairs*, 97:4 (2021), 1143–1163.

[128] Leslie Elliott Armijo and John Echeverri-Gent, "Absolute or relative gains? How status quo and emerging powers conceptualize global finance," in Thomas Oatley and W. Kindred Winecoff (eds.), *Handbook of the International Political Economy of Monetary Relations* (Cheltenham: Edward Elgar, 2014), 144–165.

[129] Ibid., 159.

economies.[130] The Governor of the People's Bank of China publicly said, "A half century after its founding, it is clear that the IMF has failed in its mission."[131] Kastner et al. argue that Beijing's desire to reform the IMF did not stem from any particular material concerns. Rather, it was tied to status. China wanted more institutional representation commensurate with its economic importance, and it wanted to break into the club of countries – comprising the United States, the EU, Japan, and Britain – whose currencies collectively provide an index of value for IMF reserves, or Special Drawing Rights (SDR).[132] In 2010, both the IMF and World Bank agreed to increase China's voting quotas. However, this agreement required approval by the US Congress, which withheld the necessary legislation for almost six years. The United States seemed unwilling to even "give China a little more say" at the IMF.[133]

Given the intransigence of the great powers, Beijing decided that it was time to establish an institutional venue where China could enjoy top billing. In 2013, China proposed a new bank to finance infrastructure-based development in Asia: the Asian Infrastructure Investment Bank. This was an indirect challenge to the international order, resulting from years of institutional closure in IFIs that was compounded by the inconsistent application of IMF rules to benefit Western countries in the aftermath of the Global Financial Crisis. "China is, understandably, impatient for change," noted *The Economist*. "It is therefore taking matters into its own hands."[134] When the United States tried to block friends and allies from joining the AIIB, Wei Jainguo, a former Chinese vice minister of finance said, "You could think of this as a basketball game in which the US wants to set the duration of the game, size of the court, the height of the basket and everything else to suit itself. In fact, the United States just wants to exclude China from the game."[135] In October 2016, China experienced "rapid elevation into the exclusive great power club" when the renminbi was included in the IMF's basket of currencies.[136] Yet, this was only one aspect of the reforms China has sought. China's voting

[130] Kastner et al., "Invest, hold up, or accept?," 165.   [131] Ibid., 170.
[132] Ibid.
[133] The Economist, "Why China is creating a new 'World Bank' for Asia," November 11, 2014.
[134] Ibid.   [135] Quoted in Layne, "The US-Chinese power shift," 103.
[136] Goh, "Contesting hegemonic order," 637.

quota has grown marginally, but it is still nowhere close to the de facto veto power enjoyed by the United States. The IMF Executive Board remains unchanged in its composition, and top leadership positions in IFIs remain reserved for the United States and its allies.

Evidence from these institutions shows that China uses institutional proliferation as a strategy to expand the ranks of the great-power club. IST can thus better explain than other theories why China undertakes significant costs to replicate existing institutions. Institutional proliferation is not a frontal challenge to the international order. Chinese leaders have repeatedly emphasized that new institutions such as the AIIB seek to complement and work with existing institutions such as the World Bank.[137] However, over time, institutional proliferation can lead to an indirect weakening of existing institutions and the overall international economic component of the LIO, as China invests more in new institutions than old ones and other countries follow suit.

Open but Procedurally Unfair Institutions

IST predicts that when an institution is open but procedurally unfair, a rising power will seek institutional reform that reframes negative evaluations of its major-power identity claims as positive. In practical terms, this involves altering the criteria by which rules are applied such that the rising power can be treated as symbolically equal to the great powers. The international climate change mitigation regime under the UN Framework Convention on Climate Change contains a set of institutions that fit this description. In the post–Cold War order, China's rapid rise has caused it to gradually become the largest national producer of greenhouse gases in the world.[138] Consequently, China has a guaranteed place in the top ranks of institutional efforts to mitigate climate change.[139] However, China – along with other states such as India, Brazil, and South Africa – sees a fundamental

[137] The People's Daily, "The AIIB is a complement rather than a competitor," October 28, 2014; Peter Guy, "AIIB not a threat to World Bank," *South China Morning Post*, April 5, 2015; Yukon Huang, "Demystifying the Asian Infrastructure Investment Bank," Carnegie Endowment for International Peace, April 21, 2015.

[138] Reuters, "China's greenhouse gas emissions soar 53 per cent in a decade, data shows," *South China Morning Post*, July 15, 2019.

[139] Jevans Nyabiage, "China's role 'critical' if world is to meet climate change targets," *South China Morning Post*, January 28, 2020.

inconsistency in the way the international climate order has developed. Namely, an emphasis on current emissions as the basis for determining international obligations unfairly singles China out as having to make sacrifices that the great powers did not make during their long history of industrialization and growth, which cumulatively contributed to global warming today.

China argues that due to their historical role in industrialization, developed nations must shoulder greater responsibility in terms of emissions reductions and technology transfer to poorer countries for climate change mitigation.[140] Over the last three decades, China has consistently emphasized "matters of allocating responsibility, and other related questions of equity" in climate change negotiations.[141] Importantly, China has chosen not to undermine the climate change regime. Xinyuan Dai and Duu Renn find that when it comes to environmental treaties, China engages in deep cooperation by signing not just the agreements but also their associated protocols that take on additional obligations.[142] China's approach to climate change obligations has also become increasingly cooperative over time, as highlighted most recently in Beijing's support for the Paris Agreement, from which the United States itself had withdrawn under the Trump administration.[143] Yet, Beijing remains committed as ever to "equity norms" in this domain, and has promoted the principle of Common But Differentiated Responsibilities to "legitimize its opposition to binding [emissions] reduction limits" as proposed by the United States and its allies.[144] So long as Beijing has access to the top tier of the global climate order, it will continue to push for fairer rules and procedures by which to adjudicate national responsibility for emissions reduction.

The domain of maritime law, particularly the United Nations Convention on the Law of the Sea, presents a similar case of an open but procedurally unfair institution (from China's perspective).

---

[140] Peter Christoff, "Cold climate in Copenhagen: China and the United States at COP15," *Environmental Politics*, 19:4 (2010), 637–656.

[141] Foot and Walter, *China, the United States, and Global Order*, 29.

[142] Dai and Renn, "China and international order," 191.

[143] Liang Dong, "Bound to lead? Rethinking China's role after Paris in UNFCCC negotiations," *Chinese Journal of Population Resources and Environment*, 15:1 (2017), 32–38.

[144] Phillip Stalley, "Principled strategy: The role of equity norms in China's climate change diplomacy," *Global Environmental Politics*, 13:1 (2013), 1–8.

Although the international order remains institutionally open in this domain, in that there is no explicit leadership club within UNCLOS, China has strongly objected to the procedural unfairness of the 2016 UNCLOS tribunal ruling in favor of the Philippines, as well as the US stance on territorial disputes in the South China Sea. China's objections have centered on three themes. First, that its own actions of island-building via land reclamation in the South China Sea are not unprecedented, since Malaysia had done the same in the Spratly Islands in 1983.[145] Second, that in bringing an arbitration case to UNCLOS, the Philippines violated its own commitments to interstate dispute resolution, according to the 2002 code of conduct for the South China Sea agreed by China and ASEAN.[146] Third, and finally, that in supporting the Philippines and pressuring China to accept the ruling, the United States was violating its own commitment to neutrality in territorial disputes in the region and acting hypocritically by "urging others to abide by the United Nations Convention on the Law of the Sea while refusing to ratify the convention to this day."[147]

More broadly, William Ziyuan Wang argues that China's declaration in 2010 of the South China Sea being part of its "core interests" is in fact an instance of China asserting its identity as an emerging superpower.[148] Chinese leaders see their state as having a natural right to dominate their maritime region and deeply resent any US efforts to intercede in the name of freedom of navigation or dispute resolution. In the aftermath of the 2016 UNCLOS ruling, China's ambassador to Malaysia, Huang Huikang, publicly decried the tribunal as an American attempt to "smear and 'isolate' China."[149] To highlight US

---

[145] Joseph A. Gagliano, "Blurred lines: Twenty-first century maritime security in the South China Sea," in Geoffrey F. Gresh (ed.), *Eurasia's Maritime Rise and Global Security: From the Indian Ocean to Pacific Asia and the Arctic* (Cham, Switzerland: Springer Nature, 2018), 113–128.

[146] Michael D. Swaine, "Chinese views on the South China Sea arbitration case between the People's Republic of China and the Philippines," *China Leadership Monitor*, 51 (August 2016), 1–13.

[147] Erik Slavin, "China accuses US of hypocrisy for not ratifying international sea law," *Stars and Stripes*, July 15, 2016.

[148] William Ziyuan Wang, "Destined for misperception? Status dilemma and the early origin of US-China antagonism," *Journal of Chinese Political Science*, 24 (2019), 49–65.

[149] Huang Huikang, "Dao inhabits people's hearts (from Chinese Embassy in Malaysia)," July 21, 2016, www.fmprc.gov.cn/mfa_eng/wjb_663304/zwjg_665342/zwbd_665378/t1383350.shtml.

"double-standards" on international law, he recalled Washington's rejection of the International Court of Justice's ruling in 1986 that the United States stop arming Contra rebels in Nicaragua and pay for the damage caused by rebel attacks.[150] Hua Chunying, spokesperson for China's foreign ministry, argued that US silence on the activities of other states in the South China Sea while criticizing China "reflects a total double standard, is unfair and not constructive."[151]

In line with IST's predictions, China's overall response to an open but unfair UNCLOS has not been to exit the institution but to try and reframe the criteria by which its rules are applied. To this end, China has portrayed its own activities as being in the true spirit of international law, regional security, and cooperation. In effect, China has attempted to alter existing evaluations of its identity claims, trying to gain regional recognition for "some type of undefined, non–UNCLOS-based, privileged right" for itself within the so-called nine-dash line that constitutes its territorial claim.[152] On the ground, however, China's actions have gone well beyond reframing and are actively breaking rules and customs pertaining to maritime law, sovereignty, and peaceful dispute resolution. Although IST does not predict rule-breaking in response to an open but procedurally unfair institution, these actions are better interpreted within the dynamics of local territorial contestation than as a concerted response to the international order itself. On the latter question, evidence suggests that China would prefer an alternative conception of maritime law that can recognize its major-power identity to a rejection of UNCLOS in its entirety. The South China Sea is not just an area of security competition but also one of active "normative contestation."[153]

Closed and Procedurally Unfair Institutions

China's response to the international human rights order embodied in UN agencies and treaties shows that when an institution is closed and procedurally unfair, a rising power will challenge it by trying to

---

[150] Ibid.
[151] The New York Times, "China's statement on its construction in the South China Sea," April 10, 2015.
[152] Swaine, "Chinese views," 9.
[153] Rebecca Strating, "Norm contestation, statecraft and the South China Sea: Defending maritime order," *The Pacific Review*, 35:1 (2020), 1–31.

publicly undermine it or by breaking its rules. For almost two decades after the Cold War, the United States and its allies led a fundamental normative transformation of the UN's human rights system. Absolute conceptions of Westphalian sovereignty gave way to more contingent notions whereby states enjoyed de jure sovereignty but their de facto sovereignty – or freedom from organized external intervention – rested on domestic human rights practices.[154] During this period, some argued that universal human rights became a new "standard of civilization," just as Christianity and scientific progress constituted such a standard when the United States was a rising power in the early nineteenth century.[155] Although the human rights components of the LIO have weakened in the years since the Global Financial Crisis, Zhang argues that the overall transformation is part of a larger shift toward "new cosmopolitan and anti-pluralist conceptions of international society in which China is viewed as the undemocratic Other, decidedly outside, or at best on the margin."[156]

Leadership of the international human rights order will always be closed to China so long as it is not a democracy. Moreover, China has been repeatedly singled out by the United States and its allies for having a deeply problematic human rights record. Beijing views this treatment as biased, especially given the extent to which the United States itself has violated human rights around the world. As predicted by IST, faced with a closed and unfair set of institutions, China has challenged them in multiple ways, often to shield itself from criticism.[157] It has used diplomacy and rhetoric to delegitimize the Western claim to universal human rights, arguing for the superiority of the Chinese approach, which emphasizes collective social and economic rights over individual political and civil liberties.[158] At the UN Commission on Human Rights, which was active from 1946 to 2006, Chinese diplomats "mastered Commission procedures" and "often used them successfully to deflect criticism" of China sponsored by

[154] Stuart Elden, "Contingent sovereignty, Territorial integrity and the sanctity of borders," *SAIS Review of International Affairs*, 26:1 (2006), 11–24.
[155] Jack Donnelly, "Human rights: A new standard of civilization?" *International Affairs*, 74:1 (1998), 1–23.
[156] Zhang, "China and liberal hierarchies," 806.
[157] Sonya Sceats and Shaun Breslin, "China and the international human rights system," Chatham House Report, October 2012.
[158] Alastair Iain Johnston, "Is China a status quo power?" *International Security*, 27:4 (2003), 5–56.

the developed states.[159] During negotiations to replace the UNCHR with a new UN Human Rights Council – established in 2006 – China pressed for a number of institutional design features that ensured that human rights practices would not be a precondition for membership in the organization, and that developing countries would have greater representation than they had in the previous organization.[160]

Although China could not muster sufficient support to raise the barriers for bringing country-specific resolutions to the UN Human Rights Council – a practice commonly used by the United States and others to criticize China's human rights practices – in the years since the UNHRC's creation China has promoted "the principle of 'universality,' which reduces the degree to which individual countries are singled out for attention."[161] It has specifically championed processes such as the Universal Periodic Review of every member's practices, including the United States, and the submission of Human Rights Action Plans, which allow each member to offer their own view of how international human rights norms should apply to their country.[162]

Beijing has also subverted and repurposed the human rights reporting practices of the United States in order to delegitimize the LIO's human rights agenda. Since 1991, China has periodically issued White Papers on progress made on human rights in China, with an emphasis on poverty reduction and social development.[163] In response to the US State Department's annual reports on human rights in various countries, including China, the CCP has issued an annual report on the human rights record of the United States, which since 2015 includes annual chronologies of human rights violations committed by the United States.[164] In the LIO itself, human rights remains an

[159] Rosemary Foot and Rana Siu Inboden, "China's influence on Asian states during the creation of the U.N. Human Rights Council: 2005–2007," *Asian Survey*, 54:5 (2014), 849–868.
[160] Ibid., 856.
[161] Andrew J. Nathan, "China's challenge," *Journal of Democracy*, 26:1 (2015), 156–170.
[162] Ibid., 166.
[163] See China Society for Human Rights Studies, "China's White Paper on Human Rights," www.chinahumanrights.org/html/special/20180305/.
[164] See China Society for Human Rights Studies, "Human Rights Record of the United States," www.chinahumanrights.org/html/PR/HRRUS/.

issue area in which China is very weakly embedded, having signed very few protocols and conventions.[165]

Conclusion

IST fares well in explaining variation in China's approach to the core institutions of the LIO. In open and procedurally fair institutions, such as the UNSC, WTO, NPT/CTBT, and G20, Beijing has cooperated (often at significant cost) to earn or maintain symbolic equality with the great powers. In procedurally fair but closed institutions – for example, the IMF – Beijing has sought to amend institutional rules to expand the top ranks of the international order as a way of attaining equality with the great powers. When institutions have been slow to change, China has paid costs to set up parallel institutions in which it can enjoy prime position. In open but procedurally unfair institutions (from China's perspective), such as the UNFCCC and UNCLOS, Beijing has used its already significant international status to push for a more equitable application of rules, while also using its power to change facts on the ground in the case of the East Asian maritime order. Finally, in closed and procedurally unfair institutions, such as the international human rights order, Beijing has mounted an outright challenge centered on tactics of delegitimation. Although this chapter does not trace the process by which changes in institutional variables over time have shaped China's status-seeking strategies, enough preliminary evidence exists from the plausibility probe presented here to warrant further study of the LIO's causal impact on China's pursuit of great-power status.

* * *

---

[165] Dai and Renn, "China and international order," 191.

8 | Conclusion

Institutional Status Theory (IST) highlights the importance of thinking about the societal nature of international relations. Materialist theories of revisionism view the international system as an anarchic realm, ungoverned by any authority above states, where states care only about their survival. By contrast, IST takes the international system to be ordered by an overarching hierarchy of power and status, atop which sits the club of great powers. There are other hierarchies in international relations and multiple international orders within an international system, but IST is concerned with *the* international order that results from the coordinated action of great powers to manage relations between themselves and in the rest of the international system. This is not a hierarchy of domination, as great powers clearly cannot simply dictate terms to lesser states. Great powers rule by the consent of the governed, which requires the international order to be accessible and fair.

IST also expands the set of things states value to include symbolic goods such as status. In thinking about the issues over which states bargain in international politics, a narrow focus on state survival loads the dice in favor of material explanations – typically wealth and security – for state behavior. Survival clearly matters, but it is not the only thing that matters to states. This is all the more so in the case of great powers and rising powers, which are better able to deter external threats than other states. Survival is rarely at stake in the interactions of great powers and rising powers for most of the duration of a power shift. It only becomes a concern as a rising power approaches parity with a great power, and that too when the rising power is dissatisfied due to nonrecognition of its major-power identity. Even this may not be sufficient to provoke a challenge to a complex and interconnected order such as the contemporary international order. As China's example shows in Chapter 7, a rising great power can be satisfied with certain core institutions of an order while being dissatisfied with others, without wanting to overthrow the order entirely.

The great powers constitute a club, which confers not just material benefits but socially scarce status on its members. Membership of the great-power club is an association good – its value depends on who else owns it. Rising powers seek to associate with great powers in order to attain the status benefits of club membership. Lacking the capabilities to match the great powers, they seek *symbolic equality* with them. Institutional rules and procedures are an important and overlooked source of symbolic equality between rising states and established powers. Theories of status in world politics highlight the importance of recognition and status parity, but they rarely consider the manner in which institutions can act as sites of highly consequential status politics during power shifts.

IST's Predictions and Empirical Validity

IST derives a set of predictions for the behavior of rising powers pursuing symbolic equality with the great powers within the international order. Two variables influence this behavior: institutional openness and procedural fairness. Institutions are relatively open if they leave a pathway for rising powers to eventually join the ranks of the great powers within the international order. Institutions are relatively fair if they treat the rising powers in a consultative, consistent, and unbiased manner. In reacting to these rules, a rising power is ultimately reacting to information about where the great powers place it in the international status hierarchy. An institutionally open and procedurally fair order is likely to elicit greater compliance than one that is closed and unfair, because the former indicates equal membership of the great-power club.

In the preceding chapters, IST's predictions were applied to three historical cases of a rising power within an international order: the United States in the Atlantic system of the mid-nineteenth century, Japan in the Washington system of the interwar period, and India in the international order of the Cold War. For ease of comparison, each case was focused on a core institution of the international order that dealt with regulating war, specifically: the 1856 Declaration of Paris, the 1922 Washington Naval Treaty, and the 1970 Nuclear Non-Proliferation Treaty. The cases were designed to examine variation in

rising power strategies – cooperation, challenge, reframing, or expansion – over time. A fourth case, of China in the contemporary liberal
international order, demonstrated the way in which IST can be applied
across issue areas and institutions within a single international order
during a particular time period.

IST's predictions fit the three historical cases better than purely
materialist theories. Without an account of status politics, it is impossible to explain why the United States, despite its material and moral
aversion to privateering, rejected a change in maritime law that would
have greatly benefited it as a neutral trading state and also abolished
privateering; why Japan first accepted disadvantageous restrictions on
its military power and geopolitical ambition only to reject them a
decade later at the risk of starting an arms race it could not win; and
why India initially renounced nuclear weapons – despite a Chinese
nuclear threat – only to test a nuclear device a decade later at the risk of
starting an arms race and inviting international sanctions.

Theories of status in world politics show that states become revisionist when their status aspirations are denied. IST subsumes these
theories by demonstrating that status concerns can elicit both conflict
and cooperation, as well as efforts at institutional reform. IST also
contributes to existing research on social identity in international relations by demonstrating the conditions under which we can expect
rising powers to pick one status-seeking strategy over another. In the
case of China in the contemporary liberal international order, IST
provides a systematic account of China's behavior across issue areas
and institutions. Finally, as discussed below, IST contributes new and
original insights to the historical knowledge of each case in this book.

The United States and the Atlantic System

The case of the United States and the Atlantic system shows how
American leaders from the very early days of the republic believed in
the future greatness of their country and undertook various policies
with an eye to securing its rank among the European great powers.
This is an uncommon account of US grand strategy in the nineteenth
century, one that goes against the conventional wisdom – at least in
political science – of the United States being isolationist and unambi-
tious prior to the 1890s. Viewing US history through the lens of status
illuminates new dimensions of historical episodes such as the War of

1812 and the Monroe Doctrine, as well as the philosophy behind
Manifest Destiny. Focusing on the only pillar of international order
at the time – maritime law – the case shows that when the rules and
institutions of the maritime order were relatively open and fair, the
United States cooperated and followed the rules set by the
great powers.

Subsequently, the Concert of Europe created a more closed great-
power club premised on monarchical and conservative principles.
American leaders sought to create an alternative basis for their claim
to symbolic equality with the great powers by contributing to international law in the name of Christianity and civilization (both essential
for membership of the great-power club at the time). These efforts went
nowhere. Instead, the great powers adopted the liberal stance advocated by the United States while shutting the door on US aspirations by
abolishing privateering in the 1856 Declaration of Paris. Privateering,
albeit an ineffective military tactic morally abhorred by most
Americans, was symbolic of US claims to maritime power. Faced with
a great-power club that now seemed deeply biased against the United
States in addition to being closed, US statesmen rejected the
Declaration at significant risk to American commercial interests.

Japan and the Washington System

Japan from the Meiji Restoration to World War II is a more commonly
known case when it comes to rising powers and status. However,
scholars generally overlook the 1920s as a pivotal period in the status
politics of the interwar order. Japan's status aspirations during the
Meiji period are well documented, as are Japan's efforts at securing
symbolic equality with the great powers at the Paris Peace Conference
in 1919 and Japan's rejection of a racist international order in the
1930s. However, it is difficult to understand the extremes to which
Japan went to challenge the international order in the 1930s without
understanding the status anxieties that led its leaders to cooperate
extensively at the Washington Conference of 1921–1922. The extent
of their sacrifices at this conference comes into stark relief when we
understand the immense betrayal they subsequently felt at the racial
exclusion of the US Immigration Act of 1924.

IST offers a comprehensive explanation for Japan's approach to the
international order during the interwar period. At the Washington

Conference, Japan faced an open and procedurally fair international order. Invited to be part of the "Big Three" at the conference, Japan was consulted at every turn and its leaders felt that the United States had been extremely fair in its own concessions. In order to avoid isolation at a time when Japan was beginning to be recognized as a major power, Japan's most senior negotiators at the Washington Conference decided to cooperate to the fullest extent possible, often sacrificing significant security interests in the process. A powerful faction in the navy, however, did not see the international order as open to Japan's rise, and began developing capabilities in nontraditional areas of naval power in order to prepare Japan for future negotiations. When the US Immigration Act officially excluded Japanese immigrants from America, widespread and sustained outrage in Japan gave this faction and its political allies the upper hand. Faced with a closed and unfair great-power club, growing domestic antagonism toward the international order eventually compelled the government to quit the Washington system for the sake of asserting equality with the great powers.

India and the Cold War

Like Japan and the United States before it, India developed a major-power identity during the Cold War. The United Nations and its associated institutions offered Indian leaders an opportunity to claim symbolic equality with the great powers. The nuclear order in particular – with the NPT at its core – was a central feature of the Cold War system. IST shows that India's decision-making with regard to nuclear weapons was influenced by the relative openness and procedural fairness of the nuclear order, particularly through the IAEA and the Eighteen-Nation Committee on Disarmament. Scholars of nuclear proliferation acknowledge status or prestige as a potential motive for the pursuit and acquisition of nuclear capability. However, few have systematically studied how the international order can impact status-seeking strategies in this domain. Historians of India's nuclear program have similarly focused on the prestige motive behind India's nuclear decision-making – at least in the early 1970s – but typically as an outgrowth of Indian exceptionalism and not a more general account of status in world politics.

IST shows that India's case is exceptional only to the extent that rising powers tend to see themselves as exceptional and destined for greatness. Critical moments in India's nuclear trajectory, involving the decisions both to pursue and to not pursue the bomb, are poorly explained by existing approaches. IST offers a more complete explanation that unites India's decision-making in two crucial time periods – the 1960s and the 1990s – in one coherent framework. In the 1950s and 1960s, when the international nuclear order seemed institutionally open and procedurally fair, India prioritized cooperation with the order over pursuing the bomb, even in response to China going nuclear. When the NPT came into force in 1970, India found that the international order had shut the door on India while admitting China into the nuclear club. New Delhi decided to reassert its symbolic equality with the great powers by demonstrating its ability to test a nuclear device. India made a similarly motivated decision to test in the 1990s, when faced with an unequal test ban treaty and a permanent extension of the NPT.

China and the Liberal International Order

China's status aspirations are well known to scholars of international relations. Yet, few attempts have been made to examine how China's desire for recognition of its major-power identity influences its behavior in the US-led liberal international order. In particular, our understanding of why China cooperates with some aspects of the LIO and not others remains incomplete. Existing studies either take a monolithic view of international order, conflating it with US-China relations and conceptualizing a potential challenge largely in military terms, or even while examining institutional variation assume only material interests on China's part, which cannot explain why China pays considerable costs to support institutions such as the United Nations Security Council or the global nuclear order since the 1990s. IST contributes to the study of China in contemporary world politics by disaggregating the LIO into its core institutions and showing that variation in openness and procedural fairness across these institutions shapes China's approach to them. IST does not rule out the role of material interests, but instead it shows the conditions under which a rising power may be willing to trade away some amount of security or economic benefit to earn or maintain symbolic equality with the great powers.

Insights from the Empirical Analysis

The case studies show that international institutions are major sites of contestation between rising and great powers during power shifts. While most existing research has focused on war, which is one possible *outcome* of power shifts, few scholars have looked closely at the *process* of power shifts. There is an entire realm of interaction between rising and great powers that takes place well before war is in the picture. These interactions can in turn shed light on why some rising powers end up challenging the international order in which they are rising, while others do not. The following are some insights drawn from the cases that point toward potential avenues for further research.

Rising Powers Can Be Restrained

Great powers often design the rules and norms of international institutions to entrench their own privileged position in the international order by raising the barriers to entry for the great-power club. Britain attempted to use the Declaration of Paris to exclude the United States and curb its rise by abolishing the practice of privateering. British leaders found the Americans to be "Vulgar-minded Bullies"[1] who were insisting on neutral rights during the Crimean War. In return, the British proposed the abolition of privateering so that they could take the moral high ground, isolate the United States, and "catch Brother Jonathan in the trap which he had laid for us."[2] Six decades later, when the United States had become a great power, it sought to use the Washington Conference to constrain Japan's naval expansion in the Far East and weaken the Anglo-Japanese relationship. During the Cold War, the United States and Soviet Union could not agree on much regarding global nuclear governance, but they agreed on the need to restrict new countries, including India, from joining the nuclear club.

Sometimes, rising powers can be restrained materially if great powers are attentive (even inadvertently) to the status aspirations of rising powers and the manner in which the rules and institutions of the international order impact them. The cases suggest that it might be *easier* to restrain a rising power materially than it is to deny it symbolic equality with the great powers. As the examples of Japan and India

---

[1] Lemnitzer, *End of Privateering*, 59.   [2] Ibid.

show, a rising power that is treated in an open and unbiased manner is more likely to cooperate with the rules and institutions of an order even at the cost of short-term insecurity or material losses. By contrast, a poorly designed order that deprives a rising power of upward mobility and creates inequalities between it and the great powers is likely to provoke resistance, as was the case with India's response to the post-NPT nuclear order of the Cold War and the United States' response to the maritime order of the Atlantic system.

Symbolic Rights Matter

Dissatisfaction is not immutable. In the mid-2000s, when the United States finally recognized India as a responsible nuclear power, India became content to cooperate with the nuclear order and uphold its basic tenets. These types of outcomes suggest that institutions are not fixed entities but rather fluid social hierarchies that can in fact be altered by their most powerful members. An appropriate counterfactual in this regard would be the case of Japan and the Washington system. It is entirely conceivable that the United States and Britain could have elicited greater cooperation from the Japanese navy through the 1920s had they modified the Washington Naval Treaty to permit Japan an equal capital-ship ratio. Although Japan did not have the resources to build at the same level as the great powers, its naval leaders greatly valued the symbolic equality of a 10:10:10 ratio.

Understanding this drive for symbolic equality is vital in all the cases. A rule that imposes little or no costs on a rising power, or that even produces significant economic benefit by way of reduced spending on armaments, will still be resisted so long as the rising power perceives the rule to be denying it the *right* to possess a particular instrument or strategic option that might give it symbolic equality with the great powers. This is the case even if the rising power has no intention of utilizing the instrument or option in question. The United States valued privateering less for its putative strategic value than for what it symbolized – it was the only naval instrument that would allow some semblance of being an important maritime player. Japan valued its right to construct capital ships up to the same tonnage limits as the great powers, even though actually following through would destroy its economy. India went to great diplomatic lengths in the 1950s and 1960s to preserve its nuclear option without ever seriously intending to exercise it, because it was the only way to maintain the most visible trappings of major-power identity while lacking the economic or military foundations.

It is telling that after challenging the international order and asserting their respective rights, neither the United States nor India went further down the path of actually utilizing the respective instruments they had sought to preserve – the United States did not use privateers after 1856 and India did not attempt to develop nuclear weapons for fifteen years after its first test, when Pakistan's nuclear weapons development left India with no choice. Had Japan's challenge to the Washington system not gotten caught up in broader geopolitical currents in the 1930s, it is likely that Japan too would not have resumed building capital ships at the scale that it did from the mid-1930s onward.

The Sequence of Status-Seeking Strategies

Regarding the choice of status-seeking strategies among rising powers, there are mixed assessments in the literature about the sequence of strategies that a lower-ranked state might follow in order to attain status. Scholars applying social identity theory to international politics have argued that states will first attempt cooperation and if that does not work, they will switch to a strategy of challenging higher-ranked states.[3] However, by not specifying the theoretical conditions under which a strategy can be deemed unsuccessful, they overlook the intermediate stage of reframing or expanding status criteria that sociologists and social psychologists emphasize. These latter theorists argue that because conflict is costly, individuals and groups will not attempt it until all other avenues are either deemed impossible or have been exhausted.[4] IST suggests that it is possible to move from cooperation directly to challenge, but only if the international order goes from

---

[3] Larson and Shevchenko, "Status seekers"; Larson and Shevchenko, "Shortcut to greatness"; Ward, "Race, status, and Japanese revisionism."

[4] Johan Galtung, "A structural theory of aggression," *Journal of Peace Research*, 1:2 (1964), 95–119; Bettencourt et al., "Status differences," 537; Tuomas Forsberg, Regina Heller, and Reinhard Wolf, "Introduction," *Communist and Post-Communist Studies*, 47:3–4 (2014), 261–268.

being open and fair to closed and unfair within a very short period of time. If only one of these variables changes, then we are more likely to observe reframing or expansion rather than outright challenge.

The evidence from the cases shows that the sequence of strategies does not always run from cooperation to reframing/expansion and then challenge. The United States and Japan did follow this sequence, for different reasons. In the US case, the slow pace of change in the international order left room for an expansion strategy, especially since the international order remained procedurally fair even while being closed to America's rise under the Concert of Europe. In Japan's case, the state was divided, and a faction in the navy pursued an expansion strategy as they perceived the Washington Naval Treaty to have closed off Japan's pathway to the great-power club. The Indian case is different. The advent of the NPT dramatically altered India's evaluation of the international order along the dimensions of both openness and fairness, resulting in the decision to demonstrate India's nuclear prowess through a nuclear test. What all the cases have in common is that changes in status-seeking strategies occurred in response to external changes in the international order, which altered one or both dimensions along which the rising powers evaluated their symbolic equality with the great powers.

Mixed Evidence on Domestic Politics

The case studies show that material interests at the state and domestic levels do not adequately explain the decisions made by a rising power when status concerns are in play. It is possible, however, for status concerns to operate *through* domestic politics. If a large enough domestic constituency seeks status, this may pressure state leaders into following status-seeking strategies. Steven Ward has found that domestic constituencies are activated in moments of status immobility, and thereby push for revisionist policies.[5] The empirical analysis in this book confirms this finding, but only in the Japan case. In the cases of the United States and India, public and (non-state) elite opinion undoubtedly turned sour toward the international order when the state was excluded and treated unfairly by the great powers. However, there is no evidence that this opinion forced the hand or played into the

---

[5] Ward, *Status and the Challenge.*

decision-making of national leaders in these two cases. Rather, national leaders *changed their minds* about the nature of the international order when they discovered that it would not give their country access to or equal treatment in the great-power club. This was also the case with key leaders in Japan, such as Fleet Admiral Togo Heihachiro, who came to see the international order as exclusionary and unfair in the course of the 1920s.

Domestic opinion did not impact the decision-making of national leaders when they decided to cooperate in the face of an open and fair international order. In the case of Japan, although the leadership in Tokyo was skeptical of the Washington Conference, the chief delegates in Washington and the Japanese ambassador in London collectively took a cooperative stance, often lobbying Tokyo for deeper concessions to the great powers. In the case of India, a large chunk of domestic opinion represented in Parliament and among journalists and intellectuals was in favor of building a nuclear device – and even a nuclear arsenal – in response to China's nuclear development. However, India's political leadership stood firm on the importance of preserving India's status as a scientifically advanced yet pacifist state whose nonaligned foreign policy granted it considerable importance in the international order. Ultimately, both cases show that when faced with an opportunity to sit at the international high table, status-based arguments for cooperation won the day within the domestic sphere. These findings suggest the need for more theorizing and empirical research on the interaction between status concerns and domestic politics.

The Security Externalities of Status

Understanding the politics of status in international institutions is vital for comprehending the security externalities institutions may produce. As IST demonstrates, a focus on the status concerns of rising powers illuminates the real material fallout of seemingly innocuous institutional variables. The fact that a successful arms control agreement such as the Washington Naval Treaty or the NPT might in fact lead to further arms build-ups or nuclear acquisition is only a paradox if one does not consider the security externalities of status ambitions. This finding suggests that a theoretical framework based on status can be used to revisit conventional understandings of negotiation success and failure in a wide variety of situations. IST shows that the study of any type of institutional interaction that does not account for status concerns is likely to miss essential causes of cooperation and discord in world politics.

Future Research on Institutional Status

There are three dimensions on which it is possible to vary the research design for testing IST: state, issue area, and time. The historical chapters in this book tested IST by holding state and issue area constant, and varying time. This method produced in-depth longitudinal case studies, each one focusing on a single rising power in relation to a single core security institution of an international order.

There are other ways in which to approach this empirical task, and one of them is highlighted by the chapter on China and the LIO, which held state and time constant while varying issue area. The result was an exploratory picture of how status concerns might explain variation in China's behavior within the LIO. Given the possibility of intrinsic differences between issues complicating this type of analysis, more focused cross-sectional research involving a single country across issue areas is necessary. For example, a research design that controls for observable differences between two issue areas and then examines variation in a rising power's approach to them would be able to isolate the effect of institutional features such as openness and fairness in a more rigorous and systematic fashion.

Similarly, one might hold the issue area and time fixed, and examine variation in the approach of different rising powers. The source of variation in this case would be the openness and fairness of an international institution to different rising powers. For example, a study of the respective approaches of China, India, and Japan to the international nuclear order in the 1960s and 1970s – a period when all three countries were rising powers –would add to IST's external validity. Although such an effort would encounter challenges of comparability across a set of very diverse countries, it is possible to design a study that could control for observable differences between these rising powers and focus on the micro-level decision-making of state leaders.

Lastly, IST assumes that at any given time, great powers – being the architects of international order – have an interest in maintaining the order and its component institutions. But what does the world look like when great powers themselves decide to withdraw from the international order that they created? The United States under President Donald Trump took this approach, and scholars are in the process of examining the impact of this shift on the international order, as well as on the grand strategies of rising powers, such as China, India, and Brazil, that have benefited from it in the post–Cold War era.[6] Future research that examines how a dominant state's changing commitment to the international order alters the status-seeking strategies of rising powers would offer important insights into this contemporary question.

Implications for Existing Theories

With regard to theories of hegemonic war and hegemonic peace, IST contributes a more direct measure of (dis)satisfaction among rising powers than alliance portfolios, economic benefits, and membership of intergovernmental organizations. Alliance portfolios and membership of intergovernmental organizations are in fact the *result* of (dis) satisfaction. Economic benefits may produce satisfaction, but they are not the only factor that matters during a power shift. Indeed, as the central puzzle of this book points out, a state benefiting more than others in economic terms should not want to challenge the international order, yet rising powers do frequently challenge it. IST adds a nonmaterial dimension to satisfaction that theories of hegemonic war and hegemonic peace have not yet systematically integrated into their respective canons.

The psychological micro-foundations of IST show that individuals and groups are dissatisfied when their status-related identity claims are not recognized by significant Others, and are satisfied when such claims are recognized. Thinking about power transitions in this way creates the possibility for future large-n analyses based on possible measures of status differentials in international institutions such as leadership positions or voting rights. IST would predict that rising states with less access to and less equal standing in the great-power club will be more likely to be dissatisfied with the international order.

IST can further draw a causal link between dissatisfaction and revisionism in power shifts. Contrary to the broader power shifts

---

[6] See Alexander Cooley and Daniel Nexon, *Exit from Hegemony: The Unraveling of the American Global Order* (Oxford: Oxford University Press, 2020).

literature pioneered by Robert Gilpin and others, IST shows that rising powers are not automatically dissatisfied with the distribution of gains and status in the international order. Rising powers may, however, feel *entitled* to want more, and IST shows that this is a function of their major-power identity. The question is: At what point does a rising power decide that making a bid for symbolic equality with the great powers is worth taking substantial risks and expending material resources? In other words, when does dissatisfaction translate into revisionism? IST offers an answer in terms of the configuration of institutional openness and procedural fairness facing a rising power.

With regard to state motivations, IST shows that assuming a state values both material and symbolic goods enhances the explanatory power of theory. At an intergroup level in domestic society, it seems intuitive that groups and their leaders value their material well-being *and* their rank in various social hierarchies. The two may even be instrumentally linked, though IST assumes they are intrinsically valued. It further stands to reason that there will be actions groups can take that will enhance both material and psychological well-being. There will also be moments when groups must trade one value for the other. IST lays out the conditions under which states, understood as social groups in an international hierarchy, will trade material gain for status. There is tremendous scope for future research to work out more precise junctures at which these trade-offs may occur, and also the conditions under which states may engage in the opposite exchange, that is, material gain in return for lower status.

With regard to theories of status in world politics, IST shifts the theoretical and empirical focus of research away from military conflict to political contestation over the rules and institutions of international order. The latter is chronologically and analytically prior to the point at which a rising power and a great power might begin contemplating war. It is significant in terms of its effects on the fabric of international cooperation, and if not resolved, can ultimately lead to major ruptures. Order contestation can also be extremely costly. For example, India's nuclear test in 1974 led to the creation of an elaborate international regime for export controls managed by the great powers; Japan's exit from the Washington system caused naval expenditures in all major capitals to skyrocket; and the US rejection of the Declaration of Paris made Atlantic commerce vulnerable to Confederate privateering in the

Civil War. By explaining the emergence and resolution or exacerbation of such contestation, IST contributes to existing knowledge of the trajectory of satisfaction or dissatisfaction that shapes the process and eventual outcomes of power shifts.

By focusing in depth on the international order and its component institutions, IST analytically separates order from the distribution of power and bilateral relations between a rising and great power. This separation highlights distinct institutional pathways by which status can matter during power shifts. This is not to say that bilateral relations are insignificant, but that a substantial part of them is mediated through the rules and institutions of the international order (as was the case of racial exclusion for Japan). The international order becomes a source of information about relative standing, as well as the object of strategic attempts at earning or maintaining status through conflict or cooperation. This mediatory role grows stronger as the order itself grows more complex. As John Ikenberry has argued, institutions are sticky and can end up constraining even the great powers that designed them.[7] IST is thus particularly suited for studying international orders since the mid-nineteenth century, when international institutions began taking on a global character.

Finally, IST expands the causal role of status from the commonplace focus on status denial and develops a broader theory subsuming a range of strategies. It shows that under certain conditions, states may cooperate or seek institutional reform in order to attain or retain status. It is not only status inconsistency that may drive a state's grand strategy, but also status consistency or partial consistency, depending on the level of institutional openness and procedural fairness in the international order. This broadening of the canvas opens up research on status to studies of particular institutions or time periods, as noted earlier, that go beyond the conventional focus on status immobility and war. Looking at the other side of the equation, a focus on the manner in which great powers perceive the identity claims of rising powers and the decision-making calculus according to which these claims are granted or denied within the international order would offer a more complete look at the interactive process of power transition.

---

[7] G. John Ikenberry, "Institutions, strategic restraint, and the persistence of American postwar order," *International Security*, 23:3 (1998), 43–78.

Policy Implications

The empirical evidence since the end of the Cold War suggests that rising powers such as China, India, and Brazil are content *not* to challenge the LIO, despite their varying levels of dissatisfaction with it.[8] Although the events of 2020 certainly revealed China's willingness to strike out on multiple fronts – including a legal crackdown in Hong Kong, increased incursions into Taiwan's air defense identification zone (ADIZ) and Japanese waters, a border stand-off with India, and a trade spat with Australia – these actions are surprising only in their simultaneity. The broader trend of China's approach to the international order remains intact, even in the realm of the World Health Organization (WHO) where China has bent the rules to serve its own interests but not challenged the institution itself. Naturally, actions of this nature damage the international order in Western eyes, but it is crucial to note that China is not mounting a challenge to the international order so much as seeking to control what already exists for reasons of both material interest and status. This objective was easier to pursue during a Trump presidency that withdrew from critical parts of the international order. The United States under President Joe Biden has recommitted to a leadership role for the United States in the LIO, which suggests that the lessons of IST remain applicable to the manner in which Washington approaches China's ambitions going forward.

Instead of frontally challenging the international order, rising powers in the post–Cold War world have adopted a free-riding strategy, that is, not fully paying the costs of maintaining the order while benefiting significantly from it. This type of strategy is what underlies China's exploitation of international trading rules, India's grandstanding on climate change, and Brazil's outsized influence relative to its economic power within the World Trade Organization. This unwillingness to genuinely contribute to the liberal order may seem puzzling,

---

[8] Kahler, "Rising powers and global governance"; Andrew Hurrell and Sandeep Sengupta, "Emerging powers, North-South relations and global climate politics," *International Affairs*, 88:3 (2012), 463–484; Chan et al., *China Engages Global Governance*; Maximillian Terhalle, "Reciprocal socialization: Rising powers and the West," *International Studies Perspectives*, 12 (2011), 341–361; G. John Ikenberry and Darren J. Lim, "China's emerging institutional statecraft: The Asian Infrastructure Investment Bank and the prospects for counter-hegemony," Brookings Institution (April 2017), 15.

given that it makes these countries diplomatically vulnerable to the charge of free riding. It is explained, however, by the symbolic aspects of the order. Put simply, the great-power club is still dominated by the United States and its allies while the distribution of power is shifting steadily in favor of the rising powers. Voting rights at the IMF, permanent membership of the UNSC, top leadership positions in international financial institutions, the official designation of nuclear weapon states in the NPT, and small-group decision-making within the WTO are some of the more prominent institutional aspects of the liberal order that rising powers to varying extents have contested as exclusionary, discriminatory, and unequal (though they do not uniformly share all these concerns). Wherever possible, they have sought to reform institutions from within. Where these efforts have been repeatedly frustrated, they have established new institutions such as the New Development Bank and the Asian Infrastructure Investment Bank, or bolstered existing forums where they already hold leadership positions such as the India, Brazil, South Africa (IBSA) group, and the Shanghai Cooperation Organization.

Membership of the great-power club brings both material and status benefits, but it also comes at a price. Rising powers are unwilling to pay the price unless they are made full and equal members, especially since material benefits already accrue to them in significant measure simply through membership in the order. For its part, the United States has been unwilling to admit rising powers into the club, questioning their ability to act as "responsible stakeholders." These conflicting incentives create a chicken-and-egg problem: Rising powers decline full responsibility without first being admitted as symbolically equal members of the great-power club, while the United States refuses them club membership without first seeing evidence of them taking full responsibility for comanaging the LIO.

IST suggests that if great powers such as the United States seek to manage the rise of new powers, they must pay attention not only to the latter's material interests but also to their status ambitions. Understanding the worldviews of rising powers is, therefore, a critical exercise for the sake of international stability. Mapping assessments of the institutional architecture of the international order among rising powers, and how they might vary from one country to the next, is an important exercise that can produce valuable insights on how to negotiate with and come to agreements with these important states.

Institutional innovations that enable social mobility for rising powers are likely to produce more peaceful outcomes and therefore lower the risk of discord during power shifts. Inviting China to be a responsible stakeholder while the United States controls the levers of leadership in various international institutions is likely to produce few results unless China is invited to genuinely become an equal partner in the leadership of the international order. US diplomacy to this date has been unable to transform the rhetoric of global partnership with China into genuine institutional innovation. The events surrounding the COVID-19 pandemic suggest that the window of opportunity for integrating China as a comanager of the international order may have already closed. Nonetheless, if reform were to be genuinely attempted, the top jobs in international institutions would be a good place to start. Similarly, US support for rising states such as India and Brazil as permanent members of the UNSC would be an important, albeit difficult, piece of institutional reform.[9] In the absence of reform, the United States can expect more institutional challenges such as the AIIB and the NDB to emerge over the coming years. Devesh Kapur frames the matter plainly in the case of international economic governance: "As the power of the Bretton Woods institutions wanes, Western countries might be tempted to hold on even more tightly to the levers of governance. But the tighter they squeeze, the less these institutions will matter in the long run."[10]

At the micro-level, the procedural aspects of negotiations with rising powers can have a major impact on the outcomes of negotiations. The type of status concerns at play during systemic power shifts have to do with rising powers seeking membership of the great-power club, or what William Thompson calls "big 'S'" status concerns.[11] These are distinct from "small 's'" concerns, or "the irritations, sometimes trivial and sometimes not, associated with states not acknowledging the status that state agents feel they deserve."[12] Nonetheless, because rising powers infer their status from institutional rules and procedures,

---

[9] Jacek Kugler, "The Asian ascent: Opportunity for peace or precondition for war?" *International Studies Perspectives*, 7 (2006), 36–42.
[10] Kapur, "What next for the Bretton Woods twins?"
[11] William R. Thompson, "Status conflict, hierarchies, and interpretation dilemmas," in Paul et al. (eds.), *Status in World Politics*, 219–245.
[12] Ibid., 222.

small "s" concerns matter more when occurring against a backdrop of changes that trigger big "S" concerns.[13]

This is not simply a matter of respect or honor – though matters of protocol can have important localized effects – but rather a matter of legitimacy. At the very least, decision-making in key global forums should *appear* consultative, consistent, and unbiased when a rising power compares its treatment with the treatment received by the great powers.[14] In some cases, this might require great powers to actually make deeper concessions than rising powers, or to favor rising powers over other classes of countries, as the United States has done by encouraging smaller groupings of high-powered countries within larger multilateral institutions in the areas of trade and climate change. In other cases, it might simply require a diplomatic style that appears to be paying close attention to the concerns of rising powers and explicitly factoring these concerns into the decision-making process, as multilateral groupings such as the Nuclear Security Summit have done. Even if some rules impose unequal obligations to the disadvantage of a rising power, it might still accept them so long as they are arrived at openly with clearly stated reasons and justifications. The great powers must, therefore, carefully cultivate the Weberian rational-legal authority of international institutions if the international order is to accommodate the rise of new powers.

* * *

[13] Ibid., 220.
[14] Stephen G. Brooks and William C. Wohlforth, "Reshaping the world order: How Washington should reform international institutions," *Foreign Affairs*, 88:2 (2009), 49–63.

Appendix
Case Selection

In keeping with scholarly practice, I divide the period from 1815 to 1990 into three distinct international orders punctuated by the two World Wars: the Concert of Europe (1815–1914), giving way to the Atlantic system in mid-nineteenth century; the interwar period (1919–1939), or the Washington system; and the Cold War (1945–1990). A fourth order, the liberal international order (LIO) running from 1990 to the present, is the subject of a plausibility probe in Chapter 7.

Core Security Institutions

The core security institutions of an international order can be defined as multilateral institutions focused on either preventing or regulating war. Institutions of the first type are managerial in nature. They require intense and sometimes exclusive involvement by the great powers, and take the form of full-fledged organizations with extensive bureaucracies. The managerial institutions in each international order are: the Concert of Europe in the Atlantic system, the League of Nations in the Washington system, and the UNSC during the Cold War. Institutions of the second type are regulatory in nature. They do not involve intense great-power involvement and take the form of agreements or treaties that stipulate rules and procedures to be followed. Historically, these institutions have dealt with the laws of war and arms control. The regulatory institutions in each international order are shown in Table A.1.

To clearly study the potential conflict between material interests and status ambitions, I pick institutions with relatively high material stakes for the rising powers. In effect, this creates a set of hard cases for a theory that predicts that states will at times prioritize status over material gains or losses. This is why although the Geneva Conventions appear in each international order, they offer a weak test of the theory. Countries had very little to lose by signing the

Table A.1. *Core regulatory security institutions*

Period	Issue	Multilateral Regulatory Institutions (by year of entry into force)
1815–1914	Laws of War	1856 Declaration of Paris 1864 Geneva Convention 1868 Saint Petersburg Declaration 1899/1907 Hague Conventions
	Arms Control	N/A
1919–1939	Laws of War	1928 Geneva Protocol 1929 Kellogg-Briand Pact 1931 Geneva Convention
	Arms Control	1922 Washington Naval Treaty 1930 London Naval Treaty 1936 London Naval Treaty
1945–1990	Laws of War	1950 Geneva Conventions 1956 Hague Convention on Cultural Property 1974 Declaration on Women and Children in Armed Conflict 1977 Geneva Protocols 1978 Environmental Modification Convention 1983 Convention on Certain Conventional Weapons
	Arms Control	1961 Antarctic Treaty 1963 Partial Test Ban Treaty 1967 Outer Space Treaty 1970 Nuclear Non-Proliferation Treaty 1972 Seabed Arms Control Treaty 1972 Anti-Ballistic Missile Treaty 1975 Biological Weapons Convention

conventions. Indeed, when war did break out in the nineteenth and early twentieth centuries, many countries disregarded the conventions. Based on these considerations, I settle on the most consequential institution in each international order: the Declaration of Paris of 1856, which regulated maritime warfare; the Washington Naval Treaty of 1922, which regulated naval armaments; and the Nuclear Non-Proliferation Treaty of 1970, which regulated the spread of nuclear weapons.

Great Powers

Great powers possess three features: extraordinary military capabilities, global geopolitical interests, and general recognition of their great-power status. I measure capabilities using the Composite Index of National Capability (CINC), a relative measure of a state's material power based on six indicators of war-making potential. Following the power transition literature, I count the most powerful state in the international system and any state with at least 80 percent of its capabilities. I measure geopolitical interests using data on diplomatic representation, assuming that states with more expansive interests have wider diplomatic networks. I count the state with the widest diplomatic network and any state with a network at least 80 percent the size of this state's network. Lastly, I measure recognition in terms of official membership of the top tier of the international order: the Congress of Vienna for the Concert of Europe, the Council of the League of Nations for the interwar period, and the United Nations Security Council (UNSC) for the Cold War.

A great power is a state that meets *at least two* of the above three criteria. Very few states meet all three, and setting the bar so high excludes most states from consideration. The great powers of each international order thus emerge as follows.

1. 1815–1914: Britain, Prussia/Germany, Russia, Austria-Hungary, and France
2. 1919–1939: United States, Britain, Italy, and France
3. 1945–1990: United States, Soviet Union, France, Britain, and China (after 1974)

Rising Powers

The literature on power shifts and transitions focuses almost exclusively on rising *great* powers, that is, states that have reached a threshold of significant capability and can pose a systemic threat to the international order. This book focuses on the earlier stages of a power's rise; hence its selection of rising powers is agnostic about the eventual success/failure of a country's rise and its eventual impact on the international order.

I adopt a two-step process for identifying the rising powers examined in this study. I rely on capabilities, since increasing capabilities are a necessary condition of power shifts. Once this approach yields a viable candidate for each historical order, I examine whether it meets two further criteria: (1) growing major-power identity (self-perception as an important global actor), and (2) growing recognition from other states (not necessarily the great powers) of the state as a major power. Rising powers are thus states experiencing sustained increases in capabilities that see themselves and are seen by others as increasingly important actors on the world stage.

In terms of capabilities, a rising power is a state that has crossed a minimum threshold of material power and is experiencing a sustained increase in capabilities. The minimum threshold excludes states starting from a small base that may be rising but are not powerful in the sense of having a discernible impact on world politics. The requirement of sustained growth excludes flash-in-the-pan rising powers that may rise and fall for idiosyncratic reasons.

To identify the universe of potential cases, I again turn to the CINC dataset and set the minimum threshold of capabilities at 10 percent of the most powerful state in the international system. A higher threshold risks excluding a number of countries that scholars have considered rising powers. Raising the bar to 20 percent, for example, leaves only the United States in the nineteenth century (after 1855), Russia in the interwar period, and China, Japan, and India in the post-1945 period. Among the more significant cases excluded by this higher threshold are Japan, a rising power in the late nineteenth century and early twentieth century; Italy, which experienced a significant rise during and after reunification in the nineteenth century; and Brazil and South Korea during the Cold War. I thus adopt a more liberal minimum threshold for identifying rising powers.

The 10 percent threshold is anchored to the capabilities of the most powerful state, not the great powers as a whole, in order to maintain methodological consistency with the power transition literature's identification of great powers as having 80 percent of the hegemon's capabilities. Anchoring the measurement of capabilities to the hegemon allows us to see if and when a rising power becomes a great power by meeting two of the three criteria laid out for great-power identification mentioned earlier.

Above the 10 percent threshold, I identify states experiencing long-term increases in capabilities for at least a decade. Although ten years is an arbitrary choice, it serves the purpose – discussed below – of weeding out short-term rising powers without being too restrictive. On the latter point, for example, raising the bar to twenty years would exclude Italy in the nineteenth century, China in the interwar period, China and India before the early 1970s, and Japan from the 1980s into the post–Cold War period.

To reduce the impact of short-term fluctuations and capture the underlying trend of a state's rise, I substitute any given year's rate of change in capabilities with the average rate of the previous five years, thus producing a moving average rate of changing capabilities.[1] It is this trend that must be sustained for at least a decade for a country to count as a rising power. Sustained growth means the moving average cannot be negative for more than two consecutive years. Allowing occasional negative change ensures that short-term dips in a country's rise do not disqualify its broader trajectory from being counted.[2]

The first cut based on capabilities yields the rising powers listed in Table A.2. It should be noted that the time periods in this table are imprecise. Rising powers do not start or stop rising overnight, or even in the span of a few months. There are undoubtedly other times at which one might observe a rising power develop and seek recognition of its major-power identity. The above exercise is nonetheless valuable for identifying the universe of potential cases and approximate points in the historical record where we can look for evidence of the institutional politics of status during power shifts.

I select my case countries from each period using three criteria. First, the timing of a state's rise should overlap substantially with the establishment and functioning of the core security institution of each order selected from Table A.1. Second, the longer a state is rising the better, so that more evidence is available for a longitudinal case study. Third,

---

[1] This method is similar to the commonly used five-year moving average of militarized disputes as a proxy for a state's threat environment. See Sonali Singh and Christopher R. Way, "The correlates of nuclear proliferation," *Journal of Conflict Resolution*, 48:6 (2004), 859–885.

[2] Although Japan in the interwar period does not fully meet this criterion due to experiencing three consecutive years of negative average growth in 1926–1928, I still code it as a rising power because the decline in each of these years was minimal (well below 1 percent) and was the result of Japan reducing military expenditure and personnel – two of the six components of the CINC index – to comply with the Washington Naval Treaty. It is precisely this anomaly of why a rising power would willingly curtail its rise that Institutional Status Theory can explain, making Japan a useful case despite this minor variance from the coding rule.

Table A.2. *Identifying rising powers: a first cut*

	Growth in Relative Industrial and Military Capabilities
Measure	Composite Index of National Capabilities (1816–2007)
Threshold	At least 10 percent of hegemon + sustained growth for at least ten years (measured as a five-year moving average)
States Meeting Criterion 1815–1914	United States (1827–1851, 1855–1866, 1872–1914) Italy (1860–1871, 1882–1891) Japan (1887–1909) Belgium (1904–1914)
States Meeting Criterion 1919–1939	China (1919–1928) Soviet Union (1920–1939) Japan (1920–1939)
States Meeting Criterion 1945–1990	China (1958–1974)[3] India (1960–1977) Japan (1958–1978) Brazil (1970–1990) South Korea (1980–1990)

to increase the theory's coverage and to avoid the effects of path dependence across orders, no state should feature in more than one period. These criteria yield the United States in the mid-nineteenth century, Japan in the interwar period, and India in the Cold War.

With regard to major-power identity, I find evidence in each case – the United States, Japan, and India – that successive generations of the rising power's leaders saw their nation as a major power that would eventually join the ranks of the great powers. This evidence is presented at the beginning of each case study in the book. As to recognition, existing literature shows that other states, including some of the great powers, recognized both the United States in the nineteenth

---

[3] According to the definitions of this study, China became a great power from 1974 onward. Chapter 7 treats China as a rising great power.

century and Japan in the late nineteenth and early twentieth centuries as increasingly important global actors.[4]

Although it belongs in the same category, scholars have not typically identified India as a rising power in the Cold War due to its weak economic growth during that period. Yet the case for India in the context of this book's research design is clearest precisely when one looks at economic growth trends for the three historical cases. Figure A.1 depicts the five-year moving average of gross domestic product (GDP) growth rate for each of the three cases – the United States, Japan, and India – during the respective periods that qualify them as rising powers in Table A.2. The underlying trend of India's GDP growth rate from 1960 to 1990 is very similar to that of the United States from 1827 to 1866 and that of Japan from 1891 to 1939 (even more so if we do not count the interregnum of World War I).[5] The compound annual growth rate for the three countries during these periods is also very similar: 4 percent for the United States, 3.3 percent for Japan, and 4 percent for India. By the definition of sustained long-term increase in capabilities subject to a minimum threshold, therefore, India in the Cold War was as much a rising power as the United States in the mid-nineteenth century and Japan in the late nineteenth and early twentieth centuries.

The case for India on grounds of recognition by other states is also clear. Numerous studies have shown that India positioned itself and was widely recognized as a leader and champion of the Third World during the Cold War.[6] India played a pivotal role in the organization of global conferences of Asian and African nations, most prominently in New Delhi in 1947, Bandung in 1955, Cairo in 1957, and Belgrade in 1961, with the latter launching the Non-Aligned Movement (NAM) – based on India's foreign policy doctrine – that institutional-ized the bloc of postcolonial states seeking to eschew Cold War power politics. For a relatively poor country, India also maintained a

---

[4] See Stacie E. Goddard, *When Right Makes Might: Rising Powers and World Order* (Ithaca: Cornell University Press, 2018), 42.

[5] Jutta Bolt and Jan Luiten van Zanden, "Maddison style estimates of the evolution of the world economy. A new 2020 update," Maddison Project Database (2020). Data for Japan begin in 1891 instead of 1887 due to the lack of sufficient data to calculate five-year averages prior to 1891.

[6] Manjari Chatterjee Miller, *Wronged by Empire: Post-Imperial Ideology and Foreign Policy in India and China* (Stanford: Stanford University Press, 2013), 67–69.

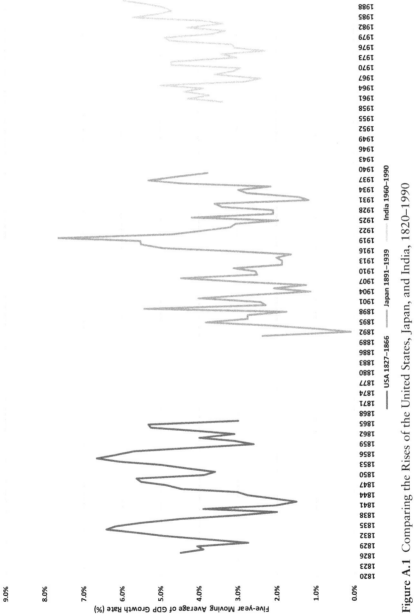

Figure A.1 Comparing the Rises of the United States, Japan, and India, 1820–1990

Table A.3. *Case studies*

International Order	Concert of Europe/Atlantic system	Interwar period/ Washington system	Cold War
Security Institution	1856 Declaration of Paris	1922 Washington Naval Treaty	1970 Nuclear Non-Proliferation Treaty
Attempt to Regulate	Maritime warfare	Naval armaments	Nuclear weapons
Great-Power Sponsors	Britain, France	United States, Britain	United States, Soviet Union
Rising Power	United States	Japan	India

substantial program of foreign aid and technical cooperation for Third World countries.[7] Altogether, therefore, India was widely recognized in the international order as a major player that was growing in importance during the Cold War.

Combining the core security institutions selected from Table A.1 with the rising powers selected from Table A.2 yields the three empirical cases of this book, listed in Table A.3.

* * *

[7] Rohan Mukherjee, "India's international development program," in Srinath Raghavan, David M. Malone, and C. Raja Mohan (eds.), *The Oxford Handbook of Indian Foreign Policy* (Oxford: Oxford University Press, 2015), 173–187.

Index

Cambridge Studies in
International Relations